THE
FIGHTERS

Americans in Combat
in Afghanistan and Iraq

C. J.
CHIVERS

SIMON & SCHUSTER PAPERBACKS
New York London Toronto Sydney New Delhi

For those who recognize these stories as their own

Simon & Schuster Paperbacks
An Imprint of Simon & Schuster, Inc.
1230 Avenue of the Americas
New York, NY 10020

First Simon & Schuster trade paperback edition May 2019

SIMON & SCHUSTER PAPERBACKS and colophon are
registered trademarks of Simon & Schuster, Inc.

For information about special discounts for bulk purchases,
please contact Simon & Schuster Special Sales at 1-866-506-1949
or business@simonandschuster.com.

The Simon & Schuster Speakers Bureau can bring authors to your
live event. For more information, or to book an event, contact the
Simon & Schuster Speakers Bureau at 1-866-248-3049 or
visit our website at www.simonspeakers.com.

Interior design by Lewelin Polanco
Maps by David Lindroth

Manufactured in the United States of America

1   3   5   7   9   10   8   6   4   2

Library of Congress Cataloging-in-Publication Data is available.

ISBN 978-1-4516-7664-8
ISBN 978-1-4516-7666-2 (pbk)
ISBN 978-1-4516-7667-9 (ebook)

"A bitter dose of truth about the wars in Afghanistan and Iraq. . . . *The Fighters* is about as accurate a depiction of combat in the Sandbox as we are going to see in our lifetimes."

—*Field & Stream*

"A chilling account of failed American invasions of Afghanistan and Iraq through the searing experiences of six fighters."

—*Kirkus Reviews*, starred review

"A Must-Read Book . . . *The Fighters* will stand as an essential record of Americans in combat in the years following September 11."

—*Men's Journal*

"The narrative he weaves is not only compelling but may change what you think you know about the American military experience in these two countries."

—*The Christian Science Monitor*

"Gripping and thought-provoking."

—*USA Today*

"*The Fighters* spares no one. . . . These are not easy hero stories with smooth edges, but in their lack of cohesion and conclusion down in the gray areas where they dwell, they shine back at us, forcing us to look at what we've done as a nation, forcing us to look at ourselves."

—*Popular Mechanics*

"A necessary, immersive narrative of what it's like for a soldier in Afghanistan and Iraq, fighting without a clear end."

—*Chicago Tribune*

"Evocative . . . This fast-paced, action-heavy work of long-form war journalism has bestseller written all over it."

—*Publishers Weekly* (starred review)

"Wonderfully engaging. Readers will empathize with the trials each faced in combat and beyond in a book that will enlighten all who read it, no matter their feelings about the wars."

—*Booklist*, starred review

"*The Fighters* is a rare book that thrusts the reader straight into the sweaty, filthy, exhausted reality of war while also revealing the broad sweep and scope of our nation's struggles. It joins the best war literature this country has ever produced."

—Sebastian Junger, *New York Times*
bestselling author of *Tribe* and *War*

"Courageous in its reporting and shining in its humanity, *The Fighters* is a defining document of what war truly is."

—David Finkel, Pulitzer Prize–winning author of
Thank You for Your Service and *The Good Soldiers*

"A riveting, heart-rending, and chastening account of the Americans who are waging wars that the rest of us have already chosen to forget. It is a gift to the nation, both deeply moving and profound in its implications."

—Andrew J. Bacevich, *New York Times* bestselling author of
America's War for the Greater Middle East

"'Fighters' is a vital text. It should be required reading for members of Congress and the national officialdom. For the rest of us, the book is a powerful tribute to our people who volunteer for military service, wherever that may take them."

—*Chattanooga Times Free Press*

"There may be no finer war correspondent today, in the classic sense of Ernie Pyle, than C. J. Chivers. He not only knows the tactics and weapons of war better than most journalists (he wrote a previous book about the AK-47 assault rifle), he has an unusually clear understanding of the men and women who enlist in the armed forces, because he was a Marine infantry officer before going to work as a reporter for *The New York Times*. He sympathizes with his subjects and portrays them as honorable fighters for a country that is careless with their lives."

—*The Intercept*

"Marine Veteran C. J. Chivers Definitively Captures the Endless Wars in 'The Fighters' . . . Chivers deftly shows how these most recent wars thrust our combatants into trying situations without all of the tools they needed to win—whatever winning has come to mean in the last decade and a half. But in telling the story through the perspective of those who actually fought it, Chivers also vividly illustrates what makes them worthy of a nation's respect and how they performed their duty as valiantly as any generation before them."

—Military.com

"Chivers' *The Fighters* has given a voice to the human component of our country's time in Afghanistan and Iraq—the troops—in a way that none before have accomplished. That voice is poignantly honest, meticulously detailed in its narrative and well worth the read."

—ConnectingVets.com

"These powerful stories show how, for some, the war doesn't end when the service member comes home. Ultimately this book does an outstanding job of putting into focus the stories of ordinary people thrust into the hardship of war. These stories are just as important to understand as how a strategy for a battle came about or the decisions a senior leader made during that battle. This is war at its grittiest."

—*Small Wars Journal*

"A forceful critique of the wars and how those leading them have failed their subordinates and the public . . . these stories begin to feel universal, representing the wars' unfathomable costs to so many Americans. These fighters have their foibles, but they are largely competent, self-sacrificing and seeking to do what's right for their fellow troops. Fatal errors seem to originate from entities unseen or unknown, often at higher echelons, baffling those in harm's way. Chivers is unapologetic in his approach."

—StarsandStripes.com

"Gritty and gripping."

—*Proceedings* magazine

ALSO BY C. J. CHIVERS

The Gun

> Why,
> it seems like only yesterday, or the day before,
> when our vast armada gathered . . .

> —*The Iliad*

> America is not at war.
> The Marine Corps is at war;
> America is at the mall.

> —*handwritten note on the wall of the government
> center in Ramadi, Iraq, in January 2007*

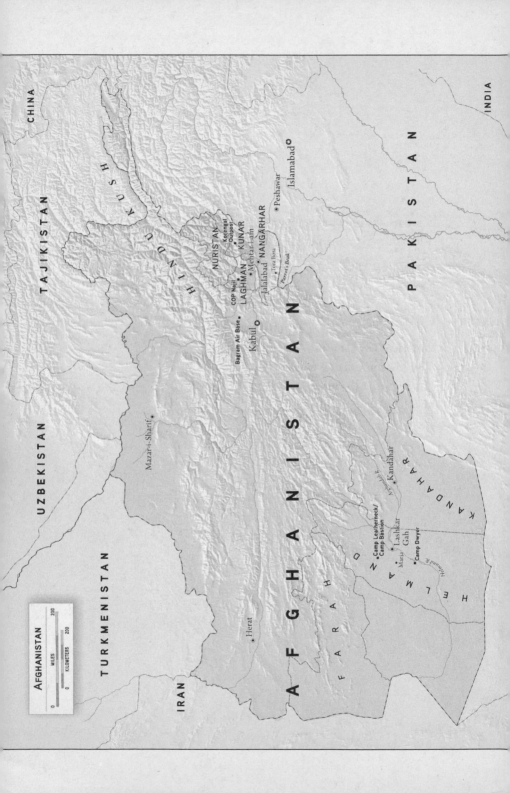

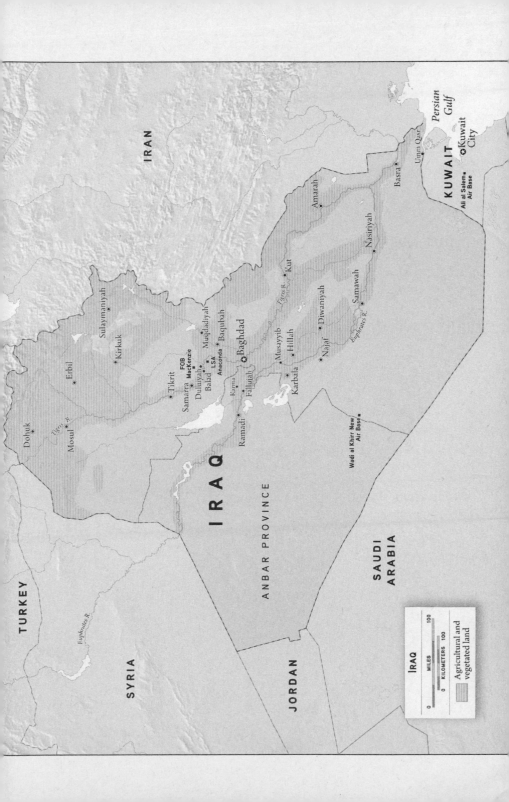

Contents

Guide to Maps

Preface

The American medevac helicopter descended toward a shattered home on the Afghan steppe, sweeping grit against its mud-walled remains. Gunfire cracked past. Inside the ruins, several young infantrymen from Kilo Company, Third Battalion, Sixth Marines, crouched near the bodies of freshly killed civilians. They had tallied eleven corpses so far. All but two were women or children.

Two American rockets had struck here a short while before, a pair of errant blows in a battle between the Marines and the Taliban that had begun in the morning of Valentine's Day. In the seconds after, as a dusty smoke cloud rose, a small girl scrambled out. For a moment she stood still. Then she ran, sprinting headlong to another nearby building, which the Americans occupied as a temporary outpost. Her father was detained inside.

Soon Marines were hustling across the field, crossing the open space where a gunfight had raged for hours. When they entered they found one more survivor—a young woman lying in a pool of blood. She was calling out children's names. The blasts had severed both her legs and one of her arms. Covered with dirt, streaked with blood, she moaned and repeatedly asked for the kids. She tried sitting up. A corpsman and a few Marines consoled her. A lieutenant and a sergeant with radios called their commanding officer, seeking a Black Hawk medevac aircraft to rush the woman to care. Around her the bodies of her family were scattered where they had died, not far from dead poultry and sheep. Gently the Marines assured the dying woman that all would be okay.

The Pentagon and the manufacturer of the weapon that struck here, known as a HIMARS,* consider its ordnance to be precise. Its GPS sensors and guidance system help the rockets fly scores of miles and slam to earth within feet of the coordinates they are programmed to hit. Each carries a high-explosive warhead and a fuze that can be set to burst in the air, maximizing the spread of shrapnel below. The manufacturer markets them as "low collateral damage" weapons. This is true on practice ranges. Battlefields rarely resemble ranges. More often they are the lands where people live and work, and in this profoundly poor village, the Pentagon's precision weapons had hit precisely the wrong place. A sniper had been firing on the Marines from near another home, but the rockets landed here. A family following American instructions—*stay inside and out of the way*—had been almost instantly destroyed.

By the time the Black Hawk arrived, the woman had died.

The aircraft flew into a trap.

Automatic fire erupted. Kalashnikov rifles joined in. The Taliban had been waiting, and ambushed the aircraft as its wheels settled toward the ground. The lieutenant and sergeant ran into view, arms waving, warding the pilots off. Their company commander shouted to a radio operator: "Abort! Abort! Tell him to abort!"

The helicopter lurched forward, gathering speed. A rocket-propelled grenade whooshed into the whirling tower of dust. An explosion boomed behind the Black Hawk's tail rotor—a near miss. The helicopter flew

---

* Acronym for High Mobility Artillery Rocket System, a product of Lockheed Martin.

across the field, banked, and put down near the company commander to pick up a wounded Marine, whom the sniper had shot. Then it was gone.

A lull replaced the din. Young men muttered curses. Inside the compound, Afghan soldiers working with the Marines covered the dead with cloth. A Taliban commander, overheard on his own radio frequency, berated his fighters in Pashto for missing the Black Hawk. He'd almost realized his prize. "That was your chance!" he said.

These Marines were almost all young men on their first enlistments, the type of citizen who serves for four years and returns to civilian life. They were thoroughly trained, visibly fit, thoughtfully equipped, and generally eager to participate in what they were told would be a historic fight, a campaign preordained for American military lore. Most of them were also so new to war that the dead women and children were the first casualties they had seen. Many of them wanted then, and still want now, to connect their battlefield service to something greater than a memory reel of gunfights, explosions, and grievous wounds. They wanted to understand accidental killings as isolated mistakes in a campaign characterized by sound strategy, moral authority, and lasting success. They didn't get this, at least not all of it. Instead, the major general commanding NATO forces in southern Afghanistan circulated a publicly palatable version. The HIMARS rockets, he said, hit the correct building after all. For years the Marine Corps and the Pentagon said little more, even as Marja, seized by Marines and then held by their Afghan army and police partners, returned to Taliban and drug-baron control.

This book is about men and women who served in American combat service in the wars in Afghanistan and Iraq that followed the terrorist attacks on September 11, 2001. It covers these combatants with a simple organizing idea: that they are human. It details personal experiences: what these experiences were, how they unfolded, and what effects they had upon those who were there. And it covers them from their own perspectives, offering their own interpretations of their wars.

More than 2.7 million Americans have served in Afghanistan or Iraq since late 2001. Many went to both wars. Nearly 7,000 of them died, and tens of thousands more were wounded. President Donald Trump's chief of staff, retired Marine Corps General John F. Kelly, who lost a son in combat in Afghanistan and under whom I briefly served three decades ago when he led the course that trains new Marine infantry officers, called these men and women "the best 1 percent this country produces." He added: "Most of you, as Americans, don't know them. Many of you don't know anyone who knows any one of them." This book is an effort to remedy that, in part through demystification. In doing so, it also rejects many senior officer views. It channels those who did the bulk of the fighting with the unapologetic belief that the voices of combatants of the lower and middle rank are more valuable, and more likely to be candid and rooted in battlefield experience, than those of the generals and admirals who order them to action—and often try to speak for them, too.

No single military unit or individual character can capture the breadth of the national projects the wars became. But the cross section of characters who follow represents the experiences of a significant portion. Many of them served in the infantry or the Special Forces or performed jobs— as a strike fighter or scout-helicopter pilot, or as a corpsman—that were closely connected with infantry life. These men and women volunteered, uttered their oaths, and entrusted themselves to politicians and officers who would decide where, when, and why they would go. Some had brief enlistments. They felt compelled to serve for part of their youth. Others chose full careers, embarked upon multiple combat deployments, and stayed beyond twenty years, returning to the wars with tiring bodies and graying hair. All of them had personally grueling wartime experiences. Most of them suffered wounds—physical, psychological, moral, or all three. Together, their journeys hold part of the sum of American foreign policy in our time.

Stripped down, such journeys also hold something else: the recognition that for many combatants the wars were for a time reduced to something local and immediate, little more than who was near and whatever happened. This human experience of combat is often unexpressed by the public relations specialists and senior officers who try to explain the *purposes* of operations rather than describe the *experience* of them, and who together drive an outsized share of the discourse of American wars in real time. The pages that follow offer personal experiences over official narratives and slogans. They are a presentation of what results when ideas about warfighting, some of them flawed, become orders.

Grunts, as members of the infantry call themselves with grim pride, live beyond the end of the road. They do not make policy. They are stuck in it, which is to say that they are the inheritors of the problems caused by the ambitions, poor judgments, and mistakes of others, starting with their politicians and generals and continuing down the line. They have jobs that are almost impossible to do perfectly, much less perfectly all the time. Even when they mean well, they are often attacked with as much ferocity and thwarted with as much cunning as when they intend to do harm. Often they are punished simply for being present, set upon for the offense of being there.

On one matter there can be no argument. The foreign policies that sent these men and women abroad, with an emphasis on military activity and visions of reordering foreign nations and cultures, did not succeed. It is beyond honest dispute that the wars in Afghanistan and Iraq failed to achieve what their organizers promised, no matter the party in power or the officers in command. Astonishingly expensive, operationally incoherent, sold by a shifting slate of senior officers and politicians and editorial-page hawks, the wars continued in varied forms each and every year after the first passenger jet struck the World Trade Center in 2001. They continue today without a satisfying end in sight.

As the costs grew—whether measured by dollars spent, stature lost, or blood shed—the wars' organizers and the commentators supporting them were ready with optimistic predictions. According to the bullhorns and depending on the year, America's military campaigns would satisfy justice, displace tyrants, spread democracy, prevent sectarian war, reduce corruption, bolster women's rights, decrease the international heroin trade, check the influence of extreme religious ideology, create Iraqi and Afghan security forces that would be law-abiding and competent, and finally build nations that might peacefully stand on their own in a global world, all while discouraging other would-be despots and terrorists with evil designs.

Little of this turned out as briefed. Aside from displacing tyrants and the eventual killing of Osama bin Laden, prominent successes were short-lived. New thugs rose where old thugs fell. New enemies emerged or multiplied, including the Islamic State. Corruption and lawlessness remain entrenched. An uncountable tally of innocent people—many times the number of those who perished in the terrorist attacks in Washington, Pennsylvania, and New York—were killed. Many more were wounded or driven from their homes, first by American action and then by violent social forces that American action helped unleash. The scale of waste was almost immeasurable. Much of the infrastructure the United States built with its citizens' treasure and its troops' labor lies abandoned. Briefly schools or outposts, many structures are now husks, nothing but looted and desolate monuments to forgotten plans. Hundreds of thousands of weapons provided to would-be allies have vanished; an uncountable number are on markets or in the hands of enemies. The billions of dollars spent creating security partners also deputized pedophiles, torturers, and thieves. National police or army units the Pentagon touted as essential to their countries' futures have disbanded, ceding their equipment as they disappeared. The governments of Afghanistan and Iraq, which the United States spent hundreds of billions of dollars to build and support, are fragile and willing to align with Washington's competitors or foes. The nations they struggle to rule harbor large contingents of irregular fighters and terrorists who have grown savvy through the experience of fighting the American military machine. The Pentagon specializes in war. Across three presidential administrations, with a license to spend and experiment unmatched by any nation on earth, it managed, again and again, to make war look like a bad idea.

More than a decade and a half after the White House insisted that American troops would be welcomed as liberators, large swaths of territory in both nations are so hostile to the United States that they are no-go zones, regions into which almost no Americans dare to tread, save a few journalists and aid workers, or private contractors or American military and CIA teams. The American fighters who do venture into the badlands operate within a dilemma. Their presence is fuel for insurgency and yet their absence can create sanctuaries for extremists to organize and grow.

Such are the legacies of the American campaigns.

To understand some of what is portrayed in the pages that follow, two elements of these campaigns demand forthright explanation here: the relations between American combat units and civilians where they operated, and the struggles of Afghanistan's and Iraq's security forces.

One of the many sorrows of the wars is that most American troops had little substantive interaction with Afghan and Iraqi civilians. Language and cultural differences, tactics, rules, security barriers, operational tempo, violence, racism, mutual suspicions, and a dearth of interpreters all combined to prevent it. The people who lived where Americans fought and patrolled, and whose protection was presented in official statements as one of the wars' organizing ideas, often were regarded by those on duty in the provinces as scenery, puzzles, problems, or worse. Citizens and occupiers had physical proximity but almost total social distance. Special Forces units, depending on how they were used, could be an exception but often were not. The result was that during action, and after, American combatants had little means to gain insight into the views or experiences of Afghan and Iraqi civilians, as is often evident in veterans' memories and accounts of their tours.

As for the Afghans and Iraqis that American forces did interact closely with—members of Afghanistan's and Iraq's security forces—many American troops, including many in this book, formed harsh views. These views were true to their time. They reflected particular circumstances during the occupations and relations more generally between American and local partner forces among the conventional rank and file. But they should not be read as an indictment of Afghan and Iraqi troops overall, especially during the most ambitious years of these forces' expansion. This is because the conventional national forces of Afghanistan and Iraq—as organized and provided for by American generals—were poorly matched for operations alongside American units. In retrospect, they were built almost perfectly to fail.

The design flaws were many. From the outset, Afghan and Iraqi volunteers were issued less capable weapons and vehicles, and fewer items of protective equipment, than their American partners. Their training was rudimentary and hurried, and opportunities for improvement via battlefield experience were undercut by competing American ambitions. (As local units became seasoned, and capable noncommissioned officers emerged, many of these promising Afghan and Iraqi veterans were offered jobs to work with American special operations forces, depriving line units of competent people.) Limited vetting of applicants ensured that the local ranks were infiltrated by collaborators and spies. Ugly disparities and unwise thrift were manifest on the battlefield, undermining morale. One example: The quality of medical care for Afghan and Iraqi service members was so far beneath the care provided to Americans that the arrangement resembled a caste system in which local lives were less valued than those of the occupying troops. This was often on display after firefights and bomb attacks in Afghanistan. Wounded Americans were rushed to modern Western military hospitals staffed by robust surgical teams; Afghans cut down beside them were flown to Afghan medical centers with little equipment and comparatively abysmal standards of trauma care. Another example: Wages for Afghans and Iraqi conscripts were small enough that their rifles and pistols could fetch several months' worth of pay on black markets—a structural imbalance that encouraged mass desertion and the flow of weapons to jihadist hands.

All this amplified the already substantial difficulties in forming cohesion between forces that did not speak the same languages and were culturally apart, and helped foster the mutual resentment evident between the forces. Nonetheless, well-intentioned Afghans and Iraqis gambled on American promises, only to suffer and die in quantities far exceeding the American loss of life. Blame for their shortfalls cannot fairly be assigned only to them. They were victims of Pentagon folly, too.

How to examine personal combat service in wars replete with miscalculations of such scale? By remembering that national failures and individual experiences, while inextricably linked, are distinct. One chronicler of prominent veterans of Vietnam called his subjects "a flesh and blood repository of that generation's anguish and sense of betrayal."* For veterans of recent American wars, the postwar experience has been different. Beyond their physical wounds and the psychological toll, the bulk of them were not betrayed in the same sense—at least, not by most of their fellow citizens, who have mostly been supportive of this generation's all-volunteer force. These American veterans confront something pernicious but usually invisible: the difficulties of trying to square their feelings of commitment after the terrorist attacks in 2001 with the knowledge that their lives were harnessed to wars that ran far past the pursuit of justice and

---

* From *The Nightingale's Song*, by Robert Timberg.

ultimately did not succeed. They were betrayed not by their neighbors, but by their leaders. Although each of the combatants in this book was different, they shared a pair of behaviors that shaped their lives and became part of who they were—a determination to serve the American public, and an intensity with which they came to their fellow fighters' aid. Selflessness in extreme circumstance was a binding, animating trait. Stripped of all other context, apart from the errors and misjudgments above them, this is what the pages that follow are about, so that their labors—what they gave in good faith—might be more fully understood, even where squandered by those who sent them into circumstances of grave danger, moral confusion, and agonizing deed.

New York, N.Y.
April 2018

PART I

Storm

ONE

INTO AFGHANISTAN

G-MONSTER—Lieutenant Layne McDowell's Quick Air War

"I have been praying for God to take vengeance, since vengeance is His. I ask that if He decides to use us to take it, then make it swift and just and let us not be ashamed, let not our enemies triumph over us."

SEPTEMBER 11, 2001
Aboard the USS *Enterprise*

All through the ship the eyes of the crew were locked on television screens. The Pentagon was burning. The World Trade Center was ablaze. The USS *Enterprise*, a nuclear-powered aircraft carrier, was steaming through the Arabian Sea.

The ship had passed through the Strait of Hormuz the day before, leaving the Persian Gulf and swinging its bow south toward South Africa. Temperatures fell as the huge gray hull entered cooler waters. The aviators and crew enjoyed a welcome sense of relief. They had been away from home for four and a half months and for the past few weeks were sleep-deprived and uncomfortable in the hot conditions and tempo aboard a warship in the Persian Gulf. All that was behind them. They were scheduled for one last stop—a port call in Cape Town—before setting course for Norfolk, Virginia, where their families would be waiting.

A few hours before, at lunch in the wardroom, the aviators were lighthearted. "For all intents and purposes, this cruise is over," one of the senior officers had said. Their most pressing duty was to spend all their training funds before the *Enterprise* reached home. In the peculiar way the United States military burns money, they would be flying to protect their service's share of the Pentagon budget.

Now sailors were watching live coverage of American citizens under attack.

The news swept away all plans. The American military was readying for retaliation and war. Emotion and anxiety rippled from unit to unit, person to person, right to the bridge and operations spaces of this ship, where senior officers were in a state of uncertainty. The Navy Command Center had been destroyed in the attack on the Pentagon. The *Enterprise's* officers had been cut off. They had no fresh orders. The ship's nuclear power plants were pushing the vessel south according to the old plan, away from where news commentators were suggesting the terrorist attacks had come.

Lieutenant Layne McDowell, an F-14 pilot, had been asleep in a three-bunk stateroom when one of his roommates, Lieutenant Patrick Greene, rushed in and switched on the television. He woke sensing Greene's heightened state of alertness.

"Something weird happened in New York," Greene said.

McDowell sat up. He saw a burning tower on the screen. Greene mentioned a plane and the possibility of a terrible accident.

A second aircraft appeared, a jetliner flying low, level, and fast. It hit the other tower and exploded in an enormous fireball. McDowell instantly knew what it meant.

This is a coordinated attack, he thought. *What's next?*

He winced as if he himself had failed. He had never felt so out of position in his life. *We're an F-14 squadron. We're supposed to be between Americans and this. This is what we're supposed to prevent.*

He and Greene hurried to the ready room, stood before another screen, and watched the towers collapse.

McDowell was a member of VF-14, a fighter squadron built around

F-14 Tomcats and part of the Navy's elite. Its aviators had combined experience spanning multiple wars. They were conditioned to attack, unfamiliar with the sensation of seeing American cities struck.

The *Enterprise* had been shuddering as it steamed south, vibrating as it moved near its maximum speed. The ship slowed. The shuddering ceased. The carrier leaned into a hard turn as its bow came around. Throughout the ready room the aviators understood. The USS *Enterprise* had changed course. It was headed in the opposite direction, toward their foes. McDowell turned to another pilot. "Somebody knows where we're supposed to be going," he said.

That night the squadron's commanding officer called a meeting. Al Qaeda, he said, was behind the terrorist attacks. Around the world, Navy ships were reacting. Schedules were being scotched. The *Enterprise* was moving north to meet another carrier, the USS *Carl Vinson*, south of the coasts of Iran and Pakistan. There the two carriers would prepare for strikes into Afghanistan against al Qaeda and the Taliban. The American military was at DEFCON 3, a heightened state of national readiness and a step closer to armed conflict. The ship and all aboard, he said, were to act as if at war. Once operations began, aircrews should prepare for the worst. There was no nearby friendly country to which a pilot might divert. Aircraft that were damaged or short of fuel would have to try heading back to the carrier, he said, and their crews would eject as near to the ship as they could.

After the briefing, McDowell reviewed maps and charts. The ships' rendezvous point, he saw, was 700 miles from the center of Afghanistan. He was one gear in a sprawling military machine and knew the opening salvos would not be immediate. While the *Enterprise* and *Carl Vinson* were almost in positions from which their aircraft could strike, the two carriers would not act alone. The retaliatory killing would be coordinated across the globe. Surface ships and submarines would launch Tomahawk cruise missiles. B-2s would strike from the United States. B-52s would carry payloads from Diego Garcia, and these planes would have to be brought there.

McDowell did the F-14 math. It was a long flight to the Afghan border, and their targets would be beyond that. The Tomcats would require KC-10 or KC-135 aerial tankers from which the pilots could refuel in flight. None of these aircraft were in place. And there would be diplomatic steps before the aircraft would fly. Afghanistan was landlocked. Approaches to its borders from the Arabian Sea passed through Pakistani or Iranian airspace. F-14s would either need permission or have to fight their way in.

As he weighed the factors, McDowell wondered whether Tomcats would fly at all. This might be a quick war, the work of heavy bombers and remotely launched strikes. Would he miss it altogether?

Layne McDowell had been seasoned early enough that his analytical demeanor and calm brown eyes could make him seem older and wiser than his junior rank might suggest. At twenty-eight years old and on his second overseas deployment, he was a veteran F-14 pilot, experienced in the particulars of air-to-ground killing in the American style. In the spring of 1999, on his first carrier tour, he had flown repeated sorties against Serbian forces in Kosovo and hit an airfield in Montenegro. He had also struck into Iraq in 1999 and in 2001. A month before the attacks in New York and Washington, he had flown in a formation of six F-14s that destroyed a fiber-optics facility at An Numaniyah, southeast of Baghdad.

Since childhood he had seemed destined for such missions. Raised on a cotton farm in the Texas South Plains, he was four or five when he first saw a crop duster buzz past his house. Years later he could still draw that aircraft: a bright yellow prop-powered single-seater with low wings and a sprayer bar underneath. It looked like a stylized P-51 Mustang. His father contracted the aircraft and its pilot, William Tidwell, known as Wild Bill, to spray fields for weevils. McDowell developed a habit. When Wild Bill approached the high plains flatland, so low that the little yellow plane scooted beneath power lines and seemed to skim grass, McDowell would run from the house into the crops for a personal air show.

The allure of the crop duster marked a beginning. Reese Air Force Base, a training base for pilots, was over the horizon to the west. Its students would scream above the cotton in white T-38 Talons, twin-engine supersonic trainers with a needlelike shape. The McDowell farm stood alone. Its big white roof acted as a beacon in a sea of green and brown.

The flight school used it as a low-level turning point to teach new pilots how to think at high speed. Formations of T-38s would blast by the house and bank, often as low as 500 feet. McDowell became sharp-eyed, picking them up on the horizon, watching them grow as they neared, basking in jet-engine roar as they blew past.

By the time he was in junior high, he had decided: He wanted to fly. One night over dinner he mentioned his ambition to his father.

"Then you need to get yourself into one of those service academies," his father said. "We definitely can't afford to both send you to college and teach you to fly."

Gaining an appointment to a service academy was difficult. McDowell built his file. He lettered in three sports and racked up achievements. He stood five feet seven inches tall but quarterbacked the high school football team, taking the snap behind linemen he could not see past.

A knee injury led to the Air Force disqualifying him. But the Navy gambled on the driven kid from the cotton farm, granting him a medical waiver for enrollment in the Annapolis Class of 1995. At the Naval Academy, McDowell completed the aerospace engineering program and graduated with a 3.84 GPA, earning a slot in the fighter-pilot training pipeline.

He soon discovered he was physiologically matched to vertiginous life in the cockpit. An early phase of the training aims to familiarize students with the effects of g-force and teaches them to prevent the onset of g-induced loss of consciousness, or G-LOC, which can lead to fatal crashes. The training is accomplished in part by seating each student in a boxlike compartment attached to a long frame that spins at accelerating speeds. Properly known as a human centrifuge, the device has another name in the aviation world: the spin and puke.

As human beings experience intense g-force, blood tends to pool in their legs, robbing the brain of oxygen for vision and alertness. The Navy's training was designed to bring each student to gray-out, then tunnel vision, so a new aviator will recognize the onset of symptoms and compensate in future flights. Many students pass out, then slowly wake, sometimes while convulsing. Depending on a person's innate tolerance and physical condition, this can happen within seconds at 4 g. It commonly begins by 6 or 7 g.

When McDowell's time on the centrifuge came, he barely reacted. At 7 g he remained sharp. His small stature helped. Blood flows more easily between heart and brain if the distance is short.

The centrifuge sped up. As the g-force intensified, McDowell quickened his breathing and rhythmically flexed his legs, buttocks, and abdomen, pumping blood up to his torso and brain.

The machine spun faster.

He was still seeing clearly. When he combined his flexing and rapid breathing with the repeated grunt-like articulation of the word "hook," he withstood 9 g over time. He was a g-monster, a pilot who via physiology and compensation stayed alert and functional in a circumstance that would imperil most peers. He was a natural for the fighter-pilot track.

Although he did not yet grasp it, he was entering a military profession that had utterly changed. Until the later years of the Cold War, aviators on bombing runs saw little of what they struck, particularly when what their bombs hit was camouflaged or small. Targets tended to pass beneath them in a most general way: an airfield, a building, a highway bridge, a hilltop upon which enemy forces were said to be entrenched. Threats from below—first gunfire and later antiaircraft missiles—could further trim an aircrew's opportunities to see what they might strike. Whether releasing from high altitude or during fast flights tight to the earth, the result was the same. It was almost impossible for aviators to observe the effects of their weapons on human beings. Often it was difficult to tell if they struck a target at all.

With the advent of forward-looking infrared sensors, GPS, and small monitors in cockpits, aviators attacking a ground target had a much richer experience. They could stare below with clear and sustained views. The sensors were coupled to new weapon guidance packages that allowed aircrews to adjust a bomb's path as it fell. The combination turned modern strike aircraft into something once unimaginable: a supersonic delivery system for high-explosive ordnance that weighed a thousand or more pounds, and could, when everything was working, hit small targets again and again, day or night.

McDowell had studied to be a fighter pilot. By the time he joined his squadron, F-14s were no longer just fighter planes. Retrofitted with targeting pods and carrying laser-guided munitions, they had become something more deadly: fighter planes that could perform as tactical ground-attack jets, and kill with an intimacy new to aviation. Aviators now saw their target—be it building, vehicle, or man—at the moment the bombs hit. Technology opened for them an experience once known primarily to snipers. They watched targets while deciding whether to kill. Then they watched people die.

With the possibility of precision came the opportunity for greater care, which in turn brought a clearer sense of responsibility. Air strikes were not visible to aircrews only in real time. They were recorded. The footage could be archived and reviewed on large-screen monitors in the safety of a ready room. This did more than give militaries another means of grading pilots. It presented moral burdens. With a larger fraction of uncertainty removed from the job, pilots could not readily disassociate themselves from their strikes, at least not in their own minds. When things went wrong, and in war they routinely do, aviators were less likely to be ignorant of the effects of their bombs.

In McDowell's view it was not problematic to enter a dogfight and kill an opposing pilot in a supersonic killing machine. The air-to-air arena pitted people who chose to fight against each other. Everyone involved accepted the kill-or-be-killed rules. McDowell yearned for this, the chance to defeat one of America's enemies in what could seem, at least notionally, like the ultimate fight. Dropping bombs was different. This was an awesome power, and it invited the gray. Combatants and civilians intermingled below. Intelligence driving targeting decisions was often insufficient and sometimes flawed. New weapons were vulnerable to failure. When fins were snatched by crosswinds or seeker heads were blinded by smoke, bombs made smart sometimes broke their high-tech leash and reverted to dumb—"went stupid," aircrews would say. These bombs would veer offscreen to strike and explode God knew where, each an outcome the Pentagon was loath to share with a public fed selectively released video snippets of successful strikes. Air-to-ground war was *surgical* now, to use one of the adjectives of choice. There was little official interest in a public accounting for ordnance that failed. And technical shortfalls formed only part of the problem. Even when ordnance worked as designed, precision munitions could not eliminate error or sloppy tactics, leaving smart bombs to channel human folly as lethally as their dumb forebears. It was possible to mistakenly target the wrong place with exacting precision, killing people you intended to protect with a bomb that functioned according to its sales brochure.

All these factors changed what it meant to be a fighter pilot. On his first deployment, in 1999, McDowell had confronted his profession's new lot. The carrier from which he flew then, the USS *Theodore Roosevelt*, was in the Adriatic Sea and his squadron was tasked with attacking the Serbian military in Serbia and Kosovo. McDowell was eager but conflicted. One moment he ached to participate. The next the idea of bombing a Christian force and a Christian nation unsettled him, and he worried about the potential for error. As a nugget, American naval slang for a pilot on a first carrier tour, McDowell was not assigned to the opening flights and had to wait for more senior pilots to fly. He alternately groused about being excluded and worried over what inclusion might mean:

> *I had a long talk with God. I'm sure there is no problem hitting all the military targets we've been given; I just want to make sure that my bombs produce no collateral damage. I don't want to live the rest of my life with the thought of having blood on my hands due to messing something up.*

When his chance came, the weather was poor and Serbian surface-to-air missile threats remained a menace, forcing him and his wingman to stay high above ground. The two F-14s were searching for four Serbian howitzers on a road near Djakovica, in western Kosovo. The intelligence photo they had been given was practically useless. What the analysts labeled as howitzers appeared as four small dots. McDowell flew lower for a closer look. He found the field but not the artillery.

He noticed something the intelligence imagery did not show. One of the dots on the photograph was within 100 feet of a home. McDowell assumed any family living there would have moved away from an obvious military target. But he could not be sure and his orders were to strike. He circled back, peering through his targeting pod. He zoomed the optics in, tightening into a soda-straw view of the ground. Even then he could not find the artillery, trucks, and other equipment he'd expect to be part of a firing battery.

He returned to the *Roosevelt* with his bombs, comfortable with his choice. "Even though we didn't drop, and I'm sure the skipper felt like it was a failure for not dropping, I actually felt good," he wrote in his diary. "I felt like we did it all right."

Several days later he had another chance. The Serbian military was basing Super Galeb light fighters and ground-attack jets at the Podgorica airfield in Montenegro. The Navy planned to attack with more than three dozen American aircraft and destroy the fleet on the ground. McDowell would fly with his squadron's commanding officer in the backseat and in control of the targeting pod. They would carry GBU-12s, laser-guided 500-pound bombs.

The formation reached the airfield. McDowell's front-seat monitor was not working, but his commanding officer had a clear view:

> *Skipper found a Super Galeb and put the bombs right on it. Right before impact I got the video back and saw our two GBU-12's completely destroy the Super Galeb. What a great shot! We were just low enough to be below the clouds and so the video came out perfect. No doubt that one will make CNN. No one was around the aircraft, but it was definitely fueled because it had tremendous secondary explosions.*

Back on the carrier his commanding officer wrapped him in a bear hug. For the rest of the deployment, their aircraft was adorned with the silhouette of a Super Galeb: not a dogfighting kill, but still a hostile aircraft destroyed.

The next day McDowell was assigned to work alongside F/A-18 Hornets and attack a bridge and highway overpass back near Djakovica. By the common line of thinking, the F/A-18 was considered more versatile than the F-14 and better suited to the post–Cold War world. It cost less to maintain and could carry a greater array of weapons. But for the war in Kosovo the F-14 possessed an advantage. A new targeting pod, retrofitted on the F-14, was not compatible with F/A-18s. This assured F-14 squadrons a busy dual role. Tomcats were not just dropping bombs in foul weather and at night; they were finding targets for F/A-18s and guiding the ordnance they released.

That evening McDowell's aircraft and his wingman converged with a pair of Hornets near a Serbian ammunition supply point that was being watched by an American special operations team. An American voice came over the radio, guiding the pilots in.

High overhead McDowell picked up a target: vehicles with men standing around, some loading crates.

From another Serbian position below, ground fire rose up.

The aviators commenced work. They selected a vehicle with several men beside it and painted it with the targeting pod laser. One of the F/A-18s released a Maverick missile. It began following the laser's reflection, downward toward the vehicle and the men.

In the intricate system of carrier-based aviation, pilots are both overburdened and striving for perfection. Much of their attention is consumed by an unshakable desire not to screw up. McDowell was at the stick of an aircraft worth tens of millions of dollars. He needed everything to be exact, and until that moment he had not had time to think about where all of this coordination led. Now there was a lull.

The targets were in the open, the ground fire could not harm him, his line of sight was clear. The missile was closing the distance toward the ground. Pilots have a word for missions that reach this stage. They are "suitcased." There was not much more to do except keep the laser on the target—and watch.

Ten or fifteen seconds passed. A few of the men beside the vehicle somehow sensed danger. They bolted for a tree line. McDowell perceived this as a smart move. Those men would live.

A thought entered McDowell's consciousness, different from any he'd ever had. It was about the men who stood in place.

I'm watching these guys' last moment on earth, and they don't even know it.

The missile struck.

A green flash briefly obscured McDowell's screen. After it passed, he saw that the men standing behind the vehicle had been blown backward and to the side. A few of them remained alive.

The missile's explosion had not been hot enough to bake the ground. Through the infrared sensor, McDowell saw human heat signatures superimposed over cold soil. They writhed. A wounded man crawled from the shattered vehicle. A few Serbs had dashed into a small building. McDowell shifted focus. His backseater redirected the laser and painted the building where they hid. A second Maverick hit it squarely.

As the smoke drifted after, the F-14s loitered. McDowell scanned from spot to spot. The wounded Serbs had died. Nothing below moved. He began the process of shutting his feelings down.

It almost felt like watching TV, yet I knew it was very, very real. It affected me in ways I did not expect. This is not the first time I've dropped a weapon in combat, or destroyed a target in combat, but it is the first time I'm certain that I've killed anyone, the first time I watched them die as a result of what I was doing. It feels different than I expected, part of me wants to spend some time tonight thinking it through, thinking about those men's families and the life they had, but a bigger part of me wants to ignore it, stay numb, and get ready for tomorrow.

On May 27, when McDowell was assigned to a midday strike on a radio-relay site in northern Kosovo, the intelligence imagery again was poor. It did not show the target clearly. Hoping not to alert Serbian forces, the pilots did not approach directly. They flew several miles to the south, then turned abruptly, giving anyone on the ground little chance to react. This tactic protected aircraft but came with a challenge: aircrews would have only seconds to find and verify a target.

The aircraft completed their sharp turn.

Serbian air defenses opened up. Incoming fire demanded McDowell's attention, leaving less time to look through his targeting screen. He thought he saw the radio-relay site, and released ordnance.

I felt good about the release, then clouds obscured the target until about 13 seconds to impact. At that time I began having doubts about the target. It didn't look right, but in those 13 seconds, I didn't say anything, and we took out what we were targeting with 2 GBU-12's.

The aircraft turned for the carrier. Freed from the demands of high-speed decision making, McDowell felt his doubts grow. It was a long flight to the ship, and he did a poor job of taking on fuel from a KC-130 aerial tanker. He flew the probe into the coupling so hard, it punched a hole in the basket. He was troubled and he knew it.

On the ship McDowell removed the electronic cartridge that held the strike's video footage with a growing sense of dread.

Viewed on a large screen with higher resolution in the ready room, the footage confirmed his fear. His bomb had not hit the target. It struck a carport beside a house. McDowell looked closely and made out signs of civilian occupation, including four bicycles standing upright in a neat row, as if their owners might be inside. Two of the bicycles were child-sized.

He felt a chill. *Have I killed a family?*

His analytical mind tallied factors: The intelligence had been poor, the imagery was bad, the tactics and the ground fire had compressed his decision window, drifting cloud deck had blocked his view. By his accounting these were not acceptable excuses. Doubt had registered in his mind during the bomb's descent. He could have dragged the ordnance off target, into a field. He had not done that. He was responsible for whatever had happened in that house.

> *Up to now, I could say positively that, while I have certainly killed Serb soldiers, I had not harmed a civilian. Now I don't know. I hope the house was empty—evacuated by refugees or the family just not there. But I just don't know . . . It concerns me . . . partly because we were sent after a target impossible to see and the imagery was bad, but also that I allowed it to happen. I can only pray that God made sure no one was there, I can only hope there is no innocent blood on my hands.*

In the weeks after September 11, after the *Enterprise* linked up with the *Carl Vinson* in the Arabian Sea, the days seemed to drag on. The squadrons trained. McDowell was agitated. The waiting bothered him.

On September 26 the senior officers on the ship called a meeting.

The admiral who commanded the strike group was blunt. American air operations had for decades been risk-averse. One objective was to not lose aircraft or crews. That mind-set, the admiral said, had been suspended. Thousands of American civilians had been killed. The Pentagon would tolerate losses as the services struck back. The flights ahead would be difficult. Some targets were more than 1,000 miles away. To reach them, aircraft would refuel with aerial tankers on the way in, then again on the way out. No one knew whether the services would manage to coordinate this kind of traffic in the skies or if the weather would cooperate. And if tanker placement was not flawless or if flying conditions turned harsh, some planes might run out of fuel.

These crews, the admiral said, would eject.

McDowell took it in. He understood how combat flights could go wrong. The presence of tankers was no guarantee of a return flight. If an F-14 were to damage a fuel probe against a tanker's trailing basket, it would not be able to refuel. Pilots would have to turn in the safest direction and fly until it was time to eject. Aviators parachuting into Taliban-controlled areas, his senior officers said, should not expect mercy. McDowell's childhood had been unusual in a suburbanizing America. He had had access to firearms and often walked far from the farmhouse to stalk small game. If he was forced to parachute into a remote area, he was confident he could survive as long as he eluded his pursuers. "Any aircrew captured there will be executed within a day or two, so there is no chance of return," he wrote in his diary. "I have no doubt that I am ready for all this and just wish that, if it is going to happen . . . we start it soon."

The wait continued. On October 2, he buzzed an Iranian tanker that ventured near the carrier group. When rigging a ship, as aviators called the maneuver, pilots approached a vessel from an angle at which they could read the ship's name and country of origin without exposing the aircraft to danger. For all the rules imposed by the Navy, this was a circumstance when aircraft safety and tactics aligned to allow some fun. McDowell flew a bow-tie maneuver far behind the tanker and then rushed forward on a heading that would take him at an oblique angle across the stern. He came in just above the water, a human arrow traveling near the speed of sound, blasting the ship with jet noise.

He did it a few more times, flying for flying's sake. He returned to the *Enterprise* for a crisp arrested landing* and headed for his bunk, wanting something more.

The next day the orders came in. The moving pieces the Pentagon required to begin attacks were in place. The carrier's air group was to link up with aerial tankers and E-3 AWACS for a night rehearsal up an air corridor through Pakistan to the edge of Afghanistan.

The flight was tense. The crews did not know what to expect from Pakistan. They flew in a defensive posture—radios silent, lights out, the pilots wearing night-vision goggles and emitting only radar. Nobody was permitted to talk, except within aircraft via the on-board intercom. The route carried them 400 miles into Pakistan, where they met tankers from Oman and took on fuel. They flew more than 200 miles farther, stopping near the Afghan border. There they patrolled, hoping Taliban pilots might challenge their approach.

Nothing stirred on the horizon.

The F-14s, out of time, retraced their route to the ship.

On October 6 new orders arrived: The air strikes would begin overnight.

Aviators gathered for updates. The beginning of the American retaliation would have many participants and parts. Targets were being divided between Tomahawk missiles, the Air Force's strategic bombers, and strike fighters on the carriers. The plans suggested that the F-14s' roles might end within weeks. McDowell wondered whether after a few days there would be much left to hit. Experience in Kosovo had taught him that air-to-ground combat in the era of infrared targeting pods and guided munitions was lopsided. *That was against a Soviet-equipped and Soviet-trained army, and we wiped them out,* he thought. Flights into Afghanistan would be harder logistically, but the Taliban was a third-world force with ancient equipment. Its fate, he assumed, would be quick.

On the opening night, VF-14 would attack behind a wave of Tomahawk cruise missiles. The aircrews were given coordinates of Qaeda

---

* Upon landing on the aft section of a carrier flight deck, fighter and attack jets are stopped by a tension cable that is engaged by a tail hook on the aircraft.

training camps and Taliban bases. By the next morning, they hoped, they would be killing the terrorists' leaders. One item carried special resonance: a list of locations frequented by al Qaeda's founder, Osama bin Laden. There was the possibility that one of the senior Navy pilots might kill him and his entourage before sunrise on the first day of a new war.

McDowell was particularly well-suited to imagine what might be in store for bin Laden. Several F-14s would carry the largest air-to-ground weapons on the ship: GBU-24s, 2,000-pound laser-guided bombs. In 1999, in Kosovo, he had dropped a bomb half that size into the entrance of a road tunnel in which a five-truck Serbian military convoy had taken shelter. His idea at the time had been "like trying to scare a rabbit out of an irrigation pipe," he wrote in his journal. After the explosion, he circled overhead and waited for the rabbit. No one came out. He reviewed the strike video and concluded that the bomb's effects had been concentrated by the tunnel's narrow confines, which channeled shrapnel, pressure, and searing heat onto his Serbian victims, ending their lives in an overpowering flash. The detonation of an even larger GBU-24 in the mouth of an Afghan cave, McDowell surmised, could kill bin Laden by overpressure wave even if shrapnel and fire never touched him.

For the first night, McDowell was assigned to be a spare for GBU-24 strikes on caves northwest of Kandahar. The operations officer drafted him to the planning team, which required hours of calculating the strikes' parameters so bombs would land at cave entrances in a manner to maximize damage inside. But even as he worked, McDowell found himself hoping that he would not fly these missions. He wanted an air-to-air chance at a Taliban MiG, one of the dated Soviet-made fighter-aircraft in a rare jihadist fleet.

He knew this might not make sense to anyone who did not appreciate the stubborn primacy of aerial dogfighting in the minds of pilots of F-14s. When he was a child in the late 1970s, and set himself on course to be a fighter pilot, the United States and the Soviet Union were squared off in the Cold War. A clash in which Navy pilots might dogfight against the pilots of a Soviet client, meeting above clouds for air-to-air battle, was more than conceivable. American fighter pilots drilled for it. By the time McDowell earned his wings, he was far more likely to participate in air strikes than to encounter a bogey. No Navy pilot had shot down an enemy fighter jet since 1991, when two F/A-18s from the USS *Saratoga* hit a pair of Iraqi MiG-21s in the first hours of the Persian Gulf War.* McDowell had flown in the conflicts of his time. But he had never encountered an enemy fighter plane in flight. Once he had a lock on an unidentified aircraft over Serb-held territory in Kosovo and cued a Sparrow air-to-air missile to down it. The rules of engagement cleared him for a kill. But something had not felt right. The target seemed too slow. He flew close for a visual and came up tight on an American Predator drone. It had not been on the flight schedule.

His restraint that day had spared him a hassle. But he still considered himself a fighter pilot, no matter that bombs hung beneath his aircraft's wings. And the Taliban, he knew, had a small fleet of MiG-21s and pilots who flew them. These pilots lacked the training and equipment to match American fighter pilots at night. But they flew by day, and some of them had been showing themselves in the skies since the attacks on September 11. When McDowell reviewed the latest briefings, he saw Taliban MiGs had flown that morning.

Let them try that again, he thought.

How easy would it be to shoot down a Taliban MiG? McDowell figured it would be simple. How difficult was it to thread antiaircraft fire at night, get a good parameter release, and guide a GBU-24 to the target nestled in a ravine? He'd done that before. It was hard. But there was nothing new there, and not much reward. Navy pilots knew the deal: Shoot down a MiG, earn a Silver Star. Smack a cave with a GBU? Go back and plan the next one.

He was content to let his older colleagues lead the cave strikes the opening night. He hoped to be assigned to flights immediately behind them. That would put him over Afghanistan as the sun rose and the sky brightened—right when a Taliban pilot might dare to fly.

McDowell slept much of the day, getting the rest he would need for an all-nighter in the cockpit. He woke as ships accompanying the *Enterprise*

---

* Lieutenant Commander Mark Fox and Lieutenant Nicholas Mongillo both were credited with the kills.

fired the opening salvo of Tomahawks. This was a historic moment, the beginning of the retaliation for September 11. He did not head topside to watch. The missiles would hit what they would hit. He focused on his role.

Pilots live by habit patterns, mastering repetitious tasks and distilling each step into a system of identical behaviors. Good habits do more than prevent mistakes; they create the possibility that a pilot will do something perfectly without thinking, even when low on oxygen and short on time.

McDowell had developed a ritual-like process for his preflight routine, and now his habits guided him.

Roughly two and a half hours before launching he attended the briefing, which lasted about an hour. He gave himself fifteen minutes to eat and use the toilet. At the forty-five-minute mark he inspected his aircraft. He read its maintenance history, checked the aircraft weight so the catapult setting would be correct, examined the tire pressure, ensured the aircraft's fuel and liquid oxygen tanks were full. He walked in a circle around the F-14 for a visual inspection and noted that all of its hatches were closed. He reviewed the ordnance sheet and looked over the bombs to be certain that they were properly fuzed. He signed an inspection and acceptance sheet.

The aircraft was now his.

At this point McDowell allowed himself a symbolic deviation. He gathered a small Bible and a 2001 quarter commemorating New York State that had been minted in Pennsylvania, and packed them for the flight. He would fly these over Afghanistan to honor the victims from September 11. Then he headed back to the ready room, where the duty officer issued him his 9-millimeter pistol and ammunition, the recording cartridge for his aircraft's targeting pod, and a blood chit—a multilingual written notice that promised a reward for assistance and a safe return that he could hand to civilians if his plane went down. From there it was a short walk to the parachute riggers' shop, where he stepped into his g-suit and torso harness, which would attach him to his cockpit seat and parachute. He slid on his survival vest, picked up his knife, emergency radio, and holster, and met his backseater.

The two of them walked to the flight deck, then to their jet.

He met the plane captain, the enlisted sailor responsible for the aircraft when a pilot was not in it. They saluted each other. McDowell reviewed the aircraft once more. He checked again the weapons' settings, climbed aboard, strapped in, and waited for permission to start its engines.

The plane captain stood at parade rest in a brown pullover shirt a few feet in front of the F-14's nose. The aircraft remained chained to the steel deck.

About thirty minutes prior to launch, the plane captain stood at attention and gave a thumbs-up. McDowell turned on the engines and switched his attention to a deck officer in a yellow shirt who would lead the aircraft to the catapult.

McDowell fastened his oxygen mask.

It was almost time to go.

Sitting in the cockpit on the flight deck, engines warm, bombs ready, McDowell did something rare. He crossed his fingers, hoping not to catapult off with the first wave. He was a spare for this bombing run. If he missed it, he would fly later on combat air patrol, with a chance to engage a Taliban MiG.

The last of the other pilots got off the carrier without McDowell being called. His F-14 never moved. He felt a surge of satisfaction and shut its engines down.

He returned to the ready room for his next assignment and was given exactly what he wanted.

He returned to the deck and found his plane. For a combat air patrol he had a full slate of weapons. Two laser-guided bombs for air-to-ground strikes were suspended beneath the aircraft beside the ordnance he hoped to use: a pair of short-range Sidewinder air-to-air missiles, a medium-range Sparrow, and a Phoenix, the longest flying air-to-air missile in the Navy's inventory, which could down a MiG-21 from such distance that an opposing pilot might not even know that McDowell was onto him.

The preflight routine repeated itself until McDowell was taxiing behind a sailor in a yellow shirt. He stopped in place above the catapult. The blast deflector went up. Engines idling, McDowell raised his hands; in this way he could not accidentally hit anything as deck crew dashed beneath the F-14 to connect the plane to the catapult's piston and arm the air-to-air missiles.

Once the last sailor was clear, McDowell lowered his hands, took the stick, released the brakes, gave the engines power, and stirred the flight controls while watching the instruments. *Good hydraulics. Good engines. Good flight controls.*

"How you looking?" he asked his backseater.

"Looking good," he heard.

It was dark. McDowell switched on the F-14's exterior lights, indicating he was ready.

The catapult controller punched a button. The catapult banged forward, yanking the aircraft by its nose along the deck into the wind, forcing it, in about two seconds, to more than 150 miles per hour.

McDowell was flying.

He stayed low to the water for a few miles, under stacks of aircraft circling the carrier, then climbed to cruising elevation for the flight through Pakistan. He entered Afghan skies before morning twilight, ahead of the usual Taliban flying times. The sky turned from black to dull gray to pink.

The Taliban's base had been getting hit for a few hours. He wondered: Would their pilots take up the challenge?

The air was empty of bogeys. McDowell did not know why the Taliban's MiGs were not flying. Their forces were under attack. He thought a sense of duty should have sent them up to fight.

His radio came alive. A helicopter was flying through a valley outside Kandahar. It was not an American or allied aircraft, the controller said. Anyone who could get a helicopter now, McDowell thought, would likely be a Taliban VIP. He signaled his intention to engage the contact. He and his wingman turned toward the valley.

Voices called out the locations, but McDowell could not find the aircraft. He had seen cases of radar having trouble distinguishing helicopters moving close to the ground from large trucks. It must be almost skimming the ground, he thought. Someone had passed through the Americans' net. His fuel low, McDowell turned back toward the sea. The window for a dogfight was closing.

———

Two nights later, the squadron scheduled McDowell for the longest combat flight of his career—from the ocean to an airfield near Herat, more than a 1,500-mile round trip to destroy Taliban aircraft idled on the ground. F/A-18s hit the airfield ahead of them, striking the runway and part of the radar system. He and his wingman then made a pass. As they dropped in, the Taliban fired antiaircraft artillery, but not high enough to menace the Americans. His wingman hit a parked helicopter. McDowell struck a radar van. They circled around for second strikes and destroyed a transport plane and seven MiGs. McDowell knew no Taliban fighter jet was likely to fly again.

On October 14, after assisting F/A-18s with strikes, he and his wingman approached a KC-135 for fuel. McDowell went first. Usually, when a Tomcat pulled behind a tanker at night, both aircraft would have their position lights on. The F-14's lights would illuminate the tanker's trailing boom, hose, and fuel basket, and the tanker's lights would allow the following pilot to see if the tanker was making turns or changes in airspeed. This allowed a midair coupling without night-vision goggles. But the war was in its early days. American aircraft still flew without lights. Pilots would have to join the fuel basket wearing goggles, which limit depth perception and narrow the field of view. On this night, foul weather and thick cloud cover obscured the horizon, making it difficult for the trailing pilot to determine if the leading aircraft was in a turn.

McDowell joined the basket. The turbulence was terrible. He could not stay behind the hulking tanker. Several thousand pounds short of a full load, he pulled back. His wingman, Lieutenant Commander Thomas Schumacher, took a turn.

As Schumacher plugged in, the tanker was either moving faster than he thought or changing heading. The hose went tight. The aircraft thumped.

"What was that?" his backseater asked.

The fuel probe, affixed to the F-14's right side, had been strained as the two aircraft drifted apart. Twisting forces had bent it. Schumacher had only begun refueling. He could not join to the basket again with a damaged probe.

This was the situation the admiral had warned of before the strikes began. They were just south of Kandahar. Far inland, hundreds of miles from the *Enterprise*, the F-14 had roughly a third of a tank of gas and no way to take on more. Their mission was over. There was only one choice: abort. Schumacher immediately turned south toward the ship. Any remaining gas would be used to get him closer to a safe place.

Schumacher ran the math, calculating the Bingo profile—the minimum amount of fuel he would need to reach the *Enterprise*. It would be close, and when they crossed the beach and the aircraft headed out over the ocean, it would be dark—poor conditions for a rescue helicopter to find aviators in the water. Flying behind, McDowell expected he and Schumacher would be told to divert to a Pakistani airfield. They'd land there. Diplomacy would sort out the rest.

Schumacher was not so sure. He had also run a fuel ladder, calculations projecting how much fuel the aircraft would burn in fifteen-minute periods, all the way to the end. Uncertainty inhabited F-14 fuel ladder math. Tomcats' fuel gauges could be off by 1,000 pounds. Schumacher still expected to reach the *Enterprise* with fuel for at least one pass. He was on his third tour, with more than 1,800 flight hours, and had done his share of difficult traps, including once with one of an F-14's twin engines down. At the speed he flew he planned to be near the ship in predawn twilight for a day approach, which meant a tighter turn into the carrier and less time with the aircraft's landing gear and flaps down. All of this would save fuel.

The two F-14s passed over the coastline and out to sea, beyond the point where they could turn back. McDowell thought through Schumacher's problem. He would get one look at the boat, one try at a trap. If he missed the wire he'd have to bolter, turn around, and fly downwind until positioned beside the hull, where he and his backseater would eject. A search-and-rescue helicopter, already in the air, would then pluck the two aviators from the water. At least there would be a little light for that.

The dim outline of the ship appeared far ahead. They'd made it to the last stage.

From above, McDowell watched Schumacher fly past the carrier, turn hard left, and line up for the descent. He landed neatly. A short while later McDowell followed him down.

It was late 2001 and the last time he would fly an F-14.

The pace of air strikes in Afghanistan was already declining. McDowell's senior officers informed him that he could now detach and go back to the States to begin postgraduate school in Monterey, California, to which he had been accepted in a dual program with the Navy's test pilot school. The Navy had plans for him. VF-14 could finish the war without him.

McDowell returned to his stateroom and packed. The next day he was to be a passenger on the COD, a propeller plane that ferried him to Bahrain, his first stop on the way home.

Washington and New York had been attacked only a few weeks before, but the United States had marshaled its military power in convincing fashion, and he was comfortable with what he had done. He had not met a MiG above Afghanistan. But he had participated in the strikes against the Taliban and al Qaeda, and he had no questions about whether he had harmed the wrong people or picked up fresh moral freight. The Taliban had been badly damaged. McDowell thought it would probably not last much longer as a viable military threat.

He considered himself fortunate. The war in Afghanistan might end soon. Not many strike fighter pilots, he thought, would get to fly over the place.

After ousting the Taliban from power in Kabul and chasing much of al Qaeda's leadership into Pakistan, the Pentagon began preparing in earnest for the invasion of Iraq. As Afghanistan's interim government tried to consolidate its post-Taliban position, the administration of President George W. Bush asserted that as punishment for developing weapons of mass destruction, giving refuge to terrorists, and defying international obligations, Iraq's leader, Saddam Hussein, should be forcibly deposed. By early 2003, political dialogue had run its course. Preparations for invasion were nearly complete. American forces were arrayed near Iraq's borders, readying for attack. Their number dwarfed the size of the force in Afghanistan, which had grown to about 10,000 troops. Afghanistan was no longer the priority. A second war was soon to start.

TWO

INTO THE KILL ZONE

Sergeant First Class Leo Kryszewski and the Gauntlet at al-Kaed Bridge

"They'll never expect us to go through a second time."

MARCH 22, 2003
Inside a darkened MC-130 flying into Iraq

Leo Kryszewski felt the cargo plane shudder in flight and knew this was his cue. The hulking propeller plane, carrying one-half of a Special Forces team, had lined up for a nighttime descent into Iraq.

His unit, Operational Detachment Alpha 572, was a twelve-soldier team entering the country apart from the main body of American forces to screen overland routes between the Kuwaiti border and Baghdad. Its mission was to find Iraqi military units on the Americans' path, focusing on an area west of the Euphrates River around Najaf and the Karbala Gap, where the Medina Division, a Republican Guard unit, had scattered its soldiers in villages and palm groves. Kryszewski was thirty-six years old and had been in the Army for eighteen years. Clean-shaven and in a standard desert camouflage uniform, he made the flight in the right front seat of an unarmored Humvee that was strapped inside the belly of the plane. The driver, a staff sergeant who served as the team's medic, sat behind the steering wheel. The team's engineer, a sergeant first class, sat in back, ready to stand in the turret with the .50-caliber machine gun.

Together the three men had nearly a half century of military experience, and had removed the truck's front doors so they could get in and out easily and fire rifles as they drove. Around them were their tools and supplies: jerry cans filled with diesel; jerry cans filled with water; small-arms ammunition; shoulder-fired antiarmor rockets; smoke grenades; chemical warfare masks and protection suits; spare batteries for radios and flashlights; a spare tire; food; first-aid gear; the team medic's trauma kit; and chewing tobacco.

The MC-130 was to land at Wadi al Khirr New Air Base, an airfield in southern Iraq abandoned by Saddam Hussein's military after being damaged by air strikes in the 1991 Persian Gulf War. Once on the ground, Kryszewski would be the team's lead navigator. The Army had issued him a handheld GPS device and equipped the team's four Humvees with an integrated battlefield monitoring system, known as a blue force tracker, which showed each vehicle's position. In theory these devices were welcome technological developments. Kryszewski considered them unproven. Having joined the Army before the GPS era, he was a creature of old habits and manual tools—the pace count, the compass, the protractor, the laminated map, the grease pencil and alcohol pen—that together informed an almost robotic mental cycle of always knowing exactly where he was. A trained soldier with a map, Kryszewski told himself, could still work when batteries died or satellite signals failed. In the run-up to the war he had spent months gathering and studying maps. They surrounded him now, at least two hundred in all.

The aircraft's adjustment in flight told Kryszewski they were only minutes away from landing. He left his seat and began to free the Humvee from its tie-down straps. In front of him was another Humvee rigged the same way. A soldier was loosening its straps, too. The MC-130, a Talon variant the Air Force used for Special Forces missions, was one of two flying without lights over the barren desert of southwestern Iraq. Still more planes were coming, each carrying Special Forces or CIA teams with missions of their own. Some teams would try to hunt down mobile ballistic missile launchers. Others were to screen different sections of the battlefield. Each was a gear in the start of a new war.

None of this was Kryszewski's business. He had expected for almost a year—since not long after his team returned from the pursuit of Osama bin Laden in Afghanistan—that the United States would attack Iraq, and that he would be among the first to cross the border. For months his team had been training for vehicle-based desert warfare. He focused on his team's job and understood the principal risk of the flight would be antiaircraft fire from the Iraqi military, which was only beginning to be weakened by American ordnance. Moreover, there had been intelligence in the days before the invasion indicating that an Iraqi mobile antiaircraft unit was operating near the airfield. Kryszewski had decided not to worry. It was beyond his ability to counter, much less control.

That's not our problem, he told himself. *That's an Air Force problem.* Everything had its box. That box was not his.

Kryszewski felt an almost mechanical sense of calm. The satellite imagery he and the American analysts had studied found nothing that led him to believe Iraqi units were stationed there. He had spent months trying to imagine how to organize the war from the Iraqi side. He assumed Saddam Hussein would not send out his military to meet the Americans everywhere. He would position them to fight at key road junctures between the border and Baghdad, and then in the capital itself. *Why would the Iraqis want Wadi al Khirr after not bothering to rebuild it for twelve years?* Kryszewski could think of no good reason. He expected Hussein would instruct his generals to let the American columns cross the border, and counter them near Karbala.

The hunch was confirmed before the flight, when ODA 572 received reports from the airfield. The company command team, Operational Detachment Bravo 570, of Company A, Third Battalion, Fifth Special Forces Group, had secretly entered Iraq two days before. Its soldiers, with Toyota pickup trucks, had been inserted by helicopters on a landing zone about ten miles from the airfield and had approached it to determine whether it was unoccupied and fit for use. They found the grounds empty, then checked its runway to see whether it was suitable for MC-130 traffic. It was not. The surface had suffered too much bomb damage from the American attacks in 1991. But airmen accompanying the soldiers determined the taxiway would do, and spent the day removing shards of shrapnel so planes might land without puncturing their tires.

Iraq had left open a side door. The Special Forces would pass through it, after a little cleaning up.

The aircraft entered a steep dive. Kryszewski's Iraq war was minutes away.

————————

A little more than a year before, ODA 572 had taken a similar ride into Afghanistan and a much different war. It was December 2001, two months into the bombing campaign against the Taliban and al Qaeda. Kabul had been captured by anti-Taliban fighters and their American partners, and another group of American operators were working in the country's south with Hamid Karzai, the Pashtun leader who would become Afghanistan's new president. In Afghanistan's northeast, Osama bin Laden had withdrawn into the mountains toward Pakistan. ODA 572 had flown by helicopter from Pakistan into the eastern city of Jalalabad to ally with a pair of warlords who said they were pursuing bin Laden and his inner circle to Jalalabad's southwest, near the village of Tora Bora.

The helicopters landed at a desolate former Soviet airfield ringed by aging minefields. A stickler for preparation and advance research, Kryszewski had been surprised by the almost surreal degree of trust required. The trip aligned with missions he considered at the heart of the Green Berets: collaborating with local forces in ground combat missions in a complicated war.

It had been a whirlwind run of weeks. On September 11, 2001, he had been among the last people allowed onto Fort Campbell, the Army post on the Kentucky-Tennessee line where the Fifth Special Forces Group was headquartered. He passed through one of the base gates and looked in the rearview mirror as the guards locked it behind him. He reported to ODA 572's team room and watched a live news broadcast as the towers collapsed. The team was almost speechless. Other soldiers began to prepare their equipment, expecting they might leave soon. As a sergeant first class and the communications sergeant, Kryszewski was responsible for organizing the available intelligence and sharing it with his team. He walked to the Third Battalion headquarters building and entered the intelligence section.

"Start getting me up to speed on Afghanistan," he said to an analyst there. "I want to know everything about it."

Then he put in a map order.

Two other ODAs from Fifth Group were ordered to Uzbekistan and inserted into Afghanistan. By November, the airfield at Bagram, once a hub of Soviet military activity north of Kabul, Afghanistan's capital, had been captured from the Taliban by the Northern Alliance and their new Special Forces allies. Kryszewski and ODA 572 were flown to Bagram and given an order: Prepare to move to Jalalabad for a linkup with Haji Hazrat Ali, a former anti-Soviet guerrilla leader who led part of the fighting in the mountains against the retreating jihadists. Osama bin Laden was said to be among them, trying to escape. With the CIA, the Air Force, and fleets of American warplanes that the team on the ground would direct, ODA 572 was to help Hazrat Ali capture or kill him. The mission had a limit: The team was only to guide air strikes. It was not to go forward and fight.

Kryszewski studied Haji Hazrat Ali, examining photographs and dossiers on the man—a survivor with a reputation for opportunism and corruption, the warlord upon whom the team and the Americans' mission would depend. This was the type of scenario that had drawn Kryszewski into the Special Forces, and the action he had sought.

The Army, in Kryszewski's view, was more than his life. It was a calling that he had no choice but to hear. The descendant of Polish immigrants and the son of a Chicago janitor, he was sure from a young age that he would enlist. As a child he dreamed of Army service in the Pacific theater in World War Two. He suspected these were visions of a previous life, that he was a war veteran reborn. His father, Leonard Kryszewski Sr., had been drafted in the Army for an unhappy tour. He disliked the Army with such passion that his son sensed he would not support his enlistment. Leonard Sr. was a stern man, up at 4:30 A.M. every day and back from work after dark. He kept a thick leather belt hanging on a door handle in the children's view. Leo spent his teen years biding his time—"bumming around," as he called it—knowing he would join the Army as soon as he reached legal age and would no longer need parental consent. In June 1985, on his eighteenth birthday, he walked into an Army recruiting station to sign up. When he returned home his father was angry. He ordered his son into the family car and went in search of the recruiter. They found the man carrying groceries. His father confronted the sergeant and demanded that he rescind Leo's enlistment.

It was too late. Leo, sitting silently in his father's car as the two men argued, was an adult. His father's objection had no legal standing. The son followed a short, straight route: Early that October he left Chicago and reported to Fort Benning, on the Georgia-Alabama line, for basic training and airborne school, and then was assigned as a paratrooper in the 82nd Airborne Division.

For a decade Kryszewski held almost every job available to an Army infantry NCO. He was a team leader, a squad leader, a platoon sergeant. He graduated from the Army's Ranger Course and served in the First Ranger Battalion. He was assigned to a mechanized unit in South Korea, where he led small-unit patrols in the DMZ.

He was eager for battle but kept missing the chance. In 1988, after Nicaragua's Sandinista government sent troops into Honduras, his battalion was among the American units dispatched as a quick-reaction force. The paratroopers landed, departed the airfield, and moved to the Honduran countryside, setting up in the mountains. The Sandinista withdrew. Kryszewski was a pawn on the global chessboard. He was not impressed. Beneath the headlines about Washington's Cold War gambit, he glimpsed his Army's caution, even hesitation, in the field. His commanders did not issue live ammunition—nothing more lethal than smoke grenades—to paratroopers on long-range mountain patrols. Soldiers walked the jungle with empty weapons, a mark of the Army leadership's distrust of soldiers and its willingness to risk lives in maddening ways. The following year Kryszewski was transferred to South Korea, and had just begun his new duties when his old unit parachuted into Panama for the invasion that deposed Manuel Noriega. He was furious to have missed the action.

In Korea he immersed himself in patrols in the demilitarized zone and had a close-up look at the United States' allies on the ground. Again he was underwhelmed. His unit included a young Korean soldier, known as a KATUSA. The United States publicly championed the augmentation program, which put Koreans in American fighting units. Kryszewski considered him worthless—a rich kid whose family wrangled the assignment for him rather than have him placed in a Korean line unit. One day the man calmly told several Americans he might betray them in battle. "If the shooting starts, I'll probably end up shooting you guys in the back," he said. Kryszewski believed him.

His tour in Korea meant he missed the Persian Gulf War—Operations Desert Shield and Desert Storm—and watched other soldiers on television on missions he thought should have been his. He arrived later, when Kuwait had been retaken and the region was quiet. He was a man who wondered whether he was a reincarnated soldier. And he was living a career without a gunfight.

His service in Korea propelled him in a new professional direction. As a paratrooper, he bristled at being in a mechanized unit. He wanted something more challenging, and with more fit and aggressive soldiers. His company commander in Korea had recently finished a tour as a Ranger and put him touch with the Seventy-Fifth Ranger Regiment's sergeant-major. With this referral, Kryszewski was assigned to the Ranger School and then to the First Ranger Battalion. The battalion handpicked members and drilled for specific missions, including airfield seizures. Haiti's government had been overthrown by a military junta in 1991, and in 1994 the American military was preparing to invade. The First Ranger Battalion was rehearsing to seize part of the presidential palace. It spent weeks practicing, including in a mock-up of the relevant sections of palace in Florida. His unit boarded the USS *America* for a voyage to the island, only to have the raid aborted when the junta's leadership ceded power.

A nomad within the Army, he had avoided soft duty and continuously honed his infantry skills. He never felt like he had quite arrived. There was only one route left to try. Throughout his years in the Army he remembered a particular sight from his first tour with the 82nd Airborne. A sergeant who had been selected for the Special Forces had returned to visit more than a year later. He was wearing a green beret. *Someday my uniform is going to look like that,* Kryszewski told himself. He was accepted for the Special Forces Qualifications Course in 1995. The Q Course, as it is colloquially called, screens and trains soldiers for unconventional warfare. Kryszewski was selected as a communications sergeant. The course lasted more than a year, capped by an exercise, known as Robin Sage, in which students operated as a team off-base in North Carolina, among

American civilians. Their mission was to infiltrate an area said to be undergoing political instability and collaborate with local guerrillas, known as the "G-force," which was in turn led by a "G-chief"—the guerrilla commander who was to be won over by the team.

Six years after he graduated from the Q Course, as ODA 572 prepared to meet Haji Hazrat Ali, Kryszewski understood that he was no longer missing the real missions. At last he was doing what the Army had trained him to do.

The available information on Haji Hazrat Ali was not promising. As Kryszewski read the reports, he saw a man of shifting loyalties. A member of the small Pashai tribe, he had fought against the Soviets in the 1980s, allied with anti-Taliban fighters in the 1990s, and then forged ties with Iran before seeking the hand of the CIA. After the attacks by al Qaeda against the United States, General Ali, as the Americans called him, voiced support for American action—a choice that stood him as a local power broker when American intelligence officers turned their attention to his turf. His bravery was unquestioned. His reliability and integrity were not. He was a gangster, more politely labeled a warlord in Western news reports. That he could summon thousands of irregular fighters to his side meant he was to be the Pentagon's latest ally of convenience. The $25 million reward the United States promised for bin Laden, and money the CIA had already begun disbursing to him, were incentive enough for him to give the arrangement a try.

General Ali told the CIA that bin Laden, pressured by airpower and the gathering strength of militias cooperating with the United States, had withdrawn with hundreds of fighters into the mountains around the White Valley. General Ali had moved some of his own fighters into the high ground in supposed pursuit. American pilots needed targets, and controllers on the ground to help them differentiate between the opposing forces—circumstances that called for hurrying ODA 572 to the battlefield, in spite of senior misgivings in the Pentagon and in the headquarters in Tampa of the United States Central Command, which was supervising the war.

The team flew from Afghanistan to Pakistan, transferred to helicopters, and was inserted at Jalalabad's airfield. The Americans soldiers, dressed in local Afghan attire, stepped off the aircraft to be whisked through a process Kryszewski, behind his straight face, found unnerving. It was December 4, nighttime, cold and dark. The airfield was desolate and looked unused. A crowd of Afghan gunmen were waiting. Kryszewski heard no English. No one in General Ali's circle had arranged for a translator. The Afghans gestured to vehicles. Soon they were all racing in the backs of trucks toward a safe house in the city, a short drive away.

Kryszewski watched as they passed knots of Afghans with assault rifles and rocket-propelled grenades. The team arrived at a small building and the soldiers were brought to a large room with richly patterned carpets and no furniture. They placed their weapons against the wall as a gesture of trust. He noticed some of the Afghans grow tense. A door opened. There stood Haji Hazrat Ali. Kryszewski walked toward the man and introduced himself.

"General Ali," he said, "we're very pleased to be here."

The general had a translator. The conversation began.

He welcomed them. His first assessment of General Ali was mixed. He sensed the man's power. But the militia leader seemed preoccupied and rude. He sat cross-legged and picked at his bare toes. Kryszewski knew the team had no choice but to work through whatever was in store. *There is no "We can't get along with this guy,"* he thought. *We have to make it work.* Kryszewski introduced the detachment's leadership—the captain and warrant officer—and eased away. They had met their Afghans. He had to set up radios and satellite phones and get a report out to officers waiting in Kabul.

The CIA had preceded the Special Forces into Jalalabad. Intelligence officers were paying General Ali large sums of cash, and had already journeyed with his fighters to frontline mountain positions. The ODA, as reinforcements, had the communications equipment and numbers to expand the link to American airpower, and it could deliver other tangible things, including airdrops of aid for General Ali to distribute around Jalalabad, and more cash. All of these could demonstrate their utility to their host.

After the first meeting, the CIA team arrived. Relations between Agency staff and the Special Forces could be strained, but not in this case.

Kryszewski knew the team from a previous assignment and liked its members and the man who led them, a middle-aged Texan who treated the military as partners. The chemistry among the Americans, Kryszewski felt, was good.

A plan took hold. The terrain where Osama bin Laden had sought refuge was a region of cragged peaks, deep ravines, and winding dirt roads. The border with Pakistan extended deep into the area known as the Parrot's Beak, which had been a major route for weapons smuggling and infiltration by anti-Soviet fighters in the 1980s. In late November the CIA's station chief in Pakistan helped prod Pakistan's military and border forces to increase their presence on their side of the border. But the trails were many, and border-straddling tribes held more local influence than federal troops. The dozen soldiers of ODA 572 could be neither shock troops nor a hunting party. They could, however, direct airpower for Afghan fighters, who would be joined by a contingent from the CIA and Delta Force, and eventually British commandos, to try to kill bin Laden. The ODA was given a code name, Cobra 72, and assigned to different ridges with different fields of view, which would be called A and B, from which to direct strikes.

On the day they were to leave Jalalabad for the mountains, Kryszewski witnessed something he found incredible. General Ali gathered the Americans into Toyota trucks and set out into the city. They drove a short distance and stopped at a small, fortresslike compound with armed men at the gate. The gate opened and they were allowed inside, where they sat with a group of armed men and drank tea. The warlord and Afghans conferred. By the time they left, General Ali had convinced four trucks of fighters to follow him. The slightly larger convoy, bristling with gunmen, stopped at another compound and repeated the process. When they left later, the convoy, by Kryszewski's estimate, had fifteen trucks, each crowded with fighters and weapons. Word traveled around the city that Haji Hazrat Ali was heading to the mountains for the big fight. The process continued for hours. By evening the trucks formed into a huge convoy that pointed at last toward Tora Bora and snaked down the roads. It drove past the city's staring residents, past tall kilns where brickmakers were at work, and out toward the borderlands, where Kryszewski knew that the Qaeda remnants would hear that it was coming. He figured General Ali had put about two thousand fighters together in a day.

In the lower ridges of the mountains, the fighters spread out uphill while the team moved with General Ali to a schoolhouse. Kryszewski put up his antennas, then set out for the long climb with the other soldiers to the ridgetop observation posts. They wore civilian clothes—Kryszewski was in a black watch cap, jeans, and green hiking pullover—topped with a chest rig loaded with ammunition and a sling for his M4 rifle. They were accompanied by about twenty Afghan fighters provided by General Ali and rented donkeys to carry heavier equipment. Kryszewski marveled at how the United States paid Afghans for services. The teams had showed up with money—all of it in $100 bills. Afghans had no smaller bills to make change. Consequently every minor purchase or rental agreement cost at least $100.

When they reached the ridgeline, he looked out at the spectacular snowcapped peaks at the border. The Qaeda fighters, to the south, had perfect positions; it would take a massive and well-disciplined force to sweep the ground in front of them. Sounds of intermittent fighting echoed from that direction. The soldiers began building their hide site, stacking rocks as windbreaks and for camouflage and protection. They set up radios, laser-guidance systems, and the largest spotting scope Kryszewski had ever seen. From more than six kilometers away Kryszewski could see cave entrances and men coming and going inside. Some had weapons—the indicator the Americans required for what came next.

General Ali's Afghan fighters needed all the help they could get. They were far from the valley's further reaches. The forces defending bin Laden had the high ground and kept them back with mortar and machine-gun fire. Kryszewski could not see how General Ali's militias would break through, or even much pressure the Qaeda positions. The Air Force controller went to work. The "stack" appeared overhead—American aircraft after American aircraft, lined up to strike.

Looking through the scope, the Americans determined the distant fighters' locations or marked them with laser designators. Airplanes began taking turns attacking; the Air Force controller talked to the pilots as they checked in for their turns. For smaller aircraft, the controller gave precise directions and laser guidance. For strategic bombers, he offered Point A to Point B spreads. The aircraft dropped every bomb on board in long rows.

Explosions rocked the valleys and reverberated off the mountain faces.

The picture began to change. Small terrain features were removed from the map. Where there had been caves, there were rockslides. Boulders became gravel, gravel became grit. Al Qaeda's fighters became harder to spot. General Ali's militias still struggled to move forward. It was Ramadan, a month of fasting from sunrise to sunset. They were hungry and tired and the ground worked against them. Each day they would arrive late in the morning and begin moving up the roads, only to get stopped in the same places by fire from above. The fighting would be intermittent and lackluster, and at nightfall the Afghans would withdraw, leaving behind any gains to break the fast and rest. In the morning the process would repeat itself.

Cobra 72—the ODA team—had been explicitly forbidden from going forward to fight. Their mission allowed only for terminal guidance of aviation ordnance. A small contingent from Delta Force arrived, with more permissive rules. Kryszewski was not sure it would matter. The space in front was too large and the Afghan militias were too unreliable, he thought, for any modestly sized force to succeed. When he watched the first Delta Force soldiers move up the same roads the Afghans had been using, he expected little to change.

They'll be turning around soon, he thought.

He heard shooting and mortar fire.

The Delta soldiers came back.

Kryszewski heard a new plan: to find a drop zone for a battalion or more American paratroopers to jump in and fight, as many as a thousand soldiers in all. From his vantage point, he thought a battalion would be too small, but the underlying idea was sound. Bring more forces to bear, block the passes, and mop up. Washington and Tampa denied the request.

General Ali had a rival, Haji Mohammad Zaman Gamsharik, a former anti-Soviet fighter who had lived in the West. Kryszewski had met him and found him to be polite, refined, and utterly untrustworthy—a criminal with intelligence service contacts. In mid-December General Gamsharik's forces moved forward and captured high ground beyond where General Ali's militias had pushed before. He promptly refused to allow anyone else onto the terrain, and announced a cease-fire to negotiate the surrender of al Qaeda's forces.

Kryszewski suspected a scam. *He's letting the targets escape,* he thought.

One of the interpreters hushed everyone. "Bin Laden is on the radio," he said.

The soldiers froze as he gave a rough translation. Al Qaeda's leader, he said, was imploring the Afghans working with General Ali not to help the Americans anymore. The transmission did not last long, and the Americans could not understand it. They were within a few miles of the world's most wanted man, so near they could hear him by handheld radio. And air strikes were idled while an Afghan commander dallied at the most forward position.

The negotiations ended. By then, Kryszewski thought, bin Laden had escaped, leaving unfinished a primary objective of the war. Soon ODA 572 headed home.

Kryszewski had not been back at Fort Campbell long when be began hearing rumors of another invasion—into Iraq. In less than a year the team was loaded onto cargo planes in Kuwait and heading into a second new war.

The MC-130 plunged downward to the Iraqi airfield, leveled, slowed, and landed. When its wheels hit ground, Kryszewski was quick to his feet. He disconnected the tie-downs and hurried back to his seat. The aircraft's tail ramp dropped. Cold desert air rushed in. The plane stopped, and the first vehicle rolled down the ramp, bounced onto the taxiway, and sped away, getting distance from the plane. The second truck followed for a short distance, then they split up to take up security positions in a different spot on the perimeter of the field.

ODA 572 was in Iraq. There had been no resistance. Kryszewski felt purposeful and alert. With no sign of Iraqi forces, he reacted to the eternal tormentor: weather. The wind was biting and dry. "It's fricking cold as shit," he said.

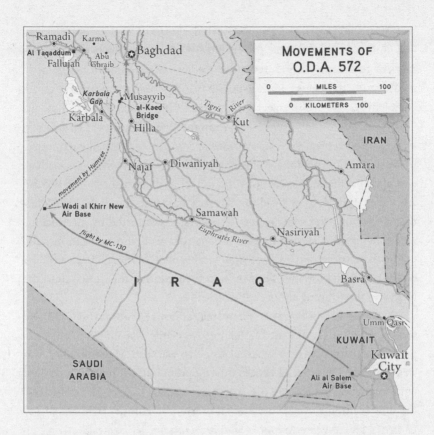

The MC-130 roared down the strip and took off, flying without light. Its engine noise grew distant. More Special Forces teams were entering Iraq on more darkened MC-130s. The soldiers stayed in place as several more aircraft landed behind them, taxied back down the strip, and took off. Kryszewski's team was given the order to move.

For months the team had trained in vehicle tactics. In the weeks before the invasion, in Kuwait, it used its time well, drilling in the desert and on the roads. The team was small and lightly armed, a force designed to search and communicate—not to fight in armored battles. And as the communications and intelligence sergeant, Kryszewski was expected to perform one aspect of his work flawlessly: finding hide sites, places where the ODA could work and rest undetected, able to defend itself if attacked, and elude a larger foe. The desert of the Arabian peninsula was new terrain for the team, so in Kuwait the soldiers had practiced. Kryszewski would study the maps and the satellite imagery of the ground around Ali Al Salem Air Base, and select spots for the four-vehicle team to hole up. The team would then drive out to examine them. The spots Kryszewski chose would typically be many miles apart. The team used each movement to practice moving in different formations and to polish immediate action drills, including reactions to contact and ambushes, near and far, and from right, left, or head-on. At each hide site the team would further drill: tying the vehicles into a perimeter supported by interlocking machine-gun fire, setting up camouflage nets and communications, and taking the steps to prepare for the inevitable next mission. These were the basics of patrol-base life. They refined their routine for weeks, until the team was functioning almost automatically.

Kryszewski was happy to be in Iraq, at last at the war the ODA had sensed coming for a year. He felt ready. While the United States appeared to deliberate over whether to go to war, the Army assumed war was coming. The Special Forces quietly prepared. Money flowed. New equipment was issued. By the summer of 2002, Kryszewski could feel his unit leaning toward invasion. It started as rumors, whispers: *The United States is going to topple Saddam Hussein.* Kryszewski at first ignored them. "Yeah, whatever, you know," he'd say. His team was fresh from Tora Bora. It had visited Ground Zero, the ruins of the World Trade Center, and been honored in a ceremony in New York. The applause was thunderous. And now they were readying for another war? This soon? And someplace else? He played it down. By summer he felt the shift. The team was told to make a list of specific equipment it might need. Kryszewski found himself doing area studies, gathering files on Iraq, and visiting the battalion's intelligence section each day, reading the classified updates on Iraq.

He knew the Army was tilting toward war when his team was issued Humvees. They had not had permanent vehicles before. The Army, he figured, did not make investments like this without reason.

Now we have to learn how to load a Hummer instead of a donkey, he thought.

Army rules mandated a three-hundred-mile break-in period for the trucks to meet the manufacturer's warranty. The team was ordered to comply. In the face of bureaucracy, the soldiers found a way. The twelve soldiers donned uniforms, formed their four new trucks into a convoy, and drove off Fort Campbell, heading south down the interstate to the Jack Daniel Distillery in Lynchburg, Tennessee. The round trip, roughly 265 miles, pushed the odometers past 300 miles. The official box was checked. Through much of 2002 Kryszewski sat through repeated briefings about the chemical-warfare threat. The military seemed certain of the risk.

Early in 2003 the soldiers were flown to the Ali Al Salem Air Base in Kuwait for their last pre-invasion preparations. Kryszewski did not have time to follow news reports or to evaluate the arguments raging around the world about the anticipated American attack. He assumed Iraq retained chemical weapons, a faith rooted in circumstance.

A few days before the attack, with American troops massed near the border, Iraq launched a long-range missile attack at the base. Kryszewski was in a mess tent eating lunch when the alarms sounded. The sound was unfamiliar, more a curiosity than anything else. Then a Patriot missile battery fired, trying to intercept approaching ordnance. Over the whooshing roar of outgoing missiles, the soldiers heard shouts. "Incoming! Incoming! Incoming!" Bedlam broke out. No one in the tent could see out. The alarm spurred action. Soldiers pulled out knives, sliced open the tent's canvas, pushed into the desert air, and ran for bunkers. *Well-rehearsed chaos*, Kryszewski thought as he sprinted.

The missile missed the base.

In the final nights before the war, some soldiers slept in chemical-protective suits. Kryszewski took a longer view. He did not want to be killed in an indirect fire attack but knew the opening days of the invasion would be exhausting. He examined the bunkers. They were too weak to take a direct hit from a ballistic missile. He remained in bed during night alarms, gas mask ready, and slept while he could.

After the last MC-130 dropped off the last Special Forces and CIA team, the order came to move. ODA 572 set out toward the Karbala gap, the strategic approach to Baghdad. The team was about twenty miles east of Najaf, and further from Karbala. The main invasion forces were heading north from the border, and Iraqi units were waiting for them in a defense-in-depth. Much of the area was barren desert, but near the cities and along agricultural canals the terrain was vegetated and green and interspersed with date palm groves. Kryszewski's team was to search around Najaf and Karbala and pass intelligence to American units driving toward the capital.

Kryszewski led the team toward the first hide site. They arrived before sunrise. The wind was kicking up. Grit moved through the air, forcing the soldiers to wear scarves and goggles. They took turns having a short rest. When Kryszewski woke just after dawn, the wind was rushing. The air seemed to hold a dull orange glow. A massive sandstorm had moved over the invading force. For two days the team was lashed by sand and dust. The team moved slowly, picking its way over the desert, wary of driving headlong into an Iraqi force and worried of being mistaken as an Iraqi patrol by an American pilot. They found nothing.

We're ineffective, Kryszewski thought.

By the third night, March 26, the weather lifted. The team was driving on the outskirts of Karbala when the horizon erupted in light. Distant flashes achieved such brightness that for a few minutes the ground around them was dimly lit. Karbala was aglow in antiaircraft fire. Short of Tora Bora, it was the largest expenditure of ammunition Kryszewski had ever seen. Its implications were obvious. Iraqi forces must be concentrated there, inside the city, where a small American patrol could not go.

The invading force's plans changed. The American strategy was reordered. The 3rd Infantry Division was ordered to continue north to Baghdad, leaving the 101st Airborne Division to clear Najaf, Karbala, and other areas, and destroy Iraqi units the lead American column had driven around.

For ODA 572 this meant a pause. Its company command element had landed outside Wadi al Khirr ahead of the invasion, secured the airfield, and returned to Kuwait. Kryszewski's team and the company command group were ordered to link up outside Karbala and Najaf and then move north to Baghdad behind the 3rd Infantry Division for a new mission:

working with local antigovernment fighters to support American forces as the Iraqi government fell.

The team waited at a temporary prisoner-of-war camp as the invasion force reorganized. Kryszewski got an update on the fighting, hearing of ferocious Iraqi resistance against Marines near a bridge in Nasiriyah, and learning that the antiaircraft light show he had seen outside Karbala on March 26 had been an ambush by the Iraqis against an American helicopter attack. The barrages had shot down an Apache gunship. Two American pilots were missing. He set about interviewing prisoners, trying to get a picture of the distribution of Iraq's forces on the roads between Karbala and the capital, a route he knew ODA 572 would soon take. The Medina Division was still out there somewhere. He wanted to know where.

The company commander arrived on March 30. His element had been flown from Kuwait by helicopter, which carried its Toyota pickup trucks—the means by which the major and his team would move. When a heavy column from the 3rd Infantry Division attacked northward three days later, capturing the al-Kaed Bridge over the Euphrates River, the Special Forces, with their lightweight vehicles, were held back. The next day they heard the division's leading forces had advanced to Baghdad. American soldiers were at the international airport. They were ordered north to catch up.

Kryszewski reviewed his maps. He was concerned. Their light vehicles would form a convoy on the highway toward Musayyib, cross the long span of the al-Kaed Bridge, and proceed north through the very territory where his previous study of the Medina Division led him to believe the Republican Guard division was operating. He knew the 3rd Infantry Division had passed through the area. They were heavily equipped, but they still met Iraqi resistance. Kryszewski suspected that few Iraqi units had been destroyed and many had been bypassed. Somewhere out there, his gut told him, much of the Medina Division was lurking—at fighting strength. And after nearly two weeks of performing a reconnaissance mission methodically and with stealth, staying off most roads, the Special Forces teams were going to make a daylight run in plain view up dozens of miles of highway? They would be twenty-five soldiers in nine light trucks, with no weapons heavier than .50-caliber machine guns and a sole

40-millimeter automatic grenade launcher. All tactics involve gambles. This gamble seemed large. He didn't like it.

The teams spent the night at an abandoned Iraqi tank maintenance base. The Air Force controller working with them plotted the route and began informing his operations center that their convoy would be running the gauntlet and American aircraft should be alerted to prevent their trucks from being mistaken as targets.

The soldiers woke at first light and organized into their convoy. They snaked out of the old Iraqi base with Kryszewski's Humvee in the lead. After a short drive they came upon two Bradley fighting vehicles watching over the road. The Bradleys were in a blocking position, and on the last piece of ground the 3rd Infantry Division held between Karbala and Baghdad.

Kryszewski asked for an update on the highway.

"Is there anything up there?" he said. The soldiers told him the road was clear.

––––––––––––

Foot soldiers know that uncertainty and misinformation stalk their ranks, from generals on down. Some soldiers fail, often spectacularly. The soldiers in the Bradleys were sharing incomplete and dated information, and it was wrong.

Units from the 3rd Infantry Division had fought across the bridge on April 2 and April 3, but the Americans drove on, leaving no forces behind to patrol the roads, much less secure them. The Iraqi Republican Guard division around Karbala, an underdog in a lopsided fight against modern Western armor protected by airpower, had been bloodied and was weakening. But it had fought cannily and remained a viable force. Confusion had since gripped the Iraqi central command. The general leading the forces between Baghdad and Najaf sought reinforcements. But Iraq's minister of defense and the chief of staff of the Republican Guard Corps, tracking the war from the capital, considered the American attacks from the south feints and predicted another prong of invaders would strike from the north. The general, Ra'ad al-Hamdani, was under orders to shift forces from Karbala to Baghdad's northern side. In spite of these orders and the dangers on the ground, he reorganized his remaining troops for the fight from the south, and dispatched troops to Musayyib to defend the bridge.

The Special Forces convoy would be driving headlong into a new Republican Guard blocking position. ODA 572 would lead, with Kryszewski in the first vehicle.

The bridge, a man-made chokepoint, was arguably the most important piece of terrain between Najaf and Musayyib.

The lead Humvee drove on. The area was heavily farmed, with high grass, palm plantations, and tilled fields. Musayyib seemed quiet ahead of them. To Kryszewski the stillness felt unnatural. *Something is not right*, he thought.

The soldiers approached Musayyib from the west. A white pickup truck appeared ahead. Its driver spotted them, performed a U-turn, and accelerated away. *Holy shit*, Kryszewski thought.

He had reviewed intelligence that said many irregular fighters loyal to Hussein were using white pickup trucks. He called it out on the radio, alerting those behind him that something might be awry.

The convoy continued on.

It reached the main intersection. A road sign showed the way for Baghdad, pointing left onto the Karbala–Baghdad highway. The vehicle swung left, toward the last stretch of road before the bridge.

In front of them were scores of Iraqi soldiers. The small American convoy had been driven directly into the Iraqi Army's midst.

Time seemed to freeze. For an instant the Iraqis and the Americans seemed equally surprised.

Someone called out in the truck. "Hey, Leo, what uniform does the Republican Guard wear?"

"Green fatigues with red triangle patch!" Kryszewski shouted back. Some of the Iraqis around them were dressed that way.

The sergeant at the turret opened up with the .50-caliber machine gun.

Kryszewski spoke into the handset. "Contact!" he said. "Contact left!" The Iraqis were firing back.

"Game on!" the driver shouted. A bullet struck the hood. Another thunked inside the truck.

Infantry troops are trained for immediate actions, including what to do in ambushes, near and far. One principle is not to hesitate. When in a

kill zone—an area of concentrated enemy fire—the best chance of survival is to fight through it fast. Turning around posed extreme risks. Hesitation often meant death.

The driver stepped on the accelerator, committing to a dash for the
bridge. Kryszewski leaned out and fired his M4 rifle as they drove past
rows of heavy machine guns, most of them idle and unmanned.

Two trucks from the convoy followed, guns firing. The trucks reached
the bridge, continued into it, and soon were over the river, driving at high
speed. Looking down at the murky water, Kryszewski wondered if they
had interrupted a Republican Guard breakfast. Maybe that was why the
Iraqis were not behind all of their machine guns.

As the lead trucks pulled away, the rest of the convoy stopped short.
The Special Forces were split—most of their trucks on the west side of
the river, three on the east. Iraqi soldiers were between them.

Kryszewski put down his rifle and picked up his map.

We need a place to regroup, he thought.

He worried about bolting too far and driving into another Iraqi unit.
We can't keep going north.

Empty white pickup trucks were parked along the road, undamaged.
Kryszewski deduced what this meant: An Iraqi force had filled in around
the bridge since the 3rd Infantry Division's soldiers crossed. The American trucks sped on, past a gas station, until beyond machine-gun range
from the bridge.

They stopped at the median. *We can't keep moving forward,* Kryszewski thought.

On the opposite side, the company commander ordered the soldiers
remaining with him to rejoin the trucks on the far side. They would not
leave their peers to fight alone.

They rushed the bridge, weapons firing, drawing fire themselves, and
reached the span. *They all made it,* Kryszewski thought. He counted them
as they pulled up and spotted the forward air controller, who was trying
to reach aircraft on the radio.

The company commander ordered the trucks to turn onto a farmer's
field and form a perimeter. The Iraqi soldiers were regrouping with rifles
and rocket-propelled grenades. The Americans' .50-caliber machine guns
gave them a degree of stand-off—unless armor arrived.

The forward air controller called for aircraft. Kryszewski heard him reach a B-52 overhead. It was not equipped for close air support, and could not help. Later he reached a pair of A-10s, formidable ground-support aircraft. But they were low on fuel and left. The teams used satellite phones and radios but could not find a ground unit nearby. The closest friendly units on their side of the river were on the outskirts of Baghdad, roughly 45 miles away. The Special Forces convoy was on its own.

Kryszewski heard more news. An Iraqi armored unit was heading toward Musayyib from the north. The teams conferred. Their first thought had been to hold their ground until another American unit could reach them. They understood now that no unit would be reaching them soon, and that they could not fight off an attack from Republican Guard tanks. The soldiers relayed information: *Fourteen armored vehicles en route.*

The Americans had only light-skinned trucks and machine guns on turrets—no match for what was coming. *There's no way we're prepared to fight armored vehicles,* Kryszewski thought. *There's no way we're going to survive that.*

But where to go? A soldier offered a suggestion. The road to al-Kaed Bridge remained open. The soldiers could always head back toward Karbala and Najaf. "They'll never expect us to go through a second time," he said.

The suggestion could have been a joke. It was not. It was a better option than waiting to die in the field. Their commander agreed. Their best chance was to attack back the way they came, straight into the Iraqis behind them, rather than wait for the tanks. They took a few minutes to prepare. They strapped on flak jackets and helmets and redistributed ammunition so every truck had an equal supply. The forward air controller explained their plan to the circling A-10s.

Kryszewski's truck would go first. He was unaware of the air support plan. He was studying the map, pinpointing the spot on the south side of the bridge where he would call for a turn, if he made it that far.

The commander said it was time.

Kryszewski's vehicle took the lead. It rumbled off the field and onto the asphalt, then turned toward the gas station and bridge. As the lead truck, it had to drive slowly to allow the other trucks to pull onto the highway. Kryszewski felt an almost unbearable tension. They were telegraphing their move. The company commander held them back until all the trucks were in formation and could attack as a unit with concentrated machine-gun fire.

The last truck reached the road. They were all in line facing the bridge.

The commander gave the order.

The driver stepped on the accelerator. The lead truck, with Kryszewski in the right front seat, started to move. Above him the turret gunner opened fire.

Gunners behind them fired, too, on their flanks, trying to force their foes' heads down. Kryszewski's truck reached the gas station and hissed past.

An A-10 passed low on a strafing run. Kryszewski felt an explosion behind him. A tractor trailer was pulling onto the road between the convoy and the bridge. It was a fuel truck. At first Kryszewski thought it was a roadblock. There was no way to get around it, at least not at high speed, because of ditches beside the road.

The American machine guns were firing. The truck's driver pulled over and allowed them to pass.

The soldiers' world was a mixed cacophony of gunfire: the heavy thump of the weapon just above each driver; similar thumps from the other trucks; the snapping and cracking of incoming Kalashnikov bullets; the booming of Iraqi PK machine-gun fire; and, high overheard, the occasional ripping roar of the A-10s' rotary cannon. It sounded like a mechanical scream.

The Humvees reached the bridge. Its defenders had spread debris on the road, trying to create obstacles. The Iraqis on the far side were ready.

Kryszewski saw them but tuned much of the firefight out. He was preoccupied. If they made it across, he would have to spot the correct turn and call it out. And then there would be one more gauntlet, running for the edge of the city, where the fighters they faced could take flanking shots from behind walls or from alleys. A disabled vehicle would mean they would have to stop and fight around their wounded.

His truck cleared the bridge and was hit with bursts of fire. A grenade landed on the ground in front of the grille and exploded. A bullet struck a fuel can inside the truck. It began to leak. The driver weaved past obstacles. The turret gunner kept firing. A rocket-propelled grenade hit a backpack hanging on the Humvee's side. The backpack acted like armor, causing the grenade to explode outside the truck and catching much of the armor-piercing blast.

Behind them, the other trucks were still driving through gunfire. Kryszewski watched the road.

Don't fuck up, he thought. *Don't fuck up.*

He barely saw the Euphrates as they passed over it. It was a green blur. He was almost detached. He had to get the intersection right.

He saw it and called it out.

The truck lurched and made the turn.

The lead Humvee rushed through town with the sound of gunfire behind it, with other trucks following. They were in the last straightaway.

Rocket-propelled grenades flew past. Bullets crisscrossed and cracked by in the air. Kryszewski tossed out HC smoke grenades, thinking they would create a screen between the Iraqis and the convoy. His idea backfired. The air of Musayyib held a morning chill. The smoke cooled and settled over the road, forcing the drivers to slow down.

Bullets kept coming. One truck was hit in the steering column, a brake line, and the cooling system. It was leaking fluids. A shoulder-fired AT-4 antitank rocket on the roof of the last truck was struck by another bullet, causing the rocket to fire unexpectedly. Its backblast knocked the turret gunner to the truck bed.

The convoy cleared Musayyib and passed out of range. Eighteen years in the Army, Kryszewski had survived his first gunfight. One of the Humvees was riding on rims. None of the American soldiers had been struck. The convoy headed slowly toward the prisoner-of-war camp they had left earlier in the morning.

Well south of the bridge, they found Americans from the main invasion force milling about. Kryszewski pulled into a compound where infantry soldiers were resting. The Special Forces convoy was a spectacle unto itself—a string of damaged vehicles, cluttered with spent cartridges, carrying sweaty soldiers back from a narrow escape.

The teams got out to collect themselves, and spotted another unit preparing to drive toward al-Kaed Bridge. It was a support unit, pulling trailers, clearly not expecting a fight. The team scrambled to warn them.

As the convoy passed by, Kryszewski ran into a field, arms waving, shouting. The convoy stopped.

Kryszewski jogged up to a lieutenant sitting in one of the trucks' right front seat. "Where are you going?" he asked.

"We're trying to go north," the lieutenant answered.

"You don't want to do that," he said.

PART II

Bad Hand

In the spring of 2003, with Iraq's ruling party and military forces destroyed and Saddam Hussein a fugitive, President Bush declared an end to major combat operations in Iraq. Though he acknowledged much work remained, the priority was to create the governing institutions of an independent state and to recruit and train new Iraqi security forces. Signs were mixed. Hussein was captured by American forces late in 2003, but violence and sectarian strife were rising, and Iraq's unsecured stockpiles of conventional weapons provided fuel for more violence. Occupation was met with armed resistance from many quarters. American casualties were rising, as was the far greater toll on Iraqi civilians. The American force was still green—led by generals and younger troops with limited, if any, combat experience. By mid-2004, the United States was eager to transfer power from the American-led Coalition Provisional Authority to an interim Iraqi government, which would hold elections and draft a constitution. The Afghan war had fallen from the news. The whereabouts of Osama bin Laden and of Mullah Omar, the Taliban's leader, were unknown.

THREE

THE ONE YOU HEAR
ALREADY MISSED

Sergeant First Class Leo Kryszewski
and the Rocket Attacks

"I have a bad feeling about it."

JUNE 16, 2004
Balad, Iraq

Leo Kryszewski heard the occasional explosions, the familiar crack and crunch of ordnance impacting around the base. He paid the noises little mind. They were infrequent and not especially close, he was busy with work, and there was nothing he could do about them in any event.

It was June 2004 at Logistics Support Area Anaconda, the Army's name for the former Al-Bakr Air Base at Balad, a city about fifty miles north of Baghdad near the Tigris River. Kryszewski was starting his third overseas tour since 2001, and in a new phase of his career. After leaving Iraq in the fall of 2003, he returned to Fort Campbell to be transferred to the Fifth Special Forces Group staff to help supervise the Special Actions cell, which organized classified activities in the Middle East. The position required him to work in a sensitive compartmented information facility, or SCIF,* which was akin to working in a vault where classified information is discussed and stored. His life became busy with meetings and hours at computer terminals, a sharp shift from his years in the field. He was ambivalent about the routine and missed being on a team. Sometimes he longed for the intensity and small-unit self-reliance he had known.

The rest of the Fifth Group headquarters was due to leave its stateside offices at Fort Campbell soon and begin a tour in Iraq. Kryszewski had flown to Balad ahead of the staff to finish erecting a special operations headquarters for the Middle East.

All around him were signs of construction. The United States had predicted a swift victory in Iraq. Now it was settling in for a long stay. Anaconda was among the busiest centers in an expanding constellation of American military installations in Iraq—a hub for air support, medical care, logistics, Special Forces operations, and conventional ground troops. It was steadily becoming denser, with new buildings, barriers, shipping containers, antennas, and tents. This high state of activity, and its growing population of troops, made it a rich target.

Insurgent groups had risen after the invasion, and those around Balad sensed Anaconda's importance and were harassing the place. Among their tactics were mortar and rocket attacks, a campaign fueled by the seemingly bottomless stores of abandoned munitions they had inherited from Iraq's military. The United States failed to secure its enemies' weapons as it routed Iraq's conventional forces the year before. The weapons available for irregular warfare in the aftermath included troves of unused rockets, grenades, artillery shells, and mortar projectiles. Scrappers and scavengers stole them and moved them on black markets, from which armed groups claimed many of them. Beyond Anaconda's blast walls, bands of fighters were roaming the fields, hiding in canals and groves, and lining up high-explosive shots. Now and then the rockets they fired rushed in unpredictably and exploded. There would be lulls, sometimes for days. Then they would start again.

Usually the incoming fire failed to harm anyone. The munitions struck

---

* Pronounced "skiff" in intelligence community slang.

runways and open ground, jarring those on duty, waking troops from
sleep, but rarely causing harm. But on occasion the weapons wounded
the base's occupants. A few times they killed. They were a feature of a
changed war, exposing American vulnerabilities and putting the base on
edge. It seemed only a matter of time before the next lethal event.

To reduce the number of attacks, an ornate game of move-countermove
took shape. The military's explosive ordnance disposal teams and ammunition specialists roamed the country to destroy munitions that had left
state custody. Ground units patrolled near old bunkers to thwart thieves
feeding the black-market trade. The Army brought counter-battery radar
systems to the theater. By recording the trajectories of incoming munitions, the equipment could calculate a projectile's path in reverse and determine possible firing points; American artillery and mortar struck these
sites with ordnance. Drones and attack helicopters were assigned to the
effort, along with ground troops who rushed out gates after attacks and
sometimes made arrests.

The attacks kept coming. The sheer quantity of unsecured ordnance
left from Iraq's vanquished military meant that belated efforts to collect
it could not keep pace. And the attackers adapted, increasing their own
battlefield longevity, too. Armed groups learned to rig rockets with timers
so their weapons fired only after those who had aimed them were safely
away when return fire struck or patrols arrived. They also fired from positions near civilians' homes, apparently hoping that the American rules of
engagement would restrict troops on Balad from striking back.

This bloody match was not part of Kryszewski's writ. He had no time to
worry about problems he could not solve. *There's nothing I can do about
these rockets coming in*, he thought. *No sense giving yourself an ulcer. When
it's your time, it's your time.*

His first tour in Iraq, which began with a forward reconnaissance for
a conventional desert invasion, had ended in an entirely different fashion. His Special Forces team had moved to Baghdad and taken up residence in a mansion formerly owned by a relative of Saddam Hussein. The
team was on hand as the city was looted. Their instructions allowed the
soldiers to use violence in self-defense but otherwise not to intervene.

Kryszewski agreed with the decision. *These people have been oppressed so much,* he thought. *They're just venting.* Soon the mood in the capital calmed. In the spring and into the summer of 2003, after President Bush had given a speech before a "Mission Accomplished" banner on the USS *Abraham Lincoln* and declared an end to major combat operations, Kryszewski's team—ODA 572—roamed the streets in seeming safety, focused on meeting the various armed factions and getting Baghdad functioning again.

Kryszewski considered it typical postwar work. Often the security conditions were not bad. The soldiers mingled openly with Iraqis. They ate in Baghdad's restaurants and shopped in its stores. He had access to the classified briefings and a well-developed sense of skepticism. He knew the situation was not entirely clear, and saw indicators of trouble. But the signs had not cohered into a picture of escalating war, much less irreversible war. At a high-level meeting with a Shiite cleric, his team was delivered a blunt message. The cleric said that for now the Shia were going to watch and assess the country's developments and the Americans' actions, and that if they became unhappy, then a new war would start. But this was not entirely an ominous sign. The Americans and their potential foes were talking. The United States had set up a provisional authority. A new constitution was to be drafted, from which a new government might rise and be given the country's reins. Scattered violence clouded the summer of 2003. But there was still time, Kryszewski thought, for the political situation to improve.

The pictured darkened on August 19 when a truck bomb exploded beside the Canal Hotel, destroying the main office of the United Nations Assistance Mission for Iraq. The bomb killed at least twenty-two people, including the UN's special representative to the country. Kryszewski heard the explosion. His team rushed to the scene. He understood the cunning behind the targeting. The UN had just opened its assistance mission. Bombing those who might provide aid was a means to choke off services and donated goods and reduce outsider influence in a nation reorganizing itself. Three days later a bomb exploded near a police checkpoint outside the United Nations headquarters in Baghdad. The UN soon began a large-scale withdrawal of its staff.

The Special Forces reacted. Two ODAs were organized into a strike force, and when the intelligence implicated a terror cell in Ramadi in the attack that killed the special representative, Special Forces soldiers were sent to raid where the cell was believed to be hiding. They hit the building before dawn on September 12 and immediately faced a fight. Two senior members—Sergeant First Class William M. Bennett and Master Sergeant Kevin N. Morehead—were killed. Both were well-known Special Forces veterans. Like Kryszewski, both had served in Afghanistan after 9/11. Bennett, a medic, had been with the team that captured John Walker Lindh, the so-called American Taliban. He had given Lindh first aid. They had been in Iraq since the start of the war and were due home soon. Morehead's team had already left Iraq; he had volunteered to stay behind to orient the soldiers who replaced his team. They were the first two Fifth Group fatalities in Iraq, and their deaths were a jolt—another sign that the post-invasion period was tilting away from a chance at reconstruction and peace.

Kryszewski's team was scheduled to rotate back to the States, too. In its last weeks in Iraq, its soldiers still drove confidently through the capital. But they were anticipating violence in ways they had not been expecting before. The troops replacing them were entering a changed war. Iraq, the departing soldiers knew, was not going to be a quick job.

———————

When Kryszewski moved to the Fifth Group staff, his aperture widened. Instead of focusing on the needs of a small team, he was helping guide operations for a large force in countries across the Middle East. But as his community was being drawn ever deeper into Iraq, soon he began the process of heading back, this time to set up the intelligence section's office spaces at Anaconda. He left in June expecting a deployment of six to nine months.

On the bus ride to the C-17 that would fly them overseas, he sat beside Master Sergeant Darrin Crowder. Like Kryszewski, Crowder was a Special Forces communications and intelligence specialist; they were part of a clique within a clique. Crowder had arrived at Fifth Group a few years before Kryszewski and mentored him. He liked Kryszewski and saw him as a quiet, detail-oriented soldier who was quick to pick up new technology and kept his calm in situations when many other soldiers could become overbearing. Crowder, too, was adjusting to career changes. He had been a team sergeant for four years but now was too senior for the job. He'd moved to the staff. His years in the Special Forces had come with costs. Twice divorced and without children, a veteran of Afghanistan and Iraq, he had given himself so completely to the Army that he was feeling empty, spiritually drained. He had recently committed to his Christian faith. But, like Kryszewski, he was also feeling lonely, and missed being in the company of a team. It was a morose ride.

"You know, Leo," he said as the bus neared the plane, "this is the first trip I have ever been on without being on an ODA."

Kryszewski had been sorting through the same sentiments. "Me, too," he said. "And I have a bad feeling about it."

He remembered the confidence and sense of security he had felt on previous deployments. *I knew as long as I was with my team that I'd never be hurt.*

He did not have that same feeling now.

"I don't have my team," he added.

Crowder knew what he meant.

———

The new Combined Joint Special Operations Task Force headquarters at Anaconda was almost completed when Fifth Group's advance party landed in June. It occupied a large clamshell structure surrounded by its own blast walls, and operated as a compound within a compound—a partially independent universe. Inside its walls, Special Forces soldiers and their support staff and contractors kept their own hours and lived by more permissive rules. Crowder rarely wore a uniform. He wore shorts and a T-shirt, like a carpenter on contract. Kryszewski was setting up his section's space, hooking up Internet cables, getting communications equipment running, and creating the sensitive work areas they would need to protect their transmissions and conversations. He and Crowder rarely left their offices. Their sleeping spaces were within their compound. Warm food was brought to them from the main chow hall. The rest of the base was not their concern.

During lunch on June 16 they made an exception. Crowder and Major Paul Syverson stopped by Kryszewski's office to say they were headed to the post exchange, the convenience store that served the base. Crowder needed shaving cream. Syverson wanted to buy a toothbrush. Kryszewski was at first not interested. He did not want to put on his uniform, but the others convinced him to go. They planned to stop at the chow hall. This was a chance for a meal fresher than the soggy, steamed entrées served at their compound.

Kryszewski and Syverson had been in different companies at Fifth Group. But Kryszewski knew the major by reputation. Syverson had fought in Afghanistan in 2001, too, in the north around Mazar-i-Sharif. Like Sergeant Bennett, who had been killed in Iraq the previous fall, he had been present at the prison uprising in Qala-i-Jangi, where he was among the soldiers who recovered the body of Johnny Micheal Spann, the CIA officer killed in the riot. Syverson had been wounded by an American air strike during that battle. He'd received a Purple Heart, recovered, and returned to duty. Kryszewski heard good things about him. Though Syverson was not scheduled for the group's deployment to Iraq, he had volunteered to fly with the advance party to Anaconda and help with the new headquarters, lending a hand for a few weeks before returning to the States. He had two children at home, one of them newborn. Kryszewski saw him as a credit to the organization.

The three men left in a sport utility vehicle a little after noon. Time was short. Crowder had to be back by 2:00 P.M. for a meeting. They ate quickly and drove to the exchange.

The PX was an older single-story tan brick structure that Iraq's military had used for offices. The Americans had converted it into a retail store. A few shrub-sized palms grew outside. It opened that spring, another sign that the American military expected a long stay, but had not yet been protected with blast walls. The approaches to its entrance were open and flat.

Kryszewski parked the truck. Crowder and Syverson stepped out and walked toward the store. Kryszewski caught up as they neared the front stoop but then stopped. He had never held a staff job before. He had always worked in the field. He was still following old habits. His professional practice—*never go anywhere without being ready for a sustained fight*—had not left him. Even on this short errand he brought a loaded M4 rifle, a pistol, a utility belt, and hand grenades. Other soldiers had been teasing him. They joked that he often looked like a military policeman, a dreaded MP. Kryszewski did not care. He did not intend ever to be caught unable to fight.

Now he had to tone it down. He did not know the rules of this place. Soldiers were loitering casually on the steps out front. Entering the store with loaded weapons might be forbidden. Just short of the entrance he paused, removed his chambered rounds, holstered his pistol, and slung his rifle behind his back. He had almost pulled even to his friends. He held his rifle magazine in his left hand and was about to follow Crowder up the steps.

A rocket landed a few yards to their left.

In the instant it exploded Kryszewski felt as if he had been hit by a huge linebacker, who was crushing him in his arms. He became weightless as the pressure tightened. He was moving somehow.

The scene turned black-and-white, then dimmed.

He lost his sense of space and time. He recognized a familiar smell. *Explosives.* The odor pulled him back. His attention snapped into focus.

He woke on the floor just inside the entrance, atop a mat of broken glass. He was flushed with adrenaline and instantly alert. He took stock. He saw that the shattered glass was what remained of the plate-glass doors. He looked at his hands. One still held the rifle magazine. The other was just starting to bleed. It meant he had not blacked out long. At most a few seconds of his memory were missing—just enough to leave him unsure whether he had staggered inside or been thrown by the blast.

Panic rose around him. The shop was crowded. People were scream-ing and yelling. The noise angered him. There must be wounded to treat. He kicked into action.

He saw Crowder beside him, in his carpenter shorts. He was near the entrance, on the top of the stairs. Crowder needed help. His left leg was torn open. Blood streamed down his face. Another man leaned down to tend to him and pulled the T-shirt over his head, using it to apply pressure on his cuts. Kryszewski pushed the man's hand away and looked into his friend's face—*he's conscious*—and started to give instructions for treat-ment. The bleeding in his leg needed to be stopped.

Blood gushed into Crowder's eyes. He could not see. "Leo, is that you?" he said.

"Yeah," Kryszewski answered.

Crowder asked if he was okay.

"I'm fine," Kryszewski said.

Kryszewski heard shouting outside and saw more wounded people out there. Other soldiers were coming to everyone's aid. Syverson was at the bottom of the steps, down, but getting medical attention. Kryszewski was methodical. He had to help Crowder. He put the rifle magazine into the pouch on his utility belt and ran through the aisles. He found bags of cotton balls, with which he might pack a wound, and a bandana, which he could use as a tourniquet.

He hurried back and tightened the bandana above Crowder's leg wound.

"Are you good?" he asked.

"I'm good," Crowder answered.

"I'll be right back," Kryszewski said.

He had to get to Syverson.

He stepped outside. He was having trouble staying conscious but had one goal: to bring the major inside. *An attack might be coming,* he thought. They needed to organize.

He tried assessing what he could see. The smoke had risen and drifted away. Wounded soldiers were spread on the steps and the sand near the entrance. There were many of them. Syverson was still on the steps. Other soldiers were helping him.

A huge soldier blocked the way. He outranked Kryszewski and was looking at him intently.

"You all right?" the man asked.

Kryszewski had no time for this.

"Yeah, I'm fine," he said. "Get all the people in."

He tried to go around the soldier. The man stopped him with a firm grip. Kryszewski pulled back. *Who is this guy grabbing me?* he thought.

Kryszewski collapsed.

A group of soldiers closed around him. He noticed he was bleeding from more places than his hands. Blood ran down his back, legs, and face.

After a while he recognized that he was being carried on a stretcher and he was not making the decisions. His weapons were gone. He was not sure where. It was not a feeling he liked.

He arrived at a medical tent, where the staff examined him. They said he had been hit with shrapnel in his back, his buttocks, and his face. One piece had passed through his left cheek and shattered teeth. He was covered with cuts from falling onto shattered glass. The staff began to sew up his wounds. He was woozy. His brain swelled. His confusion deepened.

Someone moved him to a holding area. He felt defenseless, alone. He was more scared than he ever could recall. He was without a weapon and unsure where Crowder and Syverson had gone. He had no communications equipment and no team. He hated being away from a team.

———————

War can drive the wounded to all manner of conclusions. Elsewhere in the bedlam, as Crowder was carried from the blast site, he entered a spiritual journey. He was taken to a tent with more wounded soldiers, where someone told him that others were in worse condition and the doctors would get to him soon.

"I'm fine," he said.

He watched as a soldier was wheeled past, under a blanket. His bare feet protruded from beneath the dark cloth. Silently Crowder asked the man to show signs of life. *Please move your feet,* he thought. *Please just move your feet.* The man was motionless. Crowder watched color leave his skin and the soles of his feet turn gray.

A chaplain came to check on him. Crowder remembered talking with Kryszewski; Leo had said he was okay. He asked for information about Syverson.

The chaplain said he would check.

At that moment Crowder understood—he thought he was being told by God—that Syverson was dead. He began questioning God, wanting to know why such an attack had happened and what good could come of it.

One of the people attending him removed the tourniquet on his leg. It was the bandana Kryszewski had tied above the wound. It was blotted with blood and had been stenciled with text. He unfolded it and began to read through the bloodstains.

A thousand may fall at your side,
ten thousand at your right hand,
but it will not come near you.
You will only observe with your eyes
and see the punishment of the wicked.

If you say, "The LORD is my refuge,"
and you make the Most High your dwelling,
no harm will overtake you,
no disaster will come near your tent.
For he will command his angels concerning you
to guard you in all your ways;
they will lift you up in their hands,
so that you will not strike your foot against a stone.
You will tread on the lion and the cobra;
you will trample the great lion and the serpent.

Crowder read the first words and knew them. The bandana held Psalm 91. He saw it as a sign, and felt an epiphany he could neither ignore nor deny. On the hospital bed at Balad, having just seen another man die, unsure about the whereabouts of Kryszewski, grieving for Syverson, he redoubled his commitment to a life in the service of God.

———————

Where some see God, others perceive randomness. Kryszewski, in another tent, was having a different experience. His sense of vulnerability had ceased. His Special Forces colleagues had rushed to the scene, looking for their own, and had been scouring the tents, checking for missing members of Fifth Group. They found him on the stretcher and moved him to a more thoroughly staffed hospital tent.

There Kryszewski was evaluated again. He had a concussion and more extensive shrapnel wounds than he had realized. An X-ray showed a piece of metal embedded in his lower back, less than an inch from his spine. Another had passed through his left buttock, caromed off his tail-bone, and come to rest in his right buttock. He was filthy, riddled with wounds packed with sand propelled by the blast. He understood he had been lucky. His wounds were serious but not crippling.

He could not remember any warning of the rocket. He recalled what he had long heard: Those who have survived the experience of incoming fire say that they did not sense the ordnance until it was too late. Hearing a whistling shell, a screaming rocket, or a snapping bullet means that you have been missed. The projectile headed directly your way makes no announcement before it hits.

This was the case in front of the exchange. The attackers had fired from more than three miles to Anaconda's west. Five of their rockets had landed on the base. The other four caused no casualties. But the weapon that struck beside the exchange entrance, the largest of the five, exploded in a human crowd. It was a 127-millimeter rocket, tipped with a warhead packed with more explosive power than a standard American 155-mm artillery shell. Nearly ten feet long and weighing more than 150 pounds, it landed within twenty feet of the three soldiers, just to their left. The impact caused its fuze to detonate the warhead's main charge, more than fourteen pounds of TNT encased in a fragmenting metal sheath.

One moment Leo and his colleagues had been walking. The next they were encased in the blast.

The trauma was instantaneous.

Major Syverson had been to the left of Crowder and Kryszewski. He absorbed more of the weapon's effects and blocked some of the shrapnel from striking them. Two other soldiers were killed: Specialist Jeremy Dimaranan, an Army reservist from Virginia Beach, Virginia, and Staff Sergeant Arthur S. Mastrapa, a military policeman from Apopka, Florida. Mastrapa was due to leave for home. He was outside the exchange after using the Internet to research a hotel for a birthday reunion with his wife when the rocket hit. Twenty-five other soldiers and two civilians had been wounded.

As more details were shared with him, Kryszewski's mind turned to reflections on chance. The sight* on Kryszewski's rifle had been sheared

---

* An ACOG, or Advance Combat Optical Gunsight, an accessory to his rifle. Kryszewski had slung his rifle across his back, barrel down.

off, hit by shrapnel. What if, he wondered, his rifle had been slung differently—so that its sight did not rest between his flesh and the hot metal it had stopped? Shrapnel might have passed through his torso or severed his spine. What if he had been a half step farther, or leaning slightly forward? Would the shrapnel that shattered his teeth instead have struck his temple or his throat? What if he had driven to the PX slower, or faster? They might not have been inside the blast. What if they had not stopped for chow, or had lingered longer over their meal? Crowder saw God in his survival. Kryszewski wondered about the combination of tiny choices and events, factors in or out of his control, that aligned to put them there. *If I had not been frozen in that exact position, it would have been a lot worse.*

Kryszewski and Crowder were reunited as they were loaded on the aircraft that flew them to the Landstuhl Regional Medical Center, near Kaiserslautern, Germany, where they became roommates shuttling between surgeries. Kryszewki's head was bandaged. The wounds in his back and buttocks made sitting painful. Crowder was confined to bed and wheelchair.

They were in Germany a few days when they heard that a memorial service for Syverson was to be held at Fort Campbell. They were not yet scheduled to be discharged from the hospital and flown back to the States. A Special Forces medic who worked at Landstuhl intervened. He told the hospital staff that he was taking his two friends out of the hospital for a bit of sunshine and a restaurant meal. It would help them recuperate, he said.

He brought them civilian clothes and sedatives, helped them into a car, and headed to the airport. He had purchased tickets for an American Airlines flight.

He pushed Crowder in a wheelchair through the terminal as far as he could. Kryszewski hobbled along, his face covered in bandages. He was missing teeth and gum where the shrapnel hit.

There had been a brawl in the days before at a nearby football match. The hooliganism had been in the news. At the check-in line one of the attendants asked if they had been injured at the stadium.

"Were you at the football game?" she asked.

Crowder was not sure what she was talking about.

"No," he said. "We were just in Iraq."

Her demeanor stiffened. "Oh, you were in the war," she said.

Crowder sensed disapproval.

The two wounded soldiers took their boarding passes, made their way to the gate, and lay down on the floor, waiting to board. Other soldiers heading home helped them onto the plane. Once in the air, the flight attendants invited them to sleep in the back of the aircraft, on the galley floor. They took sedatives that the medic had given them, and dozed much of the way across the Atlantic.

———

The next day Kryszewski stepped from a car in front of his house. He had a ritual with his oldest son, Travis, who was five. Over the course of the boy's life, Kryszewski had been away more than he had been home. When he returned, Travis would run to him and jump into his arms. They would hold each other in a long, primal embrace.

Through the fog of his painkillers, Kryszewski saw the child.

He was running to him.

Kryszewski was wobbly and bandaged, with shrapnel still under his skin. He could not roughhouse. He held up his hand, signaling to Travis to stop. The boy slowed, happiness draining from his face. Kryszewski was home.

By late 2004, the American forces in Iraq were mired in a spiraling war with well-established dangers. Fresh troops arrived without equipment matched to the threats, or the doctrine or cultural knowledge for common situations they would face. Roadside bombs and ambushes had become common. Vehicles lacked armor. Uniforms were flammable. The military did not have the logistics capability to keep itself supplied, and relied on private contractors to maintain its forces and bases. Objectionable actions by both sides—the mutilation and display of American contractors by militants in Fallujah, the abuse of Iraqi detainees by American soldiers in Abu Ghraib—filled the news. Roughly 130,000 troops were in Iraq, where new militant groups were multiplying. About 20,000 were in Afghanistan. Neither war was near an end. The American services labored to enlist and train recruits, rushing to fill their ranks for rotations to come.

FOUR

"IN THE NAVY HE'LL BE SAFE"

Hospital Corpsman Dustin E. Kirby and a Family at War

"Joe Dan was fucking Superman."

SEPTEMBER 17, 2004

On the Drive Between Jacksonville and Powder Springs

Dustin Kirby was feeling lucky. It was Friday morning at Headquarters & Service Company, Second Battalion, Eighth Marines, the infantry unit at Camp Lejeune, North Carolina, to which he was assigned. Word had circulated that the company's Marines and sailors would be released from their duties before lunch. This weekend's liberty, as Marines call their off-duty time, would include Friday afternoon—a welcome bonus for young men heading to war. It meant that Kirby could leave early for his drive home.

Camp Lejeune was on the Atlantic coast and the Kirby family lived in Powder Springs, Georgia—a town of thirteen thousand that fell just inside the five-hundred-mile limit the battalion ordered its members to remain within during weekends. Freed from work, Kirby climbed into his black 1995 GMC step-side pickup truck, which his grandfather had given him. He traveled with more than his off-duty clothes. He had packed field uniforms and combat equipment, too. Second Battalion, Eighth Marines, was on twenty-four-hour fly-away notice, in the event the United States needed to send Marines to a crisis. If the call came, Kirby could turn his truck around and drive straight for the battalion armory to collect his M16.

Kirby disliked this drive. But his military life had not yet eclipsed home. He was twenty years old and had been in the Navy a year, most of it in indoctrination and training. He joined his first operational unit only a few months before, as a field corpsman, a trauma medic who would be expected to treat wounds in an infantry platoon during a combat deployment the following year. It was a revered position among the grunts, and his East Coast assignment had been a good draw for a young man from Georgia. His cousin, Joe Dan Worley, had also joined the Navy as a corpsman but been sent to the First Marine Regiment in Southern California, far from home. Then Worley's battalion left for Iraq not long after he found out his wife was pregnant. He was still there, busy with the fighting in and around Fallujah. His first child was three months old. Worley had yet to see her. Kirby's duties, he knew, would take him to similar places. But for now his work at Camp Lejeune kept him close enough to home that each weekend he could make the trip.

Sometimes it felt as if he had never left. On the trip westward, Kirby would call his mother, Gail, or his brother, Daniel, or a friend. Then he'd put the phone on speaker and talk for twenty minutes or a half hour, making plans. When one call ended, he'd make another. Call by call, the highways passed beneath him until he covered the eight hours behind the wheel and was pulling into his parents' driveway.

He called his home number to let everyone know the good news. His company had let him leave early. He would be home in time for dinner.

No answer.

He called his siblings.

No one answered those lines either.

He hit SEEK on his radio, looking for whatever distraction music might bring.

Kirby's route to a Marine infantry battalion had been circuitous and yet managed to feel ordained. His family was unflinchingly patriotic and unshakably Christian, a tone set by his grandfather, William E. Kirby, who as a young soldier had been wounded in the Battle of the Bulge near the end of World War Two. William Kirby returned to the woods outside Atlanta and became a preacher in a Pentecostal church. His faith in Jesus Christ and the scriptures, along with his own admonishments about clean living, were cornerstones of the Kirby worldview. "Once you get the water on you, you're good," he taught. "But you've got to live right."

Dustin Kirby was raised in awe of his grandfather's battlefield service. From an early age he dreamed of being a paratrooper and trying out for the Special Forces. In high school he signed up for Junior ROTC, seeing it as a pipeline to that life. He was a Marvel Comics fan—Captain America, Thor, and the Silver Surfer were his favorites—and wanted to be a hero. When al Qaeda attacked New York and Washington, he had just started his senior year in high school and had already enlisted in the Army, having signed up for the delayed entry plan as a junior when he was seventeen. He wanted to be assigned to the infantry. His relationship with the Army was short-lived. After the attacks, he had misgivings about his recruiters, who he felt were pushing him for a military police or communications job. A war was starting. Kirby wanted to fight. When he graduated in 2002, he told the Army he would not show up for boot camp. He took a job as an usher at a local movie theater, biding his time. He considered college but found the prospect of four years of study unappealing. In college, he thought, he'd be bored. College was no path for a hero.

His plans crystallized after his cousin enlisted. Worley was three years older than he was, and had lettered in football and wrestling in high school. Dustin saw him as a Superman: handsome, kind, and physically imposing, but in possession of a polite and respectful demeanor. Worley had married young and started work at a metal fabrication shop that manufactured parts for Boeing. It was a good job, but repetitious, and he felt stuck in a paycheck-to-paycheck cycle. He and his wife, Angel Worley, decided the military offered a chance to reset their lives. He opted for the Navy because he and Angel thought it might be safer. In 2002, he enlisted and selected a job as a corpsman—a medical job. This seemed safer still. He was unaware that it meant he could be assigned to the Marine Corps. America's momentum toward the invasion of Iraq had begun. Worley paid it little attention. He was headed to the Navy and had a family to feed. Ground war was not on his mind. In early 2003 he shipped to boot

camp at Naval Station Great Lakes, near Chicago. He was in recruit training when his instructors announced that the United States had begun its
attack on Iraq. The country was now fighting two wars. Worley figured
he'd pass his years working in a naval hospital or on a ship.

Back in Georgia, as Worley paid Iraq little mind, the Pentagon's march
toward Baghdad cemented Kirby's choices. He would follow his grandfather's path and serve his country in war. Soon he was back at the recruiting offices, talking with the Navy about joining the SEALs. During the
entrance physical in Atlanta, the staff told him his eyesight was too poor
for the SEALs but he was medically qualified as a corpsman. He signed his
enlistment contract in May 2003 and was told to report to Great Lakes in
September. His mother, Gail Kirby, was relieved by the news. He wouldn't
be with the Army or the SEALs. He'd be away from the violence, just like
Worley, maybe even afloat. *The Navy's not that bad,* she thought. *In the
Navy he'll be safe. He'll be on a ship and not in the middle of a war. He'll be
out on the ocean. Nothing happens out on the ocean.*

Kirby's family threw a pizza party for him the night before he left. He
was supposed to be at an airport hotel that evening, ahead of his morning
flight. But the house swelled with visitors and the party dragged on so late
that his recruiter extended his check-in time. Late that night, after leaving
him at the hotel lobby, Gail and his father, Jacko, were driving back to
Powder Springs. Jacko abruptly pulled to a stop on the highway shoulder.
His eyes were filled with tears. He was consumed with sorrow, and something he had not expected: fear.

"Our little town was never going to be big enough for Dusty," he said.

Gail had not seen her husband cry before, not even when his mother
had died.

She felt a pervasive sense of dread.

———

Dustin Kirby excelled at boot camp. He exuded intensity, seemed to enjoy
the indoctrination, and frequently professed his love of the United States.
He thrived in what other sailors saw as the military's "stupid shit" and
pined for a hard assignment and a chance to distinguish himself in battle.
By then his cousin, Worley, had been selected for Field Medical Service
School, the last step before being assigned to the Marines, and an almost

sure diversion from duty in a hospital or on a ship. Kirby heard what his cousin was doing. He wanted the same kind of assignment. He ached for a place in an infantry platoon.

At the swim test, one of his instructors asked him what his job would be in the Navy.

"I'm going to be a corpsman in the Fleet Marine Forces," he said loudly, his head just above the surface. The instructor laughed derisively.

"Good luck," he said. "You need perfect vision to go with the Marines."

Kirby was crushed. That night in the barracks he made his way back to an open bay, a place where the platoon hung its mops and recruits huddled to commiserate while their instructors were away. Kirby gathered his friends and started crying, telling them he expected to be disqualified. He was nearly despondent. One of them watched Kirby's eagerness with foreboding, as if he were seeing a man willfully "heading into a meat grinder." When the platoon graduated in December of 2003, Kirby learned the swim instructor had been wrong. The Navy shipped him to Camp Lejeune for Field Medical Service School and an eventual assignment to the Marines.

Field Medical Service School is where the Marine Corps takes custody of its sailors, preparing them for life among grunts. The transition "from blue side to green side," as the Corps calls it, can be jarring, in part because the curriculum is an eye-opening tour of the brutality and trauma of modern warfare. This was the realm of sucking-chest wounds, femoral bleeding, full-body burns, blast amputations, and psychologically disoriented victims in the first moments of devastating injuries. And Kirby's training moved past treating one patient at a time in the safety of well-lit aid stations. It emphasized death-delaying steps on the ground under simulated fire and then escalated to mass-casualty drills—the aftermath of a rocket strike, a helicopter crash, or a bomb blast—when a corpsman could be thrust into danger to sort and treat a dozen or more anguished victims at once.

Where others saw gore, Kirby sensed responsibility. He felt charged by the opportunity to snatch others' lives from death while risking his own, and of earning his place on the "green side," the harsh Marine Corps milieu that many sailors tried to avoid. None of the training seemed notional. He understood and accepted that he was on an institutional conveyor belt carrying him from stateside drills to the body-wrecking firefights and roadside bombs of Iraq. The Marine Corps had not seen full-scale war since Vietnam. But Iraq, he knew, was boiling under American occupation, and around on Camp Lejeune battalions were preparing for combat tours in areas where militants were rising up. Kirby knew he would be put in a platoon and sent to clash with them. He expected to save those who fell.

By the time Kirby graduated from Field Medical Service School, Worley had already left. He arrived in late 2003 at Camp Pendleton, in California, and was put on a fast track to Iraq with Second Battalion, First Marines. The battalion had fought in the invasion of Iraq and worked in Shiite areas of the country's south before heading home for rest and refitting. Worley returned with the battalion's Fox Company to Iraq in March 2004.

They arrived to a changed war. This time the battalion was assigned to Anbar Province, an area inhabited by Sunnis displaced from power by the fall of Saddam Hussein. An initially uneasy but mostly nonviolent relationship between Fallujah's residents and American forces had broken into open fighting during 2003, and the insurgency had gathered ferocity with the passage of a year. This was not a war against a conventional Baathist military, in which American firepower could be concentrated against a visible foe. It was a campaign against shadowy enemies who engaged in guerrilla warfare and were developing a proficiency with improvised bombs. The country's stockpiles of conventional munitions, left unguarded by the evaporation of Hussein's military in 2003, gifted the militants with a seemingly boundless supply of explosives. The fuel for long-term violence was in place.

Kirby had been in touch with Worley since he shipped out, and knew something of the war his cousin was fighting. Fox Company landed in Kuwait in March 2004 and set out on the long drive to Forward Operating Base Volturno, which they renamed Baharia*, a former Iraqi resort near Fallujah, to relieve a unit from the 82nd Airborne Division. The turnover was tense. The departing soldiers, Worley thought, were spooked and unsure of their tactics. They spoke of no-go areas—places they had ceded to militants and no longer patrolled. Worley's platoon commander, First

---

* The base, when the Army lived there, was also called Dreamland.

Lieutenant Wade Zirkle, was disappointed. The Army had taken a posture he did not like, and allowed the militants to grow bold. He had a word for it: "standoffish."

The initial guidance to Fox Company's Marines was to step up the pace and ambition of patrols and thereby learn the turf and its people. It was an old formula for an uncertain occupation, mixing intelligence gathering and a show of presence with an intention of finding allies and nudging Fallujah toward order. In meetings it sounded possible. On the ground it promised confusion. The Marines were trained to fight, but there was no opposing army to fight against. And outreach and intelligence gathering were hindered by the fact that almost none of the Marines knew Arabic, beyond a few phrases on printed cards the Corps handed out. They could not talk with Iraqis without the help of interpreters, who were few.

The first large mission came on March 26, when the battalion entered Fallujah in what its senior officers said would serve as a signal to its residents that a new unit and mentality had arrived.

Worley's platoon, known by its call sign, Pale Rider Three, was given a sector to patrol. It approached the city from the north. Most of the Marines were on foot, walking widely spaced apart. Two Humvees moved with them, each with a .50-caliber machine gun. Worley liked the platoon commander, Lieutenant Zirkle, who had fought during the invasion. He joined the platoon weeks before the deployment, replacing an officer who had been relieved.

The first hours passed quietly. The militants risked only one shot: a rocket-propelled grenade fired from a rooftop, which sailed over the Marines' heads and exploded in a courtyard. As the day dragged on, Lieutenant Zirkle grew uneasy. He was having trouble contacting the company commander on the radio, and thought the captain was preoccupied with missions given to other platoons, including a search of several buildings. He did not want his Marines, most of whom had never been in combat before, wandering the streets. They were targets with no missions. He ordered the squads to move to a partially built building near a field and patrol from there. At dusk the platoon was ordered to walk south back into the city, meet the company at the main east–west corridor, and return to their base, Baharia.

Soon after stepping off, the platoon was attacked.

For fifteen or twenty seconds militants fired with automatic weapons and rocket-propelled grenades from a third-story rooftop. The Marines returned fire for about a minute, when commands to cease fire were yelled from Marine to Marine.

One of the young Marines in a Humvee, Private First Class Leroy Sandoval Jr., had been struck.

Marines shouted for a corpsman.

Worley ran to the truck and found Sandoval slumped inside. He dragged him out, pulled him behind the vehicle for cover, and examined him. Sandoval was his first wounded Marine and his first encounter with what modern weapons can do. He had at least one gunshot wound in his upper body and one behind his helmet's lower edge, on his brow. The bullet had pierced the bottom of his Kevlar. The Marines moved him into a courtyard patio and guarded him while the corpsman worked. Worley found a heartbeat and started CPR.

The heartbeat faded.

There was no saving a man wounded this badly.

The platoon loaded Sandoval into the back of the Humvee.

Another shout came. A second Marine had been hit. Worley sprinted again, this time to Lance Corporal Bret McCauley, who had been shot through his buttocks. This was a wound Worley could treat. After Worley bandaged him and Marines had carried him away, the platoon moved out of range. A third Marine had been struck, too, though not as seriously. Pale Rider Three walked across open fields to their base, unsure what it had accomplished or how the battalion would calm the city.

Five days later, four American contractors were ambushed and killed in Fallujah. A mob burned and mutilated their remains and strung them from a bridge over the Euphrates River. Outside the city at Baharia, Worley and the Marines watched what seemed like an endless loop of news footage. *American bodies being used like victory flags*, Worley thought. It had happened a short drive away.

The Pentagon and Bush administration had been insisting that the forces on the ground were succeeding and the post-invasion period was going well. The footage shattered that view. Action demanded reaction. Second Battalion, First Marines, returned to Fallujah, where Worley's platoon seized a building and formed a strongpoint. If punishment was in the works, this was not quite it. The mission was not ambitious. The Marines were not ordered into an offensive or to clear the city of militants sheltered there. For about two weeks the platoon faced probing attacks. Both sides fought in a limited fashion. *This is more about sitting around getting dysentery than patrolling*, Lieutenant Zirkle thought. By May any ideas of fighting for Fallujah had been called off. The Marines were ordered back to Baharia to give Iraqi units and politicians a try at brokering a ceasefire. Many in Pale Rider Three were furious. Departure felt like surrender. They doubted Fallujah would find peace without a fight.

The platoon settled into a draining perimeter routine, passing the summer rotating through small outposts on the east–west highway outside the city, which they called MSR Mobile.* Pale Rider Three's section was about six miles long. Its Marines did four hours on patrol and eight hours off, around the clock, and had to stand guard in the outposts when not patrolling. The two corpsmen—Joseph Santos and Worley—had even less rest. They often did a four-hour patrol and then went right back out, so that no squad was without a sailor trained in trauma care. The platoon spent two or three days in the outposts and then one at Baharia to recharge. Sleep no longer offered a chance to recover; it became a means not to become more tired. The roads remained dangerous. Insurgents had been preying on American logistics convoys (often containing unarmed civilian drivers from the private contracting firm KBR) since early in the year, and were not averse to attacking military units head-on, especially units like Fox Company, which had little armor to protect its forces when they drove down the roads.

Back at Camp Lejeune, Worley's cousin, Dustin Kirby, followed what he could of the Marine Corps' war for Anbar. He knew little beyond that he was headed there and needed to prepare.

On Monday, September 6, Worley's platoon, accompanied by several Iraqi troops, loaded into three seven-ton cargo trucks and a Humvee

---

* The military assigned its own names to Iraq's roadways, often repurposing geographic names from back home—Tampa, Michigan, Chicago, and more. Troops rarely used, and often did not know, local highway numbers or names. Mobile was considered a MSR, or Main Supply Route.

to return to its outposts. It was time to rotate back to the highway duty on Mobile.

Zirkle did not like the trucks as troop-transport vehicles; he considered them totally improper. They were outfitted with only rudimentary armor. Boarding them required Marines to huddle together in large numbers—a departure from smart tactics and best practices that made them vulnerable. Most of the Humvees available were not hardened either, and some had makeshift additions of "Hillbilly armor," as troops called hastily fitted steel plates and sandbags. But Humvees at least carried only a few people, Zirkle thought, which limited how many Marines might be harmed by a single bomb.

The seven-ton trucks stopped at Camp Fallujah, the Corps' big base outside the city, so the Marines could have a hot meal and pick up the Iraqi troops who would join them for the rotation. Worley usually rode with Lieutenant Zirkle in the lead truck. He climbed in to wait. But as the vehicles began to move, he realized he had made a mistake. The trucks were out of order. The lieutenant climbed into the cab of the truck behind him, which moved into the lead position as the convoy headed for the gate. The lieutenant would be out front without him.

By now the rotation routine was known to the militants, which created risks on the roads. The Marines understood this and spread their vehicles apart. They drove close enough to support one another with gunfire but not so close that an attack would strike more than one truck.

The highway had six lanes, three in each direction. The platoon stayed in the center, to keep a distance from roadside blasts, moving at about 50 miles an hour.

A pickup truck drove forward on the convoy's left side and pulled even to the lead truck, where Lieutenant Zirkle, ten other Marines, and several Iraqi troops were riding.

It exploded.

An enormous blast cracked the air. It heaved Marines onto the asphalt as it blew apart the truck and set its remains afire. Worley felt a rush of its pressure wave two hundred yards away. His truck stopped. He leapt to the highway and ran to his first mass-casualty event. Black and gray smoke poured overhead. Fire burned to his front. He saw carnage, strewn limbs, and chunks of flesh. He wondered if his sprint was pointless.

The lead truck was a flaming, melting husk. He came to the first recognizable human shapes: Some were decapitated, others were intact. All were motionless. He could not tell, as he rushed close, if the intact victims were alive. Worley ran closer. An Iraqi soldier who was with the platoon had survived. His femur protruded from the flesh near his hip. He was screaming, pleading for help.

There are people here alive, Worley thought.

Doc Santos was in a truck behind him, and as Worley reached the first victim, he could see Santos sprinting into the mess, too. There was far too much work for two corpsmen. They had to triage.

Other Marines converged around them. Worley and Santos went from downed Marine to downed Marine, trying to sort out their priorities. Most of the people who had been on the truck were dead, but not all of them. Bret McCauley, who had been shot in the platoon's first fatal firefight, was among the living. He had only just returned to duty. Worley found another Iraqi alive, too.

Worley was still assessing the workload, trying to determine whether any of the Marines who appeared dead were alive. He had to keep moving.

"Come over here," he said to one of the Marines, and showed him how to stop a wounded man's bleeding. "Put your hand here. If I don't see you putting every bit of pressure you can on this, I'm going to come over and hit you."

"Lay your head near his nose about every ten seconds," he said. "And if this guy stops breathing, you scream for me so loud that there's no way I can miss it."

Worley ran to the next motionless man, seeking life.

After a few minutes he and Santos had found three Marine survivors, including Lieutenant Zirkle, who had been blown out of the cab and suffered severe burns. Worley assumed he had broken bones, too. Zirkle was conscious. Santos reached him first, injected him with morphine, and removed a hot piece of metal that Zirkle had landed on and was burning through his uniform.

After rechecking every down man, Worley doubled back to help him.

The lieutenant refused medical care. "Treat the others first," he said.

Worley lost his sense of time as he worked, but he came to a moment when he recognized a helicopter had landed beside the highway to lift the wounded away.

There was no one left to help.

A solemn cleanup began. The remains of six of the platoon's Marines, the Marine driver, and three Iraqi troops were put into body bags.*

Worley was blood-soaked, exhausted, grieving, and enraged when he arrived back at Baharia. But he knew he had done what he was supposed to. He had found his reason for being in Iraq.

For ten days the survivors of Pale Rider Three remained on the base; their platoon was deemed not combat ready. Lieutenant Zirkle had been evacuated from Iraq, leaving the platoon without an officer. It was mid-September and the battalion's deployment to Iraq was almost over. It was due to leave the country within weeks. Fox Company dissolved Pale Rider Three and assigned its members to other platoons. Worley joined Pale Rider Two and prepared to rotate back out to the highway.

The platoon left Baharia on September 17 for the outposts. It was Worley's first time outside the wire since the suicide attack. He arrived to tension. His new commander was simmering. The platoon was beset by radio troubles, and the lieutenant was struggling to talk with the company and battalion.

A call came that a Marine at Post Three had cut open the back of his right leg. He needed a corpsman to examine the injury and decide on treatment. The platoon's longtime corpsman, Petty Officer Third Class Michael Meaney, was on a satellite phone call with his mother. Worley was glad. He wanted to escape the stress around the lieutenant, and volunteered for the ride to the sandbagged post to look at the Marine's wound.

The cut was deep. The Marine needed stitches, which meant Worley and the rest of the patrol would need to drive him to Baharia, about forty minutes away.

---

* The Marines killed were Lance Corporal Derek Gardner, Corporal Mick Bekowsky, Lance Corporal Lamont Wilson, Lance Corporal Quinn Keith, Private First Class David Burridge, Lance Corporal Michael Allred, and Corporal Joseph McCarthy. The names of the Iraqi victims were not recorded by the platoon.

The Marines loaded four Humvees and set out. The Humvees were not properly armored.

Near the first bridge a civilian car sped up behind them. Worley was in the rear truck. The Marines waved at the driver, warning him off. The car kept coming.

It was getting closer, ignoring signals to stay back. Less than two weeks before, a truck bomb had detonated beside Pale Rider Three. The Marines were on edge. The gunner looked to Worley, unsure what to do. When the car was about fifty yards away, Worley gave the word.

"Engage," he said.

The gunner opened fire.

The car veered as bullets struck it. It hit a guardrail and stopped. The first Marine truck was driving over the bridge.

An explosion rocked the air, away from the disabled car, from another direction. Worley spun to look forward.

The Marines' second truck had been hit by an improvised bomb on its passenger side. The device had been hidden on the bridge. The other Humvees stopped. Worley zeroed in. Smoke poured from the truck. Nothing else seemed to move.

He grabbed the forty-pound trauma bag, scrambled from his Humvee, and sprinted yet again. He ran onto the bridge and into the open—and the next stage of the trap.

Whoever was watching waited until Worley pulled even with the second bomb, which was embedded in the guardrail. It exploded about ten yards to his right.

Worley felt heat, pressure, and shrapnel as the blast blew him sideways.

Pressure wrapped around him. His big frame felt inconsequential, a feather hit by a huge puff of air. Then he was heavy. He hit the blacktop at an angle, facing about 45 degrees left of the direction he had been running.

His ears rang.

His mind, buzzing, was unsure of what had happened.

He relaxed.

For some time—Worley was not sure how long—he did not move. Smoke drifted downwind. His thoughts were peaceful, almost spiritual.

I'm as good as dead. It's out of my hands.

Until he had landed on the hot asphalt, and began grasping what had happened to him, he had not realized how exhausted he felt, how draining the experience of Iraq had been, and how vigilant and edgy all of it had left him.

Now was different, and better. Things had spiraled so far out of control that he was no longer stressed. The blast had delivered to him something he did not know he had wanted. He welcomed it as it washed over him like a wave.

It was relief.

I have done everything I can and there is no more burden to perform.

It did not last. Worley felt part of himself waking.

Other thoughts rushed in.

I need to roll over and see if I am going to die.

He forced his buzzing mind to think. His training kicked in.

I need to see how bad it is.

The pain had begun; it pulled him further toward alertness. He saw blood spreading on the road in an expanding stain. This was his blood. Chunks of hot metal had hit him. He needed treatment.

He realized he was in the kill zone, which meant he would have to treat himself.

He started the inventory of his wounds. He lifted his right hand and ran it over his face and neck. No bleeding there. He reached for his pistol, which he remembered he had fastened to his hip instead of to his flak jacket, just before returning from the stand-down. It was gone, shattered into pieces around him. It had stopped a flying piece of shrapnel and probably saved his life.

He heard Marines shouting. They were behind him.

"Doc's moving!" one said. "Cancel the KIA!"

He continued checking himself, allowing his eyes to drift down his body. His left leg, from the knee down, was mangled beyond recognition. What remained was attached by a white scrap of tendon.

Worley was thinking clinically now. *Unsalvageable,* he thought.

His abdomen was bleeding. Nothing he could do about that here. The blood rushing out his left leg would kill him before whatever was going on in his guts got the chance.

He sat up, hearing the same adrenaline-fueled shouts he recognized from so many patrols. Marines were securing the bridge, coming for their wounded and their dead.

Worley needed to do his job, this time on himself. In his right cargo pocket, beside the thigh of his intact right leg, he kept a tourniquet that he had put together in Field Medical Service School. He had carried it on every patrol. It was a simple lifesaving device made from a broom handle, a grenade pin, and a green field dressing.*

It was a talisman, his charm.

He pulled it from his pocket.

Now was its time.

He leaned over his ruined left leg, fastened it tight over the meat above the knee, and twisted the broom handle, mashing his quadriceps against his femur, cutting off blood flow. He had little time. He had to get this done, or die.

A sergeant called him. "Do you need someone?"

Worley's senses had returned. He knew he was in the trap. Maybe he was bait.

The tourniquet was in place.

"No!" he shouted back.

He flopped sideways to the ground and rolled onto his stomach. He could not walk but he could try to crawl. He started to pull himself over the ground, chest down, with his arms, through the puddle of his own blood. He wondered if he could reach the damaged truck. He had not seen anyone come out alive. The exertion raised his heart rate, causing more blood to flow from his wounds.

I will kill myself doing this.

The bombs had triggered a response across Pale Rider Two. Marines from Post Two were speeding to them in trucks. They ran onto the bridge, into the blast sites, toward him and the smoldering wreck he had never reached. Marines in a Humvee with Doc Meaney pulled up to the damaged truck, removed a wounded man, then rushed to Worley. Hands

---

* Two corpsmen who handled the tourniquet remember it differently. The description in the text is from Worley. Doc Meaney recalls a section of wooden dowel thinner than a broomstick, and no grenade pin but a ring from a Gatorade bottle.

grabbed him, dragged him clear, and lifted him into the truck. He saw Meaney and the wounded Marine—Lance Corporal Jacob Lewis, the driver of the second truck. He was bleeding heavily from shrapnel in the neck.

The Humvee raced toward Camp Fallujah. Doc Meaney leaned over him, calm. He was a friend.

"You're leaking, brother," he said.

Worley looked at his mangled left leg, the torn and blood-soaked pants. Blood still seeped. He was disgusted with himself. *If you're going to do something right, putting your tourniquet on better be that thing.* He gritted his teeth, and he and Meaney gave the tourniquet three more twists. But Meaney was also examining Worley's right leg, which had been hit by shrapnel and was bleeding, too. He took a second tourniquet from his bag and tightened it to the right leg. The bleeding slowed, then stopped.

The Humvee kept driving, with Lewis beside them, holding a bandage to his own neck. Meaney chatted with Worley as he worked. Next he tried to get an IV started, but couldn't. He felt guilty. Worley was horribly wounded and in shock. Pale Rider Two was Meaney's platoon, and ordinarily it would have been him treating the Marine who had cut his leg. It would have been him in the ambush. Now he was keeping Worley calm and talking about Worley's daughter, Abigail Magdelana. She was three months old and had been born while he was here. He spoke of Angel, Worley's wife, and how he would see her soon.

Through the haze of shock and blood loss, Worley knew what Meaney was doing. He was functioning on multiple levels: as caregiver, victim, and someone who understood exactly how this situation worked. Marines who survived bomb blasts often acted according to pattern. First they would see if they were alive. Then they would seek their weapon. Then they would ask if their genitals were still there.

He had gone through the first two steps.

He loosened his pants. He looked. There were no apparent wounds.

The Humvee drove on. Worley wanted to know about the others in the truck the bomb had stopped.

He looked at Lewis. "Was there anything that could be done?" he asked.

"Absolutely not," Lewis said.*

The Humvee passed through the base gates.

Worley was rushed inside an aid station to a doctor and more corpsmen. They cut away his bloodied clothes. He felt a catheter being pushed down into his urethra. He did not know what other wounds he suffered or what his chances were. He was losing consciousness to anesthesia, unsure whether he would wake again, knowing that if he did he would be an amputee.

Darkness had settled over the Kirby home when Dustin Kirby pulled into the drive. The house was quiet. Usually the place was bustling. He stepped into the kitchen, curious about the silence. His brother, Daniel, a high school freshman, was alone inside.

Kirby sensed something was not right.

"What's up, man?" he said. "Crazy drive home."

"Yeah, man, that is crazy," Daniel said.

Kirby froze at the tone.

Daniel blurted it out. "Joe Dan got blown up, man," he said.

Kirby's pulse spiked upward. It was as if he were suddenly in a fight. *No*, he thought. *Not Joe Dan, Joe Dan is bulletproof.*

He heard himself ask: "Is he okay?"

"He got his leg blown off," Daniel said.

"No way," Dustin answered. "No, he didn't."

He called Worley's mother. She told him Joe Dan had been hit in an ambush, lost one leg, and been shot.† He was being treated but it was too soon to know many details beyond that he was alive. Kirby thought she spoke mechanically, as if reading a news report.

---

* Two men died inside the Humvee: Sami (last name unknown), an Iraqi interpreter working with the platoon, and Corporal Christopher Ebert.

† Official accounts and news reports of the ambush say that Worley was struck by small-arms fire after being wounded by the bomb. Worley himself is unaware of any gunshot wounds, and says these descriptions appear to contain errors.

This was the reason no one had answered his phone calls. Kirby's mother did not want him to hear about Joe Dan while he was driving. She herself was shaken, unsure what to say or do. When she heard Worley had been wounded, the façade she had built for herself—that Dustin would be safe on board a ship—crashed down. Her first thought, loaded with anger at Joe Dan, had filled her with guilt: *And he talked Dusty into doing the same thing!*

Daniel called to tell her that Dustin was home, and she rushed to the house and hugged him. She was crying. Her son was with the Marines, too. He had his uniform and combat kit in his pickup truck. But maybe there was something good in this, she thought. She told Dustin that this would be it. Joe Dan had lost a leg. The family had a casualty. That would be it. Families did not have two casualties in these wars.

Dustin Kirby would be safe.

Standing in their kitchen, listening to his mother, the news fresh in his head, Kirby saw it differently. The war was upon them, and he accepted his fate. *Joe Dan was fucking Superman*, he thought. *If this happened to him, it's definitely going to happen to me.*

Confronted in 2004 by soldiers with complaints about their poor state of equipment, Defense Secretary Donald Rumsfeld had been dismissive. "You go to war with the army you have, not the army you might want or wish to have at a later time," he said. During 2005, the American forces in Iraq were slowly becoming better equipped. Heavier equipment and armor were being deployed, and new weapons and protective gear were in development. But American forces often remained overwhelmed. Many lived in large bases, yielding the cities and countryside to militants, who often operated unchallenged. Iraqis were to vote on a new constitution while the country slipped into sectarian war. The war in Afghanistan, where President Hamid Karzai assumed office in the fall, remained a lower priority, though the Taliban endured and was becoming more bold.

FIVE

DOWN SAFE

Chief Warrant Officer Michael Slebodnik and the Air Cavalry War in Iraq

"I am an American soldier."

SEPTEMBER 27, 2005
East of Samarra, Iraq

Forward Operating Base MacKenzie was a fortified compound around an airstrip in Salahuddin Province, a relic from Iraq's military buildup under Saddam Hussein. During the Iran-Iraq War in the 1980s, when Hussein spent lavishly on his armed forces, the place was known as Samarra East Airfield. Yugoslav contractors built concrete hangars and bunkers beside the runway to protect the jets with which Iraq waged war.

The American military arrived at its gate in 2003, after Hussein's military was no more, settling in for occupation by moving into the old hardened shelters and erecting temporary housing outside. The place was spartan to the point of feeling oppressively grim—a mix of Eastern Bloc drab and plywood-and-prefab American haste, ringed by fences adorned with blowing trash. The Americans gave their outpost a cheery name, Camp Pacesetter, and made it a part of the network of bases in north-central Iraq from which soldiers began working on the country's post-invasion recovery and reconstruction. The first months were manageable. But security conditions around the base soon tanked. During 2003, armed resistance rose outside the perimeter fence. Pacesetter, under constant watch, became besieged and a target for rocket and mortar attacks.

Recognizing the change, in early 2004 the Army replaced the departing units with a cavalry squadron equipped with Abrams tanks and Bradley cavalry fighting vehicles—tracked troop carriers with armor and a chain gun*—and renamed the post Forward Operating Base MacKenzie, a designation more in tune with the dangers all around. MacKenzie had been the surname of an Army officer from American frontier history, General Ranald S. "Bad Hand" MacKenzie, who was credited with defeating recalcitrant tribes and instilling the rudiments of government during the Indian Wars of the 1870s. Adequately airbrushed, his history could inspire. One of his hands had been maimed in battle as a Union officer during the Civil War, but he returned to duty, short of fingers, and led soldiers through his second war, deep into another decade. Lost in the messaging of 2004 was an uglier resonance. After suffering more wounds, including a fall from a wagon that may have damaged his brain and perhaps an infection of syphilis, MacKenzie was deemed insane. He suffered through inglorious final years, all but forgotten. His nickname came to suggest ill fortune as much as grit. In occupied Iraq, it was an able shorthand for the soldiers' lot.

Forward Operating Base MacKenzie was a concrete-and-gravel island in a zone of baked sand. Located in a parched basin near the Tigris River, it offered an empty vista for soldiers to look out upon. Fine dust blew across its runway and worked its way into soldiers' laptops, beds, uniforms, and eyes. When it rained, the dust morphed into batter-like mud. A northern section of the base, littered with unexploded bomblets from old American cluster-munitions strikes, was a cordoned-off no-go zone, lest troops be maimed or killed by their own bombs. Bloodsucking sand flies preyed on the concentrated soldiers; until troops treated their uniforms with permethrin, some fell ill with leishmaniasis, a parasitic disease that can cause lesions resembling leprosy, along with fever, anemia, and

---

* A chain gun is a machine gun that uses a chain driven by external energy, as from an electric motor, to cycle ammunition through the weapon.

an enlarged spleen. Hussein's old airstrip was a dump, one of the most
unpleasant duty stations in Iraq.

Chief Warrant Officer Michael Slebodnik landed a Kiowa Warrior
scout helicopter on MacKenzie in late September of 2005. He was a soldier in Alpha Troop, Second Squadron, Seventeenth Cavalry Regiment,
part of the 101st Airborne Division. The troop had ten Kiowas and forty
soldiers, half of whom were pilots like Slebodnik. Its immediate role was
to relieve another Kiowa troop that was rotating home, and to work with
the First Battalion of the Fifteenth Infantry Regiment, which was running
armored ground patrols in and around the nearby city of Duluiyah and
trying to keep open the supply routes upon which MacKenzie's soldiers
relied.

In his community's jargon, Slebodnik was an "IP," an instructor pilot,
a senior member in the command who trained and evaluated younger
aviators. He was thirty-six years old and had been in the Army since the
day he graduated from high school in 1987 in Gibsonia, Pennsylvania, a
rural town north of Pittsburgh. He fit one of the Army's most successful
and loyal profiles. A devotee of military history whose grandfather had
been a navigator in a B-24 bomber in World War Two, he was a career
soldier, a lifer who had never wanted another job. Alpha Troop was scheduled for a one-year tour, and Slebodnik's seniority would have him lead
two-helicopter patrols, called scout weapons teams. Only the right-seater
in a Kiowa can fire the aircraft's weapons, and nothing forbade a senior
pilot from flying left seat and allowing a younger pilot to lead a flight and
control the weapons. But Slebodnik was known among peers for never
relinquishing the right-side chair—or control of a Kiowa's machine gun
and rocket pod.

Slebodnik had been to Iraq before as part of the Night Stalkers, the
160th Special Operations Aviation Regiment, which worked almost ex-
clusively with special operations units. An assignment to the 160th was
highly respected, a stamp of Army aviator cred. But Slebodnik did not
quite fit in. He disliked aspects of the unit's stateside social life, including
weekend carousing, and disliked even more that as a clean-living soldier
he was expected to be a designated driver for others when they drank. In
2004, he left the 160th and was reassigned. His wife, Tanja, whom he married in 2003, was soon diagnosed with a viral brain infection. She suffered

from seizures. It had been a busy and difficult year, a whirlwind of family and medical needs. Slebodnik and Tanja had each been previously married. He had three children, she had twin boys, and in 2004 she became pregnant. Their new son, Michie, was born on December 31. Slebodnik's switch to the Cav allowed him to be more fully involved as a new husband and father. He was home at Fort Campbell when Tanja was diagnosed and as she convalesced, and was present for their son's birth. He then had a run of months before returning to the war.

The squadron put him in Alpha Troop, which he helped train before Iraq. Slebodnik could seem easygoing and even folksy, a balding man with a big smile and Western Pennsylvania accent, which led him to pronounce Washington "Wershington," to the amusement of peers. He took the ribbing easily. He was religious and socially proper; unlike many soldiers, he could be painstakingly polite. His understated style belied his competitive streak. A dedicated runner, Slebodnik was determined to remain in top shape in the later years of his career, even as he joked with fellow pilots that he ran so that he could keep up with Tanja, who was more naturally athletic and lean. And he was deeply invested in the cavalry ethos. The Kiowa was an aircraft he knew intimately, and the latest variant, the D model, was the most lethal version the Pentagon had fielded yet. Across his community he was considered an aggressive pilot, someone who pushed the Kiowa hard, sometimes beyond its official limits, occasionally to the point of damaging engines. This intensity had roots fellow soldiers respected and understood: He spoke often of protecting the troops on the ground, no matter what. His call sign, Annihilator 21, fit the man.

He arrived to Iraq harried. After leaving the States in the summer in 2005, Alpha Troop stopped in Kuwait and was waiting for a scheduled move north, when the soldiers were told to cease their preparations and hurry to MacKenzie. Much was rushed. Combat-loaded Kiowa helicopters can fly for about ninety minutes before needing to refuel. The troop's journey was a series of hops over the desert from one refueling point to another, a linear tour of the archipelago of bases and outposts the Pentagon had built in Iraq, the unsightly public works project of a war in progress. They flew over a universe of plywood shacks, generators, fuel bladders, sandbags, fences, and blast walls. Much of it was disorganized and already falling into disrepair. MacKenzie matched the mess. He had

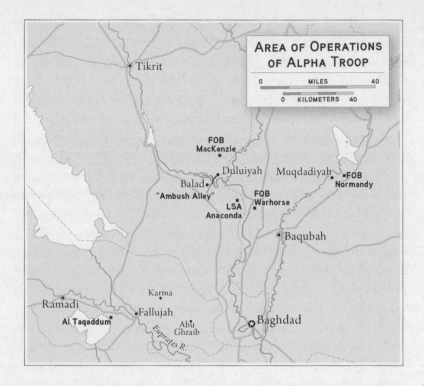

just landed at the old airstrip, and was carrying equipment to his new living quarters, when he almost crashed through the top of a septic tank. Soon after, he wrote Tanja to tell her that the first walk across his base had included a near plunge into human waste.

> *I fell in one foot in one foot out. The lid saved me from breaking ribs on the edge of the opening. Lucky for me the tank wasn't full. Welcome to Iraq Mike. Smile. I didn't get hurt.*

Alpha Troop, one part of an Army reorganizing against an insurgency it had not expected to fight, was entering a confounding war. A briefing about Slebodnik's new world contained the story of a stretched military force mired in an evolving conflict. In the first months of occupation, during 2003, the Americans at Pacesetter had stepped out to patrol the base's environs, meet Iraqis who lived nearby, and encourage them to accept Iraq's Washington-backed government. There were clear problems. The Coalition Provisional Authority's de-Baathification order, issued in May 2003, stripped the government of an experienced workforce and barred trained officers and soldiers from further service. This disrespected almost an entire governing class, and freed the remains of an experienced military for guerrilla war. Official optimism still ran high, in part because the forces opposing the Pentagon's project had started small, and in part because the military's and the Coalition Provisional Authority's internal and external messages emphasized reconstruction, political transition, and aid. But the picture was darkening. As dangers arose, the United States took steps intended to protect its forces, keeping troops inside bases and venturing out on short missions and limited patrols—a posture that ceded most of the country to armed groups and made many dangerous areas more dangerous still.

By early 2004—when First Squadron, Fourth Cavalry Regiment rotated from Germany to MacKenzie—the armed groups had grown in numbers and skill. Their ranks included area tribesmen, former Iraqi soldiers, and foreign fighters who had traveled to Iraq in what they saw as the call of jihad. These combatants were firing rockets and mortars at the base, driving the Americans into bunkers and hangars and behind concrete blast walls. The base enforced an absolute blackout at night; any light was a potential aiming point for attackers and invited more accurate fire. Other dangers could not be readily avoided. The road from the big logistics base at Balad to MacKenzie passed through the small city of Duluiyah, a warren of single-story concrete buildings and alleyways where American soldiers and the local population mixed.

Duluiyah was a Sunni town. Many of its people had been displaced, first by the fall of their patron, Hussein, and then by de-Baathification. They were angered anew by the status and powers claimed by Kurdish and Shiite parties in Iraq's government, which the Americans in Baghdad had granted in an interim constitution. Seething under foreign occupation and shifting domestic politics, much of Duluiyah tolerated, if not outright supported, the insurgents' campaign. When Americans left their base, they were often attacked by gunfire, rocket-propelled grenades, and bombs on the roads. First Squadron, Fourth Cavalry Regiment lost several soldiers and a private contractor that year.

The demands of maintaining troops in an isolated base led to gunfights timed to the resupply schedule. To keep MacKenzie provisioned, the American military sent roughly two convoys a week from its logistics base in Balad through Duluiyah to Mackenzie. Each contained ten to fifteen trucks carrying food, fuel, ammunition, spare parts, mail, and anything else the base's residents required. Often their enemies were waiting. To discourage ambushes before they occurred, when a convoy was due, the soldiers would send out Bradleys to clear the way. It was a risky routine, a forcible opening of the only ground route to the base's southern gate. The violence was such an established part of the routine that on one section of road more than three kilometers long the Americans plowed and burned all the vegetation on each side, creating standoff in a deadly corridor. The fighting could still be pitched, especially in the built-up areas through which the road passed. Earlier in the summer of 2005, one of the attackers moved close enough to throw an RKG-3 armor-piercing hand grenade onto the top of a Bradley. The grenade—a shaped charge attached to a small parachute that directs the weapon's penetrating blast—cut a hole through the armor, nearly killing a soldier inside. A week before Slebodnik arrived, a convoy of resupply trucks from KBR had been cut off and swarmed by attackers in the city, leading to a long battle between militants and an American patrol that drove to help them; several unarmed contractors were wounded or killed. Children had been involved in the attack, and some of the drivers were shot at close range as mobs rushed their trucks, adding to Duluiyah's rising tally of American lives. After the battle, survivors said Iraqi police officers had participated in the ambush. By then, the route had earned a standard name: Ambush Alley. One section, where the armed groups hid most of their makeshift bombs, carried a more menacing distinction: Death Valley. Bringing supplies to MacKenzie was a war within the war.

Recognizing that the roads to Duluiyah required more American eyes and MacKenzie needed more firepower, the Army was using Kiowas to keep the place alive. Soldiers running the Ambush Alley gauntlet tried to have two helicopters in the air around them every time a convoy was due. The relationship was symbiotic. The convoys carried the Kiowas' fuel.

———————

Slebodnik found his way to his bunk inside a shipping container along the airfield, and took a tour of his latest home. Soldiers had been busy. They had cleaned the hangars, chasing away rats and snakes, and built a nonalcoholic bar, improved the gym, and hooked up Internet and phone connections. Life on the base was safer than it had been in 2004. Kiowa pilots had been flying around the clock for most of the year. The flatlands that surrounded MacKenzie offered no place for attackers to conceal themselves, and the frequent comings and goings of the helicopters forced mortar and rocket teams to reconsider tactics. Nights tended to be quiet. The soldiers lived under a roof of black sky and bright stars.

Alpha Troop's first phase of the deployment was for familiarization and breaking in. The fresh pilots worked with their peers from the departing troop to learn the terrain and pick up the rhythm of the air cavalry's war. Each aviator adjusted to the repetitious loop of missions: where to meet for preflight briefings, where to test-fire weapons, where to refuel and rearm while on missions away, what to do when not in the air. Slebodnik was put on reverse cycle, sleeping in the container by day and flying at night. One day, to adjust, he took Ambien to sleep. The schedule was draining and the amenities were less than what was available on larger bases, but he was satisfied. There were phones with which he could call Tanja, talk to their children, and get updates on their infant son. There were computer terminals with Internet and access to email. He knew Tanja worried. He understood how silence could be agonizing. He followed a habit of notification, a ritual of assurance that their future was safe. Whenever he returned from a flight, no matter how distracted or tired, he would send an email containing two words she waited to read: "Down safe."

On those nights she would sleep.

———————

The Kiowa Warrior helicopter is a small and lightweight military aircraft, a single-engine platform in the bantam class. It stands on a pair of metal skids that span about six feet across; even with a pair of side-mounted weapons pylons attached, the aircraft is less than ten feet wide. Its four rotors beat through the air in a diameter of only thirty-five feet. The Black Hawk, in comparison, rests atop wheels nine feet apart and its rotors spread nearly fifty-four feet. (With external fuel tanks, the Black Hawk can exceed twenty feet in width.) As a single-engine aircraft, the Kiowa is also slow, reaching maximum speeds at level flight around 105 knots, compared to a Black Hawk's in excess of 150. It is lightly armored and has a large windscreen. At a glance, the helicopter can seem about as safe as a phone booth with a rotor on top, carrying a load of flammable fuel. But the Kiowa possesses a characteristic well matched to the role of protect-ing infantry: It is extremely maneuverable. When cruising at 60 knots, a confident pilot can put the aircraft through a complete 180-degree turn in about fifty feet. In this way, Kiowa pilots in Iraq could participate in firefights as small, mobile, and semi-mechanical gunfighters, hunting and turning and killing in concert with foot soldiers below. In the configu-ration that Alpha Troop used, the left pylon held a .50-caliber machine gun. The right held a Hydra rocket pod loaded with 2.75-inch rockets with explosive warheads. Above the Kiowa's rotors stood a large globe, called the mast-mounted sight, containing a thermal optic with which pilots could separate terrain from its human targets, day or night. The Army painted its Kiowa fleet a shade of dark green. With time, as the air-craft were splattered with oil and exhaust, they inclined toward black— pint-sized American machines that flitted above the infantry, frightening, taunting, hunting the grunts' tormentors, then darting away to drink fuel before returning again.

On October 6, Slebodnik woke at midnight for a 2:00 A.M. briefing and a taste of the tour ahead. After preflighting the aircraft, checking its weight and fuel, he flew to an area of the basin north of the base that pi-lots used as a test range and fired the aircraft's weapons to be sure they worked. Then he flew off with another Kiowa to cover the infantry on a cordon-and-search in a village near the Tigris River. They watched over the soldiers from 4:30 A.M. until 10:00 A.M. The search turned up a small cache of military equipment in a chicken coop, which the soldiers on the ground destroyed with explosives.

Kiowas flew at low elevation over Iraq, often less than fifty feet above the ground, which gave aircrews remarkably clear views of people below: shepherds tending goats and sheep, women doing laundry, children playing along canals. Pilots passed through the air at highway speeds, rushing into Iraqis' lives to see them only for seconds, looking down upon surprised or annoyed faces. The Americans' enemies hid themselves. The war's toll was in view. On the flight back, Slebodnik's Kiowa was thumping low over the Tigris River when he saw a corpse of a man stuck in a fishing net. His hands were bound with zip ties. Slebodnik thought he looked Iraqi but was not entirely sure. He watched the body break free and drift away, out of sight.

Many flights were uneventful. Others were exercises in frustration for a foreign force on its enemies' home ground. On October 9 he covered an infantry unit on a nighttime raid to snatch a suspected insurgent from his home. They didn't catch the man. Slebodnik listened on the radio as soldiers discussed how a Predator drone had spotted an Iraqi fleeing into a building. In the right seat, Slebodnik wore green-tinted night-vision goggles and could see the Predator sparkle the home with an infrared marking laser. The thin beam of light was invisible to the Iraqis but stark and clear to him. All of this technology, the presence of the soldiers, the stack of aircraft above, the almost incalculable expense and extraordinary synchronization of the combined fighting tools—none of it mattered that night. The man escaped. The Predator's laser was like a flashlight beam sweeping a kitchen through which a resident mouse had dashed.

Slebodnik was feeling homesick. "It bugs me that I am missing Mike grow up," he wrote to Tanja afterward. "I see him in my mind doing things."

The ground units that Alpha Troop supported were busy that fall helping Iraq's government put a referendum for a new constitution to a public vote. For the soldiers, this meant trying to provide safe polling places and protecting the movement of ballots through areas beset by hostility. It was a daunting set of tasks—simultaneous security missions spread across the country—and it forced some units to relocate troops. Slebodnik was shifted to another former Iraqi military base, renamed Forward Operating Base Normandy, northeast of MacKenzie, near the city of Muqdadiyah.

October 14 was the day before the national vote, and while watching over government trucks bringing ballots to Duluiyah, Slebodnik thought he saw a small bomb hidden against a guardrail outside the city. He called it in. Alpha Company sent a patrol to examine it. The soldiers saw wires protruding from the unknown object and thought it was a bomb, too. As they worked, a sniper fired a single shot at a turret gunner in a Humvee.

The shot missed.

Over Slebodnik's radio came a request.

The ground patrol wanted him to suppress a tree line from where the shot had come.

Although the Kiowa carried a forward-looking infrared sensor and a laser range finder, many Kiowa pilots were of an older school. They fought visually. Slebodnik had his own way. During preflight, upon taking his seat in the right side of an aircraft, he pressed his left hand—spread wide from pinkie to thumb—against a spot on the windscreen that only he knew, and drew hash marks with a grease pencil or dry-erase marker. This crude grid became his weapon sight. After taking off, he would fly to a test-fire area, fire a burst of .50-caliber machine-gun rounds, and note if the rounds struck high or low, left or right, relative to his visual guide. From there, his mind attuned to the day's Kentucky windage, he was ready to fight.

After the sniper shot, Slebodnik performed a set of aerial maneuvers he had practiced for years. He flew away from where he thought the sniper was hiding, then turned back and rushed the spot head-on. As the distance between the Kiowa and his target shrunk, he bumped the nose of the aircraft up. The helicopter climbed, steeply like a rising roller coaster encased in engine and rotor noise, until it was about 1,000 feet in the air.

There Slebodnik leveled off, pointed the nose, lined up his sight—and dove.

Using controls on the cyclic, the flight control stick rising between a pilot's legs, a right-seat Kiowa pilot can fire rockets or the .50-caliber machine gun. Slebodnik flipped a lever to the left to select for the machine gun, then lifted a safety cover, depressed his thumb on the button, and opened fire.

The heavy gun began blasting from the pylon to his left, shaking the aircraft.

Down he dropped, gun thumping, past 800 feet, past 600 feet, adjusting the orientation of his makeshift sight as he descended, lower, to 400 feet, then to 200 feet, and at last below, firing throughout as the ground seemed to rise.

At this phase of an attack, risks suddenly rise. A Kiowa cannot defend itself from its bottom, flanks, or rear, which means that overflying a target presents an armed foe with the opportunity of firing back, a potentially devastating counterpunch. And so, short of the target and at about 100 feet off the ground, Slebodnik ceased firing and performed the next step in the sequence. He banked hard right, moving away from where the bullets he fired had been thudding, and swung away from the point of greatest vulnerability.

His copilot said he saw a muzzle flash.

Someone was firing at them.

Slebodnik had been in the Army his entire adult life. It was his first combat engagement. He flew the aircraft out of rifle range, turned around, lined up the nose, attacked again, and repeated the dodge. He performed the maneuver a third time, pouring gunfire into the trees.

Adrenaline flowed through him. He felt elated. He was driving a sniper away from the grunts. He was unsure whether he had hit the man, but the soldiers on the ground were safe. "No more firing came from that area," he wrote later. "We didn't see any bodies or blood, but at least we got him to stop. It was the first time I have ever engaged an enemy force. It felt good."

Voting proceeded quietly in the areas he flew the next day. Anticipation gave way to relief.

Then came blood.

On the night of October 17, an infantry company on MacKenzie, Alpha Company, First Battalion, Fifteenth Infantry Regiment, sent out its First Platoon on a route-clearance patrol. Another logistics convoy was due in the morning. The ambush of the KBR convoy in September had cost unarmed drivers their lives, and led to recriminations and at least one investigation. The soldiers were determined not to have a repeat, and planned to clear and secure the route. The lead Bradley held nine people: three soldiers in front and five more in back, plus Bakim, an Iraqi interpreter.

While crossing Ambush Alley, it drove over a buried bomb.

The bomb exploded.

The blast had a dual effect. It perforated the Bradley's fuel tank and damaged the cable that opened the rear hatch to the troop compartment. The vehicle burst into flames. Bakim and the soldiers inside were trapped.

Gunfire broke out to the west.

Sergeant First Class Alwyn Cashe climbed down from the turret and pulled the driver from his hatch. With the vehicle commander, he put out the fire that was burning the other soldier's uniform and skin.

Diesel fuel had splattered onto Cashe. Flames spread to him. He did not stop. He returned to the disabled Bradley and, with help from a desperate soldier inside, forced open its rear hatch.

The troop compartment was an oven. Cashe helped burning soldiers out, through the smoke and waves of heat, but one of the Americans and Bakim, the interpreter, did not appear. His uniform aflame, Cashe plunged in. He crawled into the rectangular metal space, moving forward until he found the last soldier and Bakim, whom he dragged out.

Bakim was dead. The others were alive, many with severe wounds. When Cashe took his place among them, more than 70 percent of his body had been burned.

In the days after the ambush, Slebodnik began to hear of a plan by the infantry company to return to the kill zone. Cashe survived the medevac flight and the longer journey to the Army's burn ward at Fort Sam Houston, in San Antonio, Texas. But he was covered with second- and third-degree burns. Soldiers were warned he might not make it. The pilots of Alpha Troop was told to ready for a follow-up patrol. An assistant division commander wanted to tour the area. The units spent days organizing a VIP patrol. A Kiowa was set aside to fly the general over the area, and a spare helicopter was assigned to be ready if the first helicopter had mechanical problems. Slebodnik was assigned to the spare.

At midday on November 2, Alpha Company escorted the general off Mackenzie toward Duluiyah. A Bradley drove in the lead, followed by a pair of Humvees. The first held the general and the company commander, Captain Jimmy Hathaway. The second carried the sergeant major and other soldiers. The patrol rolled heavy. More vehicles followed.

The column moved past a police station, and had just passed where Cashe's Bradley had been destroyed on October 17. A rocket-propelled grenade flew from an alley and struck the third vehicle on the armored door beside the driver. Its armor-piercing warhead exploded. The blast severely wounded the driver and injured other soldiers inside.

The patrol pulled over to fight. Kiowas bore down. Several of the attackers ran to a house and the ruins of the old Baathist party headquarters, which the Kiowas circled. A British jet did a low pass to fix them in place, and was followed by F-15s that dropped a pair of 500-pound bombs, one on each building.

The fight ended.

The company set up a landing zone at a soccer field. By the time the helicopters landed, it was too late. The wounded driver was dead. The soldiers placed him on the floor of the Black Hawk, which lifted him away.

The patrol still had not reached the kill zone from the September ambush. The general asked to keep going.

"If it is important enough for a kid to get hurt out here, it is important enough for me to continue mission," he said to Hathaway.

The patrol reorganized and pushed on. The remainder of its movement was quiet. The air strikes had shut down fighting for the day.

Hathaway appreciated the general's decision. He thought it signaled to Alpha Company that its soldiers' work would not be dictated by those who ambushed them. Slebodnik thought otherwise. He saw the mission as unnecessary. The driver, Specialist Dennis J. Ferderer Jr., was from North Dakota, a twenty-year-old from a family-run dairy farm. He was the type of stock Slebodnik knew from Western Pennsylvania. His death, in Slebodnik's view, had been caused by a senior officer's urge to get a peek.

"The general went on his sightseeing tour, and 1-15 lost a guy," he wrote to Tanja. "What a waste."

Slebodnik was patriotic and committed to the Army; sometimes he groused about negative media coverage of the wars. But he was also a career soldier of the middle rank, unshakably dedicated to younger troops, and not above criticizing an officer he thought had done them wrong. "All just so the General could see what it was like," he continued. "He had a taste alright, but at the cost of one of ours."

The next day Slebodnik felt down and lethargic. He did not go to the gym or do his usual run. "It's depressing," he wrote. A few days later, word came down about Cashe, the sergeant who had been flown to the burn ward. He had died, too.*

To fight the elastic insurgency, American commanders often changed plans and shuffled forces. In November, Alpha Troop was reassigned, and flew its helicopters to the air base at Logistics Support Area Anaconda, at Balad.

Anaconda, still growing, had become a super-base—an operational and logistical hub. Built near the serpentine Tigris River, in the years since the invasion it swelled into an American military city, with compounds and housing centers protected by mazelike arrangements of concrete blast walls. Just beyond its outer perimeter was another world. Farmers tended seasonal crops on fields drenched by water pumped from the river. Date palms and fruit trees stood in groves. The vegetation and the many roads, waterways, bridges, and footpaths offered uncountable places where gunmen were shielded from view and from where rocket and mortar crews could fire. Unlike Mackenzie, where shelling and incoming rockets had declined, attacks still shook Anaconda. Troops were often alerted by alarms warning of incoming ordnance, followed by explosive blasts.

On December 5, Slebodnik led another team of two Kiowas on a flight northeast of the base, on the opposite side of the river. It was a typical scouting mission, a matter of making the rounds through areas where

---

* Sergeant First Class Cashe was awarded a Silver Star. Several of his former commanders have nominated him for a Medal of Honor, the nation's highest and most prestigious valor award.

enemy activity had occurred in the past, and checking previously used rocket firing points. In the Kiowa's left seat was Chief Warrant Officer Mariko Kraft, a young pilot on her first tour. Slebodnik had been training her. The two often flew together and had a rapport.

When the two aircraft were low on fuel, they planned to head to Forward Operating Base Warhorse, near Baqubah, for gas. It had been a quiet flight and Slebodnik and Kraft were chatting amiably. Kraft was lamenting at how little they had seen. Slebodnik was used to disappointment. Iraq was beset by war, but the insurgents were patient and knew how to stay out of sight.

"Sometimes you don't find anything out here," he said.

They were flying over farmland. They passed a white Toyota pickup truck in a field between two stands of tall trees. Three men stood next to the truck. The field was barren. Its crop had been harvested. Slebodnik came from farm country. This was an unusual place for idle men.

He brought the Kiowa around for a second look.

The men broke and ran.

Slebodnik fired a warning burst, away from the men. They did not stop. He watched them split up. Two of the men wore black and stayed together while a third man, dressed in gray, veered away. Slebodnik asked the trail aircraft to follow the men in black. They were heading across open ground for the trees to the west.

He swung back to check their truck.

Kraft called out from his left.

"I see mortar rounds," she said.

Slebodnik did not see them. He swung the Kiowa around again. "I am going to go by low and slow," he said, and asked Kraft to lean back and shield herself behind the vertical armor plate along the left-side door. "Stay in a protective posture," he said. "I don't want you to get shot in the face."

As they drew close to the truck, Kraft pointed. "Over there," she said.

Slebodnik saw them: three long, dark green projectiles spaced in a row about eight or ten feet apart. They were in a ditch by the pickup truck's front end and aiming southeast—directly at the American base.

"Those aren't mortars, they're rockets," he said.

Rockets fired at Balad often were rigged to timers that launched ordnance only after the men who emplaced them were safely gone, at no risk of being hit by return fire. These men had been far along in their task when the Kiowas happened upon them. Slebodnik radioed to the second Kiowa that the men in black were combatants and could be engaged. He turned the nose of his Kiowa toward where they had fled, to join in.

The other aircraft opened fire.

The men bolted. Slebodnik was positioned for a good view and a clear shot as his Kiowa bore down. He depressed the button on the cyclic, firing a long burst while swinging the aircraft's nose and sweeping bullets from the second man toward the first, the way a wet brush, if whipped, will sling an arc of paint.

The second man tripped. Slebodnik could not tell whether bullets had struck him.

The first man stopped in mid-stride and crashed hard; Kraft saw that his back seemed to have been torn open by a .50-caliber round.

The gun run carried them past the pair. Slebodnik came around for a second pass.

The wounded man rolled in the dirt.

Slebodnik fired more bursts. The man stopped moving.

Pilots in the other Kiowa radioed to say that they could not find the man in gray. They turned for the truck.

Slebodnik followed. He made a first pass with the machine gun, then wheeled around and attacked with 2.75-inch rockets. The first rocket was long. The second struck to the truck's right. The third was a direct hit, impacting where the pickup bed met the cab.

He yelled. Kraft was yelling, too.

As quickly as it had begun, it was over. Slebodnik and Kraft flew past the truck a last time. Their helicopter was in a condition pilots call Winchester: out of machine-gun ammunition. Both aircraft needed gas. They left the engagement area behind.

The pickup truck was smoldering, sending smoke into the air.

Slebodnik was trembling when he shut down the aircraft at the base. He shouted again with satisfaction and joy.

He had killed an enemy combatant. He had been in the Army eighteen years and felt like a true soldier at last. And it was more than a kill: They had caught a rocket team in the act of setting up ordnance, and stopped an imminent threat. He may have saved American lives.

As more information circulated from other units that visited the field, he heard that after the Kiowa team had left, the man in gray tried to return to the damaged truck. A pair of Apache gunships caught him there and killed him. A ground patrol found the bodies of all three of the men and recovered the rockets.

That night, still charged with energy, Slebodnik went looking for Kraft, who had spent the hours thinking about what had passed. She felt no sorrow for the men they had shot and had no doubts about how the team had acted; their actions fell well within the mission and the rules. But she had been wondering about the people the dead men had left behind. "I feel bad for their families," she told Slebodnik. "Why did they do that to their families? They did not just sacrifice themselves. They sacrificed their families."

Slebodnik was unmoved. Those men had pointed rockets at a base where thousands of American soldiers, including him and Kraft, lived and worked. They made choices and lost. He sat down and wrote home, sharing with Tanja a detailed account. "Today I killed a man," he began. He had trained for a moment that at last had played out in front of his windscreen. There was nothing to doubt. "My only real thoughts," he wrote later, "have been how could I have done it better to get all 3."

"I am," he wrote, "an American soldier."

———

Slebodnik had few chances to repeat the flight. Later in December he was reassigned for much of the winter to liaison duty, which required him to work from an operations center coordinating flights for Special Forces missions. He was bored and angry, and lobbied to be returned to the cockpit. He groused to Tanja and sent emails to his senior officers, pleading to be sent back to the action.

He was granted his wish in March and was soon flying missions again.

The morning of March 21 began with the familiar routine. Slebodnik and Kraft were on a reconnaissance mission before dawn, checking roads and scouting for signs of the insurgents. Just before sunrise they passed over Muqdadiyah, a city of about 300,000 people just southwest of Forward Operating Base Normandy along the Diyala River, a tributary that feeds the Tigris. They looked in on the governor's residence. They saw nothing of interest. The city felt quiet. Low on fuel, the aircraft headed to Normandy for gas, flying over farmland.

The sun was rising. The pilots stowed their night-vision goggles.

Only one soldier had come out to assist the aircraft at the refueling station. In the trail aircraft, Chief Warrant Officer Lori Hill waited while Slebodnik and Kraft filled up, with Kraft standing beside the aircraft on fire guard while Slebodnik sat at the controls.

One of the radios became noisy with chatter. The compound in Muqdadiyah used by the joint coordination center, where the local police and Iraqi and American officials worked together on projects, was under attack. An American infantry patrol in the city was alone and under fire, possibly trapped.

Slebodnik waved his arms at Kraft.

"What's up?" she said.

"Ground guys are pinned down," he shouted. "We need to get gas and go!"

Slebodnik and Kraft finished topping off. Time was pressing. The radio reports were saying the attack in Muqdadiyah was complex, and the patrol was small—only two Bradleys from the First Squadron of the Thirty-Second Cavalry Regiment—and under heavy fire. Muqdadiyah was not far, about three miles away. Hill opted to leave before her tank was full.

The two aircraft lifted off, cleared Normandy's outer wall, and gathered speed, heading southwest. It was 6:00 A.M. The light was getting bright. They needed only minutes to reach the soldiers calling for help.

Slebodnik had flown about halfway when gunfire encased them.

Red tracers streaked past the windscreen in tight, consistent lines, like machine guns, not rifles. He heard the crack of bullets going by and felt the metallic thunk of other bullets strike his aircraft.

Hill's voice sounded over the radio.

"Mike, you're getting shot at!" she said.

From his left side Kraft was yelling, too. "Break right!" she shouted.

Slebodnik turned so abruptly that Kraft thought one of the Kiowa's four rotors might have snapped. There was an explosion. A rocket-propelled grenade projectile had burst in the air nearby. Slebodnik sorted through multiple thoughts, beginning with surprise. *What are they doing here?* he wondered. *We aren't near the grid yet.*

Kraft was rushing through an assessment. The gunfire had been thick and come up at them from multiple firing points in an L-shaped formation. She recognized what was happening. Whoever was attacking the joint coordination center in Muqdadiyah had set a trap for reinforcements.

This looks pretty organized, she thought. *This is not some farmer.*

Slebodnik had laid the aircraft hard over to right and was still taking their Kiowa through the turn. The motion swung Kraft up in the air, above him, to his left. She heard the torque indicator alarm bonging and thought: *What damage have the bullets done?* Looking down, she could see Slebodnik's lips moving as he held the turn. He was mumbling a prayer. She wondered: *Last rites?*

She marveled at how much she could see and think at once, as if time had slowed or her mind had sped up.

We're going to die, she thought.

The trail aircraft opened fire with the .50-caliber machine gun and broke right, too, following Slebodnik's lead. The ambushers missed with another rocket-propelled grenade. A bullet struck the second Kiowa as it flew through the gunfire. It passed up into the aircraft, stopping about three inches behind the left seat, near the back of First Lieutenant Kevin White, who was flying with Hill.

The multifunction displays in Hill and White's aircraft, one in front of each pilot, briefly went dead.

Slebodnik eased out from the turn and leveled off.

They were clear, out of range. He turned north to regroup. Alarms sounded. His mast-mounted sight had gone blank; either it or one of its cables had been hit. The AC and DC generators were off-line. The cockpit display indicators told the two pilots that they were now on battery power. Hydraulic fluid leaked in the cockpit.

A helicopter without hydraulics cannot fly long.

Hill and White caught up. Slebodnik was talkative, awash in the wonder of being alive.

"I may have been praying back there," he said to Kraft.

"You were definitely praying," Kraft shot back.

He had choices to make. According to the alarms, the helicopters should return to base. They did not have many minutes to fly. But the two Bradleys—a small patrol led by a lieutenant using the call sign Rock 16—were a short distance to the south.

Slebodnik was the senior pilot. "The aircraft is still flying," he said to Kraft. "We can support those ground guys. Do you agree?"

"Yes," she said.

"Take your M4 out, because I can't protect you on the left side," he said.

Kraft lifted the carbine and fastened it to herself with a carabiner. She was ready to fire out the left door as Slebodnik maneuvered. The carabiner would keep the rifle attached if he turned again as he had minutes before.

Low to the earth, just above the farmers' fields, Slebodnik chose another route toward Muqdadiyah and headed for the trapped grunts.

The attack on Muqdadiyah, large in scale and well prepared, was rife with betrayal and plans for fratricide, a marker of the bitter and confusing war that had sprung up around the American occupation. Earlier that morning, as the sun was about to rise, the helicopters had flown over the participants' final arrangements. The joint coordination center's compound held a courthouse, a jail, and a station for the Iraqi police. At 4:30 A.M. Muqdadiyah's mayor, who was a member of a prominent Sunni political party, vacated the compound with his bodyguards, leaving the area to be attacked by darkness. An hour and fifteen minutes later the militant raid began, with gunmen opening fire from three nearby buildings. One building was the local headquarters of the same party as the mayor; another was the home of the deputy governor, also a party member.

Outside the city, hovering above the fields, Slebodnik checked his map, planning the angle at which he would approach. Kraft and White were trying to raise Rock 16 on the radio. Slebodnik looked north and saw a burning police truck.

The two helicopters flew toward the truck and were fired upon, this time from a tree line. Slebodnik rolled the aircraft to the right and fired. Hill passed him on his left. He had flown days without finding insurgents. Now they were everywhere. As he opened fire, the Kiowa was directly above a farmer standing in the field with a shovel. The burst startled Kraft. She shouted and slapped him on his left thigh. Slebodnik laughed.

He turned south. He was shaking. He did not know why.

He held up a hand to show Kraft.

"I'm scared," he said, but wondered if he meant it. Machine gunners were hiding in the approaches to Muqdadiyah, trying to shoot the little helicopters down. Maybe he was just excited.

Hill and White radioed to say they could see smoke rising from the compound. Hill thought the American soldiers would be nearby. Slebodnik headed that way, through more gunfire they ignored.

At the city's edge, the pilots reached Rock 16 over the radio. He said his patrol was under fire. The Bradleys had left their base before sunrise on a counter-IED patrol, an assignment to search roads for bombs, and had not been expecting to fight. Each vehicle had only one soldier in the rear troop compartment, leaving the patrol leader, First Lieutenant Chris Hume, with no forces to dismount and maneuver. The attack did not seem intended for them, but they had tried driving to the center's aid and been stopped by gunfire.

Slebodnik asked Rock 16 to protect him with covering fire as he bumped up high to have a look. The Kiowa climbed.

He saw a white building below, surrounded by concrete walls. Vehicles burned within; there was no one to fire upon. He broke right, just as more machine guns sounded below. Tracers streaked past, and he heard the crack of bullets again, and felt the impact on the aircraft as the Kiowa was struck once more. Behind him, Hill opened fire.

Someone from the Bradleys called on the radio. The helicopters had surprised the attackers around the building, who had shifted fire off the American ground troops.

"You're being shot!" Kraft heard. "You're driving them away."

"Get out of there!" she answered. "That's your opportunity to go."

A female voice cut in on another radio frequency, a growl tinged with surprise. Kraft heard its urgency and pain.

Slebodnik asked if the trail aircraft had been hit.

Hill did not answer. Slebodnik turned his head and saw Hill was still flying. Her aircraft looked intact.

Lieutenant White's voice sounded on the net. "We took some fire," he said. "We'll see you on the other side."

Hill's voice followed his. She said she had tried following Slebodnik and climbed, but their aircraft had been hit again. Now she was flying low over the buildings, a dangerous move in a city swarming with gunmen. But their Kiowa was damaged. She had no choice.

Slebodnik lost sight of her aircraft in the smoke but understood they were heading back. He followed and cleared the city, then passed out over the cropland.

Kraft was trying to get his attention. She had been watching indicator lights in the cockpit displays. One stack of lights had fallen from green to red and then to empty. It was the transmission fluid level. A blue light glowed, indicating the gauge was working. There was no pressure to measure.

"Mike, we've lost all transmission fluid," she said.

He did not answer.

She raised her voice.

"Mike," she repeated, "we lost all of our transmission fluid."

He smelled the leaking fluid now. They were a few miles from Normandy, flying on residual lubrication. They might make it before the transmission seized up. But they might not. He dropped the aircraft lower, within thirty feet of the ground, and decelerated. At that altitude and speed, if the transmission froze, they would have a better chance of surviving the crash.

The other Kiowa was flying the same way. He caught up and passed it.

Landing without hydraulics is difficult. Hovering is nearly impossible and flight controls become stiff. Slebodnik landed first, a running landing. He and Kraft stepped out from their Kiowa and saw Hill and White coming in behind. Both were at the controls, fighting the aircraft. They flew through a gap in the trees around the base so as not to have to climb, cleared the outer wall by inches, and landed just behind them. *Expertly,* Slebodnik thought.

Hill staggered out her helicopter's right door and fell to the ground.

Slebodnik did not understand. Neither did Hill. She had felt an object slam into her foot as she flew, which caused her to growl in pain as bullets hit her aircraft and tracers zipped by. She thought perhaps something had been knocked loose in the front of the aircraft.

Slebodnik and Kraft ran to her. She sat up, clutching her right ankle in pain. Blood dripped from a hole in the bottom of her boot.

"Lori, your heel is leaking," Slebodnik said.

Now she knew what had happened. "I got shot," she answered.*

The bullet had passed through the sole of her foot and exited through her ankle. They pulled off her boot and rolled away her bloody sock, revealing a foot streaked in blood. "At least I painted my toenails," Hill said.

Slebodnik had forgotten his camera. He borrowed hers, took several photos of the wound, and helped Hill to the operations center, where they called for a medevac.

He talked by radio with a pair of Apache pilots, to direct them to the fight at Muqdadiyah, where Lieutenant Hume's patrol was still fighting to relieve the besieged coordination center. Then he called his headquarters, seeking a maintenance officer from Balad to fly to Normandy and begin the repairs on the two shot-up Kiowas by the refueling point. He was frustrated. He paced, as if caged. He wanted to get back to the battle down the road. It was 6:30 A.M. Only thirty minutes had passed since they set off for Muqdadiyah, and he was a cavalryman with nothing to ride.

Both Kiowas were repaired by the evening, and at 5:00 P.M. Slebodnik and Kraft flew the short hop back to Balad and headed to the Alpha Troop area. Other pilots told them that Hill was going to be okay. The brigade commander, a colonel, congratulated them and suggested that the four pilots on his team had followed the traditions of the Army's cavalry, pushing into uncertainty to help their own, and should be commended for judgment, valor, and skill. Slebodnik was annoyed. He felt he had not done enough. There had been so many insurgents out there, in the tree lines, fields, and city, and they had been shot up and forced to turn away.

---

* For her actions on this flight, Chief Warrant Officer Hill was awarded the Distinguished Flying Cross in October 2006.

Reinforcements from Forward Operating Base Normandy had at last reached Muqdadiyah, and with Lieutenant Hume's patrol the ground units pushed through the last of the resistance. Once the Americans reached the compound, they understood the militants' motives. They had raided the place to free captured fighters from the jail. Some of the police inside survived by barricading themselves in a building. But the attackers killed as many as twenty Iraqis and freed thirty-three inmates before vanishing into the city and countryside.

Slebodnik felt tired. He had managed to fly the broken helicopter, empty of transmission fluid, back to base. He had seen masterful flying by Hill. But Hill had been wounded, and the insurgents, moving almost openly in their safe haven in the Diyala River valley, had replenished their ranks. It had been the most intense mission of his career. He had a message to send to Tanja.

Down safe.

Voters elected a Parliament in Afghanistan in the late summer of 2005, seating many former or active warlords in a process that lent them and the government a degree of official authority. But the Taliban was regrouping, attacking American forces more frequently and with more vigor than in any year since the war began, and using an increasing numbers of improvised bombs. The American force remained under 20,000 troops, about one-seventh the size of the force in Iraq, and faced enemies who found sanctuary in Pakistan. Fighting and terrorist attacks in Iraq continued apace. Afghan and Iraqi security units, which the Pentagon was trying to recruit and deploy into areas where government authority was weak, were disorganized, underequipped, and prone to brutality and sectarian loyalties. In the United States, career officers and noncommissioned officers were realizing the campaigns in Afghanistan and Iraq would likely dominate their professional lives. The United States was mired in two wars, with no clear path out of either.

SIX

G-MONSTER

Lieutenant Commander
Layne McDowell's Dream

*"I have proudly fought for my country in the skies over
Kosovo, Iraq, and Afghanistan without regret."*

JANUARY 2006
Naval Air Station, Lemoore, California

Layne McDowell was back in a combat unit, preparing to head overseas.
More than four years after leaving the USS *Enterprise* during the opening attacks on the Taliban and al Qaeda, he was thirty-two years old and
a lieutenant commander, newly transferred to VFA-97, a strike fighter
squadron stationed in central California. Known as the Warhawks, VFA-
97 had formed in the 1960s. For most of its existence it had flown the
A-7 Corsair II, a subsonic attack aircraft dubbed by aviators the SLUF,
for "short little ugly fucker," owing to its dumpy appearance and inelegant
lines. In 1991 the squadron scrapped its Corsairs and transitioned to F/A-
18s, the supersonic fighter-attack jets that were also replacing the Navy's
fleet of F-14s. Its next rotation was to be a tour at an air station at Iwakuni,
Japan, where it would work beside Marines from Okinawa and be part of

the American forces arrayed near the Korean Peninsula. Its Pacific crossing was scheduled for February.

The squadron was grieving. In mid-January, its pilots temporarily
relocated to Southern California and were flying practice bombing runs
at the Navy's complex of air-to-ground ranges at El Centro. One of Mc-
Dowell's peers, Lieutenant Commander Frank Carl Wittwer, had been
on a night bombing run when his aircraft malfunctioned after releasing
a practice bomb. Wittwer's jet had been pointed at the ground when the
malfunction occurred, putting him into immediate out-of-control flight.
He ejected. The aircraft hit a farmer's field. Wittwer's chute only partially deployed. McDowell had fallen ill with food poisoning that night
and missed the training flights. But he was the squadron's safety officer,
and was rushed by Marine helicopter in the morning to the crash site
to begin the investigation and recover his friend's remains, which he escorted to the air station and then to Wittwer's hometown, DeRidder,
Louisiana.

McDowell had lost peers before, including one of his closest friends,
who had been in an F-14 that hit the ocean in 2001. He was adept at com-
partmentalization, at doing what needed to be done. Wittwer was married
and had left three children. After the memorial ceremonies, the squadron's calendar marched on. McDowell followed the pattern pilots use to
survive. He focused on work. A pilot with a growing supervisory role, he
had to plan a flight of six aircraft that he would lead across the Pacific.
The F/A-18s would complete the journey in three legs, trailing an aerial
tanker and taking turns refueling while McDowell plotted routes dodging
storms. He turned his mind to this.

As the United States settled into its fifth year of war in Afghanistan
and was about to mark its third year in Iraq, he personified American naval
aviation success. He had graduated at the top of his class at Annapolis,
earned pilot wings in an F-14, and served two tours on nuclear-powered
aircraft carriers in the Persian Gulf and the Mediterranean and North Arabian Seas. He had dropped ordnance on four countries in three different
military campaigns, and wore the medals and ribbons that marked him
as a member of his community's seasoned core. He'd earned a master's in
aeronautical engineering and qualified as a test pilot. Recently promoted,

he was in the small pool of Navy pilots being groomed for space shuttle flights or aircraft carrier command.

He and his wife, Jolene, had also started a family, timing the birth of their first son, Landon, in late 2002 with a seam in his fast-paced schedule that allowed more space for a home life. When Landon was born, McDowell was a student at the Naval Postgraduate School in Monterey, working on his master's—a routine that allowed him to be with Jolene almost every night. It had been a year to remember. He enjoyed academics, found the classwork satisfying, and rode a bicycle to and from class every day. Later, when he looked back at his time in Monterey, he realized it was the only year of his life in which he could not recall routinely being in either a cockpit or a car.

His period of study aligned with the run-up to the invasion of Iraq, which put McDowell in an unfamiliar position: watching the United States prepare for a war in which he was not involved. He had supported President Bush's call to overthrow Saddam Hussein, and found the question of whether Iraq retained an active chemical weapons program a distraction. McDowell believed in consequences and in justice, and thought that credible deterrence was both an essential element of global security and the responsibility of a superpower. By his measure, the Baath Party was illegitimate and egregiously brutal, a criminal enterprise that ruled by violence and fear. Its repeated use of chemical weapons in the Iran-Iraq War in the 1980s, and then against Kurds, was grounds enough for removing it from power. The many crimes against Iraqis inherent in Baathist repression, he thought, strengthened the case. When the invasion seemed imminent, McDowell's principal feeling was disappointment that he was not there. He yearned to be assigned to the first strikes, to be reviewing targets in a ready room and then catapulted toward them, where the threat would be real. This was not only what he had trained to do. It was consistent with his experience, which had conditioned him to a life in the center of the action.

He was busy with his engineering courses but closely followed the news, anticipating the opening attacks. When home, he studied in a walk-in closet in the apartment where he and Jolene lived. In the manner of a Navy pilot accustomed to confined spaces, he had converted it to a small office, a place where he could concentrate undisturbed.

About ten days before the invasion, McDowell was reading news online when he saw an article about Natalie Maines, the lead singer of the Dixie Chicks, an alternative country band. A few days before, at a concert in London, Maines had spoken against the impending war and derided President Bush. "Just so you know," she told the crowd, "we're on the good side with y'all. We do not want this war, this violence, and we're ashamed that the President of the United States is from Texas." The outcry was swift. Fans renounced her, radio stations were refusing to play the Dixie Chicks' music, and tour sponsors faced calls for boycotts. The uproar prompted Maines to release a statement. "As a concerned American citizen, I apologize to President Bush because my remark was disrespectful," it said. "I feel that whoever holds that office should be treated with the utmost respect. We are currently in Europe and witnessing a huge anti-American sentiment as a result of the perceived rush to war. While war may remain a viable option, as a mother, I just want to see every possible alternative exhausted before children and American soldiers' lives are lost."

McDowell read the apology while studying in his closet. He felt stung. He and Maines came from the same part of Texas. They had been near contemporaries in school. He was a fan of the Dixie Chicks and considered Maines a local artist who had made good. He was astonished that she would be divisive just as American troops were about to go to war, and was irked that her apology managed to imply more criticism. He read news from Texas. The country radio station he had listened to as a child, KLLL-FM, was soliciting comments. It was all the invitation McDowell needed. In ten or fifteen minutes he had completed an open letter and sent it.

Earlier this week, while performing in London, you stated that you were ashamed that our President is from your home state. I wonder if you realized how many Americans would be listening. This American was listening. This Texan is ashamed that you come from my state.

I serve my country as an officer in the United States Navy. Specifically, I fly F-14 Tomcats off carriers around the world, executing the missions that preserve the very freedom you claim to exercise.

I have proudly fought for my country in the skies over Kosovo, Iraq and Afghanistan without regret. Though I may disagree wholeheartedly with your comments, I will defend to the death your right to say them, in America.

> *But for you to travel to a foreign land and publicly criticize our*
> *Commander in Chief is cowardice behavior....*

McDowell did not think words alone were strong enough. His hometown radio station had pulled the Dixie Chicks from the air. He thought he could do more. "In a separate correspondence," he wrote,

> *I am returning to you each and every Dixie Chicks CD and cassette*
> *that I have ever purchased.*
>
> *Never again will I allow my funds to support your behavior. All*
> *you have done is to add your name to a growing list of American "Ce-*
> *lebrities" who have failed to realize that they have obtained their suc-*
> *cesses on the backs of the American blue-collar workers such as our*
> *servicemen and women.*
>
> *To Natalie Maines: This Texan—this American will continue to*
> *risk his life to guarantee your freedoms. What will you do to deserve it?*

After KLLL posted the letter, it became a minor Internet hit, picked up by blogs and shared on forums. McDowell received emails from across the country thanking him for speaking up and for sharing the insights of an officer who had been to war and come home proud. One young man informed him that the letter inspired him to enlist.

McDowell's words were sincere. But he had written impulsively to a small radio station and was not expecting a larger stage. He had neither the time nor inclination for politics or more public discussion about the commander in chief. Under the Navy's traditions and rules, this was beyond a young pilot's purview. He kept to his work and put the attention behind him.

The Iraq war joined the Afghan war in the aviation community routine. The Navy played the long game. Its personnel bureaucracy kept its own clock and continued to move officers step by step through the arcs of peacetime military careers. McDowell remained in a development phase, attending classes, filling stateside jobs, being readied for larger responsibilities in later years.

His next assignment, at U.S. Naval Test Pilot School, was so demanding that he saw little of his family. It was the hardest year of his life, rivaled only by his Annapolis plebe year. He practiced spin training, the process of recovering a jet from uncontrolled flight, on the way to qualifying on nineteen different aircraft, including two helicopters, three gliders, multiple jets, and an Albatross, a lumbering twin-engine floatplane. Among the jets he flew was the T-38 Talon, the aircraft he had seen over his farm as a child, attracting him to flight. The school lived up to its reputation as an exhausting grind, a test for even the highest achievers. McDowell absorbed the work and found it priceless. By the end of the course he could walk up to an aircraft, look at it, and anticipate how it would fly.

He graduated in mid-2004 and moved to VX-23, the Navy and Marine Corps' strike aircraft test squadron, where he remained until late 2005. Iraq had slipped into intractable violence and sectarian war. He wanted to be there. But if the Navy had other designs for McDowell and deemed it too early to send him to a strike fighter squadron, test-pilot life was his ideal substitute. The squadron was used to evaluate the suitability of new technologies, ensuring that any avionics boxes or flight-control algorithms under consideration for the fleet could withstand carrier landings, catapult shots, and dynamic combat flight. Test pilots would deliberately make mistakes, like new pilots, jerking planes around, putting them through hard landings at nearly twice the angle of normal descent. Sometimes they broke aircraft in the process. McDowell, the fighter pilot with no regrets, was having so much fun that he was disappointed when the call came for him to rotate on.

The timing of his arrival to VFA-97 was good. The Navy's F-14s were gone; he had to transition to F/A-18s for the remainder of his career. But the squadron was entering a six-week training exercise, the Strike Fighter Advanced Readiness Program, in which aircrews study the weapons and tactics associated with the F/A-18 and then hone skills at ranges and in dogfighting drills. The program gave him a chance to practice using the F/A-18 to fight. By the end, he felt ready. He was back.

Before departing overseas, McDowell was in an unusual circumstance. He was not overwhelmed with work or school. Much of the intensity of his past years was lifted. His mind had time to roam. Sometimes he found himself revisiting one strike in Kosovo in May 1999, during his first tour. That day he had attacked the wrong place, hitting a building with a

500-pound laser-guided bomb. McDowell replayed the sequence in his mind, tallying the conditions that had contributed to the error. A low ceiling. Poor weather. Incomplete intelligence driving his unit's decision to strike. He had been assigned a mission and performed it. He remembered his misgivings in the minutes after the explosion. He recalled reviewing the video of the strike back on the ship, on a large monitor, and discovering what he had not seen on the cockpit display: four bicycles parked in the carport where the ordnance hit.

An old question returned. Had he killed civilians inside?

The Navy had shown no interest in finding out whether anyone had been harmed. There had been no push to dissect the strike and tease out what had gone wrong. McDowell had been neither reprimanded nor suspended from flying, even for a few days. He had been told, simply, to prepare for his next flight. *There was no desire to make sure that it did not happen again,* he thought. *The desire was to get back out and strike.*

McDowell believed without qualification that the air-to-ground campaign against the Serbian forces had value. He understood that permissive rules could save lives. The faster that Western aircraft drove Serbian forces out of Kosovo, the sooner the war would end, and the fewer civilians might die. But he also thought mistakes should be examined, learned from, and, when appropriate, punished. He wondered who had parked those four bicycles there. Were they inside when the bomb struck? If they were, then he had killed them, and was responsible for their deaths. The Navy paid this possibility no mind. *It was almost as if these lives did not have value,* he thought.

Just as he believed that Saddam Hussein should be held accountable for his brutality in Iraq, McDowell thought his own errors merited examination, and perhaps punishment. He wished something had been done. He had not even been benched, even for a while.

One night, asleep in his apartment, McDowell dreamed that he was looking at the building just after the bomb had hit.

Somehow the building was intact. He was standing outside, sure this was the place, wondering how its walls still stood. He stepped in, moving past four damaged bicycles by the door. Smoke obscured his vision as he walked through the rooms. Boards, blasted from walls, littered the floor. Insulation and wiring dangled from the ceiling. Dust covered the scattered debris.

Sorrow rose in him, and regret. Minutes before, from the cockpit of an F-14, he had struck this building with a 500-pound bomb. He had struggled to find the target, and after he released the bomb, while the ordnance rushed downward, doubt had registered in his mind. Still he had guided it, all the way to here.

Now he ached with a solitary wish: to turn back time. He needed only five minutes to do things differently. Given a second chance, he would not release the bomb. Or he would steer it harmlessly into the field.

This building would not be shattered and spewing smoke.

McDowell kept moving, searching, needing to know what the bomb had done.

He saw a child curled in the corner, a small boy coated with dust.

The boy was breathing but gravely wounded.

McDowell lunged to help, realizing as he moved that he recognized the child's clothing, hair, and face. Then he knew it. It was Landon, his son.

He lifted the boy to his chest, tightly for a hug, cupping his hand behind the child's little head, to hold it. The back of his skull was gone.

———

McDowell woke.

PART III

Counterinsurgency

Criticized by Congress and the public, Secretary of Defense Donald Rumsfeld resigned in 2006. The generals commanding the conventional forces he had sent to war had pushed units off large bases and distributed them in Iraqi neighborhoods and along roads. Notions for defeating militants were reorganizing around an updated counterinsurgency doctrine, and its ambitions of protecting civilians and supporting governments in Iraq and Afghanistan until they could stand on their own. Special operations forces were engaged in targeted killing campaigns against insurgent leaders. The leader of Al Qaeda in Iraq, Abu Musab Al-Zarqawi, was killed in mid-2006. His followers fought on, as did insurgents in other militias and terrorist groups, including Shiite organizations supported by Iran. The war had a fresh urgency for all sides. In Afghanistan, Osama bin Laden and Mullah Omar remained at large. Al Qaeda's militants in Iraq had taken a new name: the Islamic State of Iraq.

SEVEN

ON AL QAEDA'S TURF

Dustin Kirby and the
Route Chicago Shooting Gallery

"I thought it would be cool to save a life."

AUGUST 2006

The Marines assigned to drive through Karma called it the Chicago 500, their nickname for running motorized patrols on the road connecting the small Iraqi city to the country's highway network. At a glance, Alternate Supply Route Chicago, as the highway was labeled on American military maps, could seem unremarkable. It was two narrow lanes of asphalt running over farmland and small bridges and passing through the eastern edge of Karma's business district, where it became a dusty slot between storefronts and auto repair shops. Marines weaved their gun trucks through civilian traffic, watching over the people they were told to protect with suspicion and an expectation of the worst. The Iraqis, for their part, generally ignored the Americans and often refused to acknowledge them. Their coldness was one of the indicators. The tired body language of the farmers beside the road's shoulders, the sleepy look of the fields scorching under a desert sun, the bustle in the shops and crowds at the street corners—all of this was deceiving. For almost its entire length Chicago was a zone of ambushes, precision rifle fire, and hidden bombs, a gantlet of lethal traps coordinated by informants and spies, and aided, many of the Marines thought, by the Iraqi police with whom they lived. For the young Marines of Weapons Company, Second Battalion, Eighth Marines, the Chicago 500 felt like a pointless routine and a bloody lottery. They lived in two crude outposts beside the highway and drove it coiled, waiting for the blast or the shot.

Petty Officer Dustin "Doc" Kirby had his first taste of the Chicago 500 in the summer of 2006. His battalion pulled into Camp Fallujah in late July, just as American war plans were changing again. Neither military campaigns nor political transition had calmed Iraq's violence. The Marines returned to Fallujah in late 2004 and drove many militants out. The area's population had not crossed over to the new government's side. The province had resoundingly rejected Iraq's constitution in a referendum in 2005; 97 percent of the votes cast were against ratifying the new document. And the Pentagon's practice of concentrating its ground combat power on large bases had given insurgents and terrorists freedom to move, helping create an environment in which armed groups had grown confident and strong. The groups near Fallujah included Al Qaeda in Iraq, the franchise that once swore loyalty to Osama bin Laden, but under Abu Musab Al-Zarqawi had broken the leash and led a multipronged campaign against Iraq's Shiite population, its government, and foreign troops and aid organizations, including the UN. American forces had killed Zarqawi in June 2006, just before Kirby arrived. Sunni militants no longer had an unchallenged enclave in Fallujah's streets. But his followers fought on. Many of them had survived the fighting in Fallujah, escaped from the city, and clustered around Karma, keeping the Chicago 500 what it was: a punishing ribbon of asphalt.

The battalion arrived as the Pentagon was moving to check the groups' growth and begin rolling them back. American troops had been ordered off super-bases and into small outposts, from where they were instructed to follow a set of ideas the military called COIN, its acronym for a hastily assembled counterinsurgency doctrine that generals hoped would stop the country's bloody slide. Iraq had descended into civil war. Its new security forces were unreliable and weak. Kirby and the rest of his unit were told that their mission now was to protect the Iraqi population from militants, build relationships with Iraqis, and help the country's government reestablish some of the order the invasion had destroyed.

That was the plan. Many of the young Marines did not pretend to understand it. It sounded like so much officer school theory, which it was. Even if the doctrine was sound, which much of the rank and file doubted, the Marines patrolling Karma felt shorthanded. The battalion's turf, Operations Area Redwolf, was roughly three hundred square miles of farmland crisscrossed with canals, dotted with villages, and bordered by desert. The battalion had only a thousand Marines, many of whom were occupied with outpost defense or quick-reaction-force duties, or busy in operations centers and the logistics depots on Camp Fallujah. This left few Marines for work on the roads or in villages. It limited where the Marines even tried to go. "Economy of force," the corps called it—a euphemism for counterinsurgency with a skeleton crew.

The shortage of Marines was especially pressing in and around Karma, where Weapons Company worked, which was among Redwolf's most dangerous ground. Before leaving the States, the company, which traditionally had been organized into mortar, heavy machine-gun, and antitank missile platoons, was rearranged in full. It became a motorized infantry force of five mobile assault platoons, each consisting of about a half dozen trucks with machine guns on turrets, thirty Marines, and a corpsman or two to handle ailment treatment and trauma care. Kirby was assigned to Mobile Assault Platoon 2. The Marines also set aside their usual camouflage utility uniforms and donned tan flight suits like those worn by aviation crews. The suits were fire retardant—safer than normal utilities, which in a burning vehicle were prone to bursting into flame. The officers spoke of COIN, of interacting with villagers and seeking partners in a new Iraq. The uniform swap, like the referendum vote tallies showing 3 percent support for the political project in Baghdad, said something else: *You're not going to find many friends in Karma.*

Kirby picked up other ominous signs all around. After the battalion flew from the States to Kuwait and drove to the big Marine base outside Fallujah, the platoon met its counterparts in the battalion it was replacing. For a few days the fresh Marines accompanied the departing unit on its last missions, part of a handoff of duties called "left-seat, right-seat" patrols. The idea was straightforward: Incoming Marines were to get a crash course on Redwolf's lethal geography, learning areas where ambushes had occurred and bombs had often been laid. As his platoon's sole trauma care specialist, Kirby wanted to know what to expect, so he sought out one of the departing battalion's docs. He was jolted by the man's bluntness and brevity. "Stock up on tourniquets and bleeder kits, bro, and get ready to do your job," the man said.

At first Kirby was angry. *That's it?* he thought. *That's all you have for me?* Then he heard the corpsman had worked on a fatally wounded Marine shortly before. Having a Marine die under a corpsman's care was his community's nightmare. Kirby's anger subsided. He filed away the other corpsman's words, and dour mood, as lessons. *He's not in the proper place to give me a turnover. But he is in the right place to let me know that I'm in a bad place.* Weapons Company was headed into a lethal puzzle with a feel-good doctrine and a small crew.

Karma, the line went, *is Bad Karma.* Kirby had no illusions. The foreboding feelings fit.

Within days the company relocated to Karma's small center, turning north onto Chicago from the highway linking Abu Ghraib and Fallujah and passing through a small industrial zone before crossing a bridge over a winding waterworks. Previous Marines had given this ditch a name: Shit Creek. From here Chicago was about six miles long as a bird might fly. As far as Marines were concerned, it was all bad.

When Weapons Company rolled into Karma, there was not enough infrastructure for its Marines. The police station was too small for the full American force, and Outpost Omar, farther north up the road, was only partially built and not ready to be occupied. The company set up its office at the police station, a grubby concrete building ringed by blast walls. Inside its lobby was a mural of a silhouetted Marine in mourning, the work of a previous unit. Out back were free weights and Porta-Potties that were cleaned by transferring their contents into barrels and burning the sludge with diesel fuel. Several times a day the air filled with Arabic as loudspeakers on mosques broadcast prayers and anti-occupant screeds. Sometimes the company's interpreters said the voices urged Karma's residents to fight. Just up the road a circular concrete sign bore Arabic script. One Marine asked a translator what it said, and was told it was a greeting

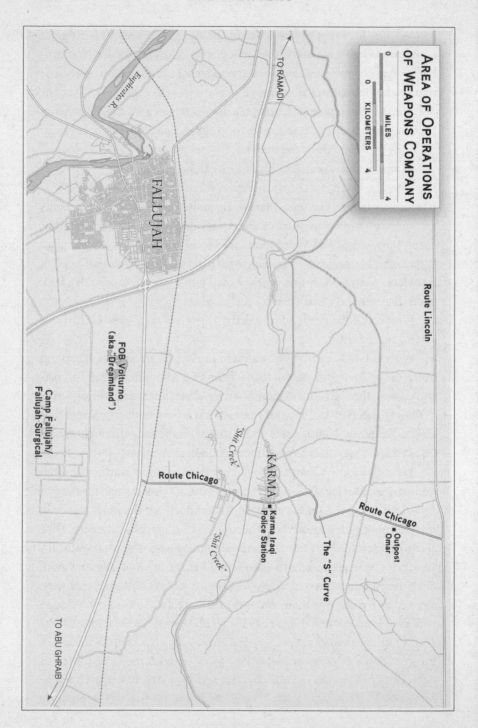

AREA OF OPERATIONS OF WEAPONS COMPANY

MILES
0   4

KILOMETERS
0   4

Euphrates R.

FALLUJAH

TO RAMADI

Route Lincoln

FOB Volturno (aka "Dreamland")

Camp Fallujah/ Fallujah Surgical

"Shit Creek"

Route Chicago

KARMA
■ Karma Iraqi Police Station

Route Chicago
■ Outpost Omar

The "S" Curve

"Shit Creek"

TO ABU GHRAIB

welcoming people to Karma. It was not. It was the beginning of Al Imran 103, a Koranic verse urging Islamic solidarity—an implicit call for resistance scrawled in front of the American post.* The Marines called the sign the Lollipop.

For the first few weeks, with few bunks to sleep in, the Marines of Mobile Assault Platoon 2 drove the Chicago 500 almost constantly. Sometimes, when the need for sleep grew too great, they would pull onto farmers' fields and form the trucks into a circle so everyone could rotate through brief rests. The platoons called these hasty patrol bases a "coil." There were living quarters in the police station, and a few times the platoon parked behind the blast walls to try to find cots before another group of exhausted Marines would get a turn. But the space was small and the chance of finding a spot slim. *Musical bunks,* Kirby thought. Other times the platoon assumed duties in the bunkers protecting the police stations—posts made of lumber and sandbags, ringed by mesh to stop rocket-propelled grenades.

Kirby came to accept that he did not quite grasp the overall mission. The intelligence was unclear, the enemy rarely visible, and the doctrine longer on theory than a coherent vision for the troops' day-to-day. The company had been told it was trying something that had not been tried in Iraq before: a security mission with a focus on protecting the population. But what if the population did not want this protection? Kirby heard contradictions at every turn. One day, he thought, senior Marines would say it was going to be easy. The next they'd say everyone was going to be knee-deep in blood and shit. Some instructions felt habitual, as rote as a weekend safety brief: *Don't go anywhere alone, don't leave the wire without permission, keep your equipment close.*

Kirby stuck to what he knew: being ready to treat Marines. He also gave himself a personal mission: to be his platoon's motivator, the man

---

* Al Imran 103: "And hold firmly to the rope of Allah all together and do not become divided. And remember the favor of Allah upon you—when you were enemies and He brought your hearts together and you became, by His favor, brothers. And you were on the edge of a pit of the Fire, and He saved you from it. Thus does Allah make clear to you His verses that you may be guided." (Sahih International translation)

in the ranks who kept everyone else upbeat. He was well suited for this. Kirby was a believer in the Marine Corps, and driven to do well. He thrived in the military's culture and was in peak physical shape. He'd developed a swagger and gregarious personality. His loud Southern accent, his near-perpetual state of motion, his enthusiasm and ability to weather bullshit, his in-your-space approach to his Marine peers—these combined to make him a palpable part of Weapons Company's personality. Everyone in the battalion, it seemed, knew Doc Kirby.

His assumption of a larger role had other roots. Mobile Assault Platoon Two was led by a gunnery sergeant, Shawn Dempsey, whom Kirby respected and liked. But the company's leadership was an uneven lot. The first lieutenant who commanded Weapons Company was tall and imposing, a quiet presence who spoke few words and rarely smiled. He had spent most of his career as an enlisted Marine, and was commissioned as an officer in his thirties. Marines considered him competent and legit, though many kept their distance, finding him stern and unapproachable. They called him the Shark, a reference to his blank-faced alertness and habit of quietly making rounds to look over each post himself, a process they called "The shark on patrol." When he roamed the positions at night, they whispered between themselves, "The shark's in the water." The commander's senior enlisted partner, the company's first sergeant, exuded a different type of presence altogether. He was noisy and brash. He had come from the Marine Corps drill fields, where the habits of power and harsh indoctrination were given license, and had not previously served in the infantry. When he was out of earshot, Marines said he seemed uncomfortable on the occasions when he patrolled with them. Sometimes, they said, he overcompensated and gave unsound instructions, like telling Marines to keep a symmetrically equal dispersion between them when they walked, as if they were part of an introductory tactical demonstration on the grass at Parris Island, and not on the ever-varying ground of a real war, where grunts move between pieces of terrain and cover. His tendency to revert to a loud and all-powerful drill instructor persona on the outposts sat wrong in a combat zone. No one liked a random haze. In an abruptly reorganized company, with a confusing mission for which they were understaffed, Marines defaulted to the battlefield's baseline mentality: They looked after themselves, platoon by platoon, squad by squad, truck crew by truck crew, each Marine having the other's back, and staying wide of the higher-ups. Kirby's role, the sailor who wandered the ranks, checking on every man, gave him influence beyond his rank.

———

For Kirby, Karma was a new Iraq. In 2005, the year after his cousin, Doc Worley, was wounded and lost his leg, Kirby's battalion had been sent overseas, but not for ground combat. The Marine Corps was still busy with its routine of packing battalions aboard ships for rotations in floating task forces. Kirby embarked aboard the USS *Kearsarge*, an amphibious assault ship, and headed across the Atlantic. Shipboard life was tedious but the months were not entirely boring. The Pentagon's wartime posture meant the battalion did more than training visits with allies. In the summer of that year, Kirby was part of a detachment sent into southern Iraq to work beside British forces around Basra. And on August 19, 2005, while tied to a pier in Jordan next to another ship, the *Kearsarge* was attacked by ground-to-ground rockets fired from a warehouse in the city. The rockets missed the ships, though one killed a Jordanian soldier, and the *Kearsarge* departed with such speed that Kirby, who was on a working party on the pier, was left behind. The attack gave his family a taste of the Pentagon's habit of speaking in partial truths: His mother and father received an email assuring them that all the sailors and Marines on the ship were accounted for, even though, as far as Kirby was concerned, the Navy had steamed away without him. It was six days before a ferry ran Kirby and the other abandoned sailors and Marines out to sea to climb back aboard the *Kearsarge*.

The deployment to Karma augured more action. And then it seemed not to deliver. Nothing spectacular happened in the first weeks of the company's patrols. Some of the Marines began wondering if the threats they had been warned of had been overstated. They found IEDs, and had occasional incoming mortar rounds or bursts of small-arms fire. But these attacks were largely ineffective. Some days passed quietly. A few admitted to themselves that they felt complacent. It was August in Iraq, under a searing sun, and the viciousness they had been warned awaited them did not materialize. *Mostly*, Kirby thought, *it's just stupid hot*.

After a few weeks Weapons Company moved its headquarters to

Outpost Omar, a small walled compound north of the city in open fields laced with canals. A few other buildings were within range of a rifle shot. The outpost's history was subject to debate. Some Marines heard that its main building had been a poultry-processing house. Others, trading an apocryphal story, said the place had formerly been a funeral home. In grunt-speak, the tales allowed for a pitch-perfect one-liner: *We live in a morgue.* The outpost's opening brought rounds of new labor. When Weapons Company settled in, engineers had already installed a generator and wiring and built exterior walls. But the company had to choose and establish its own defenses—and then build the group of small bunkers in which the Marines would stand post—to be ready to repel any attack. Between patrols and time on watch, the Marines built Omar into a lone fortress in Anbar Province, wedged between two asphalt lanes and a field. Kirby was kept busy by the tasks he shared with Marines, and by tending to minor medical problems—cuts and colds, sprains and intestinal infections—that are among the low-grade and persistent hassles of infantry life.

And then it began.

On August 23, Mobile Assault Platoon Five set out to meet with a gas station owner who they heard wanted to discuss problems with extortion and black-market fuel. The meeting was a short drive up Chicago to the T-intersection with Route Lincoln, which ran parallel to a large canal. The canal marked the edge of the irrigated zone. To the north extended a landscape of sand and stone—an area with almost no Marine presence that the battalion suspected insurgents used for training and weapons storage.

The T-intersection was a busy hub, a rest stop with a gas station and food kiosks.

The platoon positioned the trucks around the gas station so the staff sergeant could go inside to talk with the man. Other Marines stepped out, making a show of presence.

Lance Corporal Donterry Woods was standing with Lance Corporal J. D. Hirlston, who was taking pictures. The two men were talking about photography, bantering in the small talk of Marines on perimeter duty.

The platoon heard a single loud crack.

Hirlston stiffened, remained momentarily upright, and fell.

Woods jumped to help. A bullet had passed through Hirlston's head and exited near the base of his skull.

Woods was a big Marine, upward of 200 pounds, muscular and lean. He began to drag his friend. He saw the wounds and knew Hirlston was dead. Gun trucks pulled around them, cutting off a follow-on shot.

"Get him the fuck in here!" Woods heard.

Another Marine, Lance Corporal Daniel Strauser, leapt down from a turret and helped lift Hirlston into the truck. One of the platoon's trucks opened fire to the north, from where the shot had come. Its machine gun roared.

Hirlston was inside, motionless on the seat. The platoon collapsed the cordon and sped away, heading south down Chicago, past Omar, through a sweeping bend they called the S-curve, headlong into Karma, passing the police station and racing on.

They were headed for Fallujah Surgical and the doctor there.

They drove with fury, the fine points of the rules for interactions with civilians on the roads forgotten.

After Karma, the trucks turned west on the highway and sped in the gates of Camp Fallujah, lurching to a stop at the surgical center, where several Marines carried Hirlston inside.

All at once there was nothing left to do.

Woods and Strauser and the rest of Mobile Assault Platoon Five waited, looking around, splattered and soaked by blood.

Someone suggested they clean up and change clothes. They headed to the supply section for clean flight suits. Woods felt dizzy. He suspected that the platoon had been lured to a meeting, with a sniper waiting, across the canal. They had been set up.

Kirby was seething. He arrived on Camp Fallujah just before the corpsmen were to transfer Hirlston's body to mortuary affairs, where he would be processed for the flights to Dover Air Force Base and onward to his home in Tennessee. He all but stormed in. Weapons Company had not yet suffered a loss, and he was furious that Hirlston had not received life-saving care. It was a corpsman's job to save wounded Marines. His anger masked complicated feelings. He and Hirlston had quarreled before leaving the States, and for stupid reasons. Back in the barracks at Camp Lejeune, where the Marines were safe and relaxed, Kirby had eaten a few of Hirlston's Oreos. Hirlston had retaliated by eating Kirby's stash of ramen noodles. The two locked in a standoff for weeks.

Then came Karma, where there was less room for bullshit. Hirlston told Doc he was sorry and that it had been a ridiculous fight. Kirby was moved. "Motherfucker, I was going to apologize first," he replied. The feud ended. The two men were good.

Hirlston was gone?

Kirby was incensed.

He stepped into the room. Hirlston's body was on the table. Kirby's anger evaporated as he examined the wound. He felt a flash of acceptance, even calm. Hirlston had been killed instantly. *The only way a corpsman could have saved him,* Kirby thought, *would have been to be there two seconds before it happened and push him out of the way.* The corpsman in Mobile Assault Platoon Five never had a pulse to work with, or a life to save. *There wasn't shit he could have done.*

Kirby strode back to his own platoon, changed. He had sworn oaths to himself that none of his Marines would die. But there were things a corpsman could not do.

The killing of Hirlston marked a shift in the company's tour. It was as if the insurgents had studied the Marines' tactics and routines, sketched the layout and defenses of the Karma police station and OP Omar, and were now ready to fight. Two days later there was an attack on the Iraqi police station, where many Marines lived. In late August an RPG was fired at one of the mobile patrols. The next day a sniper fired on an explosive ordnance disposal unit as it was trying to clear an IED on Chicago. Three Marines were wounded when an IED damaged their Humvee. By mid-September Omar was receiving mortar fire and the police station was occasionally targeted by rifle grenades, lobbed into the compound. Violence was spiking. The Marines were finding more IEDs—including a truck bomb they discovered ahead of an attack—and were frequently coming under fire when outside their bases and out of their trucks. Al Qaeda in Iraq had lost its leader. Its fighters were still active, and close.

On September 17, the company commander had to fill in on short notice for the battalion commander at a meeting with a council of the city's residents. This was part of the effort to have Karma accept the Americans and to work with the police to restore government to the city. He asked Kirby's platoon commander, Gunnery Sergeant Shawn Dempsey, to set a cordon of security around the building where the meeting would be held.

Dempsey rounded up the platoon but left Kirby and his truck behind. Inside Karma he positioned the trucks at each intersection near the building, blocking alleys from which attackers or a car bomb might approach. The company commander and first sergeant stepped inside, leaving the platoon to watch the streets. The Marines put out traffic cones and stood behind the trucks, expecting people would keep back, as they usually did.

After a short while a boy, perhaps seven years old, calmly walked past the cones and the first truck, into the area where only Marines were standing. It was odd. This child was either clueless or bold. Dempsey held up a hand.

"Hey, stop, little dude," he said. The boy looked up.

Dempsey motioned to the boy to follow him, led him to the edge of the cordon, and pointed him up an alley. They were side by side. Dempsey stepped up onto a curb and turned to direct the child down the sidewalk and out of the way.

He heard the shot.

It sounded like a rush of air—a hiss and whack. The bullet hit him.

Dempsey fell to the ground and scrambled behind the truck.

A turret gunner shouted from above: "Gunny got shot!"

Dempsey could feel where the bullet had struck squarely in his back. But he was breathing, and alert. He stood. The patrol burst into action. Engines started. Marines rushed to seats. The commander and first sergeant ran from the meeting to organize the medevac. The interpreter panicked and bolted ahead to the company commander's truck, climbed in, and shut the doors. There was no time to argue. The commander pushed his way into Dempsey's truck. The patrol accelerated away, leaving its orange cones behind.

Dempsey was on the radio, calling in the casualty. The Marine receiving the report asked for a kill number, the code assigned to each Marine.

Dempsey gave his own.

The radio went quiet.

"Say again kill number," the call came back.

A gunny calling in his own medevac did not make sense.

Dempsey repeated it.

The trucks rushed into the police station, where Kirby removed his equipment to find that the bullet had been stopped by the ceramic plate that hung behind his shoulders. A large welt was forming across Dempsey's back, as if he had been hit with a baseball bat. He had been spared.

Kirby looked him over. With the medical equipment in Karma, he said, he had no way to be sure Dempsey was not bleeding internally. He recommended Dempsey be evacuated for a more thorough exam.*

Word spread as the platoon settled down: *That kid set Dempsey up, just like the guy who set up Hirlston.* Weapons Company's mood was darkening. Its younger Marines had joined the Corps after the terrorist attacks in 2001. Many of them wanted to be hunters, to find and bring Osama bin Laden to justice. In Karma it seemed the war worked the other way round. They were in a town rippling with hostility, under rules and theories that ordered them to be nice, and in regular contact with some of Iraq's most savvy and violent militants. Instead of doing the hunting, it was as if they were the hunted. They did not see many signs of help from the Iraqis they were told would be allies.

Bad signs were not confined to the people of Karma. The Iraqi police unit, already thinly staffed, was shrinking due to desertions and abductions. The remaining police were afraid. They spent most of their time inside, effectively under Marine guard. The Marines suspected some of them were informants for the insurgents; one man in particular slipped off into the police station parking lot, out of earshot, and made a phone call whenever a team from the battalion sniper platoon showed up. The Marines thought he was warning the insurgents to stay away until the precision shooters left. And even if the police wanted to fight, they possessed almost no material ability to participate. There were fewer police officers than police trucks, which were damaged when an incoming

---

* Although ceramic body-armor plates often prevent penetrative injuries from bullets, shrapnel, or other projectiles, survivors can still suffer organ damage or other severe wounds, a phenomenon known as behind-armor-blunt-trauma, or BABT.

grenade exploded within the walls, riddling their pickups with shrapnel, perforating their tires, and further idling the fleet. As the police received more equipment—pistols, machine guns, bulletproof vests—it tended to disappear. Even success was followed by betrayal. Intelligence reports that included photographs of militants often showed them in orange prison attire. These men had been taken prisoner before and had either escaped from Iraq's jails or been released to continue their war.

In this dysfunctional system, the job of exerting influence over the area fell almost entirely to the Marines, who faced militant tactics that taught residents to keep their distance from the Americans. On one patrol, Kirby's platoon rode out at about 3:00 A.M. to Omar's north, past the intersection where Hirlston had been killed. At sunrise they began the return drive.

In the back of the convoy, Kirby heard a radio call. Up ahead the bodies of three young Iraqi men were lying in the intersection, set down in a row.

The platoon stopped. Kirby jogged out to examine the remains.

The three men had been shot, once each in the forehead. Papers covered their faces. Their bodies were warm. Kirby figured they had been alive minutes before. He looked closely, trying to glean more of the crime. Thin fibers of blue cloth lined the entrance wound in one of the men's skulls. He had been blindfolded, then shot through the cloth, and his killers had removed the blindfold before displaying the bodies for the Marines. The papers on their faces declared the reason for the executions: These men, the Arabic script said, had spoken with the occupiers. Kneeling over the bodies, at the center of the grisly display, Kirby understood. Whoever had done this had watched the Marines pass by and acted quickly, putting the corpses in the road between the time the patrol had passed the intersection and the time it returned. They were probably watching Kirby right now.

The insurgents grew bolder. On October 19 they attacked OP Omar in force. Their assault began with mortars, followed by a dump truck laden with explosives. A platoon had several trucks outside the base as the attack escalated. Marines near the outpost's entry point opened fire, filling the driver with bullets.

The truck exploded—a blast and ball of flame, but short of its target.

The mortar and rifle fire continued. Omar's posts ran low on ammunition. Kirby ran from post to post, shuttling ammunition and water to Marines. An American fighter jet came low for a fast pass, roaring over the fight in a show of force. The militants withdrew. The fields around OP Omar fell quiet. Traffic on Chicago slowly resumed, picking its way around the husk and scraps of the ruined truck.

Weapons Company had repelled the attack without injury.

Its luck did not hold.

Not long after the attack, the battalion passed intelligence to the company about a house the militants were using as a base. The officers had to decide between raiding the place by night or by day. By 2006 Karma's insurgents were survivors of three years of fighting. Many had moved to the farmland after being forced by other Marines from their urban hideouts in Fallujah. They knew that Americans often raided by darkness, trying to kill or capture militants beside their beds when night-vision equipment gave conventional forces an advantage. Many of them did not stay in homes at night. The officers opted for Weapons Company to sweep the house by day, hoping to catch their suspects when they least expected it.

The raid force departed the morning of October 30. The first phases of the raid proceeded as planned. With drivers and turret gunners watching from the dirt road, and a pair of helicopters overhead, Marines from inside each truck leapt out and ran to the house for the search.

It was a tan-brick building beside a canal. A cinder-block wall defined part of a yard, which gave way to muddy fields with a few scattered palm trees. No one was home when the Marines burst inside. But the signs indicated that their battalion's intelligence had been correct: This was a small insurgent base. Marines found folding-stock Kalashnikovs and a PK machine gun hidden in the home and under a pile of livestock feed outside, a chest rig for carrying rifle magazines, and an ammunition can. They also found spools of electrical wire and base stations for Sanyo cordless telephones—common components in local IEDs. A sedan outside had been stripped of interior seats. This, they presumed, was a car bomb in the making.

Marines on the outer cordon could see Iraqi men milling about, watching. The Marines raised their rifles and watched through scopes. The men drifted out of sight.

Kirby gathered the captured weapons, and he and Dempsey stowed them in the back of a Humvee. The company commander ordered the Marines to wrap up. The helicopters departed. The job seemed done.

Kirby had taken a seat in his truck when he heard the shot.

It was audible inside the vehicle even over the diesel-engine growl. Outside, Dempsey dove behind a tree, then popped up, looking for the shooter, expecting a fight.

Kirby tensed. *This is where shit gets interesting,* he thought.

Throughout Mobile Assault Platoon Two, radios crackled with reports letting Dempsey know that his crews were okay.

"Truck Six good."

"Truck Five good."

"Truck Four good."

"Truck Three good."

Weapons Company waited for the pause. Dempsey did not have time to ask. A shout told him a Marine needed help: "Corpsman up!"

Marines passed it along, shouting from turrets, speaking into radio handsets. "Corpsman up!"

Kirby leapt out the door, running through shouts from Marines in the column. They were guiding him, demanding his presence, pleading for him to hurry to a downed man.

"Corpsman up!"

"Truck One!"

"Get up there!"

Kirby ran, a mad sprint, passing unhurt Marines, heading to the truck where someone had been shot.

"Truck One!"

"Get the fuck up there!"

It was a fifty-meter dash to the first truck. Someone opened a door for Kirby as he arrived. He heard a voice.

"It's Smith," it said. "Smith got shot in the head."

Lance Corporal Colin Smith had been in the turret. He was lying across the gunner's stand in the back of the truck. For an ephemeral moment, Kirby had a vision: Sitting beside Smith, an arm's length away and intruding on the Marines, was a strange young man in a black hood with a taut face and brilliant blue eyes. The man's arm reached out. Kirby met the man's gaze. He was young and looked annoyed, as if the corpsman had interfered. Kirby had never seen him before, but knew him at once: the Grim Reaper. *You can't have him*, he thought.

The man disappeared, as if he had not been there at all.

Kirby climbed in. Smith had been his roommate in the barracks at Camp Lejeune. A Marine was cradling Smith's head like a baby's. He looked at Kirby with desperate, reddened eyes.

"What do I do?" he said. His hands were coated in blood. Fear was contagious. Panic bred mistakes. Calm allowed people to think, and to work. Kirby knew he had to project calm.

"You did good, man," he said. "You did good."

He pulled Smith close and looked down. Smith's eyes were closed. A thin stream of blood trailed from the right side of his head down his face. The exit wound on the opposite side of his skull was about the size of a fifty-cent piece, aligned with Smith's frontal lobe.

He is my friend, Kirby thought.

He rested Smith's head on his groin protector and forced himself to focus. To do this right he had to suppress unnecessary thoughts and resist the paralyzing emotional shock rising within. *He is my friend.*

He swept that away.

Smith was a patient. The patient needed care.

He pulled back Smith's eyelids. Both pupils were dilated. He shined a flashlight down. Both eyes constricted as light hit them. It was the sign Kirby hoped for. Kirby felt for Smith's pulse. It was strong. Smith's jaw was clenched. But he was breathing, audibly and hard.

Kirby reached into his medical kit, removed a pressure dressing, and gently wrapped it around Smith's head to cover the entrance and exit wounds. He had two ambitions, one medical and the other social. He had to keep impurities out. He also wanted to protect the platoon from seeing what he had just seen.

Smith stopped breathing. Kirby was in a zone. He leaned over, pressed his lips over Smith's mouth and gave him two rescue breaths, and pulled back.

Smith gasped. Kirby repositioned his head, lowering it, creating a straight neck, and ensuring the airway was as open as it could be. The labored breathing settled into a quieter rhythm.

Kirby looked up. Dempsey's face was there. He was peering into the vehicle, watching Smith and the corpsman and the spreading blood, getting his bearings on what to do next. He asked for an assessment.

"His pupils are responsive," Kirby said. "He has brain activity."

Dempsey nodded. With good news came an urgency not afforded the dead. If Smith was alive and could survive, then any evacuation must happen promptly.

They needed a helicopter.

Now.

Smith peed himself, soaking his flight suit in a spreading stain.

Kirby wondered if this signaled the end. Was his friend voiding himself as he died? He kept a straight face. His mind screamed. *God fucking damn it! God fucking damn it!*

Smith's breathing labored on.

The company had radioed for a medevac. The two helicopters that had been watching over the Marines during the raid heard the call. They turned around and were back.

Dempsey jumped onto the hood of the truck and told the driver to move to the field beside the house they had just searched. Kirby held Smith tightly as they bounced over the dirt. Dempsey tossed a red smoke grenade. Its plume climbed in the air. The helicopter, a Huey, touched down.

The Marines loaded Smith onto a poleless litter, lifted him, and rushed to the aircraft. It was a Huey gunship, not a medevac bird. Smith was still breathing when they laid him inside. Kirby's job was done. He had to hand over his friend. Over the roar of the engine, he shouted lifesaving steps to the door gunner, tapped Smith on the leg, and ran clear. The blades swept up dust and grass and blew the red smoke away, scattering it in pink wisps. The helicopter moved low over the field, gaining elevation, cleared a date palm grove, and was gone.

Suddenly there was nothing for Kirby to do. He ran back to his truck and plopped onto the right front seat. The company began moving. Someone said a car had sped away after the shot, heading to a house that Weapons Company would now search.

Kirby sat in the front seat, his hands and arms and legs wet with his friend's blood. It was clotting, sticky and still warm. He held Smith's helmet. He turned it over to look at where the bullet passed through. The bullet rolled inside. It was an armor-piercing 7.62x54R round. It had zipped through the front of the helmet and then the top of Smith's head. Kirby lifted it out and inspected it, rolling it in his hand. It had kept its shape. He put it in his pocket.

Nausea came in waves.

Outside, Weapons Company's Marines were rushing into the house where they had heard the sniper might have hidden. They detained two men. Kirby had not been ordered out. He stayed in his seat, listening to the radio reports, waiting to be called, trembling with an energy that he could neither channel nor contain. Tears streamed down his face. He stared at his bloody hands, and at the stains on his legs and lap, where he had cradled Smith's head.

He shook uncontrollably. He rocked back and forth in the seat.

Never before had he saved a life. He had thought it would be cool. Instead he felt guilty. He had seen the entrance and exit wounds and the torn brain matter, and had a sense of what was missing. Some of it was inside the helmet on his lap. Kirby could visualize the path of the steel bullet through his friend's skull. If Smith survived the trip to the first hospital—if he made it through stabilization and surgery and the transfer to Germany—what kind of life could he expect?

Kirby had acted in the moment, holding emotions in check so he could do his job. Now his emotions broke free. He had a chance to think past the second-by-second sequence and tasks of lifesaving steps. He was not sure what saving a life meant.

Did I do that for me? Kirby wondered. *Or for him?* He did not know whether Smith was even still alive. There was no medic on the Huey. He might die on the way.

Kirby had done what he had most wanted to do, and was trying not to vomit.

The hours passed quickly. The company drove its two prisoners to the police station. A warrant officer took the bullet from Kirby and bagged it for evidence. The platoon drove back to Omar, where Kirby showered, threw away his bloody flight suit, and was issued a replacement.

The company commander met with the Marines to tell them that he had received information: Smith survived the flight to the doctors and was stable and in surgery. The Shark seemed warmer than usual. Inside the command post, one of the platoon's drivers, Lance Corporal Daniel Nicholson, opened a pocket-sized Bible and led the Marines in prayer, verses from Psalm 91, a counterpoint to Al Imran 103.

"Thou shall not be afraid for the terror by night, nor for the arrow that flieth by day," he said. ". . . For he shall give his angels charge over thee, to keep thee in all thy ways."

Kirby found his bunk. Now was his chance to rest, to sleep.

He could not. Contradictory feelings plagued him. Marines snored. Kirby waited for news, half expecting someone to step into the bunk room and say that Smith had died. Sunrise found him drained, an insomniac rising for another day. He felt locked inside his own head. He was excoriating himself, reliving the sight of his friend's wound, replaying his own actions, feeling anxiety, dread, and doubt. He wondered about the vision of the man in the black hood beside Smith. He assumed he had hallucinated; the vision was the product of an overwhelmed mind. He could still see those blue eyes. Kirby was in a daze, a state of physical exhaustion and moral turmoil. That night he volunteered for guard duty, knowing he would not sleep. *What had Smith's life been saved for?*

For more than a week Kirby felt mechanical, moving from duty to duty, patrol to patrol, event to event, outwardly present, inwardly withdrawn, always sleep-deprived. He thought saving a life would be validating and satisfying, a test that, if he passed it, would infuse him with wisdom and meaning. It was none of these things. He was stalked by a mix of self-loathing and worry about what Smith's life now held.

Most men who had been shot like Smith had died in prior wars. Through luck—the bullet had been just high enough, the lifesaving steps had been just quick enough, the helicopter had been just close enough— Smith had survived. *But for what?* Each day Kirby waited for the news that Smith was dead. Outwardly, he kept up appearances; he had to be the corpsman who could be counted on. Internally, he was numb.

A week later he was in a motorized patrol heading to the police station, in the back right seat, still dazed.

The trucks were in a column moving south down Chicago, nearing a road juncture Dempsey called the Evil Intersection. Several auto garages were just off the road's west shoulder. Traversing the intersection was a gamble. If Marines left the trucks to search on foot—a predict-able behavior—they risked being shot by a sniper. If they drove straight through, they risked being hit by a bomb. It was only steps from the police station—the Chicago 500 distilled.

Dempsey decided to drive it. He gave the word.

The police station was 300 yards away. The column of trucks sped up. Kirby was in a vehicle near the end of the column, ready to react. The lead truck passed safely. The second followed not far behind. Kirby saw the auto garages drawing near. The structures offered cover to anyone who might remotely detonate an IED. The other trucks made it.

His truck came even with first of the garages. They were a ramshackle mess, littered with garbage, grimy barrels, and idled cars.

A bomb exploded to Kirby's right. Two 130-millimeter artillery shells, wired together, had been detonated by someone watching the Marines.

A pressure wave slammed against the passenger-side doors. Kirby was near the explosion. He felt the vehicle absorb the blast, almost as if it might flip, and heard shrapnel splatter against armor. When the truck glided to a stop, he looked himself over. He was intact. He felt alert.

He spun to check the others.

The vehicle commander, Corporal Drew Upton, was unconscious. In the driver's seat, Lance Corporal Nicholson, the Marine who had read the Psalm after Smith was shot, was screaming and touching his face. The turret gunner, Lance Corporal William Thorpe, was thrashing. Kirby felt both woozy from the blast and fired by adrenaline and purpose. The Ma-rines' needs snatched him from his funk. He opened his door and swung himself out and onto his feet, carrying a medical bag. Thorpe was waking up. Kirby looked at him. He was whole. Kirby saw no blood. Thorpe spoke.

"I'm fine," he said. "I'm fine."

Triage, Kirby thought.

He ran to the opposite side of the truck and pulled open the driver's door.

Nicholson looked up.

Kirby's mind formed its own thought. *Fuck*.

Much of Nicholson's face had been sheared away. Shrapnel had hit a seam above the right-side doors, where the armor was weaker, and skipped inside, striking his head. From the ear to an eye and then over to his upper lip, his face was a partially connected mask, hanging like a flap. Kirby glanced down at Nicholson's equipment harness. Teeth had fallen onto it.

"Hey, man, I got you," he said.

He opened a pressure dressing, pressed it against the wound, and asked Nicholson to help. "I need you to hold this right here while I do some stuff," he said. Nicholson took the dressing and pushed up against his face.

He was over the surprise of being hit and was registering what he knew. He had calmed himself. "Doc, I think I am missing some teeth," he said.

Kirby added the words to his inventory. Nicholson was coherent, talking, making sense. *Amazing signs,* Kirby thought.

"You are going to be fine, bro," he said. "You are going to be fine."

The truck's entire crew was moving now. Upton had come more fully to; he reached across the vehicle to pull gauze for Kirby out of Nicholson's first-aid kit. Thorpe, the turret gunner, climbed onto the hood, jumped down to the road, and fell over. He rolled into a prone position with his rifle aimed out, ready to defend the truck. Blood stained the back of his trousers.

Iraqis watched the wounded Americans from up and down the street. The broken truck of Mobile Assault Platoon Two was the latest bloody spectacle on the Chicago 500, another scramble of bloodied men beside a smoking hole and a damaged ride.

The rest of the platoon swarmed them.

The crowd kept away as they charged in.

Dempsey appeared in Kirby's field of view. He had run from another truck.

"Gunny, we're going to need an urgent surgical," Kirby said.

"Got it," Dempsey answered.

They loaded Nicholson into another truck and sped the last few hundred yards, into the station, and led Nicholson out back to wait for the medevac. Kirby stayed with him until a helicopter came and lifted the Marines away. Kirby was ordered to Camp Fallujah, where an exam determined that he had suffered a concussion. The military was beginning to force soldiers to slow down and rest, and undergo evaluations, after concussions from bomb blasts. He was told he would need to spend a week on the base on light duty, under close watch.

Light duty required Kirby to be idle. Without the distractions of patrols and platoon life, his mind resumed its tour of guilt. He played the sequence after Smith had been shot over and over in his head. He had faced the Reaper and done all he could to save his friend. He had lived up to everything a corpsman assigned to Marines was supposed to do. Marines were looking up to him, thanking him, expressing admiration, respect, even love. And yet Kirby was depressed. He berated himself. People told him he had acted selflessly. He felt the opposite. He had acted selfishly. By keeping his friend alive, Kirby had established his own worth and cemented his place as a corpsman before his Marines. What did Smith get out of it, with a brain trauma like that?

He was given a bunk at Camp Fallujah and told to convalesce. He had recurring headache and ringing ears. Time dragged. He wanted to go back to Outpost Omar, where there was work to be done. While waiting to be declared fit to return, another corpsman came to him with word: There was a call for Kirby at the aid station. The aid station had an international telephone line. The doctor used it for his casework—to gather information with which to brief the battalion's officers on the conditions and prognoses of wounded Marines, and to pass information to doctors in the States. It was not a line that Kirby ever used. He asked what was going on.

Someone wanted to talk with him, the corpsman said.

In the office, Kirby was told Lance Corporal Smith's father, Bob Smith, was on the line. Kirby took the handset, wondering what to say, heart pounding. "Yes, sir, this is Petty Officer Kirby," he said.

He heard a man's voice, clear and strong. "I want to thank you for saving my son's life," he said.

Lance Corporal Smith had arrived at the Naval Hospital at Bethesda, his father said, and he was with him now. He told Kirby that when he looked into Colin's eyes, he could see him in there.

Kirby could hear it. The voice on the other end was breaking. Bob Smith was talking through tears. He pushed on. "My son would not be alive if not for you," Smith said. "And as long as I am breathing, you will have a father in Ohio."

Kirby's guilt began to lift.

A few days later Kirby passed the concussion protocols and returned to Outpost Omar and the Karma police station. His life on the Chicago 500 resumed: standing post, patrolling, tending to the company's Marines, marking days off a combat tour. In early December, Mobile Assault Platoon Two came off patrols for a rotation at the police station. There were no other Marines there beside the guard force, which meant the platoon might have the bunk room to itself and get proper sleep. One of the Marines had a DVD of a season of *Family Guy*. Kirby and several Marines clustered around a screen watching episodes, laughing, carried away from Karma a session at a time.

During one of the episodes, the ground shook. It was like the tremor of an earthquake, detectable through the feet.

The sound of the explosion followed behind, a heavy crack, then a rolling rumble.

The Marines were up before the shouting began. "Get your shit on! We gotta go."

The blast had been to their north. They heard clods of dirt landing. When they ran to their trucks, they saw a tower of smoke climbing in the sky.

Someone had been hit by a massive IED on Route Chicago.

Regret washed over Kirby again. He felt like he had let Marines down. When the bomb detonated, they had been enjoying *Family Guy*, tuning out the war, which continued right outside the police station's blast walls.

Somebody just died, he thought. *We were laughing right then.*

The platoon sped to the blast site, turret gunners ready, and came upon a pair of Abrams tanks. They were stopped. They seemed to be intact.

The militants often went quiet when Marine tank patrols moved through. Abrams were immune to most light weapons, and were imposing in a way Humvees never would be. On this day the tanks had been moving north on the road, past the police station, and crossed without incident through the juncture where Nicholson had been wounded. They continued toward Omar. At the S-curve the bomb exploded under the trailing tank. By local standards it was huge. Its explosive charge, perhaps 250 pounds in all, had been stuffed into a drainage culvert—a job that must have taken those who had hidden it there considerable time. A fine copper wire ran from the crater to the west toward a watching triggerman who had initiated the blast.

The crater was roughly twenty feet long, fifteen feet wide, and five feet deep.

The rear tank was damaged but its crew was not seriously wounded. The platoon guarded the site until a recovery vehicle retrieved the tank and an explosive ordnance disposal team investigated the site. The bombers had chosen their target poorly. Attacking a tank was tempting, but the Abrams withstood the blast and would be repaired. Had the same bomb detonated under one of Weapons Company's Humvees, the vehicle would have been blown into chunks. All the Marines inside might have been killed.*

The bombs kept coming. A truck in another platoon was hit by an IED in the northern stretch of Chicago near where Hirlston had been killed. The truck was badly damaged, and the platoon sergeant, who had been riding shotgun inside, appeared stunned when he returned to Omar. Kirby examined him. The sergeant looked tense and ashen. Kirby had no formal say in another platoon's affairs, but he told the sergeant to go to Camp Fallujah, as Kirby had, for rest and observation.

The sergeant refused. "Go fuck yourself," he said.

Kirby backed away. In mid-December the same sergeant lost his M4 rifle on patrol—a violation of the Marine culture so egregious that it was beyond an embarrassment. It was an all but instant end of a career. Whispers traveled among the company's Marines about how it had happened. Some said the sergeant had leaned it against his truck during a stop at a police post in Karma and forgotten it when the patrol drove away. Others said the sergeant had set it on a bumper to urinate and

---

* Arabic-language video of the attack on the tank bore the logo of the Al-Furqan Foundation for Media Production, a propaganda wing of Sunni militants and terrorists in the area. The same organization would later become a primary producer of videos for the Islamic State of Iraq and Syria. This was consistent with events of which the Marines of Weapons Company were as yet unaware. While Weapons Company was strung along Route Chicago, Al Qaeda in Iraq rebranded itself as the Islamic State of Iraq. The company was among the first American units to engage with the Islamic State, in its early form.

stepped back into his seat without it. Whichever story a Marine believed, the effect was the same. The sergeant was immediately relieved of duties and sent to Camp Fallujah in shame. The Marines then heard that the battalion was asking whether he had suffered a brain injury that had undermined his memory and caused his inattentiveness, and been a factor in the rifle's loss.

The sergeant's lapse ushered in fresh hassles for everyone else. Weapons Company, stinging at the loss, entered a period when it repeatedly counted its equipment. Marines were required to prove they had all of their issued items. Constant inspections fueled anger and distrust. And some Marines worried about grimmer effects. In the bunk rooms and in trucks, where Marines were close and spoke with candor, they asked: What might the missing rifle's next chapter be? It was equipped with an infrared laser target pointer and 4-power optical sight. Would one of Weapons Company's own weapons be turned against them?

In the cold hours before sunrise on Christmas morning, Petty Officer Kirby made a mistake. He woke inside a trailer in Camp Fallujah, stood half-dressed beside his rack, and groggily urinated into an empty water bottle. Working hard days in Iraq's dry climate, Marines and corpsmen drank large quantities of water. This was seen as a duty, necessary for heading off dehydration and avoiding collapse. Heavy intakes created hassles, including frequent urination. The portable toilets were outside and often foul. Waking at night and walking into blackness to use them disrupted sleep—which, for Weapons Company's Marines, was already in short supply. The workaround was simple: Many Marines kept empty water bottles by their bunks and at night would reach to them for relief. The practice was both common and forbidden, considered an affront to discipline and close-quarters hygiene. On Christmas morning Kirby was caught.

A sergeant discovered Kirby's water bottle filled with pee. The two men argued. A few hours later, the sergeant asked for Marines to stand post. Another member of the platoon volunteered. The sergeant who was angry at Kirby had a different idea. He told the corpsman he would stand the extra duty—a shift in a two-man bunker on the roof.

"You're going up there, and you fucking know why," he said.

The particular post was a sparely built box of framing lumber ringed by a low sandbag wall. Salvaged bulletproof windows from vehicles offered a measure of protection, but the place had an otherwise partially made feel. It lacked camouflaged netting to break up the Marines' outlines or a heavy metal screen to catch an incoming rocket-propelled grenade. For weeks Marines had groused about it. They thought it was unsafe and should not be occupied. Lance Corporal Anthony Santos, who was assigned to the post with Kirby, loathed the place, which he thought resembled a cheap closet with no door.

Kirby took his turn behind the tinted bulletproof glass late in the morning, the punitive replacement on a shift that had been scheduled for his driver. The day was quiet. It felt like a holiday lull. He passed a few hours chatting with Santos. The two men talked about movies, and joked, and griped about Doc's misfortune, of being punished on Christmas Day. In the afternoon, his time up, Kirby stepped from behind the barrier and into the open, ready to dash the few steps to the stairs leading to the ground.

A bright light flashed in his eyes. He felt a jolt to his head. There had been no warning.

"What the fuck happened?" he said.

He did not recognize his voice. Its Southern twang had been replaced by mumble.

He looked back. Santos was staring out of the bunker, directly at him.

"Shit, you're bleeding!" he said. He was wide-eyed. "What do I do?"

"I'm bleeding?" Kirby said. Again his words did not form. *What the fuck's going on?* He leaned forward and held his left hand under his mouth. A single drop of blood landed on his palm. A flood followed. In a hot gush, Kirby's hand was covered.

He heard someone yell.

"Doc Kirby got shot in the face!"

Kirby tried to guide his mind away from panic. Hunched over, staring at his soaked left hand, he needed information. *How bad is it?*

A chunk of bone fell into his palm.

He worked his jaw, trying movement he had always taken for granted. His jaw did not seem attached. More blood sputtered out, mixing foam and meat with shards of teeth and bone. Kirby retched. Out dropped a larger chunk. It was a piece of his jaw, holding an intact tooth.

Kirby swore.

The dark puddle expanded beneath him. He knelt and felt an impulse to gather everything solid. This was his face, his mouth, his teeth—all glistening on the roof. He needed these for the doctor. He started pushing it all together, forming a small pile.

A frantic bustle surrounded him. Santos pressed close.

Kirby heard shouted orders, calls for help. Someone was talking about how to get him off the roof. A voice called for litter bearers.

Ordinarily when Marines were wounded, their treatment and evacuation would be Kirby's job. But Kirby was detached. Details of his own case seemed merely overheard. He was transfixed, busy with other things. He picked through the puddle, collecting the pieces of his mouth. More fell out.

The company commander bounded up to the roof and stood beside him. He asked for all of Kirby's serialized equipment. Kirby returned to the moment. He was astonished. These were not the words he expected to hear. *This is what we talk about when a man gets shot?*

He saw it as more fallout from the lost rifle.

He complied. Blood rushing from his face, he handed over his rifle, unfastened his lanyard, and turned over his pistol. He pointed to the pouch, now bloody, that held his night-vision goggles. He was insulted. He had lost nothing and right now did not want to talk about gear. Blood rolled down his chin.

He punched the pile of his own flesh, smashing his fist downward, striking knuckles into blood. A sergeant asked him to calm down.

Kirby took a few breaths, pushed himself away from the pile, stood, and faced the stairs. He started to walk. He met the litter-and-security team coming up with a stretcher. He walked past them under his own power.

Their faces told Kirby what he needed to know.

I look nasty.

This is bad.

People parted as he walked, clearing a path.

He stepped into the company office. A sergeant said a helicopter was on its way. Kirby took a seat on a case of water. He was hot, terribly hot. But it wasn't a hot day. He thought he was supposed to feel cold as he lost blood. This fevered feeling surprised him. He unzipped the top of his flight suit and tied its sleeves in a knot around his waist. His T-shirt, from neck to navel, was a stripe of blood. Kirby wanted a mirror. He asked for one. No one seemed to understand.

Within minutes a helicopter landed on Chicago. Kirby refused a stretcher. He thought if he lay down he would choke on flaps of meat and blood. That's not how he wanted to die.

He walked up the aircraft's tail ramp, sat down, and held on.

A procession of Marines had followed him, and stopped near the helicopter, in silent awe. *That man walked out after being shot in the face*, Santos thought.

Rushing air blew over Kirby as the aircraft took to flight. It felt good, a relief from the strange fever.

Kirby knew he had little time. The trip to the surgical team at Al Taqaddum Air Base was short, but while en route there was no way to apply a tourniquet, and the bleeding from the tearing was too extensive and too hard to reach to be stemmed with pressure bandages. He needed surgery fast.

A corpsman on board the aircraft stood above him, but the two men could not talk, and Kirby insisted on sitting upright. *He's waiting for me to pass out*, Kirby thought.

He held a bandage to his face, feeling the minutes ticking by, evaluating the patient he had become. The fact that nobody would let him see himself told him he looked worse than he guessed. His wounds were still bleeding heavily. The volume stained his chest and lap. He could feel it on him, warm and sticky, down his neck, under his shirt, between his thighs. He looked at his flak jacket. The groin protector—the Kevlar flap that covered his genitals, where he had rested Smith's head in October—was solid red. Blood filled Kirby's mouth, demanding his attention, forcing him to breathe through his nose. He could feel himself weakening, his consciousness ebbing, his sense of control fading even as he was carried closer to medical care.

His mind told him that the details added up to one thing: He was soon to die.

This is it, man, he thought. *This is it.*

He wondered if he could accept this. He was away from Weapons Company, away from friends to whom he was supposed to provide care. None of them would see him. He could let himself be human now, and be weak.

The aircraft cleared the blast walls at Al Taqaddum and set down beside the surgical center. This was where Kirby's previous patients had gone, one of the entrances to the Anbar Province casualty pipeline. He'd made it this far and knew the routine. The hour ahead would determine whether his next stop was a larger hospital or the morgue. Litter bearers rushed to the aircraft's tail ramp. Kirby waved them off. He would not lie down. He staggered off the aircraft and faced that look in everyone's eyes again. People froze at the sight of him. He walked to the litter bearers' vehicle and saw the crew had come out with a body bag. He sat beside it.

The vehicle lurched into gear and sped to the surgical center's entrance, where he walked toward the first person he saw. People were scrambling around him.

"No, no, no!" he heard. "Not that way! Go there!" Someone pointed him to a gurney and nurses and doctors eased him down.

His anxiety was rising. He had to let go now and yield control to a surgical team. Their hands were on him.

He was a corpsman. He was trained for this situation, and these people were not doing it how he liked. He tried to speak. *Y'all need to calm down a little bit, because you are starting to freak me out.*

The words did not form.

The staff cut away his clothes and started an IV.

As if a switch had been tripped, Kirby's pain began. He was lying on the gurney, sweaty, naked, exposed, in agony. His face felt as if it had been torn open and set afire. Someone said they had to remove his bracelet, a piece of braided parachute cord that he had worn for years. It was an amulet, his good-luck piece.

Kirby signaled that he would do it. But he had lost strength and dexterity. His fingers could not manipulate the loop. The man snipped it off with medical scissors.

Kirby snapped. He rolled toward the man and swung, trying to punch his face. It was pointless. Speed and power had left him, and he sensed himself lurching in a slow-motion roundhouse. He saw the staff close in, felt them holding him down. He pulled his hands back and covered up to defend himself, recoiling into an almost fetal pose. He noticed he was trembling uncontrollably. *What the fuck's going on?*

"Hit him!" he heard. "Hit him!"

The world went black.

With President George W. Bush's second term ending and the Democratic nominee for president, Barack Obama, campaigning in part on pledges to commit more resources to defeating the Taliban, public attention was turning from Iraq back to Afghanistan. Bloodshed in Iraq was declining, the result of many factors, including the deployment of more American troops (a renewed effort nicknamed the "Surge"), large cash payments to insurgents to cease fighting, and demographic shifts as the country became more segregated between sects. The Pentagon, facing a skeptical public and a Congress that had long called for troop withdrawals, was forming plans to begin bringing home the more than 160,000 troops participating in the surge. The forces in Afghanistan, just over 30,000 troops in all, were much smaller, and faced seemingly intractable rural resistance and terrorists in cities. But resources and attention were shifting. American units were soon to rejoin the war in earnest.

EIGHT

"I'LL FLY AWAY"

Chief Warrant Officer Mike Slebodnik and the Air Cavalry in the Eastern Afghan Valleys

"Let's go back in and see if we can draw fire."

SEPTEMBER 9, 2008
Forward Operating Base Fenty, Jalalabad, Afghanistan

The joke was working. For days Chief Warrant Officer Sokol Cela was pondering whether he was in trouble. A Kiowa Warrior helicopter pilot, he had been home in the States for two weeks of leave when emails from Michael Slebodnik started landing in his in-box. Slebodnik was one of Cela's bosses and the senior warrant officer in his air cavalry unit— Charlie Troop, Second Squadron of the Seventeenth Cavalry Regiment. He wanted to know when Cela would be back at Jalalabad Airfield, where both men were nearing the end of a one-year combat tour.

Cela was unnerved. Slebodnik was not one to waste time on unimportant details. Questions formed in his head. *Why is Slebodnik asking? What did I do wrong?*

The journey from the United States to Jalalabad was at least a five-day trip. It began with commercial bookings out of the States and shifted in the Middle East to flights on military aircraft, hopping from base to base as seats became available on aircraft making runs into Afghanistan. There the returning soldiers fanned out, each shuttling to smaller satellite bases as spare seats opened up. It was an unpredictable means of travel, an ever-changing air traffic lottery dependent upon weather, operational tempo, and luck, even in early September 2008, when the skies over Afghanistan were busier than ever with American helicopters.

As Cela got closer his anxiety grew. Each note from Slebodnik forced him to wonder: *What does he want?*

Finally Slebodnik told him: A journalist was writing an article about their troop, and Cela had been nominated to be profiled. They needed to get the interview done.

Cela was both relieved and annoyed. He liked Slebodnik. They were friends, and lived in neighboring rooms inside a B-hut, one of the eighteen-by-thirty-six-foot wooden shacks that dotted the base. But Cela was traveling, and tired, and did not want to deal with a reporter. He griped back on email. He just wanted to get back out on missions, he said.

The reply was terse: *Well, you don't have a choice.*

Cela had spent a career in the Army and was used to its bullshit. But Slebodnik was not like this. Cela was confused. *What's going on here?*

He made his arrangements for the last leg of his trip, not suspecting that his fellow pilots were setting him up.

American Special Forces and CIA teams had first arrived at the former Soviet air base in Jalalabad in 2001, chasing Osama bin Laden during the opening months of the war. Immediately afterward the Afghan countryside seemed quiet. But as years passed and the Pentagon focused much of its attention on Iraq, the Taliban reorganized and resurfaced, and Afghanistan's new government and the United States struggled to counter its influence and spread. The Pentagon adjusted troop levels upward, to 25,000 by 2007, and the deserted airfield at Jalalabad resumed a level of activity not seen since Soviet forces had left. Renamed Forward Operating Base

Fenty* after an infantry officer killed in a CH-47 crash, it became a head-quarters and hub for an expanding set of outposts in the mountains. Most of these posts, at the bottom of narrow canyons or built into the sides of steep-walled valleys, were isolated. Many were remote.

Slebodnik and his fellow Kiowa pilots landed in Jalalabad in early 2008 to run reconnaissance missions around the positions and cover patrols and convoys on the ground. They lived on the tarmac in a cluster of B-huts, each with eight single-occupant rooms furnished with a crude bunk and desk. Their rooms amounted to little more than sleeping cubicles with walls that stopped above head height, leaving airspace overhead.

It was here that some of the pilots' practical jokes originated. Beneath their self-contained exteriors, many had long histories of flying combat missions in Iraq. They could feel taut and be jumpy. Sometimes they tossed laundry over the walls or playfully teased one another. In August, right before Cela departed on leave, he lobbed an empty water bottle over the wall into the room of another pilot, Chief Warrant Officer Jeremy Woehlert.

The bottle landed on Woehlert's head.

The B-hut filled with Woehlert's curses, and laughter from everyone else.

The plot to get even began immediately. Woehlert and Slebodnik conspired. *Cela likes bottles? We can help him with that.* They printed signs and posted them around the base. "RECYCLE," they said.

CW2 CELA NEEDS EMPTY (CLEAN) WATER BOTTLES . . . HE DID NOT WANT TO SAY WHY, BUT HIS INSTRUCTIONS WERE TO SAVE AS MANY AS POSSIBLE WHILE HE IS ON LEAVE. PLEASE SAVE SOME IN BAGS AND THEN JUST DUMP THEM INTO HIS ROOM. HIS GOAL IS TO HAVE ENOUGH TO FILL HIS ROOM UP PRIOR TO HIS RETURN FROM LEAVE AROUND THE 6TH OF SEPTEMBER.

---

* Lieutenant Colonel Joseph J. Fenty, killed with nine other soldiers on May 5, 2006, in Kunar Province.

While Cela relaxed back in the States, soldiers from across Fenty filed to his B-hut with their empties. Some showed up with thirty-gallon garbage bags, stuffed. The plywood door to Cela's room was padlocked, so the visitors swung their garbage bags over the wall and shook out their contents. Cela's bed and desk were soon buried. By early September the walls of his room crested with bottles, a cache of trash seven feet deep.

When Cela landed at the airfield on September 9, Slebodnik was standing on the tarmac in a gray T-shirt and black shorts. He had just finished a workout. He didn't usually meet pilots returning from leave. Cela asked if something was up.

"No, no," Slebodnik said. "I was just coming back from chow and heard you were coming back."

At their B-hut, another pilot was in the corridor. "How was leave?" he asked.

"It was good," Cela said. "Got some recess."

He tried sliding open his door. A strange weight shifted on the opposite side. A lone bottle fell to his feet with a plunk.

"Shit," he said, perplexed.

He looked through the crack in the doorway. Before him was a wall of empty bottles, thousands in all, rising over his head.

"Oh, no!" he shouted. "No!"

He looked up, into his friends' video cameras, fooled.

"You motherfuckers!" he shouted, and pulled back the door. An avalanche of bottles rumbled out.

Charlie Troop was feeling good, and so was Slebodnik. He grinned and waded through the mess. His time was almost up. He was due for his own family leave in a few days, and when he returned, Charlie Troop would have only weeks until the end of its tour. The soldiers would pass duties to fresh pilots and go home. With twenty-two years in the Army, Slebodnik might even retire.

———

Charlie Troop was part of the Pentagon's belated effort to restore momentum to the Afghan war and help the post-Taliban government take control of its own land. Political discussion in the States had shifted with the presidential election campaign, in which Senator Barack Obama, the

Democratic nominee, was pledging to draw down forces in Iraq, add combat brigades in Afghanistan, and make "the fight against al Qaeda and the Taliban the top priority that it should be."* The American military was reorienting, and the political reemphasis was coinciding with the decline of bloodshed in Iraq during 2008. American officials attributed the drop to counterinsurgency tactics and the deployment of more troops, an offensive the Pentagon called the "Surge." The reasons were more complicated than that, involving shifts where Sunni and Shiite populations chose to live, the sectarian victory of Shiite groups in Baghdad over their Sunni neighbors, an American special operations campaign that killed insurgents in raids, a timely cease-fire declared by a prominent Shiite cleric, and the practice of paying Sunni tribes, including some thick with militants, to align with the government and become the authorities over their own ground.

Whatever the relative weight of each factor, one result was beyond dispute: The pause in Iraq filled some of the American military's leadership with confidence, no matter the grim situation evident all around. The Pentagon's Afghan campaign had stalled, the Taliban was reestablished, and large swaths of the country had no government presence at all. The pivot to Afghanistan was nonetheless buoyed by institutional faith. Most of America's general-officer class had little firsthand experience with small-unit warfare; they had served the early years of their careers after the Vietnam War. But the middle and lower ranks were an experienced force, populated by officers and noncommissioned officers seasoned in Iraq. Technically and tactically tested, with better equipment than the forces of 2001, they formed a class of professional fighters, men and women who had seen years of combat and were volunteering to go back. The Pentagon's messaging was bold: *We're here now. We know what we're doing. And the Taliban will soon pay.* Even the labels suggested an eagerness to meet the Taliban on its turf and roll it up. Charlie Troop flew under the call sign Close Combat, part of an air cavalry task force known as Out Front.

In early 2008, part of the troop settled into Jalalabad. The first Kiowas to deploy to Afghanistan since 2005, they took their place alongside

---

* Campaign speech by Senator Obama, July 15, 2008, Washington.

CH-47 utility helicopters, Apache gunships, and Black Hawk troop transport and medevac birds, all under the command of another Kiowa pilot from Pennsylvania, Lieutenant Colonel John Lynch.

The area around the base was a large open bowl. To the north and east, the Hindu Kush mountains rose toward the sky. The range drained to the city's basin through a watershed of rivers and streams that had carved canyons into stone. Upstream from the base, smaller cities straddled the valley floors. Farther up, ancient villages clung to mountain walls. Throughout the rural zone, Afghan farmers diverted water to irrigate hand-fashioned terraces dense with crops. Shepherds roamed the hills. Hunters and woodcutters worked the mountains, harvesting old-growth trees, some with stumps as thick as cars. Together it formed a tableau that seemed to many Westerners to be from another time, green agrarian lowlands beneath ancient forests that gave way to snowcapped stone peaks—a harsh, gorgeous, and primeval landscape, thoroughly claimed by its own people, who knew its ways better than any outsider ever could.

The American and Afghan governments were extending their influence up the rivers to patches of Nuristan, Nangarhar, Kunar, and Laghman Provinces, an area of operations the military dubbed N2KL. They held a string of outposts in valleys few Americans had heard of before: Kunar, Alishang, Alingar, Pech, Watapur, Waygal, Korengal. Senior officers who organized the Army's day-to-day called the arrangement a defense-in-depth intended to force the Taliban to fight away from population centers. The new war was to be fought around tiny villages— Kamdesh, Ganjgal, Najil, and Kamu, to name a few—where American troops and Afghan soldiers and police officers now lived. "Taliban magnets," one colonel called them. The troops sometimes used another name: "bullet sponges." The Americans could reach their bases in the lower valleys over land. But as distances stretched, roads grew worse and dangers climbed. For the air cavalry, the result was a demanding set of missions in a complicated airspace. Many outposts were resupplied almost solely by helicopter. Apache attack helicopters and Kiowas watched over patrols and helped troops fight off ambushes or coordinated attacks. Medevac aircraft were always on call, crisscrossing the airspace to pick up the wounded and the dead. In some valleys—so narrow that helicopters were imperiled by gunfire and rocket-propelled grenades from their sides,

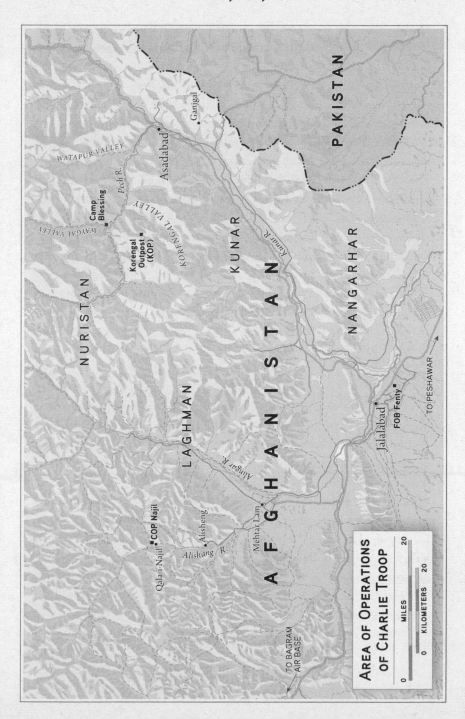

or even from above—the Army dispatched routine flights only by night, to reduce the likelihood of aircraft being shot down.

Charlie Troop started its tour in winter, when days were short, the weather was cold, and rivers were prone to flooding. The first weeks were slow, allowing pilots a chance to learn the valleys before the fighting picked up, and adjust to the Army's frustrating rules. Jalalabad was about 2,000 feet above sea level. The terrain where American troops roamed climbed to several times that. Since the Kiowa struggled for power at high elevations, the Army issued a guideline: Kiowas could not fly above 6,000 feet. The ceiling excluded Charlie Troop from many of the most menaced outposts and areas into which American soldiers hoped to push. It struck some of the pilots as arbitrary, a restriction that overreached. The frustration was compounded by more math: Task Force Out Front had only six Apaches to cover four provinces. With crew rest requirements, and maintenance, and two Apaches being held on call around the clock for quick-reaction-force duty, it felt as if there were too few helicopters to red-line the Kiowa fleet from some of the most dangerous turf. *Why have us here,* pilots asked, *to hold us back?*

———

On January 31, Slebodnik led one of the first Kiowa flights up the Kunar Valley. It was a two-aircraft reconnaissance mission to check out new ground. The aircraft flew to Asadabad, the capital of Kunar Province, took on fuel, and continued upstream. Slebodnik piloted the lead helicopter, making note of firebases and outposts, and examining roads, including stretches where the intelligence briefings had noted that the Taliban repeatedly ambushed patrols. Just north of Asadabad the confluence of valleys required a choice. They could turn northwest and head up the Pech Valley or continue following the Kunar River to the northeast. Slebodnik chose northeast.

They were overflying farmland when Slebodnik spotted a jumble of mud and stone ruins.

He turned for a closer look. Woehlert, in the second Kiowa, followed behind.

As Slebodnik circled about 150 or 200 feet above the site, Woehlert saw an explosion on the ground, just behind where the first aircraft had been.

"Hey, something just blew up," he said by radio to Slebodnik.

None of the pilots had seen the incoming shot. Slebodnik flew a low pass over the impact crater and told Woehlert that a rocket-propelled grenade had hit there.

Weapons ready, the pilots scanned ridges and fields. There was nothing to fire back at. They resumed their reconnaissance. The landscape was beautiful. It looked pastoral and peaceful. Their welcome had been an RPG.

The schedule became busy at once. Kiowas fanned out for four- to six-hour flights. Their mission was a cavalry standard: support ground commanders with reconnaissance information and provide firepower when needed. They often escorted convoys and protected patrols by flying tens of feet above the ground, searching for fighting positions and signs of improvised explosive devices. When patrols entered villages, they watched over surrounding terrain, trying to prevent fighters from maneuvering against the Americans. Left-seat pilots carried digital cameras and took photographs of anything potentially interesting to the grunts. They often found themselves looking directly into the faces of startled Afghans, especially in the first weeks, when many Afghans had never seen a Kiowa before. Some of them stopped to stare, registering in their minds another new sight in the Pentagon's rollout.

Slebodnik established a regimen. When he was not flying, he worked out in the base's gym or ran the trail around the airfield perimeter, retracing routes that might have been run by Soviet helicopter crews a quarter century before. He was turning forty that fall and in impressive condition, perhaps the best shape of his life. He was eligible for retirement, a pension, and lifetime health care, but had opted to remain in the Army for another combat tour. He told his peers that he needed to support his family, including helping his children through college, but also was in Afghanistan because he believed in the cavalry's mission. What kind of cavalry soldier would pass up America's bid to prevail in the Afghan war?

Still, in quieter moments, Slebodnik spoke of retiring to his family's hometown in Western Pennsylvania, where he might take over his father's asphalt paving business. Often he called Fort Campbell to talk with Tanja and their children. Her friends and coworkers considered her a lucky wife: She had a husband who regularly checked in. She sent him packets of dried lemons for his tea. He sent flowers back, arranging delivery over the Internet and never missing a significant date. He was not of the common Army cut. In a culture of profligate swearing, where profanity passed as punctuation, Slebodnik rarely cursed, even mildly, and almost never resorted to the harsher forms. He swapped in folksy substitutions. "Gosh-darnit," he would say, or "G-zip."

Among the troops he was seen as a leader who had not forgotten his own first enlistment. He expected no special treatment or privilege, and was approachable and interested in young enlisted soldiers. The word around the brigade was that Charlie Troop was professional and well run, aggressive on mission but under control. Much of the credit, thought the task force commander, Colonel Lynch, went to Slebodnik, who had transferred to the unit from Alpha Troop after a successful tour during some of the worst of the violence in Iraq. He had also flown previously in Afghanistan, with the 160th. The experience showed.

Not all was serious—at least, not all the time. To escape the cramped quarters, Slebodnik would turn up in a B-hut used as a small chapel, where he made music. Several musical instruments were stored there, including a mandolin. Slebodnik played well, and became an instructor for Jonathan Miller, a specialist who worked in the operations center, helping to track and direct aircraft around the valleys.

Miller was having an unhappy deployment. He felt depressed, worn down, and not his best self. He had an acoustic guitar that he was just learning to play. After a few jam sessions in which he hung back, watching and listening as Slebodnik worked through gospel songs and Johnny Cash, Slebodnik asked him to play with him. Across the rank boundaries mandated by the Army, the two formed a connection that felt like friendship. Slebodnik taught Miller twelve-bar blues, and had Miller accompany him in a gospel standby about ascending to heaven, "I'll Fly Away."

He and Miller played it again and again, getting it right.

Just a few more weary days and then, I'll fly away
To a land where joys will never end, I'll fly away

Slebodnik had never trained to sing. He barely carried a tune. Miller was impressed that a senior soldier in such a high-pressure job, closely watched by younger soldiers, was so visibly at ease with himself. Here was a pilot with combat experience and stature but who was not tightly wound. He was a boss to whom a regular soldier could relate.

———————

As the weather warmed, enemy action increased. The Americans became more aggressive, too. In April a joint Special Forces and Afghan National Army (ANA) force raided one of the region's no-go zones: the Shok Valley, the stronghold of Gulbuddin Hekmatyar and Hezb-i-Islami Gulbuddin, the militant group he led. Hekmatyar had been a prominent commander against the Soviet Union in the 1980s, only to be marginalized in the 1990s by the Taliban. He emerged locally as a powerful force against the Afghan government and its American and NATO sponsors. His valley redoubt, more than 8,000 feet above sea level, remained beyond American ambitions for years. But in early April a Special Forces team and Afghan commandos flew to the canyon and tried to capture the elusive leader. A battle erupted. The Americans, protected by fighter jets and repeated runs of Apaches, withdrew under fire. The lesson was inescapable: As Americans stepped up their side of the war, many militias were not yielding.

The pace of fighting quickened. Hot spots made themselves known. Among them was the small Watapur Valley. The upper reaches of the valley exceeded 6,000 feet above sea level, which restricted Kiowas to working in the valley's mouth, where it opened to the Pech Valley. American patrols often faced gunfire here, which made it a regular area for Kiowa reconnaissance.

In June, Slebodnik was flying in the valley with Jonathan Cooney, a pilot on his first tour. A rocket-propelled grenade exploded just behind the aircraft. The Kiowa shook from the blast.

"Fuck!" shouted Slebodnik, the man who almost never swore.

He broke right and down, into a dive.

The shot had been close, almost close enough to knock the helicopter from the air.

Woehlert was in the trail aircraft. He climbed and nosed over for an attack, plunging toward the ridge from where the projectile had been fired.

Slebodnik made a tight turn. The valley filled with the noise of rotor blades chopping hard.

"Let's go back in and see if we can draw fire," he said.

Flying headlong toward the ridge, he changed his axis and pitch erratically, making the aircraft unpredictable. The Kiowa reentered the range of a rocket-propelled grenade.

He rushed the ridge, ready to fire, looking for a kill. Whoever fired did not try again.

Slebodnik broke right and continued the patrol, having survived another near miss.

The next day Slebodnik was headed back to Watapur Valley with Jason Sharp, another young pilot, in the left seat. Sharp knew of the close call the day before. He was curious why Slebodnik was still flying when he was past retirement age.

"How many years you been in the Army?" he asked.

"Twenty-two," Slebodnik said.

"Man, don't you ever worry about something happening?"

Slebodnik shrugged. "Not really," he said. "I don't think like that."

Sharp wondered how that could be. The more hours, the more combat flights—the more risks added up. The math demanded acknowledgment. It merited respect. "If I make it to the twenty-year mark as a helicopter pilot, that's it," he said. "I'm done."

Slebodnik was the air mission commander that day, the second aircraft in the flight, following the other Kiowa's tail, ready to cover if it was attacked—just as Woehlert had done for him the previous day. It was the hottest mission Sharp had flown: about 100 degrees Fahrenheit outside at 4,000 feet, conditions that reduce air density and helicopter performance.

The two Kiowas flew up the Kunar River to Asadabad, turned along the Pech River toward Watapur, and were called to help a ground unit taking fire from one of the ridges.

They rushed to the fight, climbing to 6,000 feet as they moved up the valley.

The lead aircraft attacked first and came under fire. Slebodnik hurried to cover the first Kiowa's break, the moment when it would turn and be at risk. Rising over the ridge, he entered a 20-degree dive, oriented at the target as he dropped, and opened fire. The Kiowa's tracers slammed into a group of trees.

Slebodnik kept firing until he was about 300 feet above the ridge. Then he broke. Terrain limited his choices. Instead of breaking right and pulling out and up as he usually did, he turned hard left, rolling the aircraft over with Sharp below him. He pulled back to power the climb.

Sharp waited to feel the aircraft rise.

The Kiowa kept sinking.

He looked to the right seat. Slebodnik was fighting the controls, pulling the cyclic back between his legs with his right hand and raising the collective with his left, trying to marshal all of its power, trying to get lift, or at least to stop the dive.

The aircraft continued to fall. It was mushing and not fully responding to controls. Cockpit alarms sounded in multiple tones, a series of warnings in loud bongs and whoops.

Slebodnik and Sharp were about to hit the mountain, loaded with fuel, at about 100 miles an hour.

Sharp looked down. The ground was rising to meet them. He heard his own voice talking to himself, urging the aircraft to react. Only three words came out.

"Come on, baby, come on, baby, come on, baby, come on, baby," he said.

He couldn't stop.

"Come on, baby."

He grabbed his seat and braced for impact. Slebodnik still worked the controls.

"Come on, baby."

The radar altimeter indicated they were below 100 feet, with a second or two left to live. The Kiowa's skids brushed a tree. Sharp heard a sickening, rasping sound and waited to die. Only a few more feet to the ground.

The descent stopped.

The aircraft stabilized. The helicopter began to rise, pulling up and away from the tree. Sharp took his eyes off the rocks and spun his head to his right.

They were straight and level. Slebodnik had found just enough power. The Kiowa was responding to his controls.

Sharp's heart pounded.

"Did we overtorque?" he asked, wondering if Slebodnik had strained the engine. This could make the aircraft unsafe.

"Are you kidding me?" Slebodnik said. "You didn't hear all the bells and whistles going off?"

Sharp had been watching death rushing up for them in the shape of tree branches and boulders on which the Kiowa had almost broken and burned.

"I didn't hear shit," he said.

Slebodnik flew the aircraft down the valley, out of the Watapur, for the brief flight to Asadabad, where they could land and wait for the mechanic. He emanated calm.

Sharp remained in a state of disbelief. "That was a close one, wasn't it?" he said.

"Yeah," Slebodnik said. "We almost died."

By midsummer Slebodnik was having premonitions of his own death, which put him in an awkward state of mind. He did not want to spook younger pilots who looked up to him. He had few people to confide in, but at last, while walking across the runway with Woehlert, in a place where they could not be overheard, he opened up.

"I'm having these dreams that I don't make it back," he said.

Woehlert chuckled. "We all have those dreams," he said.

The violence in the valleys was unrelenting. All of the pilots of Charlie Troop had seen the grunts' firefights beneath them, the daily medevac runs, the bodies of soldiers passing through Jalalabad, the medevac crews rinsing away the blood. Almost everyone had had close calls. Danger amped and warped emotions. Even the most hardened pilots, who remained composed around others, could find fear stalking them when they slept. Woehlert was haunted, too, visited by dreams of gunfire, crashes, and crippled aircraft out of control. His dreams were starkly realistic, gripping, and recurring. Sometimes, in his tiny room in the B-hut, he woke suddenly, drenched in sweat.

He told Slebodnik not to put stock in nightmares. They were natural, part of the price. "Everybody gets them," he said.

Slebodnik did not want to hear it. He wanted to talk. The dreams contained visions of his end. He asked Woehlert to tell him who he was.

"What do the younger pilots think of me?" he said. "I know I am a stick pig and always fly right seat."

"They love you, man," Woehlert said.

This was true. Woehlert did not share the rest. *Everybody loves Mike,* he thought, *but nobody likes to fly with him.*

It was not that Slebodnik was not trusted. He was alert to everything around him and capable as each situation unfolded, a brave and savvy pilot. In Slebodnik, Woehlert saw the quintessential manifestation of the air cavalry, the Army's update on a species of soldier who rode horses into battle, leaning into incoming fire. And in the era of militants with shoulder-fired rockets and machine guns hidden along flight paths, Slebodnik's manner of flying was safe. He flew so aggressively, was so exuberant at the stick, that a Kiowa under his control was hard to hit.

But Slebodnik's skill came with another effect. To sit in Slebodnik's left seat was often to feel queasy. He made fellow aviators airsick. Woehlert heard the talk. Some of the left-seaters took Dramamine when they flew with Slebodnik, to keep their equilibrium in check and avoid being ill. Woehlert had flown with him once and not taken a pill. He had managed not to vomit, but barely. He remembered the flight as miserable. He knew the troop's fuller view: Riding left seat with Slebodnik, trying to hold down a meal, was a feature of service in their unit, further ingrained because Slebodnik was known to find reasons not to let another pilot into the right seat. The right seat was his. He was a stick pig, the pilot who did not give up the primary chair.

Now Slebodnik told Woehlert why. He himself, he said, was prone to airsickness. Woehlert did not buy it. *No fucking way,* he thought.

"You don't get sick," he said.

Slebodnik insisted it was true. If he sat in the left seat, he said, at the mercy of other hands on the controls, there was a good chance he would throw up. A standardization pilot could not be seen this way.

"I don't want to look like a pansy in front of the younger pilots," he said.

The walk across the tarmac was ending. Before they were close enough to the B-huts for anyone to listen in, Slebodnik revealed a purpose in sharing his secret. Woehlert was to tell no one, he said, about his reason for being a stick pig unless he had retired—or been killed.

The walk was over. The conversation was closed.

Early one morning at about the same time, Specialist Jonathan Miller left the operations center after twelve hours of continuous duty. Overnight shifts were a grind. Miller was tired and feeling blue.

The sun had yet to crest the mountains in the east. Though the sky overhead was bright and the day already hot, Jalalabad remained in shadow. He saw Slebodnik, in black shorts and gray T-shirt, facing the horizon, waiting for the sun.

" 'I will lift up my eyes to the mountains,' " Slebodnik said.

It was a strange thing to say.

"What?" Miller said.

" 'I will lift up my eyes to the mountains . . .' " Slebodnik said. " 'My help comes from the Lord, the maker of heaven and earth.' "

Now Miller placed the words. Slebodnik was reciting a Psalm.*

He followed Slebodnik's gaze and saw light spreading on the valleys. Internally, Miller acknowledged that Slebodnik had keyed him to this beauty, which he might have missed. But he was stumped by Slebodnik's words and by his relaxed good cheer, and did not know what to say.

Slebodnik smiled, his blue eyes bright, and walked away.

By then Cela was due back from leave. Slebodnik busied himself with the final details of his practical joke, trying to pinpoint the schedule for Cela's return. He was interested in Cela's travel dates for other reasons, too. Slebodnik had let the other pilots take their leave first, and once Cela was back in flight status, he could take his own vacation home. Slebodnik had only to complete a four-day flight schedule with Captain Brian Meyer, one of the troop's platoon leaders. The troop was preparing him

---

* Psalm 121:1–2:
I will lift up my eyes to the mountains; from where shall my help come?
My help comes from the Lord, who made heaven and earth.

for pilot-in-command status, and Slebodnik was evaluating him. The two pilots arranged to fly together from September 10 through 13. Slebodnik was to depart for home right after. He would return in October for the last two months before the task force packed out for Fort Campbell.

On September 10 the two pilots planned the days ahead. Slebodnik proposed that they would alternate. He would fly right seat the first day, and the next day they would switch. Meyer would be the primary pilot and run the weapons while Slebodnik coached and observed. Meyer agreed.

After the briefings, they took off on their first flight and headed to the test-fire area south of the base. Slebodnik flew a pass and fired a short burst with the machine gun. Everything was in order. He surprised Meyer by informing the other aircraft that they were going to make a second pass. He looked to his left.

"This time I want to see you engage," Slebodnik said.

Meyer was not sure how he was supposed to do that. He could fly the aircraft with the left-side controls. But a Kiowa's weapons can be fired only from the cyclic stick on the other side of the cockpit, in front of Slebodnik.

Slebodnik was insistent. No matter where Meyer sat in a helicopter, he said, he needed to be ready for anything.

"Let's assume I got shot in the head and you have to engage," he said. What would Meyer do then?

Meyer assumed control of the aircraft and lined the Kiowa up for a gun run. As he nosed the aircraft over, he leaned across the cockpit, took Slebodnik's cyclic, and opened fire with the machine gun.

He released the right-side cyclic, sat upright on the left side, and broke. Slebodnik looked on, approvingly. A pilot in command, he said, needed to handle whatever came up.

The flight that day was a routine area security mission. A ground unit was meeting with Afghans in a village. The two Kiowas were to fly around the outlying terrain and discourage would-be ambushers. The hours passed uneventfully.

The next day was the seventh anniversary of the terrorist attacks in Washington and New York. Early that morning, before Tanja went to sleep at home in the States, Slebodnik called to let her know he would be flying in a place where it was usually quiet. He expected an easy flight and said he would send his usual note—"Down safe"—when he got back.

The pilots showed up at their briefings with several American flags. These they would carry in the cockpit and later share as gifts—flags the cavalry had carried over eastern Afghanistan on the anniversary of the day the towers fell and the Pentagon was hit by a passenger jet. Meyer had five flags and Slebodnik had three. *We'll be able to hook people up,* Meyer thought.

Before the briefings Slebodnik pulled Meyer aside and asked for a change to the flight plan. Captain Hayden Archibald, an Australian pilot assigned to the troop as an exchange officer, was scheduled to be the day's air mission commander, which meant he would be flying in the trail aircraft, and Slebodnik and Meyer would be in front.

Slebodnik, as a senior pilot, gently asked Meyer if he could sit in the right seat again in the lead aircraft. "Hey, sir, I know we agreed," he said, "but I never get to fly right-seat lead anymore, because I am too senior."

Even though he was approaching his own check ride, Meyer agreed. Slebodnik was the standardization pilot. He could do what he wanted.

The first leg of the mission was a reconnaissance along the Alingar River, which fed into the larger Alishang River to Jalalabad's northwest. With Slebodnik at the controls, Meyer took digital photographs of bridges and culverts. He did not know why the grunts wanted the photographs. Perhaps it was to measure development, he thought, or maybe a unit was planning an operation out that way.

Upon returning to Jalalabad to refuel, the mission changed. Over the radio the aircraft were told that an infantry unit had heard explosions farther to the northwest, in the Alishang Valley. The operations center asked them to check it out.

The two Kiowas lifted off and headed that way.

They flew up the Alishang River past the junction with the Alingar River, where the pilots had flown earlier in the day, then several miles more, to a narrowing area where drainage valleys converged in a Y-shaped confluence at Qala-i-Najil. The last American combat outpost in the watershed, COP Najil, overlooked the village from above the eastern fork. This was a crest in the Afghan surge—a small fortified encampment held by a lone platoon, which used the call sign Joker.

The Kiowas approached Qala-i-Najil in the early afternoon and checked in with the patrol from the outpost that had reported the explosion. Joker had sent a quick-reaction force to examine the noise, too. It had stopped along the road when the soldiers thought they found a bomb. The Kiowas flew around the soldiers for about fifteen minutes, watching over them until they were satisfied that there was no bomb in their path. Then the pilots turned north, up the western fork, toward where the soldiers said they had heard the blast.

The military considered the western fork to be a transit and staging area for Taliban fighters, who rarely had to worry about Americans showing up.

A few miles upstream, the aircraft approached a small village with a government compound. Slebodnik flew by it. Nothing seemed out of order. The compound looked secure—perhaps abandoned but secure. It had not been bombed.

They banked and flew away to check up a slot canyon. That area was also quiet. Slebodnik doubled back, returning to the government center for a more thorough look.

Flying low over the village, they spotted a man in black clothes with a blanket draped over his shoulders. A rifle muzzle protruded from the blanket.

Under the rules of engagement, the man could not be fired on. His identity was unknown and he was not acting clearly hostile. Slebodnik had no authority to attack. The man walked into a house. Slebodnik orbited over the building, about forty feet up, while Meyer took a photograph and made note of the location.

The man stepped out the back door with no weapon. He was unarmed now. It was as if he knew the Americans' rules. He walked away.

Slebodnik moved east, deeper into the village, where he and Meyer saw two men talking on handheld radios. This was a bad indicator. The village had no Afghan government presence beyond the silent government compound. There were no signs of Afghan forces. Civilians seemed to be hiding inside. Meyer felt uneasy. *There is probably some shady stuff here,* he thought.

A Kiowa is lightly armored and can fight only to its direct front. Meyer picked up his M4 carbine, ready to fight to their left flank. Rifle on his lap, he took a few more photographs and marked down more grids.

The reconnaissance had turned up no sign of the explosion—no damaged structure or vehicle, no smoke, no crater, no leads. Slebodnik banked away from the village, flew to the river, and turned south, back toward the Joker patrol downstream. The trail helicopter followed behind.

The valley was a mix of boulders and tall stands of soon-to-be-picked corn. Slebodnik flew over the lower valley just west of the road, keeping the road surface near Meyer's left door, moving about 60 or 70 knots, about forty-five feet above the ground. They were almost skimming the corn rows, scanning for anything unusual. Meyer clutched his carbine.

They had almost reached the river junction when Meyer heard gunshots.

Pop. Pop. Pop. Pop.

It was very close, almost directly beneath the aircraft, a rapid staccato rising from a blind spot at about their four o'clock.

A bullet smacked the windscreen in front of Meyer's face.

Slebodnik yelled in pain.

"Oh my God!" he said.

A Kiowa's underside is armored with plates that can stop a bullet. But one bullet had found a small gap between the horizontal plate and a side panel, entered the aircraft at an angle, and missed the right-side pilot's seat, too. It hit near Slebodnik's buttocks, high up on the bottom of his right thigh, passed out the top of his leg, continued through the plastic glare screen, and made a small exit hole in Meyer's windscreen.

Meyer dropped his rifle and grabbed the left-side flight controls. They resisted his inputs. For an instant he thought the helicopter was damaged. *Have we lost hydraulics?* he wondered. Then he grasped what was going on.

Blood gushed from Slebodnik's upper leg. But he was still flying. They were low, moving at about 70 knots, and Slebodnik would not let the aircraft crash.

"Hey, Mike, I got 'em!" Meyer shouted. "I got 'em!"

Slebodnik let go. The aircraft responded to Meyer's commands. The flight was his.

"Get a tourniquet on," he said.

He juked the helicopter to evade further gunfire, accelerated, and radioed Archibald in the trail aircraft.

"Mike's hit," he said.

He looked at Slebodnik. The wound was bad. It had been only seconds since the gunfire. Already his lower flight suit was soaked with blood.

Meyer knew what this meant: There was no time.

He had decisions to make. Should he fly for Mehtar Lam, about fifteen minutes south? Or should he land now and give Slebodnik first aid? Combat Outpost Najil was nearby, a minute away at full speed. They would have a medic and aid station there. That was the best call: Joker Platoon could do more for Slebodnik, and faster, than Meyer could do himself.

He radioed ahead. "This is Close Combat 24," he said. "We've got a pilot with a gunshot wound to the leg. Have medics on the LZ."

Slebodnik was staring down at his wound. "Oh, please, God," he said. "Not now. Not now."

The outpost was close. Flying as fast as the Kiowa would go, Meyer spoke in reassuring tones.

"Hey, man, you're good," he said. "Just stay awake."

Slebodnik's eyelids drooped. He slumped in his seat. Perhaps a dozen seconds had passed.

Rounding the corner at the river junction, Meyer saw the outpost, perhaps thirty seconds away. He was flying so hard that cockpit alarms were sounding.

"Hey, stay awake," he said.

Slebodnik did not answer.

"Hey, talk to me," Meyer said.

Slebodnik was silent.

Captain Archibald, the Australian pilot, called from behind. "Make sure you safe your weapons, Brian, before you land," he said.

Meyer was in a circumstance resembling what Slebodnik had coached him for the day before. His lead pilot had been shot, and as a left-seater Meyer now needed to handle the flight alone. He reached to his right, to the center of the cockpit, and flipped a lever down, moving the weapons from ARM to STANDBY. He leaned back into his chair, banked for his approach, and descended fast, looking down upon soldiers bunched underneath on the landing zone.

"Stay with me here," Meyer said to Slebodnik.

The helicopter touched down. "Stay with me."

The grunts were running toward them. Meyer had done what he could do. They and their medic would take it from there.

Back at Jalalabad Airfield, Colonel Lynch was having a meeting in his office at task force headquarters when an officer entered the room.

"Hey, sir, first report," he said. "Not a lot of information, but Mike Slebodnik got shot in the leg."

Lynch took the news easily. He was a Kiowa pilot himself and knew a few pilots who had been struck by gunfire in the cockpit. Foot and leg wounds were the common outcome. Slebodnik, Lynch figured, was the latest.

He's going to be pissed, he thought.

He headed for the operations center to listen to the task force retrieving one of its pilots for care.

Outside Lynch's headquarters, two Black Hawk crews were on standby for medevac flights. Chief Warrant Officer Joseph Callaway heard the call.

Urgent medical. One coalition force wounded. COP Najil.

He ran to the operations center for information and a glimpse of the intelligence. Someone said a pilot had been hit in the leg by small-arms fire. He asked who was down. *Mr. Slebodnik,* he heard.

Mike, he thought.

I'm going.

Callaway knew the routes and the passes between Jalalabad and Najil. His mind laid out the puzzle. The fastest evacuation, he thought, would be if Slebodnik were flown in his own Kiowa to Mehtar Lam while Callaway was en route. Once there, Callaway's medic and crew chief could pick him up on the landing zone of the American base and transfer him to the faster Black Hawk for the run back to Jalalabad.

"Have the copilot meet me in Mehtar Lam," he said, and dashed out the door. His Black Hawk and a chase bird were warmed up. He climbed into his seat and strapped in. They'd be in the air in no time.

The operations center said Slebodnik was at Najil.

Callaway had already thought through plan B. To reach Najil, there was a route through a mountain pass he could fly instead of following the valleys. It would shave time. Either way, Callaway thought he could have Slebodnik to Jalalabad in less than forty-five minutes, maybe within thirty.

He was worried about Slebodnik losing a leg. They needed to go.

Engines running, rotors spinning, his medic and crew chief strapped in, he was about to fly. He radioed the operations center for permission to take off.

The voice came back flat. "Stand down."

The medevac for Slebodnik was being assigned to two aircraft out of Bagram. The medical planners wanted him treated there.

Callaway was astounded. Bagram was too far from Najil—at least a forty-minute flight. By the time an aircraft from Bagram picked up Mike and returned with him to the base's hospital, ninety minutes would have passed. That was too long.

"Are you fucking kidding me?" he said.

The reply was inflexible.

"Stand down, Joe."

Callaway would not accept it. If he took the mission, his aircraft would have Slebodnik in the care of a surgeon at Jalalabad before an aircraft from Bagram even reached Najil. There was no time to argue. He was right. He needed to fly.

"It's going to take those assholes forty-five minutes to get there," he said. "In forty-five minutes I can have him here."

The voice repeated the order.

"You've got to stand down."

Fuck this, Callaway thought. *FUCK THIS.*

Callaway's crew was tense. He knew they wanted to go, but had to be silent. He was the mission commander. This was between him and the boss.

"What are you going to do if I launch?" he said.

"Joe, you have to stand down. We've been told you have to stand down."

Goddamn bullshit.

"It's fucking stupid," he said.

"Joe, you've got to stand down," the voice said. "The mission went to Bagram."

The other aircraft were in the air.

Callaway climbed out and stormed into the operations center. The room was on edge. For a few minutes, seething, he listened to the radio traffic. Heart pounding, doing nothing, he could not take it anymore. He was doing no good. He was just in the way. He left the room to pace and to curse.

———

Staff Sergeant Pamela Paquet, a flight medic, was on the ground at Bagram when the call came in. She was a crew member in Dustoff 31, one of two pairs of Black Hawks on the base dedicated that afternoon to medevac flights. Her aircraft had just returned with an Afghan soldier who had been wounded by gunfire. She had worked furiously on him throughout the flight back, performing CPR. She could not resuscitate the man. Not long after litter bearers at the hospital had lifted him from the Black Hawk and run him inside, she heard he had been pronounced dead. She was drained, drenched in sweat, and soiled with the man's blood. *I just want to get this off me,* she thought.

But she was still on shift and had to keep working. She restocked her medical bag. The summer had been horrible. Call after call had come in. The next call could come in a minute or an hour. Paquet could not expect a break. She returned to the aircraft as radio chatter began.

"We've got a nine-line in progress," someone said, using the terminology for a medevac request. It came from way out—from Najil.

Najil? Paquet had never flown there. Few pilots had.

Chief Warrant Officer Matt Cole, the pilot of the chase aircraft, which would accompany the medevac Black Hawk, checked the grid on the map. It was far up the Alishang Valley, in the boonies.

"Why the fuck are we going all the way out there?" he said, as they ran for the aircraft. Cole was known for flying hard, and not one to give up a flight to someone else. But he wondered why the mission was not being assigned to aircraft from Jalalabad. The map showed it was much closer to the wounded man.

The day was busy. Americans and Afghans were being wounded across the operations area. The two other Dustoff aircraft from Bagram were on a mission. The Black Hawk Paquet was assigned to would take this one. In the aircraft the blood from her last patient had not yet been rinsed away.

More information came in. "We've received word it was a downed pilot," she heard.

Almost immediately her aircraft was in the air, nose down, flying fast.

The news moved quickly. Woehlert and Cela were working out in the airfield gym. A captain rushed in. Mike had been shot in the leg, he said, and everyone needed to head to the command post. The captain seemed agitated, but there were hints in the way he spoke that the situation was not dire. Slebodnik was going to be flown to Bagram. "He gets to go home early and see his family," he said.

The information that reached Robert Minton, another senior Kiowa pilot, sounded the same. He walked the short distance uphill, to the airfield's coffee shop, and bought an iced tea. Slebodnik liked his tea. Minton planned to give his standardization pilot a hard time. He'd greet him with an insult—*You fucking pussy, this is how you get out of the deployment?*—and hand him his favorite drink.

The duty of manning Combat Outpost Najil on September 11, 2008, fell to a platoon from Headquarters and Headquarters Company of Third Battalion, 103rd Armor Regiment, the unit from the Pennsylvania National Guard that called itself Joker.

Living in a tiny outpost, and facing guerrilla-warfare tactics on the few roads nearby, the soldiers felt a special gratitude to the Army's scout and attack pilots, who were the most visible form of support they saw. When the voice of Captain Meyer came over the net saying Close Combat had been hit and was heading their way for medical aid, the soldiers ran to their places.

"We got a bird coming in!" one of the sergeants shouted.

The outpost had no doctor. It was outfitted with only a small aid station. If the Kiowa was heading to them, and not to Mehtar Lam or Jalalabad, the situation must be grave. The wounded pilot was too badly wounded for the flight down the valley.

He needed lifesaving steps now.

With a patrol out, there were few soldiers present—several men on guard duty and radio watch, others performing menial tasks. Many were in shorts and T-shirts. They huddled at the landing zone with a stretcher as the Kiowa appeared.

The aircraft was on their radio frequency. They heard one pilot imploring another to stay alive.

"Hey, man, you're good," the voice said. "Just stay awake."

Corporal James M. Adams looked up at the Kiowa descending. The left-seat pilot was flying. The pilot on the right seat was hunched over, unconscious. He looked waxen.

The aircraft landed at such high speed that it skidded and overshot the waiting soldiers. They squinted into grit and bolted forward. Meyer, with his left hand, spun the throttle on the collective clockwise, putting the rotors in idle. He reached over and released Slebodnik from his belt.

Soldiers swarmed around. Slebodnik slouched in his seat, eyes open, pale. Blood pooled at his feet and coated the aircraft's pedals. Adams wore only his workout clothes. He had no first-aid kit. He shouted to their platoon sergeant, who was in uniform.

"Belt! Belt! Belt!"

The sergeant slipped off his belt and handed it over. Adams looped it around Slebodnik's upper leg and cinched it tight, pulling with all of his strength.

Slebodnik gasped.

Maybe he's alive, Adams thought. He felt a flash of hope.

The soldiers lifted Slebodnik, settled him onto their stretcher, and rushed him to the aid station, running so hard that one of the lead soldiers slammed into the door frame as they entered.

Adams tried keeping his fist pressed down on the wound to prevent further loss of blood.

Inside the aid station, the soldiers laid the litter onto a pair of sawhorses. The medic cut away the lower section of the flight suit and examined the wound. Adams loosened Slebodnik's chest rig and vest.

The wound was near the pelvis, a place where no tourniquet could stem blood flow. Slebodnik's pulse was weak and erratic.

Adams slid the helmet off Slebodnik's head and heard a second gasp. *I gotta talk to him,* Adams thought.

"Hey, you're going to be okay," he said. "We got you, man, you're good."

The medic started CPR.

Adams and the medic made eye contact. Adams understood. *It's not good.*

"We got you," Adams said. "Doc's a good doc. We got you."

Soldiers stood outside, unsure what to do. Someone ordered that all the local Afghans visiting the base be escorted off. After a few minutes the word went around that any soldier with an O-negative blood type, the universal donor, should be ready to donate. Soldiers lined up. But this was the Afghan wilderness. There was no means for a transfusion.

Joker Platoon looked down the valley. Soldiers strained their ears, listening for the distinctive sound of Black Hawks.

Minutes passed like days. And then they heard it—aircraft engine noise.

"Go!" the soldiers shouted, and began carrying Slebodnik back to the landing zone.

One of the Black Hawks broke toward the outpost. The other circled as the first aircraft touched down.

Staff Sergeant Paquet leapt clear and met the men running toward her with the patient. She looked down at him and thought he had the most brilliantly blue eyes she had ever seen. His pupils were fixed and dilated. He was pale. She reached for him. His skin felt tacky.

Even if you know what death looks like, she thought, *you still work it.*

Soldiers were relaying the case information. Someone said Slebodnik had no pulse and was unresponsive to CPR. Then they were in the air, turning, gaining speed. She was with a flight surgeon, a captain she admired. The two instantly were at work. She did a pulse check. Nothing.

She looked at the entrance and exit wounds near his groin and knew that
no tourniquet would have worked and that he must have lost an enormous volume of blood. *Catastrophic,* she thought.

They administered epinephrine and continued the CPR.

Bagram was a long way off, more than half an hour. She did not like
the math.

Far downstream, in the operations center at Jalalabad, Colonel Lynch
monitored the radio traffic and watched the movement of aircraft on his
digital board. The Black Hawks pulled away from Najil. Slebodnik was on
his way to the best hospital in the region. At last his vital signs were read
off. Lynch wondered if he had heard the numbers right.

I thought he was hit in the leg, he thought. *Holy cow. What's going on?*

Captain Emmitt Furner II, an Army chaplain assigned to the aviation brigade, was working on Bagram Airfield when his cellular flip phone rang.
The medevac commander was asking for him at the base hospital.

Furner regularly tended to patients there, and he also tried to check in
on medevac pilots and flight crews. These soldiers, he knew, had some of
the most difficult duties in Afghanistan. They rushed every day into the
most traumatic scenes in the country and into others' gunfights, in which
they and their aircraft were targets for Taliban fire. Then they picked up
the dead and the wounded. Their peers sometimes died in their arms.
The work was as emotionally freighted as any in the war.

Furner hurried to the medevac hangar, wondering why he had been
summoned this time. An officer told him that Slebodnik had been hit and
it did not look good, and that Paquet, the medic working on him in flight,
had lost a patient earlier in the day.

He rushed to the emergency room and found Slebodnik had already
arrived. He was on a table, surrounded by the medical staff. Paquet was in
the room, wearing bloody latex gloves and shouting at the doctors, telling
them the patient history and what she and the flight surgeon had done for
Slebodnik in flight.

The trauma doctors and nurses were giving him a cardiac massage.

The room was noisy. The staff called out instructions. Monitors beeped. Furner heard Slebodnik had been given transfusions.

Doctors were shocking his heart to restart it. Other doctors and nurses, and several soldiers from the aviation brigade, stood silently on the edge of the activity. Some held hands. A few were crying.

Paquet looked over at Furner and felt deflated. Their eyes met. She interpreted his look; it said what she knew. She understood why he was there. *My gut was right*, she thought. She quietly left, stepping outside to cry.

The noises became fewer.

Furner prayed softly.

After about fifteen minutes, the activity around the table ceased. The room fell silent. They were declaring Slebodnik dead.

A doctor spoke.

"Chaplain," he said.

Furner stepped forward and took Slebodnik's hand. He found his voice and began to speak in a free-flowing Southern Baptist prayer. He thanked Slebodnik for his service, and thanked his family for their service and sacrifice, and expressed sorrow for the grief they would soon feel. He thanked the medics, nurses, and doctors for their efforts. He prayed for perhaps a minute, then stopped and held Slebodnik's hand while the staff disconnected him, cleaned him, and covered him with a cloth.

Head bowed, praying, Furner stayed with the man. He did not release his hand until the soldiers from the mortuary had wheeled Slebodnik to their truck, the first leg of his journey home.

President Barack Obama took office in 2009 declaring that he would refocus the foreign policy establishment on the Afghan war. By the spring, American troop numbers had climbed past 50,000 in Afghanistan, and were continuing to rise. Violence in Iraq had stayed relatively low. Official optimism for a turnaround in Afghanistan was high. But as troops moved from large NATO bases into smaller rural outposts, they were unable to quell the fighting or the Taliban's campaigns against Afghans who collaborated with them. The military, saying it had not reached the troop density required to stabilize the country, was also expanding its efforts to recruit and train Afghan police and army forces. As it had in Iraq, it moved with a haste that limited the vetting and training of its partners. American casualties were climbing.

NINE

"WE'RE HERE BECAUSE WE'RE HERE"

Specialist Robert Soto and the Ghosts of Korengal Valley

"Tell my family that I love them and this is probably going to be the end for me."

APRIL 10, 2009
On a West-Facing Slope over the Korengal River,
Kunar Province, Afghanistan

Second Platoon did not hide its attitude. It was early in the afternoon and its soldiers had just waded across the swollen Korengal River to begin a long climb. They were thirty men in all, a rifle platoon reinforced with a team of scouts, a mix of original platoon members and replacements who filled gaps in the squads left by the wounded and dead. Their mission was to ascend the lower face of this mountain and lie in wait at a foot trail to ambush the Taliban at night. Many of the soldiers thought the plan was foolish, a draining and dangerous waste of time, another example of a frustrated Army unit trying to show activity for the brass. Some were in dark moods as they walked. But Second Platoon was experienced and well trained, not paralyzed by its unhappiness. Its soldiers moved steadily, striding toward their mission with the sinewy, late-deployment fitness of infantry squads seasoned by war.

Specialist Robert Soto had been haunted by dread as he left the relative safety of the company's base, the Korengal Outpost, or KOP, and trudged downhill to the water. He cursed repeatedly. His low morale was tied in part to the fact that Second Platoon was tired, and not because its soldiers had not slept enough as they prepared for the patrol. Theirs was a deeper weariness—the mind-numbing exhaustion of being worn down by a sustained and bloody combat tour. The platoon had been in the valley nearly nine months, one of three platoons in Bravo Company, First Battalion of the Twenty-Sixth Infantry. It had started with three squads but suffered so many casualties, including the death of Soto's squad leader and two of his closest friends, that even with replacements filling in for those the medevac helicopters had carried way, it now mustered at about two-thirds of its original strength.

With attrition came knowledge. Soto understood the many ways the Korengal undermined American plans. He knew his platoon's war did not resemble the cheerful and carefully considered national project the generals and their spokespeople relayed to the American people in the news. For him the Afghan war was a matter of surviving each day as the days cohered into a tour—a malleable unit of military time that could give a year a higher degree of order than it possessed in fact. He was doubtful. One more high-risk day, he thought, in the service of public affairs and waste. *There's no fucking way this works.*

Some of it was the topography. The valley was a curved chasm, with almost all the Americans arrayed on the slopes of the western side. The river flowed beneath them, cold and swift. In places the valley floor was less than one hundred yards wide. From the eastern side, which the soldiers considered hostile territory, the residents of multiple villages gazed from primitive stone homes directly at the American outpost. By day they could see the soldiers' movements, mocking any hope that a platoon might pass undetected in the light. Some of it was the villagers' prevailing attitude. A mountain people, the Korengalis had fought Soviet soldiers and their Afghan proxies in the 1980s, and had remained suspicious of outside authority after their communist occupiers left. Why the Americans believed they would be received differently was not clear. Senior officers spoke of Afghans who could be coaxed toward allegiance to the government in Kabul. To Soto, the valley felt like a network of watchers who set up his platoon. The trails were busy with Korengalis tending sheep and harvesting wood. Many of them doubled as spotters for the Taliban, relaying word of the Americans' activities to those who were laying traps. Goat herders, farmers, gatherers of firewood. All were suspect.

The platoon stepped out of the rushing water and began the uphill climb. Soto walked on, scrambling and moving higher, sensing eyes following the platoon, expecting the worst.

Everybody can see us.

Soto was nineteen years old, but at 160 pounds and barely needing to shave, he could pass for someone two years younger. He'd joined the Army at seventeen—a drama major from the Bronx who wanted to punish those who carried out the World Trade Center attacks. He was nobody's archetype of a fighter. He had an enormous smile, which came to him almost unprompted. He liked to sing, and he sang often. His memory had at its command a vast repertoire of lyrics—R&B, rap, hip-hop, the blues, his personal collection of gems—which he would sing, no matter what anyone else thought. Robbie Soto joined the Army upbeat, fast with that grin, the guy who made others feel good. He planned to become an actor if he survived the war—a dream that sounded like a fantasy to some of his peers but that he was not afraid to share. All of this made him popular in the platoon.

On this day his smile was less bright. The soldiers of his platoon were adjusting to the Army's latest surprise. A new platoon leader had turned up at the outpost: Second Lieutenant Justin Smith, a freshly minted officer straight from Ranger School. Smith had been placed in charge of Second Platoon. He was a former staff sergeant, which lent him a degree of credibility new lieutenants do not usually get. But he had not previously served in the infantry. The platoon was not inclined to give him a pass.

Smith had led them on three patrols so far, an insufficient sampling from which to measure a wartime boss. Many of his soldiers were wary. They did not know his motivations or have a firm sense of his character. All they knew was that he was confident and fit, and exuded enthusiasm for infantry tactics. Such traits were not unusual in new officers. They also were not enough. Second Platoon had no idea how Smith would behave under fire or how much he would stand up for his soldiers—the things that matter most in an infantry unit, and that in too many officers were in short supply.

Like a horse unsure of its new rider, the platoon bristled and flexed.

Smith prepared his soldiers for the ambush by issuing a by-the-book operations order in front of a terrain model in the company's gym, a small stone-walled room with an assortment of weights. Someone had written on a wall with a black Sharpie, declaring the only two reasons for a man to work out: TO LOOK GOOD NAKED AND TO PUNCH A HOLE IN ANOTHER MAN'S HEAD. This was not officers' school. It was their place more than his.

After the op order, Smith took them to the outpost's landing zone and walked them through the rehearsals for each phase of his plan: the foot movement across the river and up the hill; the leader's reconnaissance of the ambush site on the ridge; the triangle-shaped patrol base they would occupy astride the militants' trail; the placement of the automatic weapons and the establishment of the listening post that would give the patrol warning of the approach of its foes; the signal initiating the killing. The soldiers listened politely. Some liked what they saw. Smith knew his tactics and was giving this patrol his all. Others went along with the latest as best they could. Viper Company, as Bravo Company called itself, had set many ambushes in the valley. Not once had the Taliban walked headlong into the traps.*

"All right, men," Smith said, "it's just like Ranger School."

This was too much for Specialist Steven Halase, the platoon's radio operator, who would walk alongside the lieutenant on the patrol. He was the radio voice of Second Platoon, Viper Two.

"Yeah, except at Ranger School you don't get shot in the face," he said.

For a moment no one knew what would happen. Second Platoon tensed. Halase figured he deserved it if he got written up.

The lieutenant let it pass.

---

* On September 17, another infantry platoon, Viper Three, wounded a man in an ambush near a bombed-out house that militants used as a fighting position. The range, about 200 meters, was not short. The man escaped. First Lieutenant John Rodriguez, who kept records of the company's activities, remained unsure whether he was a Taliban fighter, a spotter, or a civilian.

Soto watched, not saying a word. He was willing to respect Smith, but only so far. He liked Halase and agreed with him. Smith was a bit too much. *I get that you're new. I get that you've got fresh legs and you're fresh out of Ranger School. We're just trying to get out of here in two months. And I don't want to lose another friend, or lose my own life, because you're trying to look cool.*

———

It would be difficult to trace a more direct route from childhood to the grunts than Robert Soto's. He was ten years old on September 11, 2001, sitting in social studies class in Middle School 118 in the Bronx, when his teacher unexpectedly left the classroom. She returned and told the students that an aircraft had hit one of the World Trade Center towers. Soto was not sure what this meant. Then came news of another aircraft, and of a second burning tower.

The rest of the morning was a slow-motion evacuation in a rising nervous pitch. Parents streamed to the school. Name by name, Soto's classmates were announced over the intercom. Soto's turn came after most of the others had left. His father, who had spent nearly a decade in the National Guard, was in the corridor. The man was his role model, a rock of stability. His parents had never married and lived apart. Soto's mother was mostly not present in his life—she was a "dancer," he would politely say. He saw her only occasionally. His father had custody of him and his brother, and worked as a doorman at the Milford Plaza hotel in Midtown Manhattan. He and Soto's grandmother held the family together. They were examples of clean living and hard work. Now his father sat in the car, explaining that the United States had come under attack. Soto knew his father had served in the Army, a background that added stature to the man. But he sensed fear, something he had never seen in his father before.

A few months later, Soto took the subway to Manhattan to visit the pile of rubble where the towers had been. It was an overpowering sight, this mountain of concrete, ash, and steel. Soto felt solemnity in the air. He listened to a man who stopped passersby for impromptu tours, telling them how tall each tower had stood, the square footage, the number of windows, detail after detail of symbols destroyed and lives lost. Soto felt a desire to participate in whatever the United States was doing to prevent another attack. He made up his mind while standing at Ground Zero. When he was old enough, he would enlist.

The neighborhood outside his home was rough. During adolescence Soto watched friends drift into crime. By thirteen they were smoking marijuana. Some joined the street gang Dominicans Don't Play, or DDP. Their local crew was in a bitter rivalry with another Latin gang, the Trinitarios. The two sides clashed with fists and knives.

Soto kept his friends. They'd grown up playing Wiffle ball together, and over the years he had eaten many meals in their homes. Loyalty mattered. But his father and grandmother were strict. He did not want to disappoint them. He was not interested in gangs or drugs.

He began at the Professional Performing Arts School in Manhattan in September of 2003, not long after the United States invaded Iraq. He majored in drama but was disoriented, not part of the school's mainstream. His classmates were neither skirting gang involvement nor inclined to serve in the military. Everyone, it seemed to him, planned on attending college. They were different from him, somehow able to disassociate themselves from the memory of New York City being attacked. Soto tried following the path the school's ethos presumed. When he graduated in June 2007, at age seventeen, he enrolled in summer classes at Lehman College, telling himself he would work toward a bachelor's degree. But he felt unsettled. Weeks before he started class, his closest friend was hurt in a machete attack by the Trinitarios. And he still felt drawn to the Army. There were two wars on. What was he doing, sitting around?

Shortly after starting his college coursework, Soto walked out of math class and strolled into the Army recruiting station at the Grand Concourse. He told the first soldier he saw that he wanted to sign up.

Too young to enlist without parental consent, he went home and showed his father the papers the recruiter had given him. His father looked ashen. The news from Iraq had been grim for years, and the surge was just beginning to have an effect.

"No," he said. "I don't want you to do this. The war is getting completely crazy."

The calendar gave Soto leverage. He used it. "We can do this now, or we can do this in a few months when I turn eighteen," he said. "But that makes no sense."

His father signed the forms.

The path to the ranks was short. Soto passed his physical at the Military Entrance Processing Station at Fort Hamilton in Brooklyn the same month, and volunteered for the infantry. He accepted a slot in basic training for August, allowing himself only a few weeks to train. He tipped the scale at 140 pounds when he arrived at Fort Benning for One Station Unit Training, a pipeline to the combat divisions that combined indoctrination and basic infantry skills, molding replacement grunts quickly and at low cost. His transition was jarring. He was still a few months shy of eighteen. Every other recruit but one seemed much older. Soto was cut off from the world, surrounded by men, and given the simplest label a human being can have: Roster Number 242, written on a strip of tape on his plain green Kevlar helmet.

Emotionally, he shut himself down and focused on passing requirements and meeting standards. Several sergeants who trained him had been to Iraq and Afghanistan. To Soto, they were the most impressive people he had ever met. As the weeks continued, he began to realize that much of what he thought he knew about toughness was wrong. He saw strong and cocky men falter and grow timid. He watched less physically impressive men excel. The instruction moved past the rudiments of military life to the technical and tactical fundamentals of American war: the basics of machine gunnery and of patrolling and ground combat tactics. He approached each lesson seriously.

If you are not prepared, he told himself, *you are preparing to fail.*

Soto returned home in the late fall, a soldier with orders to report to Fort Hood, Texas, after the new year and join the First Infantry Division. The Bronx seemed different. He could not relate to many of his old friends, with their poor discipline and neighborhood lives. He was part of something larger, something he believed would help keep America safe. He stayed home through Christmas morning. That afternoon his father walked with him to the Metro-North station, where he took a train to Connecticut to meet another new soldier who had been assigned to the same base. The two drove to Texas together.

Soto was given his place in Bravo Company's Second Platoon and greeted by the Second Squad leader, Staff Sergeant Nathan Cox. Cox was lanky, with graying hair and an easygoing confidence. He welcomed Soto with a smile and a straightforward Midwestern manner. The contrast between him and the sergeants at Fort Benning was drastic. The platoon sergeant, Sergeant First Class Thomas Wright, had the graceful bearing of an athlete, and did not seem to be impressed with his own rank. He told Soto to expect a difficult period of prewar preparations and put him in a weapons squad as an ammunition bearer in a machine-gun team, a position for a FNG—"fucking new guy." He told him the battalion was traveling soon to Fort Irwin, California, for a brigade exercise in the desert, and would be deploying to Afghanistan later in the year.

Soto was on the fast track to war. He was relieved to have landed in a solid unit.

Viper Company's winter and spring were busy. By May rumor circulated that the company was being sent to the Korengal Outpost, an American foothold in a place with a chilling nickname, the Valley of Death. *Vanity Fair* had published an account of the fighting in the valley. A few of Viper's young soldiers passed around a copy. Soto was not interested. He told himself to tune out distraction. He'd be there soon enough.

It doesn't make sense to read and to worry.

Noise. Always block out the noise.

The article still had its effect. The mood of the company shifted. Viper was headed to one of the most violent spots on the Afghan map, a place of minor notoriety. Haranguing became routine. Warnings were constant. "You guys better start paying attention, because these guys get mortared every night," a sergeant would say. "Wake the fuck up, because that place is no joke." Harsh climate, punishing terrain, an isolated outpost harassed by a persistent enemy who chose carefully when to fight. The works.

Soto tried to keep Viper's anxiety from infecting him. He had signed up to fight, and was doing his best. *I'm already paying attention.*

As more FNGs joined the unit, thickening the ranks, Soto was transferred to a rifle squad, taking up duties as a squad automatic weapon gunner in one of Sergeant Cox's fire teams. His duties increased. Wright chose him to attend an emergency medical technician course, for training in trauma care. Soto was to be one of the platoon's backup medics.

In July, the soldiers flew to Manas International Airport, in Kyrgyzstan, where the Air Force operated a transit center, part of a logistical wheel moving people and material into and out of Afghanistan. Within days the platoon was flown to Bagram, the main American base in Afghanistan, and settled onto bunks in a transient tent. Soto's stay was short. The unit Viper Company was replacing—Bravo Company of the Second Battalion, 503rd Infantry Regiment, known as Battle Company—was completing its tour. It was impossible to replace them all at once. The military organized a sequential swap, known as a relief in place, in which small groups of Viper Company's soldiers would fly in and small groups of Battle Company's soldiers would fly out. Soto was assigned to one of Viper's first groups in, part of his platoon's advance party. He boarded a CH-47 for the trip.

The helicopter pounded up the Kunar River valley, wide and green, between forested slopes. When the aircraft turned left up the Pech Valley, the world seemed to shrink, narrowing between peaks. At the final turn, into the Korengal Valley, Soto's heart beat fast. The valley was magnificent, a beautiful zone of ancient forest bisected by a cascading mountain stream, a place beyond the experience of a young man from the Bronx. There was almost no sign of modernity except the helicopter he sat inside. Soto was sweating. The stories of the Korengal had had an effect.

The aircraft banked. Soto looked down upon the outpost's perimeter. Dirt-filled walls and bunkers surrounded small stone buildings and plywood shacks. The aircraft touched down. Soto and the other soldiers charged out to the first barrier wall. He reached it, noticed the grim faces of his sergeants, and went down to one knee, rifle in hand, face beading sweat, waiting for instructions. Soldiers from Battle Company laughed.

Viper.

Viper Two.

The name sounded impressive. They were FNGs now.

Soto learned the lay of the land. The Korengal Outpost was the main American position in the valley, part of a terrain grab that in retrospect had been unwise. American Rangers, Special Forces soldiers, and Marines occasionally ventured up the Korengal River after forcing the Taliban from power in Kabul in 2001, typically on patrols or brief operations. The valley did not gain larger notoriety until 2005, after Operation Red Wings, when three SEALs were killed in an ambush and a helicopter that came to their aid was shot down, claiming sixteen more American lives. In 2006 an American brigade situated the more permanent outpost on a low ridge with a gently sloping crest, downstream of most of the valley's population. On a tactical level this could seem to make good sense. The place was both supportable and classically defensible—a position overlooking the river and local trails that also had enough space on its crest for helicopters to land. With time the limits of such thinking became clear. On a social level the siting of the KOP could not have been much worse. The buildings and the ridge the soldiers occupied happened to be the grounds of a sawmill and lumberyard operated by Haji Mateen, the valley's timber baron. The Americans had seized a local source of income and employment, putting many of the valley's toughest and most able-bodied men out of work.

Military minds had chosen the place. Standard military tactics would have to defend it. To protect the outpost as the inevitable fighting flared, troops built other, smaller posts so their occupants could support each other with machine-gun and mortar fire and watch over more of the riverbed. In Kabul, NATO officials spoke of forging alliances in the rural badlands. But the American presence in Korengal felt more like a crude fortress than a diplomatic outpost. On the ridges upstream, troops erected two bulwarks, Observation Post Dallas and Firebase Restrepo. A small team of fresh Marines who worked with Afghan soldiers occupied Firebase Vimoto, a third position built beside the river-hugging dirt road in the village of Babeyal. Across the valley, the Americans established two more positions in the hills, Combat Outpost Vegas* and Observation Post Rock. Taken together, they worked as a network of besieged and

---

* Firebase Restrepo was named for Private First Class "Doc" Juan Sebastián Restrepo, a soldier in the 173rd Airborne Brigade Combat Team who died of gunshot wounds received in the village of Aliabad on July 22, 2007. Firebase Vimoto was named for Private First Class Timothy R. Vimoto, a soldier in the same unit, who died of gunshot wounds received in the valley on June 5, 2007. Combat Outpost Vegas took its name from Las Vegas, part of an earlier American post-naming scheme that borrowed city names from the United States. Although Vegas was formally a combat outpost, the soldiers of Viper Company called it Firebase Vegas, including painting the informal name on the outpost's sign. (Firebase Vimoto was originally called Firebase Phoenix.)

interlocking bunkers that did not align with the official message of courting Afghan hearts and minds.

By the time Soto arrived in 2008, the place had sunk into stalemate. The early briefings were bleak. The Americans and the Afghan unit partnered with them were capable of limited ground movement. Haji Mateen, formerly of the sawmill, commanded many of the valley's fighters, most of whom fought under the banner of the Taliban. Other groups fought here, too, and al Qaeda's operational chief in Kunar Province, Abu Ikhlas al Masri, an Egyptian, circulated through the action.* The Americans met with village elders, urging them to help calm the valley down. The *shura*, a local leadership council, was ostensibly led by Haji Zalwar Khan, who brought complaints to Battle Company, discussed the Americans' initiatives, and played the role of local sounding board. The Americans considered him dual-hatted. He led the *shura*, but also served as the emissary of Nasrullah, the Taliban's local political leader and, as far as the Americans knew, the *shura*'s shadow leader, too.

Second Platoon's advance party took it all in. The riverbed, roughly 4,500 feet above sea level, formed a green stripe of cropland beside a snowmelt stream that twisted its way down from the peaks. Terraces of stacked stones climbed in stair-step fashion up to the bottoms of the hills. From there the ground rose steeply in mud-and-gravel slopes dotted with small trees. Impoverished villages clung to ledges overlooking the riverbed, each comprising stone houses and livestock sheds. Farther up the mountains rose, sheer and uninhabitable escarpments of stone, buffeted by wind.

---

* Al Qaeda's presence in Kunar Province during the busiest period of American involvement there featured large in some contemporaneous news reports but appears to have been small. Of the nearly 2,600 active militants the Afghan intelligence service claimed to have documented in the province, roughly 50, about 2 percent, were in al Qaeda. More than 75 percent, in contrast, were aligned with the Taliban, many of them in the valleys of the Pech River system. The Qaeda fighters were concentrated in and near the Watapur Valley, not far from the Korengal. The numbers above are taken from "Anti-Coalition Militia Order of Battle, Konar Province, Afghanistan," prepared by the U.S. military, with information from the Afghan Directorate of National Security, in 2009. The document provided a roster of the militants' leadership down to squad-sized fighting groups.

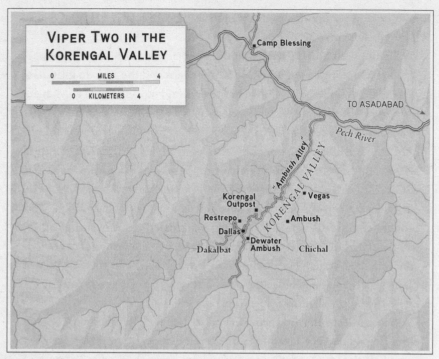

VIPER TWO IN THE
KORENGAL VALLEY

0 MILES 4

0 KILOMETERS 4

Camp Blessing

TO ASADABAD

Pech River

"Ambush Alley"

KORENGAL VALLEY

Korengal
Outpost

Vegas

Restrepo

Ambush

Dallas

Dewater
Ambush

Dakalbat

Chichal

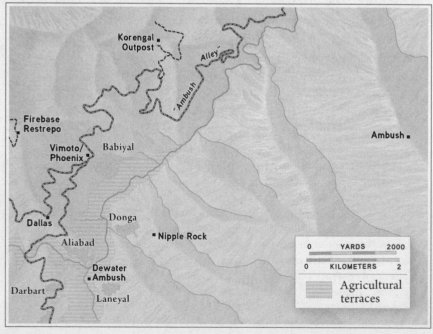

Korengal
Outpost

"Ambush
Alley"

Firebase
Restrepo

Ambush

Vimoto/
Phoenix

Babiyal

Donga

Dallas

Nipple Rock

Aliabad

Dewater
Ambush

Darbart

Laneyal

0 YARDS 2000

0 KILOMETERS 2

Agricultural
terraces

At first Soto found it breathtaking, a valley locked in former times. As he learned more, he saw it through military eyes. The outpost and observation posts were ringed with heavy machine guns, including MK19 automatic grenade launchers, which could fire bursts of high-explosive 40-millimeter projectiles across the valley. This seemed formidable, but was only a fraction of the firepower that could be brought to bear. Inside the outpost's operations center, computers showed a topographical overlay by which this terrain was more fully unpacked. Using aerial photographs and global-positioning satellites, the Americans had charted and numbered every building in the Korengal Valley. Their maps showed numbers on each structure's roof. The main buildings of Aliabad, a midsized village south of the outpost, were labeled 1 to 75. Labels superimposed on the other villages worked the same way: Chichal's list went to 103, Darbat's to 88, Dakalbat's to 31, Donga's to 69, Karangal's to 47, Laneyal's to 25, Laui Kalay's to 105, and so on. The numbers were a part of a fire-support overlay that covered hundreds of structures in all, a targeting template overwritten upon homes. The Korengal Valley, Soto saw, was no longer a land that time forgot. It was a tiny space that was intricately mapped and closely watched by layers of surveillance equipment and weaponry. Around the homes, the hilltops and ridges were also labeled and marked, each a precise spot on the earth that the American weapons were ready to hit. Viper Company kept two 120-millimeter mortars at the KOP, and one 60-millimeter mortar each at Vegas and Restrepo. When these weapons were not sufficient, the same targets were registered with 155-millimeter howitzers at Forward Operating Base Blessing, at the valley's mouth, and Asadabad. They could also be struck by Apache gunships and attack jets, including F/A-18s from aircraft carriers in the North Arabian Sea, by B-1s flying from outside Afghanistan, or by drones remotely piloted from the United States, along with more locally maintained A-10s and F-15s. The machine had done its homework. Looking up over the battle-scarred walls of their outposts, the soldiers saw an almost primeval wonder. Looking down at the computers in the operations center, they saw targets.

Two days after stepping off the helicopter, the soldiers of Second Platoon's advance party participated in their first combat patrol. Battle Company was sending soldiers across the river to Laui Kalay. Soto was told that patrols there often came under fire, so Battle Company had developed standard tactics, posting other soldiers along a road near the outpost. This was overwatch. It provided soldiers walking into Laui Kalay a modicum of protection against attackers from higher ground. To learn the routine, Second Platoon's newly arrived troops were provided a Humvee with a .50-caliber machine gun and assigned their spot. Soto took his place in the turret. Staff Sergeant Cox was the vehicle commander. Another young soldier, Kyle Stephenson, drove.

The patrol began quietly. The soldiers on overwatch picked their way along the mountain road to their places. Soto's truck stopped on a perch where he could readily fire at the eastern side. He had been shown the target reference points from where the Taliban typically opened fire.

It was a beautiful day, bright and dry. The mountains were almost bewitching. Soto was stern with himself, telling himself to concentrate.

Pay attention.

He scanned the valley, facing the expected threat. He was amped, a young soldier on his first patrol in a war.

Stay alert.

Gunfire broke out. Soto heard it but saw nothing suspicious—just the hillsides and villages to his front.

A bullet whizzed past and thudded into the dirt behind the truck. Radio noise filled the air. A voice said there was a sniper. More bullets came by, single shots. Each was followed by a pause, then another. Whoever was shooting was taking time to aim.

A bullet passed closer, making a sharp crack.

Cox shouted up to him from inside the truck.

"Hey, you okay?"

Soto was traversing the machine gun, looking for targets. He saw no one to shoot.

"I'm okay, I'm okay!" he shouted back.

"Can you see where it's coming from?" Cox asked.

Soto could not. The hill across the valley was vegetated, offering many places for a man to stay concealed. Their attackers were firing from under the trees or behind rocks. There were villages, too, with windows beyond counting. Gunmen could be firing from most any of them. Soto was annoyed. His machine gun was useless.

Where the fuck are they?

Another bullet cracked past.

Soto returned fire, aiming bursts at spots he had been shown before the patrol. Suppressive fire, the Army called it; it was a widely accepted way of shooting, a practice almost as old as automatic weapons. The machine gun bucked. Heavy bullets flew out in tight groups. But Soto felt strange. For all he knew, he was shooting at nothing.

The shooting stopped.

The Taliban switched off its attack. Its fighters were too experienced to remain in place as the Americans massed fire.

The valley was quiet. Soto was not sure how long the firing lasted. He thought it might have been five minutes. He was unharmed and flushed with energy, experiencing, at age eighteen, the dizzying joy of surviving a gunfight. Sweat poured down his face. Inside the truck, Stephenson was singing a lyric from a rap song.*

Many men wish death upon me
Blood in my eye, dawg, and I can't see.

It was 50 Cent. Soto smiled. He could finish that song in his head.

He laughed and followed Stephenson's lead, changing the original lyrics as he sang. Soto's turret was his club.

Many men wish death upon me
Sweat in my eye, dawg, and I can't see.

The machine-gun barrel was warm. Half a can of ammunition was gone. Soto sang. The patrol was over. A voice on the radio told them to head back. Soto's first firefight was behind him. Adrenaline pulsed through him, like a drug.

---

* "Many Men (Wish Death)" by 50 Cent.

More of Viper Company's soldiers arrived as July passed. Battle Company's numbers dwindled until they were gone. Viper Company was granted no break-in period. Soon Soto was back on the same road, looking across the river to the village of Donga. Again the militants attacked. A rocket zipped across the open space and struck beside his truck. The explosion's blast wave shook the truck and peppered its side with rocks and shrapnel.

Soto spun the turret and watched a small cloud of dust rising from the opposite slope.

He shouted down to the driver. "Move!"

The vehicle lurched into motion.

Soto opened up, pouring out .50-caliber bullets, aiming just below the dust. He fired an entire can, then half of another. Like the first time, he could not see anyone there.

Ghosts, he thought. *Motherfuckers are sneaky.*

The Taliban and Viper clashed repeatedly. Viper's officers examined the patterns and saw the rate of violence had risen sharply since Battle Company left.* It was as if the militants considered the new American unit to be green—easier to fight in their first weeks than they would be later. They also seemed to have a thorough grasp of American response times. Often the Taliban fought hard and with clear coordination for several minutes, firing from multiple positions simultaneously. Then they would stop and move away before the artillery responded. They had studied the Americans' way of war, and fought within its seams.

Soon after Viper settled in, Soto was temporarily reassigned from

---

* In mid-August, First Lieutenant John Rodriguez, who led Third Platoon until becoming Viper Company's executive officer, examined the trends for Taliban action in the valley. The reports showed that from November 2007 to July 2008, one of the previous company's platoons had been in thirty-eight fights, roughly four a month. In the few weeks since Viper Company arrived, the pace had increased manifold. "We have had 29 since we've been here," he wrote in his journal. It worked out to several gunfights each week, and some days more than one, for a single Viper platoon.

Second to Third Squad. Third Squad was being sent to Observation Post Dallas, the smallest and southernmost post, and had no medic or soldier with medical training. Soto was to be its provisional medic. Dallas was a machine-gun position with a commanding view and a crude environment. Only the small latrine and noisy generator made life there anything more than camping. About a dozen soldiers alternated between shifts on the radio and behind the guns. They slept on cots under a sandbagged ledge.

At first Soto disliked the place. The routine was dulling. Soldiers had little way to wash. They grew filthy and were swarmed by fleas. They urinated and defecated in a barrel, which attracted flies that buzzed around the bored soldiers. But as he spent more time there, Soto saw the post had certain qualities. Soldiers at Dallas were away from most supervisors and the endless work of soldiering. It offered young grunts freedom from patrol duties, a chance to slow down and talk.

Soto was drawn to Specialist Marques Knight, a soldier with a previous tour in Iraq. In the States, Soto had thought Knight was dismissive of FNGs. But the two had spent time together at Bagram and discovered they had similar taste in rap. At Dallas, Knight loosened up more. He confided in Soto, telling him of a difficult past and an unsettled family life and about noncommissioned officers he did not like or fully trust—a subject that would have been untouchable before Afghanistan, when Soto was new. Knight was thin as a rake. He wanted to pack on muscle. He worked out every day and scrounged for extra rations, trying to build his body. Soto saw a more complete and sensitive soldier than the taciturn veteran at Fort Hood. Knight eventually shared a plan to which he clung. When his time came for leave, he said, he was going to visit Brazil. *Brazil,* Soto thought. Knight wanted to see more of the world than Iraq and Afghanistan, and be someone other than an occupying soldier among a people who did not want him and wished him dead.

The Taliban capitalized on Viper Company's isolation. The outpost was out on a string, reachable by a single dirt road that climbed out of the Pech Valley. Supplies had to be flown or trucked in. American units had used the same path intermittently for more than a year, sending convoys of contracted Afghan cargo trucks about once a month. Often they were accompanied by attack helicopters and armored Humvees. A route-clearance platoon frequently led the drive, looking for bombs. But the road had to be driven slowly so soldiers could search for IEDs. These were the conditions under which the Americans were forced to operate. They allowed ambushers hours to prepare. One spot on the road, which was out of view of all their posts, was especially dangerous, and given a designation used repeatedly by Americans on occupation duty in Afghanistan and Iraq: Ambush Alley. Soldiers hated going there. The Army, given to tone-deaf messaging, even internally, called the road by a groan-worthy official name, Route Victory.

The battalion dispatched Afghan trucks up Route Victory with a lighter-than-usual escort on August 16.

A Taliban trap was waiting.

As the convoy neared the Korengal Outpost, in the heart of Ambush Alley, the last Humvee was stopped by an explosion caused by a pair of stacked antitank mines that had been rigged to be detonated remotely. The explosion killed Staff Sergeant Kristopher D. Rodgers and wounded two other soldiers.

Both Viper Company, in the Korengal Outpost, and Charlie Company, in the Pech Valley at Forward Operating Base Blessing, sent quick-reaction forces to the convoy's aid.

The militants were a step ahead. They began a determined assault against Combat Outpost Vegas, the Americans' main position on the east side of the river. It was the largest attack Viper had seen, involving as many as fifty fighters. Viper Company's mortar section fired 194 high-explosive 120-millimeter rounds. Artillery outside the valley fired another seventy shells, including a handful of incendiary white phosphorus rounds, which set the hills ablaze. Two American machine guns jammed. The attackers drew so close that an American sergeant was throwing hand grenades.

The outpost held.

The message to Viper was unmistakable: *We do not fear you, and we know your patterns.*

Two days later Third Platoon waited in an ambush site near the outpost. They were ten heavily armed soldiers hidden along a trail. They used camouflage netting to cover themselves, and set four claymore mines along the path they thought the Taliban might take. They were in place by darkness, ready to kill.

No one came before sunrise, and during the day the militants bypassed the ambush site and attacked the outpost the soldiers had left three times. As Viper Company fought off the final attack, two of its high-explosive and two white phosphorus rounds sailed more than a kilometer away from their intended target and struck a home in Kandlay. No one knew whether the explosions had killed or wounded civilians. The next morning, elders from Kandlay came to the gate to complain, saying the ordnance had damaged property and nearly killed women and children. Viper Company sent a patrol to survey the damage.

Soto's first rotation at Dallas had ended. He had returned to the outpost and rejoined Second Squad. That day his entire platoon headed to Aliabad. In this way, as Third Platoon walked back from Kandlay, the valley would be covered.

Not everyone was acclimated to the thin air and terrain. One team, including Staff Sergeant David L. Paquet, lagged behind. Paquet was struggling for breath. Another sergeant carried his pack and then took his rifle. Paquet fell to the ground.

Other soldiers rushed to him. He was lifeless, without a pulse.

Word traveled quickly. In Aliabad, Soto heard the talk over the radio. There was a soldier down.

A Black Hawk medevac helicopter rushed up the valley. There was no place to land in the riverbed. The crew winched Paquet aboard and turned away, headed to Jalalabad.

It rounded the turn, passing out of sight and then out of earshot, leaving Viper Company and its scattered soldiers to their thoughts. Huddled with other soldiers in Aliabad, Soto momentarily felt disoriented. Paquet had no history, as far as he knew, of being weak. Soto pushed his questions from his mind. *Ignore the noise.*

Second Platoon had to make its way back to the outpost. Soto was expecting to be attacked. He chastened himself, told himself that now was not time to grieve. *Block,* he thought. *Block, block, block. Shut down emotions. You can't dwell. You can think about this now or we can get back safe and you can think about it later.*

Soto chose later. He was eighteen years old. He had learned how to switch himself off.

———————

With his first rotation at Dallas complete, Soto's Korengal Outpost routine resumed. The days were a series of walks to the valley's villages, efforts to ambush militants along their trails, long shifts on post watching and waiting to be attacked. The attacks could proceed as if according to a guerrilla handbook. The Taliban would fire from hiding. The soldiers faced the threat and fired back. Then the attackers withdrew—as the Americans massed their mortars and artillery, before an aircraft strafed the hills or dropped bombs. Both sides moved as if by choreography. Patrols had a practiced feel, too. Afghans in the Korengal were against the Americans. The indicators were everywhere—from cold looks to villages empty of fighting-age men. It could seem that the Korengal was a valley of women, children, and old men. Everyone knew where the local men were. They were hiding in the mountains. The only time the Americans could expect to reliably see them was on Friday, when many Taliban fighters set aside weapons to visit the little mosque in Babeyal for prayer. Sometimes the Americans and Afghan National Army soldiers stood outside the place and watched their foes file past.

After prayers, the Afghan men would stroll back out, faces expressionless, walk by the loitering Americans, and return to the hills.

Little about this sat well with Soto. He had joined the Army to protect America. He was unsure how the Korengal Outpost served that end. The circumstances in the valley, and many of the missions his platoon was ordered to perform, caused him to wonder what the Army was thinking. In an outpost with a purpose that felt poorly conceived, Soto reduced the mission to its most basic rationale. *We're here because we're here.* If nothing else, the soldiers could fight for one another. That was something worth fighting for, and with a tangible purpose and a defined end.

One type of patrol seemed to him particularly ill-conceived: the sweeps of the road toward Combat Outpost Blessing. The company had no visibility on Ambush Alley. Its means of preventing traps from being laid was to go look for them on patrols called counter-IED (CIED) missions. They were the least popular missions in the company. Soto rode in the backseat of Staff Sergeant Cox's Humvee on a few of them, with his aid bag, listening to noncommissioned officers grouse. *Why drive into an ambush site as a way to prevent an ambush? Why the fuck are we going out to find IEDs that way? The only way we are going to find an IED is with our bodies.*

Soto shared this view. *What's the point of this? I thought CIED was to prevent IEDs from hurting us. This will get us killed.*

Other patrols were not much safer. On September 6, Second Squad walked from the outpost to Donga, across the river, and up a steep tree-shaded hill. Third Squad set up a support-by-fire position on the west side, in the same place where Soto had come under sniper fire within two days of arriving in the valley.

Soto and the rest of Second Squad crossed the river and reached the village. As was often the case, the homes they reached in Donga were mostly abandoned. Above them, in the hills, the militants opened fire.

The bullets were not coming Soto's way. Second Squad was safe. The Taliban were trying to hit Third Squad, on the opposite side. There was nothing for Soto to do. He could see no targets or positions to rush. The Taliban fighters were on another ridge.

More fighting was raging on a hilltop, between First Platoon and another group of Taliban. Viper Company was being attacked in two places.

The gunfire stopped.

Soto sensed something was wrong.

He watched Cox listen to the radio, hunched over with another sergeant. Their faces were harsh. They shook heads and swore and clenched their fists. They told the squad to get ready for the return walk.

It was late afternoon. The Taliban had the high ground. Second Squad crossed the river under the shadow of Aliabad and climbed toward the road. Third Squad had already left. Helicopters were swarming overhead, a mix of Black Hawks and Apaches.

Soto was growing angry. *There's a lot going on and we're not hearing it.*

He thought he knew why.

Someone was dead.

The squad reached the Marine and Afghan National Army position at Firebase Vimoto and filed inside. Once Soto was safe within the wire, freed from the mental demands of patrolling, his anger surged to fury. He confronted a sergeant.

"Tell me," he demanded. "Fucking tell me! Who got hit?"

"It was Knight," the sergeant said.

The words hit Soto like a punch. He remembered all Knight had told him at Dallas. The sergeant said there was more. First Platoon had also taken casualties. Its platoon leader, its radio operator, one of its squad leaders, and a medic had been wounded, along with three other soldiers, one of whom, Michael R. Dinterman, an eighteen-year-old private first class, was killed. First Platoon was on a hillside when it was attacked, and unable to move all of its casualties. Sergeant John M. Penich, a team leader, took charge of the fight, and organized the evacuation.* The helicopters had come to hoist them away. An Apache had been shot up and forced to make an emergency landing in Asadabad.

The sky opened up soon after Soto heard the news, splattering the valley with rain and hail. It was about a fifteen-minute patrol from Vimoto to the outpost in the dark. Soto walked forcefully, soaked and cold, alternating between numbness and lucidity, driven to pay respects to his friend.

Knight was in a body bag in the mechanics' bay, waiting to be flown to the morgue. Soto stood over the bag, speaking softly. He was thinking of the trip to Brazil that Knight would never take, of the family Knight would never have.

Others soldiers had told Soto that Knight had been killed in a vehicle turret, behind a machine gun. Soto heard he had died instantly. The soldiers inside the truck simply saw his legs slump. He never moved again.

Soto unzipped the top of the bag.

Knight's face was clean and looked calm, and his eyes were open. Someone had washed him, giving him the care he deserved. Knight was a fastidious, self-conscious man, and Soto was glad he had been cared for in this way. He leaned in tight to say good-bye. "Damn, I love you," he

---

* Sergeant Penich was awarded the Silver Star for his actions that day. The medal was awarded posthumously; by the time it was approved, Penich had been killed by American mortar fire in a mishap on October 16.

muttered, and fell into a soft stream-of-consciousness riff, unsure whether he was praying, singing, or babbling.

When the rain let up, Viper Company gathered outside on the cold gravel and mud for a memorial. From the mortar pit, soldiers fired two 120-millimeter illumination rounds. Each was a bright white flare suspended beneath a fluttering parachute. They opened high overhead, ignited in a brilliant glow, and slowly descended, issuing a slight whistling sound and casting shadows that spun and danced. Each round burned for about a minute. The soldiers stood motionless, watching them drift down. In sequence they burned out. The valley was black again.

Soto felt a heavy weight of gloom.

Knight was a great soldier, he thought. *What does this mean for the rest of us?*

Not long after the two soldiers were killed, Soto learned that Third Squad was returning to Observation Post Dallas and that he would join them there again. He did not want to go. He was part of Second Squad and there was a major mission coming up—already the talk of the company. He hoped to be with Cox on it. But Sergeant First Class Wright would not change his mind. He, too, was going to Dallas, he said, and the soldiers there would need Soto as a provisional medic. "You're coming with me," Wright said.

There was no point in resisting.

On September 20, while Soto was on watch at Dallas, a counter-IED patrol from his platoon drove north from the Korengal Outpost toward Ambush Alley. As the day dragged, Soto intermittently heard the now-familiar sounds of violence. Occasional gunfire and a rocket-propelled grenade. A helicopter dropping supplies at Combat Outpost Vegas came under machine-gun fire. And he heard Sergeant Cox calmly leading the patrol on the road.

The day quieted down. The patrol radioed that it had crossed safely through the most dangerous stretch of road, continued north, and turned back around. Soto spent the hours on radio watch.

A loud explosion rocked the valley.

It was a few kilometers away, to Dallas's north. Soto knew where it was and guessed what it meant. A Humvee in the counter-IED patrol had hit an IED.

Dallas was farther from Ambush Alley than any of Viper's positions. Rushing to the struck soldiers would be another unit's job. All Soto could do was listen.

Multiple voices came up on the radio. Soto recognized them, one by one. At first the situation was uncertain. Soto waited for more information, and for Sergeant Cox's voice to relay information and instructions. But Cox was absent. Ordinarily he would be calling in updates.

Other soldiers in the patrol backtracked to the blast site and began describing what they saw.

Two soldiers had been wounded, they said. Two others were dead.

The triggerman who had detonated the IED—using a yellow wire that ran from the road downhill—had waited for the last truck, to make his escape easier. The IED exploded under Cox's Humvee and heaved the truck off the road, throwing the gunner, Private Joseph F. Gonzales, from the turret and scattering the vehicle's armor, roof, and doors down the slope.

Gonzales and Cox were killed instantly. Private Keith Young and Private First Class Sean Hollins were wounded. Young was covered in oil, screaming that he had been blinded, and had a broken hand. Hollins was awake but dazed. The first soldiers to reach him feared he had a spinal injury.

High on the mountain to the south, unable to see the blast site, Soto listened to the radio. When he heard the battle roster numbers of the dead, his eyes welled with tears.

As Soto wept, the Army mobilized. The quick-reaction force arrived from the outpost, followed by an A-10 attack aircraft. Far overhead, a Predator looked down on Afghans its remote pilot thought were more militants, massing and watching the soldiers scrambling to give first aid to the wounded and recover the dead. The A-10 dropped a 500-pound bomb, then followed up with a strafe with its 30-millimeter cannon. A helicopter flew into the valley for the casualties.

Soto remained at the radio. He was quietly despondent, and pensive. His mind had come to a soldier's timeless realization: The battlefield did not care about reputations, appearances, or wishes. It simply snatched lives. Knight was gone, and now Cox and Gonzales. Knight and Cox had been the soldiers whom Soto had looked up to most; Gonzales was a friend. It made no sense that they had died. *The best guys always seem to lose,* he thought. *The guys you think are equipped mentally and physically ready for war—the guys you think are going to come home—aren't the guys to come home.*

Soto usually sat directly behind Cox in the Humvee, with the first-aid bag. If Sergeant Wright had not insisted on taking him to Dallas, he would have been in Cox's truck. He had been saved by a personnel shuffle. His friends had died while he listened from afar.

He was not sure what to feel.

The Taliban could fight as it pleased, but the Americans were bound by rules. There were rules limiting soldiers' ability to enter Afghan homes, rules governing when they could use their weapons, and rules governing how firepower could be applied. The soldiers were drilled to be polite and show manners and restraint. All of this created circumstances Soto considered absurd.

The only thing saving Viper Two, he thought, was that the Taliban were poor shots. Many of them carried Kalashnikov rifles and fired from hundreds of yards away, ranges at which such weapons are inaccurate. They did have other weapons, including at least one heavy machine gun, and they had weapons captured from previous American units, including an M14 that Battle Company had lost and a captured M240B machine gun. But they almost always missed. Why were they so hard to beat?

Sometimes at night, Soto looked across the valley and saw flashlights bobbing and flickering in the forests and along the trails. He was sure these were Taliban moving ammunition and heavy weapons into position. The Americans did little about it. Soto found it maddening. The Taliban had developed such a finely tuned understanding of American behaviors that it flaunted its command of the gaps. As Soto saw it, the Army treated Viper like a boxer told not to use his fists. No wonder it was losing fights.

In December, Sergeant Wright pulled Soto aside and shared bad news: Soto's half sister Ashley had died. She was fourteen and had suffered from ovarian cysts. Wright told Soto to pack and fly home. The Army was giving him emergency leave.

Soto's mother had had six children, two with his father, the others with other men. Soto knew Ashley but not well, and by the time word of her death reached the valley, her funeral had already been held. He did not want to go home. He told Wright his loyalty was to the platoon.

"I can't change anything there, but maybe I can change things in the Korengal," he said.

Wright was gentle. He told Soto he would not help him make decisions he would later regret. He ordered him to take the leave.

The trip out was jarring. Soto was flown to Jalalabad, then to Bagram. The valley had changed him. As he traveled he absorbed the sights: the dining facilities heaped with food, the PXs stocked with sundries, soldiers in lines at beverage shops, no one waiting for the abundant showers. He saw neat uniforms and clean boots. *These dudes throw away food,* he thought.

He passed his time in New York aimlessly, feeling guilty and out of place. He was relieved when it was time to return to the valley.

He landed in Afghanistan for more bad news. Three soldiers in his platoon had been shot on a patrol. And a CH-47 helicopter carrying supplies for Restrepo had been hit by a rocket. The damaged aircraft lost control and crashed near Firebase Vegas.* Most of the crew and passengers scrambled out before fire consumed the wreckage, but one soldier, Sergeant Ezra Dawson, had been killed.

The downing of the CH-47 exposed another weakness in the American ambition for the valley, and for Afghanistan as a whole: the reluctance of the Afghan National Army. The helicopter was hit above Firebase Vimoto, over the heads of the Marines stationed there, who watched the crash. Vimoto was an Afghan National Army position. No distress could be more pressing than that of a downed aircraft. As the flames climbed,

---

* The Department of Defense deployed euphemism to describe the downing, announcing that Dawson died after an aircraft "made a hard landing under combat conditions."

the Marines tried to rally the Afghans to go to the aid of the passengers and crew, and work alongside the soldiers from Vegas.

The Afghans refused.

The patrol, they said, was not on the schedule.

Soto had already taken his stock of the war. But as he heard more stories, and saw more missions, his views hardened. He did not consider himself a disrespectful person. He had volunteered for war, eager to serve, wanting a tangible role. He'd stayed out of trouble almost all of his life and kept a positive attitude as he trained. But he'd grown disillusioned and was unwilling to suppress what he knew. To him the Army's counterinsurgency doctrine made no sense. Foreign soldiers were not going to win over the Korengalis with sweet talk and projects, and they were not going to defeat them by hanging around in outposts and trying to visit them by day. Viper Company's missions seemed designed more to show activity for the bosses than to accomplish anything real, much less lasting. Soto had faith in many of the sergeants and officers in his company. They were as stuck as he was. He thought they did their best. But he had developed a deep distrust of the Army's brass. *They take care of themselves,* he thought.

When a colonel came to visit the Korengal Outpost and wanted to do a short foot patrol, the company assembled soldiers to take him out. They waited to leave until after attack helicopters arrived, to protect him.

He's afraid, Soto thought.

Squads went out every day without air support. *What's so special about him?*

As spring arrived, Soto's disappointment bordered upon disgust. He tried to contain his feelings. But he sensed that many senior officers had little idea what was going on. They said what they needed to say—about Americans coaching Afghan forces, about Americans winning over the Afghan population, about the Taliban losing ground. He read the optimistic prospects for an Afghan surge under President Obama. The official message was positive. What the brass didn't mention, or tried explaining away, was what Soto saw: that most Afghans in the valley were not interested in getting along and that the Afghan National Army was a lackluster force that survived because it was under American protection. These twin

factors ensured that their campaign would fail. And the Army offered no
better ideas. *We're here because we're here,* he thought. *We're here because
another unit came here and set up, and we replaced them, and no one knows
what else to do.*

Soto saw his Army as a huge, self-administering organization, high on
slogans and trafficking in talking points. The grunts lived the unforgiving
details of a plan that would not work. *I'll never do twenty years in this organization,* he thought. By April, when Lieutenant Smith checked in, Soto
was the type of grunt that long wars make: the young enlisted soldier, sick
of bullshit, who fought just to keep his friends alive.

Then came the order for the ambush patrol high on the opposite
ridge.

Oh, great, Soto thought.

Soto kept climbing uphill, slipping on loose rocks, feeling his quadriceps
and calves driving him on. Sweat soaked his limbs and back. He wore a
helmet and a harness that held bulletproof plates tight over his chest and
back, and he carried a first-aid kit and a small backpack loaded with extra
machine-gun ammunition and everyday essentials of grunt field life: dry
socks and T-shirt, bottles of water, a fleece skullcap, protein bars mailed
to the platoon by appreciative American citizens back home. He carried
a rifle, which from time to time he had to switch between hands so he
could scale the slope. The load slowed him. He cursed. But for all of his
sour attitude, he was acclimated, lean and taut, elastic with youth and in a
functional state of mind. With almost nine months at the outpost, he was
past struggling, and had become mechanism as much as man. He moved
steadily and almost unceasingly, gaining altitude, sure of himself, pushing
on—a creature of his place.

Soon he would be carrying more weight. He had been selected as Second Platoon's new radio operator. The soldier currently in the job, Steven
Halase, was being promoted to fire team leader. This ambush patrol was
to be Halase's last turn with the radio. Soto was to take it when they got
back in the morning.

The squads climbed separately, making time.

When Soto took the radio, he would be Smith's right-hand man. He was glad to have more responsibility but not thrilled with the circumstance. Soto figured Smith was competent. Smith's problem, in the eyes of a young enlisted soldier, was that he was a few notches too motivated. That gung-ho vibe and can-do attitude, that by-the-book faith that today was the day—Soto had seen this before. He had reason to doubt it. *He's like we were when we got here.*

Soto was interested in more important things than the plan: looking out for his buddies and leaving a strong personal record. The war was the slate upon which his reputation would be written. That much, at least, still mattered. It might even be achievable, unlike the Pentagon's Afghan daydream. Second Platoon was living day by day. *Now we're tired,* Soto thought. *Now we're hungry.*

Soto had watched Smith at the terrain model, issuing the operation order. It was done to the letter. *He seems like a kid on Christmas morning,* he thought. *We already know how this shit goes down.*

He saw the real patrol ahead, not that sand-table version. *We'll set in, no one will come, and we'll get hit on the way back. We'll take cover, fire back, come home. If no one gets killed, we'll catch up on sleep and get ready to go do it again.*

Smith kept the platoon moving.

As far as Soto was concerned, the American hearts-and-minds campaign, the counterinsurgency campaign, had little chance. Pretending it did served up soldiers for ambushes, allowing their enemies to pick away at the platoons. The doctrine was a recipe for delivering American soldiers to Afghan traps. *Why the fuck am I patrolling? Why am I going out to these villages in the middle of the day?* Soto was a junior soldier. He had been in Afghanistan less than a year. He could see a better way. *Why aren't we doing more direct action? Leave at night, knock down doors, and be back before sunrise.*

Walking around by day like this is stupid.

He had no say in such things. He was a rifleman and an ammunition bearer, a pack animal for the soldier beside him, Specialist Arturo Molano, who carried an M240 machine gun.

Soto's pack was heavy. It strained his legs and pulled at his shoulders. As the terrain grew steeper, he reached places where he had to strap his rifle to his back and struggle forward with all four limbs, using his hands to hold roots and boulders, and his quadriceps to force himself higher. Molano, with the machine gun, had it worse. The two men fell into a rhythm. One man would get over a particularly hard patch and turn around and extend a hand to the other.

"Hey, man, you good?" Soto would ask.

Molano would say he was fine.

"You want me to carry the gun?" Soto would offer.

Molano declined every time.

Tough motherfucker, Soto thought. *He'll never let me carry it.*

Soto liked being partnered with someone like this. He expected to be attacked before Second Platoon made it back. He liked having a strong soldier nearby. He loathed the Taliban, saw them as punks, guys the platoon would tear apart in a head-to-head fight. But the platoon never got the chance. The Taliban fought on its terms, and would wait for an advantage before firing the first shot. Meanwhile its spotters observed the Americans' movements, telling the valley where Viper roamed.

These guys are watching us, Soto thought. *They see us.*

After a few hours, Second Platoon reached the crest. The soldiers stopped. They had not been harassed on the long climb. Soto inhaled deeply, taking in the thin air while a few soldiers went forward with Smith to check the trail. He had been on this ridge before, after being inserted by helicopter, but had never climbed to it from the riverbed. His muscles were flushed. The air tasted clean, away from the Korengal Outpost's pits of burning trash and barrels of human waste.

Smith returned. He had found a trail intersection and seen fresh tracks. This could mean everything or nothing. It might be a sign of militants. It might be a sign of loggers. But it meant Second Platoon was not alone up there after all.

The soldiers rose. Smith led them toward the trail juncture, where they followed the plans rehearsed back on the landing zone. Almost without talking, they arranged themselves in a triangle astride the trail. In the infantry vernacular, this was known as a patrol base. After the soldiers settled in, Smith circulated along its inside edge, checking the position of each man and paying particular attention to the location and orientation of the machine guns. He put Molano at one end of the triangle, and Specialist Oxman at another, with their machine guns angled back toward each other. In this way, their fire would create an interlocking zone of flying lead across one side of the patrol base.

Soto found a mound of dirt beside Molano and looked uphill over its top. A footpath came out of the trees and followed a course between rocks and trees straight to where Second Platoon had set up. The area was vegetated, but not heavily. If anyone came from above, he and Molano would have a clear shot for at least thirty yards. He neatly arranged belts of ammunition, then grabbed his night-vision device and fastened it to his helmet. A sergeant came through and double-checked Soto and Molano's shooting sector, a cone extending uphill. This was their piece of the kill zone.

The plan called for the scouts to find a protected position up the slope, alone, out of the way if Second Platoon opened up, and watch the trail, ready to give warning if anyone approached.

Other soldiers set claymore mines on small stands. On command, their directional explosive charges could blast small steel balls to the platoon's front. Smith took a spot in the center near Halase, who operated an encrypted radio on the company's tactical net.

Everything was set before dark.

The air was chilly and the mountain ridge raked by cold gusts. Smith told the platoon to go to 50 percent watch—with every other man behind a weapon. Soto was soaked with sweat from the climb, and shivering. With Molano watching, he put down his rifle and pulled a dry undershirt and socks from his backpack. He changed clothes, ate a protein bar, and washed it down with a bottle of water. He lifted his rifle so Molano could have a turn doing the same.

The sun was dropping behind the western ridge. Soto could see the Korengal Outpost below him, across the open air. He realized this must be what it looked like to militants when they attacked.

Farther downhill, he saw tiny outlines of Afghans moving about their villages. Smoke rose from wood fires in houses and in yards outside. A distant call to prayer floated on the mountain air.

The light dimmed to a soft yellow, then to gray. A deepening blue gave way to black. Soto lowered his monocular night-vision device so it rested in front of his shooting eye. He turned on his AN/PEQ-15 aiming laser, attached to his rifle. A fine green line extended through the night. It moved with his rifle's muzzle—invisible to anyone without night-vision equipment, brilliantly bright to Soto and the rest of Second Platoon. His weapon was ready now; he could use it effectively at night.

Stars appeared. The platoon had spent the day playing the new lieutenant's Ranger games, Soto thought, but at least no one had been killed. He expected tomorrow morning would be dodgy. Second Platoon could almost count on being hit during the walk home.

These motherfuckers know exactly where we are, he thought.

He peered through his sight at the stillness to his front. His sector was a quiet green world, glowing dully in the small circular screen before his right eye.

We're wasting time. Fuck this place.

————————

Lieutenant Smith followed the playbook. He let his soldiers change into dry clothes with the last of the light. Then came stand-to, a period of 100 percent alertness during which the soldiers were forbidden to move. All were motionless at their fighting positions, weapons pointed into sectors. The silence was total. The drill—as if bracing for an attack—was part of infantry life, a means to focus the platoon. The lasers formed a web of green lines. It was a purposefully assembled geometry of Second Platoon's close-range killing potential, a prediction of what its bullets might do should anyone wander into its kill zone. It did not include the claymore mines and high-explosive grenades, or the scouts who soon would be leaving the patrol base to hide by the trail. It also omitted the vast apparatus of firepower that Smith and the platoon's radios could summon on short notice. This was the firepower that routinely killed the Taliban in small quantities and kept the outposts from being overrun. Smith was ready to call it down, onto this ridge.

After a few minutes, stand-to ended.

Smith dispatched three scouts up the slope to find their vantage point.

They stepped off into the night in single file. Soto figured they would find a spot about one hundred yards away, behind terrain that could block the platoon's gunfire and claymores, and settle in until morning.

Second Platoon was in position. A night of boredom was ahead.

———

Near the center of the patrol base, Specialist Halase sat on cold ground beside the radio. The scouts had just left. He had spread out his poncho liner and opened an MRE. He was thinking he'd pass an easy run of hours, now that the difficult walk was over.

Smith rushed toward him. He had his own radio for talking with the scouts and squad leaders. He was earnest and animated, whispering fast. He had just heard from the scouts. "Dudes are coming down the trail," he said.

Halase wondered what Smith meant. *Dudes coming down the trail?* He asked the lieutenant if the scouts were coming back.

"No," Smith said. "The Taliban."

The lieutenant dashed away to take his place on the line.

———

Soto heard movement behind him. Smith was crouched between him and Molano. He practically hissed. Scouts had just reported gunmen walking this way, he said, ten or fifteen people in all.

"Molano, you got the gun up?" he asked. Molano said he did. Smith was gone.

Adrenaline rushed through Soto. His heart rate spiked. His muscles seemed coiled to pounce. *What the fuck.* He entered the peculiar mind-set that can settle over a combatant in the seconds before battle, a feeling of absolute, intoxicating clarity. Viper had shuffled the deck, and the roles in the valley had been reversed. This time it was the Americans with the advantage. Someone else was walking into a trap.

His breathing quickened. He pressed his chest to the earth and adjusted himself so the barrel of his M4 was parallel to the dirt and aligned with the trail. He flipped its selector lever off safe. He went still. His world shrunk to what the rehearsals had drilled him for: peering into his sector, weapon ready to kill.

Seconds passed. Soto knew the scouts were not far. If they'd seen men, those men would be getting very close.

Soto's job, for now, was to wait. Smith alone was to decide whether anyone approaching was a combatant. If he decided they were, then he had to decide the moment to begin shooting. By the rules of the ambush, which he had said over and over in the operations order and the rehearsal, only the patrol leader could initiate fire.

The other soldiers were to remain motionless until released.

Soto's heart thumped in his ears.

His kept his eye close to his night-vision monocular. It showed what he had seen during stand-to: a lethal green matrix, set. All was as it had been.

His right eye picked up a change.

Something was moving. It moved again.

Into the dim green glow of his eyepiece stepped the shape of a man. He was carrying a rifle and wore ammunition pouches across his chest. He was about thirty-five yards away, walking gingerly.

Another man emerged behind him. He carried a rifle, too.

Two more men stepped into view.

The first man paused.

This one looked older than the others, with a thick beard. He pointed a small flashlight at the ground, switched it on, and quickly switched it off.

The Taliban fighters were ghosts no more. They were people like any others, dealing with what every soldier dealt with. This man was trying to be sure of the trail. For a moment Soto was detached, in a meta-state, both there and away from there. He felt vindicated. He had been right all along when he saw flashlights in the hills and suspected that the Taliban was so cocky, so familiar with the limits of the American rules, that its fighters moved openly at night.

Fuck. These are the dudes we've been trying to catch.

The man had found the trail. He started walking again, into the intersecting green lines of the platoon's night sights.

Calm settled over Soto. Surprise tonight rested with Viper Two.

These four approaching men were about to die.

A fifth man stepped into view.

Soto's shooting eye surveyed the group. A rocket-propelled grenade protruded from one man's back. Another draped a PK-style machine gun across his shoulders. After the first two men, the others did not have their weapons ready to fire. Some had their rifles slung. Their body language was relaxed. They walked side by side. They weren't ghosts. They were a mess. They had grown too confident. They had no idea of the danger they faced.

Emotions raced through Soto. First surprise, next anger, then disgust. He'd never seen the Taliban so closely, at least not with their weapons. Were these the guys who had killed his friends? They did not look like the mujahideen of legend. *You got me on the other side of the world, on this mountain, fighting these guys, and they don't even know what they're doing?*

The lead man was perhaps twenty yards away.

Soto had to choose whom to shoot. Lasers had already settled on the first two men. A green line stopped on the forehead of the man with the flashlight in the lead; another traced a figure-eight pattern on the same man's chest. The second man was similarly marked. Other soldiers had chosen them.

They're gonna get wasted, Soto thought.

He moved his weapon toward the third man. This one had the machine gun across his shoulders. He balanced the weapon by gripping its barrel with one hand. He had no beard and no headdress. Soto moved his aiming laser to his upper chest, squarely between the straps of the man's tactical harness but above any equipment that might turn a bullet.

The man did not seem alert but his machine gun was a significant weapon. Soto would make sure he could not put it to use.

The gunmen drew nearer, inside of fifteen yards, then inside of ten. More Taliban fighters filled in behind them.

Soto kept his laser trained on the third man. It was time.

Where was Smith? he wondered.

Hurry up.

Hurry the fuck up.

The man with the machine gun was maybe twenty feet away. The soldiers were silent.

Where's Smith? C'mon, dude.

Smith had not given the sign.

Do it, Soto thought. *Do it.*

Fucking do it.

The man with the machine gun was less than fifteen feet away.

Do it already.

Soto's heart felt like it might rupture his chest.

Fucking do it.

To his right, another soldier switched his rifle from safe to fire, making a slight metal-on-metal click.

The lead Taliban fighter stopped.

Shit.

Other fighters behind him paused. For a second the scene was frozen. Had they heard it? The gunmen in the kill zone were motionless. Trembling green lasers rested on their faces and chests, invisible to the Taliban, bright and hot to the soldiers hiding in front of them.

Soto wanted to scream.

C'mon, c'mon, c'mon, fucking Smith, c'mon—

An explosion shook the forest.

Steel balls slammed into the Taliban patrol. Smith's voice sounded in the darkness.

"Fire! Fire! Fire!" he said.

Viper Two came off its leash.

Soto pulled the trigger, sending his first bullet into the chest of the man carrying the machine gun. He fired several times more, eyes on his victim, hearing the rest of the platoon firing all around him.

The man fell to his knees. Soto kept shooting. The man crumpled the rest of the way to the ground. He did not move.

Halase radioed the company's operation center, checking in as Viper Two. "We're in contact!" he said.

Viper Company's commander, Captain Jimmy Howell, radioed back. "You need HE?" he asked. "You need Willie Pete?"

The mortar pit was ready with high-explosive and white phosphorous rounds.

Gunfire tore through the kill zone and across the trail. Halase could tell, from the angles of the aiming lasers, that this was no situation for mortars. The two sides were yards apart.

"No, they're too close," he said. "We need Apaches. Now!"

Along the line where soldiers were firing, someone shouted to Sergeant

Craig Tanner, who was ready with a claymore that one of his soldiers had hidden beside the trail. It was a command in the dark: "Hey, Tanner, they are running down your side! Blow the claymore!"

Tanner detonated it, shaking the hillside again.

Looking for another man to shoot, Soto scanned a green pandemonium—the grisly confusion made visible through a night-vision device. A few of the Taliban fighters had dropped in place on the trail. Others were staggering and scattering. Bright tracers slapped and skipped off rocks, spinning out over the ridge in hot arcs. The Taliban fighter on point had somehow dashed sideways, sprinting to Soto's right. Soto had heard Specialist Robert Oxman's machine gun roaring as the man headed toward it. Others ran between the thick trees, back to where they had come from.

Soto fired at them. He thought he hit them, but wasn't sure.

The man Soto had shot first rose. He was upright, directly in front.

Soto spun left and fired into him again. The man dove away, into the brush to Soto's left.

Someone threw a grenade. It shook the forest anew.

Soldiers heard familiar voices.

"Where you at?"

"Check that way!"

"How much ammo you got?"

"You good?"

"What do you see?"

Soto yelled he was fine. He checked Molano, changed his rifle's magazine, and kept his eyes facing out front.

Smoke hung low over the underbrush.

The shooting slowed.

The shooting stopped.

Not a single shot had been fired back.

An American voice called out a warning.

"Get ready for a counterattack!"

Soto's ears rang. The platoon was jumpy. Barrels were hot. He remained pressed to the ground, not wanting to rise and be mistaken for an Afghan.

A voice called out from uphill, in a language the soldiers did not know.

They heard four syllables, broken into what sounded like two words: *Delta rasha!**

The voice sounded again: "*Delta rasha!*"

It sounded plaintive and scared.

Soto kept his rifle aimed uphill. He had no idea how many militants were on the ridge. His mind cycled through possibilities. Maybe the platoon had killed only the first men of a larger force. If someone ambushed Viper like this, Viper would send out a quick-reaction force.

He braced for a counterattack.

The sergeants moved through the patrol base, checking each man.

Soto asked what was up. Someone said none of the Americans had been hurt. Word passed between the troops. Specialist Oxman said that the Taliban's point man had managed to survive for several paces. "This guy kept running toward me and I kept lighting him up," he said. He had finally fallen directly in front of Oxman's muzzle, so close that Oxman reached over to check his pulse.

An explosion boomed over the valley. From afar, soldiers in Viper Company had seen fighters fleeing. Captain Howell had cleared an F-15 to hit them with a 2,000-pound laser-guided bomb.

Second Platoon followed the next steps as rehearsed.

A sergeant led Soto and two other soldiers into the kill zone to search the dead. Just off the trail, Soto found the body of the machine gunner he had shot. He was sprawled in the underbrush. He looked sixteen years old. They found more bodies—one shot through the brow, another missing limbs. One man's face was a death mask, eyes opened in astonishment. A sergeant put on latex gloves and turned the dead fighters' heads to photograph each face.

The sound of helicopters thumped overhead. A pair of Apaches had come.

Throughout the valley the Taliban was suffering a breakdown in discipline. Its fighters frantically used two-way radios to find out what

---

* Different soldiers recall hearing "*Delta rasha*" and "*Delta lashka.*" One plausible explanation is that a surviving gunman was trying to round up other survivors, using the Pashto phrase *dalta raasha*, which means "come here."

had happened, and were having trouble getting answers. Viper Company eavesdropped, receiving translations of the intercepts. One of their commanders, a man American intelligence knew as Hamkar, had been with the ambushed fighters. His peers were not sure whether he was dead.

Captain Howell relayed another translation to Halase, from a fighter hiding on the ridge. "Tell my family that I love them and this is probably going to be the end for me," the man had said.

An Apache fired a 30-millimeter chain gun. The pilots had found a militant, they said, and killed him.

Second Platoon reorganized. The search team had stacked the weapons they captured into a pile. There were too many to carry. They permanently damaged most with thermite grenades, rendering them useless, and selected a few to bring to their outpost.* Smith and the sergeants counted every man and told the first soldiers to begin the walk home. They had killed more than ten Taliban fighters in what might have been the most successful conventional infantry ambush of the Afghan war. Now they had to get back behind their blast walls before sunrise to avoid suffering casualties of their own.

The scouts went first. The rest of the soldiers worked their way down the slope behind them.

Gunfire broke out again. It sounded like American weapons, but from his position back in the formation Soto was worried. *They regrouped and scouts got fucked up,* he thought.

---

* Among the Taliban weapons and equipment later turned over to Viper Company's intelligence section were thirty box magazines for Kalashnikov rifles. Of these, seventeen contained ammunition identical to that purchased by the United States for issue to Afghan security forces. This was a bitter revelation and pointed to more problems. Ammunition supplied to Afghan allies was leaking to the Taliban. American logisticians were indirectly supplying America's foes. Much more of the ammunition may also have been purchased by the United States, but was of types that were more common in Afghanistan and could not be conclusively linked to Pentagon procurement. (Personal survey of the ammunition by the author.)

He and the soldiers near him slid downhill, grabbing branches in the brush to break their falls. The shooting ended, over in less than a minute.

Soto's squad caught up to the scouts. They stood over three more Taliban bodies.

The soldiers searched the freshly killed men, then kept moving.

The adrenaline high had worn off. Soto's mind wandered. The lopsided violence seemed unreal. He felt proud as a soldier. Vengeance was satisfying. This night, he knew, was payback. It might even be more than payback. The Taliban's losses, he thought, could hurt the Taliban's ability to fight. *This might calm shit down.* As for Smith, the ambush on the ridge forced Soto to rethink his view. He had to square his feeling of the past days with what had happened in the past hours. Lieutenant Smith, he now knew, was legit. He had organized the platoon in a way that had torn a Taliban unit apart.

The soldiers arrived at the riverbed in the hours before dawn, waded across the frigid stream, and weaved their way uphill and into the outpost's gate. It seemed like everyone was awake and waiting for Viper Two—the Marines who mentored the Afghan soldiers, the mechanics, the company's officers, soldiers on guard and from the mortar pit. People were shouting to them, cheering. Soto heard people saying that what Second Platoon had just done was monumental. *That was some crazy shit.*

The platoon walked to the operations center and laid the captured equipment on the ground outside its door.

The cooks had prepared a hot meal, and the soldiers from the patrol clustered around one another, trading details, eating, chugging water, talking fast. After a while Soto drifted away. He was dehydrated. His legs quivered with cramps. His brain hurt. He had been working in gore. He washed himself by standing naked and dumping water bottles over his head, and headed to the B-hut where he lived. He cleaned his rifle and lay down on his plywood rack. Smith's bunk was directly above. He had not come in to rest.

The sun was up. Euphoria had passed. Soto's mind was still working, trying to decide where the ambush fit. His feeling had changed. Now he doubted the killing would change the company's circumstances. The valley did not work that way. A thought arrived unsolicited, and stuck.

They're going to get us back.

Soto woke to spectacle. Residents of the villages were ascending the foot-paths to the ridge where Second Platoon had left the bodies. Some carried makeshift litters, including one that looked like a bed. The Korengalis were retrieving their dead. The Americans watched with spotting scopes and binoculars. As hours passed, the Afghans descended in groups, walking slowly, carrying bodies wrapped in sheets.

Elders from the villages appeared at the outpost gate and asked to speak with Captain Howell. They were subdued. In ordinary circum-stances, such long faces might command people to hush. But the outpost was ebullient. Viper's morale had been buoyed by the settling of a score. Soldiers strutted and grinned.

An awkward meeting followed. Howell greeted the elders politely and took a seat among them. The old men said the Americans had made a terrible mistake. A young girl had gone missing while gathering food on the mountain, they said, and villagers organized a search party to find her. The Americans had ambushed the search party, confusing local men for the Taliban.

Howell was expressionless as the account took shape. He waited until the last of the elders had spoken, and the group was satisfied it had made its point. Then he spoke. The elders' tale, he said, was one of the most ridiculous lies he had ever heard.

After the ambush, Soto took over duties as Smith's radio operator. Halase had been training him for about two weeks, teaching him the particulars of the eight-pound Harris VHF radio, known as an ASIP, and the various reports and procedures Soto would be expected to follow.

He was part of the platoon's command group now, the human con-nection between the platoon and the company. He would be expected to know the platoon's exact location at all times, and its orientation relative to each of the Taliban's firing positions and the target reference points. He also had to consider the balance between being the communications link and working the odds to stay alive. The ASIP had an extendable antenna. For short distances and when the platoon was in line of sight of another radio, a minimal amount of antenna was fine. The antenna would not be flopping overhead, signaling to the Taliban that he was a conduit to fire support. But as the kilometers stretched out, or when the platoon ventured into the hollows upstream, Soto would have to extend the antenna farther and farther. He would be advertising his role.

On his first patrol, to Babeyal, an old woman complained that the Americans had killed her son in the ambush. The platoon faced no attack. His next patrol, to Donga, was also quiet. A wizened man stepped outside and spoke with Smith and Sergeant Wright. He claimed to know nothing of the ambush or of the men killed in it.

The next patrol was to be more serious: a walk to Laneyal, across the river from Aliabad. The company planned this mission carefully. When Second Platoon descended to the rushing water beneath Aliabad, it would be vulnerable to gunfire from multiple directions, including from many of the Taliban's usual firing positions. Captain Howell ordered soldiers at Dallas and Restrepo, and the Marines and Afghan National Army soldiers at Vimoto, to be ready to help Second Platoon. He also sent along Lieutenant Rodriguez, the company's executive officer, to walk with Smith, who was still learning the turf.

Soto readied the radio. Getting to Laneyal, he knew, involved just about all of the valley's risks. They would have to walk along the road or trails on the western side of the river, which the Taliban often raked with gunfire. Then they would have to pick their way down the slope to a fork in the Korengal River, where two branches met. The path was narrow and known, a predictable route on which to lay traps. The river was brown and swollen with snowmelt and spring rains. The soldiers would have no choice but to cross both branches via small wooden footbridges. The first bridge was perhaps two feet wide. The second was nothing more than a plank. In the low ground, as they crossed it, the soldiers would be exposed from almost all sides.

On the day of the patrol, when the soldiers assembled at midday outside their wooden shacks, Sergeant Wright issued a warning. They needed to move fast, he said, and stay alert. The Taliban would be seeking revenge.

Second Platoon departed the outpost in a chilly drizzle. Sheets of mist drifted across the valley. Small clouds clung low to the slopes.

The soldiers moved briskly south. The mud was slick like grease. They passed Firebase Vimoto, where the Afghans and Marines were covering their movement, and came to the edge of Aliabad, a village of buildings built into the slope and made of meticulously stacked stone. The soldiers filed through muddy paths between them. Dogs barked. One, tied to the front of a home with a closed door, snarled at each man moving by.

At the top of the stone staircase, Second Platoon stopped. The valley dropped before them like a gorge. The soldier stood among twisted, leafless trees. Down in the lower ground, in terraced wheat fields and the almond grove, other trees were in bloom. People were hiding inside. The landscape seemed deserted, left for the dogs.

The fire teams arranged themselves behind cover and aimed their weapons across. They were in position so the lead squad could start crossing.

It led the descent, with the lieutenants and Soto following behind, along with Private First Class Roger Webb, the artillery forward observer. The radio signal was starting to fail. Soto extended the antenna. It rose about three feet above his head.

On the way down the stairs, the soldiers met one of the elders of Aliabad, Zarin, coming up. Zarin was a lithe man, more agile than his years would seem to allow. His beard was stained red with henna.

Lieutenant Rodriguez knew him. The two men chatted in the light rain. Zarin said he had just come from Laneyal, and the path was safe. He adjusted his cloak against the chill and bounded up the steps.

The platoon continued down.

The first bridge, at the bottom of the stairs, spanned the western fork of the river upstream from the junction. After scooting across it, about eight feet above the flow, the soldiers turned left, moving in a single file until they came to the eastern fork. There they turned right and walked to the second footbridge, the plank.

Second Platoon slowed, briefly bunching up to allow the soldiers to cross, one by one, balancing on the slick board above noisy, cascading water.

Smith and Rodriguez stopped at the junction, in the center of the platoon. They would let one squad cross, then direct the rest of the platoon to the other side.

The first soldiers reached the opposite bank. It was a short uphill walk to the first terrace. Laneyal loomed overhead.

Soto crossed with the radio. They needed to leave this low ground fast; it was no place to loiter.

An IED exploded on the trail, blowing soldiers over and heaving a cone of smoky dirt into the air.

In the moment after, all was still. Soto had been stung with dirt and small stones. His ears rang. He realized he was alive.

The soldiers waiting to cross the bridge, exposed in the rocky riverbed, knew what to expect: the rest of the ambush. They bolted, sprinting for cover.

Bullets snapped down toward the trapped men. The din rose, building to a crescendo of fire. The radio antenna rising above Soto marked him as a target.

Soto pushed himself to his feet and ran, downstream, leaping over boulders as he gained speed. There was a pile of logs ahead. He headed there. Bullets smacked dirt and stone. Soto's antenna swung.

He reached the logs, finding cover among the wood. He took a knee and aimed his M4 up, looking for targets, and fired.

Beside the river junction, Rodriguez leaned into a dirt slope and radioed to the company.

"IED on the west side"—he corrected himself—"east side of the river, over."

The platoon was taking fire from every direction except within Aliabad. From his position in the center of it all, Rodriguez could see this fight was unusual. Ordinarily the Taliban did not shoot from houses; doing so invited mortars and air strikes on people's homes. Today they were shooting from homes in Donga, Darbart, and Laneyal, as well as the usual positions on the hills.

Viper Company reacted. Its machine guns and grenade launchers on the high ground answered back. Marines and Afghan soldiers from Vimoto were doing the same. Down in the riverbed, Specialist Oxman crouched behind a boulder and fired bursts from his machine gun, trying to give the soldiers across the river the opportunity to escape.

Smith called to the squad that had crossed the river. "Lead element, I need you to bound back," he said.

Rodriguez stopped him. He knew the patterns. He figured this would not last long. Once the Americans attained a superiority of fire, and aircraft showed up, the Taliban would vanish. It was too dangerous for the platoon to maneuver out of the riverbed before then. Its soldiers would have to expose themselves by wading the river or crossing the plank. He suggested to Smith that he wait.

Soto crouched with an American news photographer accompanying the patrol. The two men could hear the shooting but could not see who was firing. Their ears were buzzing from the blast. The river and gunfire drowned out other sound.

Smith shouted from the river junction.

"Stay there!" he screamed. "Stay! There!"

Soto could not hear him. He thought they were too vulnerable where they were. He needed to bring the radio to the platoon.

"We gotta move!" he shouted.

The two men stood and ran away from the woodpile, a few paces down the bank. They jumped into the river. The photographer hit the water first. It was chest-deep. The current was violent. It pushed him downstream and pulled him under until he found footing.

Soto followed him in.

Cold water wrapped around him like a blast. He felt the weight of his pack and radio working against him, and tried to stand. His feet found bottom. Soto kicked against the flow. A stone building stood across the river, less than one hundred feet away. Soldiers were huddled behind it. The photographer was headed there. Gunfire chattered. Soto pushed himself across the stream, struggling to stay upright, and not have the radio and plate carrier pull him down. The photographer cleared the water on the other side on all fours, scrambled upright, and ran to the waiting soldiers.

Soto reached the shore a few seconds behind, and dashed into place.

They were safe.

From Dallas, soldiers fired two Javelin missiles, one into a house in Darbart and another into a house in Laneyal. An Air Force sergeant notified Rodriguez by radio that a plane was about to release a 500-pound bomb.

"They're going to do the drop in, like, thirty seconds!" Rodriguez shouted to Smith. "Let your boys know!"

The bomb whooshed in and exploded, reverberating like thunder over the riverbed. A mushroom cloud rose where a building had been.

The company told Rodriguez over his radio that the plane had more ordnance. It would strike again.

Viper's firepower advantage was now established. The scattered pieces had come together.

After the second strike, the Taliban fire subsided. The platoon's enemies pulled back. Two rocket-propelled grenades flew down from the hill and zipped by the lieutenants. They struck the river-bank and exploded, far enough away from the soldiers that no one was hurt.

Smith told the soldiers pinned under Laneyal in the wheat field to be ready to withdraw. Rodriguez had made a good call. They had found a stone wall that offered protection and remained safe while the Americans massed their fires.

Now was their chance. They threw smoke grenades. As the plumes rose, obscuring them from sight, they retraced their steps along the trail. Rodriguez and Smith jogged forward from the slope they had been crouched against, and heaved a pair of smoke grenades near the plank bridge. More smoke billowed on the almost motionless air.

The soldiers reached the river's first fork, and crossed. Viper Two was contracting. Smith ordered the soldiers up into Aliabad. Winded and angry, covered in mud and drenched in rain and sweat, they climbed the steps and clustered in alleys on the slope. They slapped one another's backs and swore.

Roger Webb approached Soto. He had seen Soto in the kill zone, running for his life, then pinned behind the woodpile.

"Man, I thought—" Webb said.

Soto finished his sentence. "You thought I was gone?"

He flashed his big smile.

The mood lightened.

Corporal Sean Conroy, a Marine advising the Afghan soldiers at Vimoto, wandered through the platoon, followed by several Afghans in mismatched uniforms carrying warm machine guns and rifles. Conroy emanated the attitude of someone who enjoyed gunfights. He was often unshaven and out of uniform; sometimes he was shirtless and showed his tattoos. He and the Afghans had been firing into the villages to help the trapped platoon escape. Its soldiers were here around him, looking good. Conroy grinned and walked among them in a casual strut.

The platoon went through the ritual of a head count before returning to the outpost.

Squad and team leaders checked each man and tallied ammunition. Many had fired much of their load. Oxman had left the outpost with about eight hundred rounds for his machine gun. He was down to his last hundred, and in conservation mode. Another soldier had twisted his knee. He could barely walk.

A voice called out.

"Dewater?"

There was no answer.

"Hey, anyone seen Dewater?"

Soto looked around. *Dewater.*

Private First Class Richard Dewater was one of the platoon's combat replacements. There was no sign of him.

Shouts grew sharper. Where was Dewater?

Nausea swept over Soto. He radioed to the outpost, in case Dewater had somehow walked back. Word came back. Dewater was not at the outpost. He was MIA.

———

Captain Howell ordered action. He sent the Afghans to comb along the river, working upstream toward Aliabad, to see if Dewater had been swept away. He readied his other platoons to search villages on the east side. If Dewater had been captured they would scour every home and recover him before the Taliban could move him out of the valley. He sent Second Platoon back into the kill zone. Maybe Dewater was still there.

It was evening. Darkness was near. Zarin, the man who had told them the path was safe, had returned, and Rodriguez had told him to wait for questioning. He stood among the soldiers who remained in Aliabad as the rest of the platoon moved down the staircase again.

They suspected him of having led them into the ambush. "Fucking worm," one said. "I'd like to put a fucking bullet in that bastard." Zarin did not speak English. The hostility was palpable, clear no matter the tongue. He remained in place, waiting patiently, secure in the rules. He had heard American anger before.

On the way down to the river, Sergeant Tanner heard a soldier call out. Someone had found the buffer spring from an American rifle on the stairs. It was a distinctive part, and freshly oiled and clean. It meant a rifle had been broken apart and the spring had flown free.

This is bad, Tanner thought.

Down below, in the riverbed, Soto took point as the soldiers moved across the bridges. The sun set. The ambush site turned black.

The platoon spread through wheat fields, looking for signs. They found the blast hole. Was this where Dewater had been standing? Soto stood beside it, trying to work out what might have happened.

Where the fuck could this guy be?

Where?

This is where the attack started.

They had not seen any Taliban fighters down low on the trail. How could anyone have been captured?

"I found him," a voice said.

Soto spun around.

Sergeant Tanner was there. Dewater was not.

"Where?" Soto said. "Where is he?"

"Look up," Tanner said. He swung the beam of his flashlight overhead, into the branches of a tree.

Dewater's body hung from a branch. Tanner figured it was about two stories up. In a dimly lit glimpse Soto saw Dewater had only one leg. His uniform had been stained. He still wore his helmet. Its strap had held.

Soto went down to one knee. He raised his radio handset to his mouth.

"Break, break, break, break," he said, using the convention for interrupting all traffic with important information.

Dewater, he knew, had died instantly.

The frequency went silent, letting Second Platoon send its message. Smith was beside him. He took the radio.

"We found him," he said. He told Captain Howell that Dewater was in a tree and that the platoon would retrieve his remains and carry him back.

"Understand all," Howell replied.

Another sergeant, Matthew Kuhn, climbed up the trunk and worked Dewater free. The soldiers placed him in a litter and lifted him. Slowly, in a processional, they made their way across both forks of the river, up and over the muddy and slippery switchback trail, to the staircase. They stopped repeatedly, panting, struggling to keep their friend on the litter.

On the staircase, Afghan soldiers watched. One raised a camera. Something in Soto snapped. He stepped between the lens and Dewater's body.

"What the fuck you doing, man?" he shouted. "What do you think you're taking a picture of? We don't take pictures of you. Put that camera down."

There was a language barrier. Soto was not getting what he needed. The soldier stood there, seemingly unsure what Soto wanted. Soto shoved the man. "We'll fuck you up!" he said.

The Afghan soldier lowered the camera.

Soto seethed. He figured the soldier would sell the photograph. *What, motherfucker? You want to show that picture to your stupid-ass Taliban friends? And you think you're going to show that like it's a fucking victory? You killed one guy with an explosive. After we just killed like sixteen of your guys. You had a big, complicated ambush and after that explosion you couldn't even hit any of us?*

Fuck you.

Fuck you.

Get back.

The Afghan soldiers parted. Viper Two's processional reached the road and turned north, walking in the dark.

American troop numbers in Afghanistan in 2010 were rising toward 100,000, giving commanders more ground units to clear some of the most dangerous areas of the country—places where previously over-stretched forces had rarely gone. Troops called the push into Taliban badlands another surge, this one for Afghanistan. In Iraq, the American military withdrawal was accelerating. Units were packing up. The last combat brigade was to depart the country during 2010. The remaining troops were primarily for training and advising roles, and force numbers were to be reduced below 50,000 by the end of the year. The switch was clear in the casualty numbers. In 2009, the number of Americans killed in Afghanistan exceeded the number killed in Iraq for the first time since the war began in Iraq.

TEN

THE PUSH

Lieutenant Jarrod Neff and a Battle to Turn the Tide of the War

"No lieutenant has ever had to learn faster."

FEBRUARY 14, 2010
Marja, Afghanistan

First Lieutenant Jarrod Neff woke in the blackness before dawn, switched on a headlamp, and looked around the cold room where he had slept. It had been dark when he unrolled the sleeping bag a few hours before, and he had been so tired that he noticed little more than that he was in the company of Marines. Now he discovered that he had passed the night face-to-face with the skinned head of a goat. It stared up from a bowl beside him, guarded by mewling cats. Its cold eyes glittered in the flashlight beam, welcoming Neff to Valentine's Day.

The Afghan home where he had passed the night, listed on his map as Building 187, was a mud-walled compound in a field near a dirt road. It was one of two temporary outposts held by the infantry unit Neff commanded, First Platoon of Kilo Company, Third Battalion, Sixth Marines. The Marines knew little of the place beyond that they had chosen it for its location. A day before, helicopters had brought Kilo Company to the poppy fields of northern Marja, an irrigated area of Afghanistan's south-western steppe, and much of Neff's platoon had rushed into Building 187. Before the aircraft touched down, a study of satellite imagery told them that from inside they would be able to watch over a bridge and a cluster of shacks to the north. The shacks served as a bazaar, a small retail market for families on the farmland. The shacks and bridge were Kilo Company's conventional military objectives, the terrain it had been ordered to seize as part of the start of Operation Moshtarak, the most ambitious operation to date in the Marine Corps' Afghan campaign.

In a time of confusing counterinsurgency doctrine, in which American military actions typically were carried out on a small scale and with an ostensibly light touch, Operation Moshtarak was old-school stuff. It sprang from the conventional playbooks of an earlier generation: a helicopter insertion and an overland assault into a Taliban sanctuary to demonstrate that no place lay beyond American reach. Its ambitions were total: a riflemen's sweep of enemy-held ground to kill those who dared resist, the introduction of national police forces and a new governing order, the beginning of the end of the area's entrenched opium poppy trade. Among senior Marines, Moshtarak was spoken of with a sense of purpose resembling reverence and fate, a case of the Corps leading NATO to a new and higher crest in President Obama's Afghan surge.

Kilo's opening piece was simple. The bridge and bazaar near Building 187 were controlled by the Taliban. Kilo's Marines were to take them away. Such thinking matched an infantry unit's mentality and skills. Sergeants could circle the objectives on a map, go there, fight, and run up a new flag. To this straightforward action the military in Kabul had added a twist that blended public relations with a doctrinal shift. The ultimate purpose of the attack, it said, was to protect the Afghan population—whether the population wanted the protection or not.

Neff and his Marines were assigned a central role in January when they were told they would participate in the largest Marine helicopter assault since Vietnam. Their destination had an imposing aura. Marja, the briefings said, was an impregnable no-go zone, one of the most defiant Taliban strongholds in Afghanistan, and a challenge to the idea that the Corps could fully exert influence over Helmand Province. Its fall would augur a turning point in the war and fill new chapters in Marine Corps lore, signaling to the world that Afghanistan could be lifted from decades of conflict with the smart application of Western force.

The operation's opening day had been less violent than expected, and provided Neff with his first views of Afghanistan outside of bases and training ranges. Building 187 offered a picture of Afghan rural agrarian life, a meager assortment of dented pots, threadbare rugs, chests of brightly colored clothing, and a few pieces of furniture shared by a multi-generational family. There was no electricity. Outside, where a few goats and chickens ignored the Americans who had crowded in, the air was dry and bitingly cold. The platoon had converted the home to military use, superimposing over it the feel of a patrol base. Dim light rose from flash-lights and plastic chemical light sticks as Marines engaged in the ordinary activities of troops in the field. Some snored as they slumbered on the dirt floor, getting two or three hours of sleep. Others were on watch at porta-ble radios. Marines stood outdoors on post, weapons ready, facing out. A few hacked and coughed. For more than a week, a barracks infection had gripped the ranks.

Neff slipped into his equipment: flak vest with bulletproof plates, harness laden with a first-aid kit, ammunition and grenades, topographic map, and black-and-white satellite photographs of the roads and buildings outside. He looked at the goat head and guessed it had been left behind by the Afghan family that First Platoon had displaced the day before. The family must have killed it shortly before the Marines arrived.

The family had no way of knowing the home had been designated a Kilo Company objective at Camp Leatherneck, the big Marine Corps base. They did not know that the bazaar would be within range of the M240 machine guns, making their home a "support-by-fire" position, from where one set of grunts could watch over the bazaar while others advanced across open ground. But to the Marines this was Tactics 101, and so early the previous morning a group of Neff's Marines and several Afghan soldiers had hustled from the helicopters to the compound's door. The family spanned three generations: an elderly man, an adult son, and their wives and young children. They gazed at the Americans.

Neff had a platoon to run. He was supposed to be sweeping the ground between the other platoons and the bridge. Kilo Company's exec-utive officer, First Lieutenant Cory Colistra, met with the family's elder,

Haji Mohammad Karim, to explain what was happening, and why a foreign military force had just commandeered a private home. Via an Afghan interpreter, Colistra said the Marines planned to stay briefly and would leave once the bazaar was secure. He offered the family sole use of a few of the house's rooms, and promised they would be undisturbed.

"You're safe here," he said. "We will be here. We will not look at or talk to your wives, and we will respect you."

The Afghan men listened. Colistra waited as they conferred.

Marines had searched the home and not found any weapons.

They're farmers, Colistra thought.

These men might work with the Taliban or local drug bosses, but there was no outward sign of them being combatants. They were the people Operation Moshtarak was supposed to help.

Colistra hoped they would accept his offer. Kilo Company had fanned out from multiple landing zones, and Colistra knew the plan. Most of them would converge around these fields soon. Fighting was inevitable, but no Taliban force was going to overwhelm the Americans in strongpoints like the one Neff's platoon had made in Building 187. If the family left, they would be at greater risk outside. Colistra told the elder that the Marines meant him no harm.

"We are here not to hurt you but to help you, to protect you from the Taliban," he said. "We need to find the Taliban and neutralize them."

Mohammad Karim was composed. His demeanor betrayed neither fear nor outrage. The interpreter provided Colistra his reply.

"We are farmers and we don't know any Taliban, and we need to get the women and children out of here," he said.

Colistra said he could not allow the younger man to leave, and if the women and children departed, they would be on their own. He asked them to reconsider.

Mohammad Karim was firm. The women and children would move, he said, until the Americans left.

After the sun rose, the women gathered the children and hurried out the gate. They were about ten people. Some of the children were small—toddler-sized or just older. They proceeded across the fields to the next building, Building 284 on the Marines' map. It was perhaps four hundred yards away. The road and trails outside were empty, devoid of human life. The population was hiding. Brushed by wind, the landscape seemed ghostly.

Officially, the Marines called Marja a town, sometimes even a city. It resembled neither. It was an expanse of lone compounds and small hamlets surrounded by flat steppe that had been made arable by irrigation canals built with American Cold War funds decades before. The canals carried water from the Helmand River, which ran a serpentine course through the province. As part of the project, Pashtun families had been given land grants in the newly tillable fields. Generations later their descendants remained, and the project had taken an unforeseen shape, enabling crime at an international scale. Marja was an opium poppy belt. The latest generation of American officials, the inheritors of a problem a previous generation of American officials had made, said the opium trade served as an economic engine for the Taliban, and was guarded and ruled by fighters. Colistra called it a hornet's nest, necessitating a large Marine attack for the Afghan government to move in.

After the women and their children left, Neff moved with First Squad, led by Sergeant Wesley Laney, through clusters of crude buildings surrounded by fields. Many fields were bare. Others were covered with the ankle-high leaves of recently sprouted poppy plants. Neff and his squad walked briskly. They were scouring for the Taliban, waiting for the rest of Kilo Company to appear.

By the ordinary means that the Marine Corps manages its officers, Neff was not supposed to be there. He was an intelligence officer by profession, not an infantry officer, and had not been placed in charge of a platoon when he joined Third Battalion, Sixth Marines, in late 2008. The battalion had recently returned from Iraq. Neff took up duties as a staff officer working in its intelligence shop and had no thought of commanding a rifle platoon. Even an Afghan tour was not ensured. Throughout 2009, rumors circulated that the battalion might be sent on a six-month rotation in Okinawa and miss the Afghan war outright.

Even wars managed by bureaucracies are prone to surprises. Late in 2009, as the battalion was in its final pre-deployment preparations, the infantry lieutenant leading Kilo Company's First Platoon was stopped by the police in North Carolina and charged with driving while intoxicated. Neff was passing a night as the duty officer at the headquarters when the battalion commander, Lieutenant Colonel Brian Christmas, showed up at his door.

Christmas was an energetic man with a strong Marine bloodline. His father had commanded a rifle company during the Battle of Hue City in Vietnam, was gravely wounded, and was awarded the Navy Cross for heroism. He rose to the general ranks. Both Brian and his brother James had become Marine infantry officers, too. Brian had an offer for Neff.

"We have a platoon commander position opening up," he said. "Do you want it?"

Neff knew which platoon was available, and why. He also knew that the colonel's offer was a vote of confidence. The Marine Corps infantry worked like a club; not just anyone was allowed in. He did not let emotion run ahead of him.

"It depends, sir," he said. "It depends on what we're doing."

Neff asked if the battalion was going to Afghanistan. If it was, he said, he was interested. If it was headed to Okinawa, he was not.

Christmas looked displeased. He told Neff that he did not know where the battalion would deploy, but either way the platoon needed to be led. He gave Neff until the end of the day to decide.

Neff was different from many Marine officers. He had signed up in search of something beyond the Corps, and had no plans for a military career. A native of Everett, Massachusetts, he played four years as a linebacker and tight end on his high school football team, and thought often of joining the military. His father had served two tours in the Army Air Cavalry in Vietnam, including one as a door gunner. Neff was raised watching war movies, intrigued and excited about enlisting, too. He and a friend had discussed joining the Corps after graduation in 1998. His friend signed up. Neff opted out. He had been recruited to play football at Stonehill College in Easton, Massachusetts, and enrolled in the criminal-justice degree program there. He was six feet two inches and 200 pounds, and planned to pursue a law-enforcement career.

He graduated to a tight job market and a country fighting two wars.

Neff submitted applications to local police departments but came nowhere near getting hired. Two uncles and two cousins had jobs as police officers or firefighters in Massachusetts. Insider connections did not help. He took a position as a security guard, hoping it would gain him the experience needed for a police job. He worked for two years as an unarmed guard at the Prudential Center, then started as an armed guard at the John F. Kennedy Federal Building in downtown Boston. But as the years passed, his prospects grew worse. The departments to which he was applying gave preferential points to military veterans, and by 2005, when Neff had two years of security-industry experience, the wars in Afghanistan and Iraq were churning out war veterans. Neff could not compete. He was passed over repeatedly.

In late 2006, Neff was at work with two former Marines who were in line ahead of him for Massachusetts police jobs. One of them suggested that if he really wanted to be hired then he should do a military tour, too. Neff accepted the advice and opted for the hardest route he knew: joining the Marines. If he were to do this, he would do it full bore. In early 2007 he met with a Marine captain who ran the Corps' officer recruiting in Boston. The captain had him step on a scale and told him he would have to lose ten pounds to meet weight standards. Neff put himself through preseason football routines and in March showed up to his physical at 230 pounds, within the weight standard allowed for his big frame. He was offered a slot at officer candidate school in June.

Neff graduated late that summer and moved over to the school for new lieutenants, where he sought an assignment to the military police. But the Corps had only one MP position for 250 lieutenants and gave it to another officer. He opted for a ground intelligence job. The position required two more schools, one a grueling field-and-weapons course with infantry officers, the other learning the intelligence trade. At the infantry course he finished fifth out of dozens of officers at the opening day's endurance test taken while carrying a combat load. He was not fast, but he was a bull when weighted down, and could outlast many peers. He reported to Third Battalion, Sixth Marines, in late 2008, figuring he would deploy on the battalion staff, return to the States, pick up his honorable discharge, and move to the front of the line at a police academy back home.

The Marine Corps is dominated by its infantry officers, college-educated Marines who have been told that they and the grunts under their command are the center of their service and the reason all of the support jobs exist. Lieutenants in infantry battalions who do not come from the infantry school or who work on the staff—those who specialize in communications, logistics, and transportation—sometimes labor in the shadows of these peers. But at least one of the battalion's infantry lieutenants, Cory Colistra, liked what he saw in Neff.

Colistra, who had deployed once to Iraq, played football at the Naval Academy, and had decided over time that a jock personality did not always translate well to the seriousness of war. He first met Neff at a party. Neff wore his college football sweatshirt. Inwardly, Colistra sagged. He knew the type. *This guy is going to be a jerk,* he thought. Colistra started a conversation and discovered Neff did not match the stereotype. He was a listener more than a talker and maintained a quiet bearing after a few beers. Neff was twenty-nine, older than most other lieutenants. Colistra thought it showed. He left the party telling himself, *I can work with this guy.*

After the First Platoon commander was arrested for drunken driving, Colistra approached Kilo's company commander, Captain Joshua Biggers, and suggested he lobby Colonel Christmas to have Neff transferred to the vacant platoon. The company would be deploying soon. Most of the unit training had been completed. Whoever was assigned to the platoon would have only a few weeks before they shipped out, and no time at all in the field. Colistra told Biggers that Neff seemed like someone they could coach, a mature officer who would take advice.

"Sir," Colistra said, "I think Jarrod would be a great fit."

After Christmas offered Neff the job, Colistra followed up, pushing Neff to accept it. Before he left that day, Neff had agreed.

The next day Neff stepped in front of First Platoon. Its Marines were waiting for him outside their barracks in a semicircle, warily assessing their new officer. Neff had left a meeting with Biggers, who told him he would succeed only if he jelled with his Marines, who might not accept him at first.

Be humble, Biggers told him. Learn from your Marines.

The platoon was not privy to this, and waited skeptically. Many of the Marines were inexperienced themselves. They had come to the battalion straight from boot camp and their own infantry course, and wanted a boss with real experience in a rifle company. All around Camp Lejeune, units were being sent to Afghanistan, and these Marines hoped their battalion would be sent there soon, too. There would be no time to break in an officer.

The older Marines, those who returned from Iraq the previous year, were frustrated by stateside life. Their stay at home, they thought, had gone on too long. The veterans had passed too many drunken nights. They wondered if First Platoon had lost its edge. When they heard that their old lieutenant had gotten jammed up by the police, they dreaded the idea of having to figure out a replacement. Kilo Company was shorthanded and had already been told to expect new Marines from the infantry school to arrive before deployment. They spoke of the idea derisively. "Christmas presents," they called anyone who would check into the unit right before it deployed. *Boots*, they said, using their service's derisive term. Nobody wanted to go to war with boots. Now they found out they were not going to be led by a grunt. The ill will was deepened by recent history. A Marine in First Platoon had been arrested for drunken driving a few weeks before, and the old lieutenant punished everyone else with a thrashing—an especially hard physical-training session. Now that same lieutenant had been caught in a drinking incident of his own, and the battalion was cycling in a fresh face. There is an ordinary level of hostility to any newcomer in a platoon. But this case seemed extreme. Talk in the barracks was unkind.

We're getting an intelligence officer? This is what we're going to Afghanistan with—an officer who has been sitting behind a desk?

Sergeant Laney, the first squad leader and the Marine in the platoon with the most experience in combat, found the entire situation absurd. *This is just wrong*, he thought.

Neff knew he'd never bluff his way past thirty grunts. He kept it brief. He introduced himself and said he knew what they were thinking.

"I'm not coming to you from the infantry," he said, "I'm coming to you from the S-2 shop." He let that sink in. "I'm not going to pretend to know everything, because I don't," he added. He spoke bluntly. "So I'm going to stay out of your shit. The platoon sergeant will be the platoon sergeant, and the squad leaders will be the squad leaders, and that's how it will be."

He did not tell the platoon that he had graduated from the same infantry course that all Marine rifle platoon commanders attend, or how he had outperformed many officers there. It was an important point. It meant he was just as certified, and had as much technical and tactical training, as any lieutenant they would get, even if he had spent most of his brief career in an office. But now was not the time to play a qualification card. These Marines would not care how he did in school. He had missed their workup. He'd be accepted only if he performed.

He returned to his theme: The platoon's sergeants, and its veterans from Iraq, would wield the authority they deserved. "The only time I am going to step in is if I don't think something is right, or if something is going off the plan," he said.

"Now, anybody with a joke about the Red Sox can come talk with me personally."

This much, he knew, was unlikely. He was the biggest man in the platoon.

He left the semicircle and headed to his new office.

Some of the Marines gave him a nickname: "Masshole." It matched his Boston accent and was a worthy label for any officer boss. Others gathered in the barracks, wondering whether they had just been impressed. Their new lieutenant said he would look to them for guidance. He did not act like some of the medal chasers they knew. Maybe, they thought, First Platoon would be okay.

The next morning Neff was on base early, determined to stay low-key. He was so determined not to draw attention to himself that he withheld news of his new assignment from his girlfriend and his family. They had no idea he had taken one of the most dangerous jobs in the Corps. As far as they knew, he remained at his desk on the battalion staff. Neff did not want to trouble them, and had enough on his mind. He had a rifle platoon to lead and had to figure out how.

The rumors of the battalion's next assignment were replaced with orders: It would be going to Helmand Province, Afghanistan, after the new year, so soon that there would not be time for Neff and his platoon to work together in the field.

Captain Biggers arranged tactical decision games, in which Neff and the platoon sergeant, Staff Sergeant Matthew Dalrymple, could talk through missions with their squad leaders and practice planning, issuing orders, and organizing fire support and medevacs. Biggers had been enlisted before becoming an officer, and knew what made platoons work— getting the noncommissioned officers in sync with the lieutenant. He pulled Dalrymple aside and asked him to do all he could. They would be in Afghanistan in a blink. "This is a very tough situation," he said. "No lieutenant has ever had to learn faster. Help the dude out."

A few weeks before the battalion was to depart, Colonel Christmas ordered all the lieutenants to report to work on a weekday well before sunrise. He wanted to test their skills and talk with them about the tour ahead. About thirty young officers showed up. One was late and smelled of alcohol. Christmas stood in the darkness, in running shoes and shorts, and told them to follow him. He did not address the lieutenant who had been drinking. He knew what would happen.

Christmas began to run.

He set a quick pace, starting at a six-and-a-half-minute mile. Most Marine infantry lieutenants are fit; many are exceptionally so. Almost all of the battalion's platoon commanders kept tight. The officer who had been drinking soon straggled, then fell far behind. Christmas said nothing. He maintained his pace, running until reaching a point about two and a half miles away. There he turned around and headed back. He ran past the straggler wordlessly. About a mile from the battalion's headquarters, Christmas kicked into higher gear and pounded out a faster pace. Many of the lieutenants still hung at his heels, striding behind their commander in the predawn glow. Others could not keep up. This group stretched behind like an accordion. Among them was Neff. He was sober and fit but large. He could not run at the same pace as the smaller men.

Back at the battalion area, Colonel Christmas stared at those who were behind. They trickled in over the course of a few minutes.

When the group was intact, Christmas gave a brief speech. The battalion was headed to combat, he said, and its officers needed to lead. Marines deserved officers who would be in front in everything they did, and ready for anything they might face. He walked the lieutenants to a display of equipment and ordered them to demonstrate that they could assemble and operate the battalion's suite of radios and weapons, and call for a simulated artillery mission or air strike.

The commander departed, having made his point.

Neff remained. His knowledge of the battalion's weapons was high; his infantry-school training came back. He passed all the drills, including those that tested his skills at calling for fire support or arranging for casualty evacuation. He left determined to work on the medevac procedures even more. *That's an important one,* he told himself. *I need to be savvy at that.*

Kilo Company arrived at Camp Bastion just after 3:00 A.M. on January 10, descending to NATO's main base in southwestern Afghanistan on a flight from Kyrgyzstan. The landscape was almost unlit. It looked as empty and uninhabited as the surface of a moon. It was as if the company had "gone back in time about 10,000 years" in "only an hour and a half," one Marine wrote in his journal. Their combat tour had begun.

Bastion and the attached Marine Corps base, Camp Leatherneck, formed an expanse of runways, plywood shacks, and tents. Ringed by walls and wire and guarded by towers, the complex was an on-ramp to an invigorated war. Under the Obama administration's plan, the Marine Corps had shifted its attention from western Iraq to Helmand Province and was pushing its units through. Marine infantry battalions tended to serve seven-month tours and operate at a fast pace. By 2010, as Kilo landed, many battalions were relieving others, inheriting areas that had already seen an American presence. This was not to be Kilo Company's fate. The Corps had spent much of the previous year preparing for its assault into Marja. The attack was planned for February, and Kilo was to be one of two companies that would be helicoptered in ahead of the main force—dropped onto Taliban ground to capture and hold part of the main road network until other units arrived.

Kilo's Marines began preparing, first with classes on detecting hidden bombs and on the rules of engagement, which a Marine lawyer told them would be relaxed, giving them greater latitude to fight. Next came weapons training and tactical drills. On January 17 the company was flown to another Marine base, Camp Dwyer, which was home to an Afghan National Army force. There the company met the Afghan soldiers who would join it in the assault, and began side-by-side training.

Outside the base, the Americans had built shooting ranges where grunts could adjust the day and night sights on their weapons and do combat drills. For the first time Neff had a chance to observe his squads maneuver and to see his team leaders act. He had expected this to be an important day, perhaps his only chance to see how his squads worked under arms. But his eyes were drawn less to his own platoon than to the contrast between Kilo Company and its Afghan counterparts, who seemed almost untrained.

This is not good, he thought.

The war was nearly a decade old. The United States had spent billions of dollars on Afghanistan's military and police forces. Senior officers and spokespeople in Kabul and Washington spoke of Afghan units as partners who would lead Afghanistan out of gangsterism and war. The Afghans Neff saw bore little resemblance to what he had heard. They were marginally equipped and poorly led. Many did not aim their weapons when they fired; they pointed barrels in the general direction of targets and pulled the trigger, doing little more than wasting ammunition and making noise. The one clear accomplishment of their American-led training had been to teach them the English language's foulest words. Neff noted exceptions. A few soldiers were in possession of basic military skills, and when they spoke through interpreters they had powerful personal stories, of families in remote provinces whom their army wages would feed.

But Neff had a bad feeling. The Afghan platoon did not function as a platoon. Its soldiers did not have night-vision equipment. They relied on the Marines for food, water, and nearly everything else. They were in infrequent communication with their higher units and had little awareness of what other Afghan platoons might be doing. They all but destroyed Kilo Company's portable toilets, soiling them with feces. And their leader did not seem concerned: As long as his soldiers acted as his servants, he was in good cheer. Some of the Marines suspected the Afghan platoon of harboring spies. Lance Corporal Niall Swider, a member of Third Squad, picked out one Afghan soldier as an informant. Each day he sat in the Marines' smoke pit for hours, not smoking, just listening. Staff Sergeant Dalrymple watched the Afghan platoon closely and decided that its greatest competency was as part of the enemy's infiltration operation. It carried moles hardwired into an American force. He shared as little information with the Afghans as he could. As Operation Moshtarak approached, he withheld details of the Marja plans, lest they immediately travel to the Taliban.

———

As the day for the assault neared, intelligence officers and Special Forces soldiers met Kilo's officers and senior noncommissioned officers for briefings on the Taliban's numbers and tactics, and to show them a videotape a confidential source had made of the Afghan bazaar. The source had driven through Marja on a moped with a hidden camera attached. The militants, according to the briefing, had toggled in and out of sight, setting up temporary roadblocks to search cars, then disappearing into the population. In all, Kilo was told, they could expect a Taliban force of hundreds of men organized into small groups, each familiar with its own turf. These cells had mastered the use of hidden bombs, including how to install pressure plates in roads and doorways and place explosives in walls that would decapitate people passing by. Some of them had machine guns, including heavy machine guns that might knock helicopters from the air. When American reconnaissance units had probed Marja's edges by day, they were typically discovered and met by reaction forces, often within ten or fifteen minutes. At the tactical level, the briefers said, the Taliban was impressively organized.

The platoons received maps and satellite image printouts called gridded reference graphics, or GRGs, of the area where helicopters would leave them. Kilo's area covered two large GRG sheets, about seven and a half kilometers across. It included a dirt highway that led toward Lashkar Gah, the provincial capital, about twenty miles to the east. A radio tower overlooked the bazaar, and a dirt road headed south into the poppy zone. Other paths formed a matrix of motorcycle and farm-tractor trails.

Plans sharpened. Kilo was to land by darkness. A rifle company from another battalion from Lejeune, First Battalion, Sixth Marines, would be flown to the south at roughly the same time. Other companies would approach Marja overland from the open desert, eventually linking up with those flown in on the first day. No one knew how long it would take, but Kilo expected to be surrounded and alone for days. Once the initial fighting ended, the two battalions would establish headquarters and disperse their forces to build small outposts and patrol bases from which to reach out to farmers and their families. This last phase was intended to create what General Stanley McChrystal, the war's latest American commander, dubbed a "government in a box"—a small official Afghan presence under American protection. In the eyes of the brass, eager to signal that the war was making progress and the host government was competent, this Afghan participation was critical—so critical that it became the basis of a lie: According to the public-relations talking points in Kabul, the Afghan military would lead the whole operation. This was crude propaganda. Everyone in Kilo knew it. Operation Moshtarak was shaping up to be a Marine operation with a few Afghan soldiers in tow.

Kilo Company had more pressing matters with which to concern itself. Its young Marines were getting their first exposure to war via reports of casualties outside the base, including an IED that killed two Marines and wounded others from First Battalion, Sixth Marines, on January 24. These Marines had been chased into a trap. They had come under fire and sought cover in a building that had been rigged to blow. It was a chilling report, a detailing of foes capable of anticipating American movements and preparing complex defenses and attacks. Two days after hearing of it, several of Neff's Marines watched an armored truck that had been damaged by a buried bomb being towed onto the base. Only two of eight wheels remained on the mine roller on its front end. Helmand was becoming a meat grinder, and they were about to plunge into one of its most dangerous areas. And many of Kilo's Marines were unwell, weakened by bronchitis and strep throat—illnesses that spread in the close quarters of tent life.

The company was a mix of contradictory moods. Some were excited. *This is happening,* thought Corporal Ray "Chief" Charfauros, who led one of First Platoon's squads. *This is crazy.* Others felt dread. *We're flying into antiaircraft fire, and we might land in a minefield,* thought Edwin Harger, one of First Platoon's corpsmen. He spent his days gathering bandages and mentally preparing for the trauma aid he expected to be giving to his friends. For Lance Corporal Mark Hummel, a team leader in First Squad, everything he had heard told him that Kilo Company might be outgunned—an unusual worry for a large unit at this late date in the war. *There's a thousand Taliban waiting for us,* he thought. Marines were given instructions to make arrangements for their own deaths. "Write your letters," they were told. "Write your letters home."

By early February, Kilo Company's plans assumed final shape. The bridge, the bazaar, the hilltop with the radio tower—these were judged essential to controlling Marja's main road. The helicopters carrying Kilo Company would not land directly on them. Their landing zones would be offset in farmers' fields, to avoid bombs or air defenses.

First Platoon, led by Neff, would land closest to the highway in a landing zone called Eagle. One rifle squad and a machine-gun squad would seize the small farming and residential compound, labeled Building 187. Another rifle squad would head southeast, to a compound along the road, labeled Building 316, where they would block an intersection to prevent Taliban fighters from hitting the company's flank. Neff and the remaining squad would spend the first hours ensuring the others were in place and then clear a route to the bridge for the rest of Kilo Company, which was landing to the west. He would have about seventy Marines or sailors under his command—his three squads plus machine gunners, a Javelin missile detachment, corpsmen, snipers, and others from intelligence and radio intercept units. An Afghan squad would fly with the platoon, too.

The Marines were told to be ready to attack by February 12. On February 6, while they were rehearsing at Camp Dwyer, two tilt-rotor Ospreys landed beside them. Out stepped General James T. Conway, the commandant of the Marine Corps. The company gathered for a pep talk. The commandant's appearance surprised Neff. *This is a bigger deal than I knew,* he thought. At the platoon level, where practicalities mattered more than platitudes, not everyone was impressed. Some Marines groused that they were being flown into Marja with so much equipment they would hardly be able to move. "Didn't leave a warm and fuzzy in me whatsoever," Swider wrote in his journal that night. "They have turned us into

human pack mules for the push." Swider estimated that his load topped ·
145 pounds.

On February 10 Kilo Company flew back to Camp Leatherneck,
moved into large rectangular tents with rows of cots, and was locked
down—sequestered before the assault. The Marines and Afghan soldiers
were allowed to visit only the chow hall and portable toilets. Lights were
switched off at 10:00 P.M. Marines were ordered to sleep while they could.
Speaking was forbidden until morning—a rule that forced an anxious
unit to rest. Kilo had reached the end of its pre-combat preparations. Each
night, with the young men wondering if these nights were their last, Marines on duty paced the aisles between the cots with flashlights, ensuring
that the company slept and deterring Afghan soldiers from stealing gear.
The hours stretched long. The stillness was broken only by the footsteps
of the guards and the wet coughs of the company's sick troops.

For three days the company waited. The moon phase and weather were
right. NATO was dropping leaflets from planes and broadcasting radio
messages urging civilians to remain in their homes and to avoid helping
the Taliban. The Marine Corps had been giving repeated notice during
the run-up that it planned to assault Marja, hoping that the area's elders
might broker a deal to allow the Afghan government to enter the poppy
production zone without force. The outreach failed. The message was
now different: *We're coming, so stay inside.* Neff and his platoon reviewed
plans, talked over the maps, played cards, and read books. Sick men rested,
hoping any delay would grant time for fevers to recede and lungs to clear.

On the evening of February 12, Captain Biggers told the Marines
their wait was over. After one last warm meal in the chow hall, the platoons dressed for battle and boarded old buses for the drive to the cold
landing strip. Hours passed. After a shivering wait in darkness, and a short
meeting with the pilots, Marines and Afghan troops crowded onto aircraft. Each man carried a pack that felt like an anvil. The first Marines
found seats. But as more filed in, they added more equipment: spare ammunition, explosive charges for breaching lanes in minefields, five-gallon
jerry cans of water. The aircraft was overstuffed. No seats remained. More
people were still pushing in from outside. The aisle between the benches

that ran the aircraft's length had already filled with equipment and with ladders for crossing canals and scaling walls. The last Marines climbed onto the pile. They would ride like cargo. Neff was in the front, farthest from the tail ramp—a position from where he could wear a headset and talk with the aircrew. Standing upright, encased in a shifting pile of backpacks, weapons, and men, he was immobilized. He felt almost crushed.

The helicopters rose, banked slowly, gained speed, and moved in formation through the night. One aircraft was so crowded that Corporal Charfauros dangled his feet over the tail ramp, arms interlocked with Swider's, whose grip saved him from falling to the earth.

Neff pushed his night-vision monocular over his shooting eye and looked across the aircraft's interior. The faces of his Marines and Afghan soldiers were focused and set. After a half-hour flight he'd be leading them for the first time in the field. His first patrol would be in one of the largest operations of the war. Captain Biggers had joked that he was like a football player whose first game was the Super Bowl.

The helicopters passed over the arid flatland. Kilo was aware that its foes were waiting and may have been tipped off by Afghan soldiers. Would the Taliban know the landing zones? Would they have machine guns at the edges of the farmland? Neff liked this possibility the least of all—to lose Marines in a fiery crash before reaching the fight. But he figured the chances were small. The Taliban possessed many machine guns. And there had been a complex ambush with heat-seeking shoulder-fired missiles in 2007 in Helmand Province that had claimed a NATO helicopter and killed seven Western troops. But now, in the cold hours between midnight and dawn, only a disciplined force would be organized enough to defend a large area in the dark. And the Taliban often avoided night combat. Its fighters lacked night-vision equipment and were vulnerable to Western forces' thermal sights. Neff expected something else: Their local cells would have put belts of IEDs at the places they expected the Marines to try to claim, and would have cut firing ports— murder holes—in walls and buildings from which to fire on the Marines after they landed. The Taliban would fight the way they knew how. Neff watched the flat terrain roll by below, waiting for the dash out into the poppy field.

The helicopters passed above the first canal of Marja's outer ring.

Neff's view changed from pale sand to dark tilled fields. The canal was a twinkling black line between worlds. Neff saw mud-walled compounds, and dirt trails, and warrens of short walls. It was all perhaps one hundred feet below. It seemed utterly still. No one fired up.

The aircraft turned to descend. Dark earth rushed up. Wheels settled down.

Shouts rose over engine noise. "Go! Go! Go!"

The space around Neff loosened as everyone ran out the back ramp. He charged behind them, leaping onto damp soil and running for about twenty yards until clear of the helicopter's rotors. He looked back. Only the door gunners remained behind. In Marine jargon, the landing zone was cold. Kilo had met no resistance. The door gunners had not fired a shot. The aircraft rose on a cold blast of rotor wash and bitter exhaust, and vanished from view. Operation Moshtarak had begun.

First Platoon was arrayed in a rough circle. The air was hushed. The ground was damp and furrowed. Through Neff's night-vision monocular it looked like green frozen waves. His radio crackled with information: The rest of the company had landed to the west. Kilo Company was on the ground. He needed to pass up a report.

Neff asked for a head count and discovered an ordinary level of infantry confusion. One of the interpreters was missing; he had run from the helicopter to the wrong squad. Afghan soldiers, who did not have night-vision equipment, were huddled in hesitant knots, unsure what to do. The platoon was solving its problems without its lieutenant. Marines were already rounding up the Afghan soldiers and arranging them in columns. Others tracked down the interpreter and put him with the right squad. Neff called the company and told them First Platoon was in place with all of its people.

Neff knew that the aircraft had woken everyone up, probably for miles. All through Marja civilians would be waiting for the Americans' next move. And the Taliban would know where First Platoon was. If the platoon stayed put, Neff expected it would come under fire. The field had been freshly pumped with water; its mud was soft and clingy. The Marines were burdened by heavy equipment, and on ground upon which it would be hard to run. Neff gave word for the squads to leave the landing zone.

With First and Third Squads, he set off to the south to claim Building 316. Marines led Afghan soldiers by hand through the night.

Colistra, the executive officer, and Second Squad headed north to Building 187 and entered it, finding a nervous family. Through the interpreter, he told them that the Americans would be operating in the area and urged them to stay inside for a few days.

Charfauros's squad entered Building 316. A family was huddled inside, too. Several Marines took posts along the walls, looking out and over. To the south was a larger hamlet with a dense cluster of houses. Through night-vision devices it looked empty. Nothing moved there.

The head of household was a sullen young man, and as Marines scoured the compound for weapons, they found photographs of him posing with armed men. They looked like a motorcycle gang with Kalashnikovs and RPGs. *This guy's shady,* Charfauros thought. *He's Taliban.*

The man answered few questions.

Through an interpreter, Charfauros told him that his family could leave but he could not. The man's wife and children gathered a few belongings and headed for the hamlet to the south. Charfauros ordered the man to be zip-tied and held in a room.

A Marine who worked in civil affairs interrupted.

"You can't do that," he said.

Charfauros looked at the Marine coldly. He was not part of Kilo Company. He was temporarily assigned for the operation. Charfauros barely knew him and did not like being undercut.

"This is my mission," he said. "You're just an attachment."

Charfauros was not going to have a Talib loose among his squad and would not release the man to tell his friends where the Marines were and how many men and weapons they had.

The squad lashed the man's wrists tight, led him to a room, and placed him under guard, out of sight.

A short while later, while searching the perimeter of the compound, Charfauros found a loose string in the field near the gate. He had been raised on a farm in Alabama and thought the string had been left behind by a farmer after using it to line up rows of crops at seeding time. He had reached down to roll it up.

An explosion erupted on the road, knocking him to the ground, peppering him with dirt. He rolled over and checked the Marines with him. No one had been injured. They had been just far enough away.

Laughter and curses gave way to recognition. The Taliban had prepared defenses and the road was booby-trapped.

Later that morning, Charfauros looked outside and saw a line of Afghan men staring at the compound. They were unarmed. The Marines stared back. It was an odd standoff, an encounter made possible by American rules of engagement: As long as these men were not carrying arms, the Marines did not have authority to shoot. The two sides looked at each other coldly, sizing each other up.

Kilo had landed in Marja unchallenged, and the Taliban had not started to fight. While Charfauros's squad faced the line of Afghan men, Colistra was in Building 187, trying to convince the family to stay put, and Neff was with First Squad, going from home to home.

To their west, beyond a slight rise, the rest of Kilo Company was doing the same things. Marines were searching compounds and choosing temporary bases, caching their equipment and readying for the push to the bridge. Afghan men on motorcycles moved in the distance. Others watched the Marines over walls. It went on throughout the morning, as if their enemies were tallying the Americans' numbers and mapping their whereabouts.

By late afternoon the watchers were less numerous. Enemy gunfire began, directed at Charfauros and his squad in Building 316 and at Marines in the company's positions to the west. Mostly it was scattered shooting from a few hundred yards away. By evening, First Platoon's radios carried news that Third Platoon had been skirmishing to the west and that part of Second Platoon had been ambushed. The Taliban knew the Marines' locations. But so far its marksmanship was poor. No one had been hurt.

Captain Biggers called Neff on the encrypted radio with orders: Kilo would link up with Neff at a compound southwest of the bridge in the morning, and Second Platoon would assault the bazaar while Neff's Marines stood ready with covering fire.

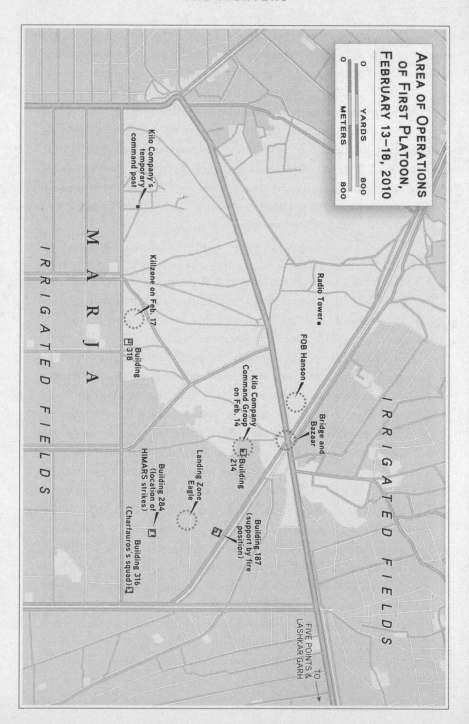

AREA OF OPERATIONS
OF FIRST PLATOON,
FEBRUARY 13–18, 2010

0   YARDS   800
0   METERS 800

Kilo Company's
temporary
command post

M A R J A

I R R I G A T E D   F I E L D S

Killzone on Feb. 17

Building
318

Radio Tower

FOB Hanson

Kilo Company
Command Group
on Feb. 14

Bridge and
Bazaar

Building
214

I R R I G A T E D   F I E L D S

Landing Zone
Eagle

Building 284
(location of
HIMARS strikes)

Building 187
(support by fire
position)

Building 316
(Charlauros's squad)

FIVE POINTS &
LASHKAR GARH

TO

The company settled in for the night, ringed in by foes, its Marines on watch with night-vision devices.

———————

Neff woke ahead of the sun and gathered First Squad for the walk to meet Biggers and Second Platoon. The morning was cold and windy. The squad stepped out into breeze. First it checked compounds around the landing zone to make sure no Taliban had moved close overnight. At Building 284 it was greeted by an old man and the displaced family that had opted to leave its home when Colistra and Second Squad moved in. Neff had slept beside the head of their goat. The man wore a gray coat over a white robe, and had dark brows over a pale beard. Through an interpreter, Neff told him the Marines hoped not to occupy the home across the field for long, and that the family would be able to move back soon. A few women milled about, keeping distance from the Americans. Children watched. All seemed calm.

Across the landing zone to the west, the ground climbed slightly uphill. A small hamlet rested on the knoll. First Squad spread out and crossed the open expanse. It stopped at a compound, Building 214, near where Neff planned to meet Kilo's assault force.

The hamlet looked like a suitable place from which Lieutenant Gordon Emmanuel, who led Second Platoon, could push for the bridge. The compound Neff chose had been planted with poppies, which rose to the Marines' shins. It resembled bright green lettuce. Another old man stood near the entrance. Children gathered around him. They greeted the Marines with smiles, amused by the big foreigners. Some of them chased each other in a game of tag. The easy vibe was a good sign. Neff felt safe. This would be a good spot for a linkup. The second day in Marja was proceeding according to plan.

Marines from Second Platoon began to appear in the hamlet and filed into the compound. The lead Marines had a metal detector and had swept their path for IEDs. It was about 8:30 in the morning. Northern Marja, so far, was the battle that wasn't.

Squads took positions along low outer walls, which offered commanding vistas across to Building 187, where the support-by-fire position was ready to cover Second Platoon's next move, and to the southeast, about a kilometer away, where Corporal Charfauros and his squad held the company's flank. The wind blew strong and cold, pushing dust. Marines scanned for threats. Several other buildings stood on the steppe. The canal running east–west to the south marked a line of demarcation. Beyond the canal, anyone could move unchallenged. Vegetation along its bank shielded the area from view.

Standing in the poppy field inside the compound's walls, Biggers called his lieutenants into a circle. Neff's Marines handed an explosive charge to Second Platoon, and Neff described the path he and Sergeant Laney had reconnoitered through the last hamlet before the bazaar. The Taliban had been casing Kilo Company, staying out of range. There had been no sign that it had massed to defend the bridge. A Reaper drone reported to the company that it could see fighting positions at the bazaar but no one who looked like a threat.

Marines on the outer walls reported seeing a column of civilians leaving a home. They were heading north, carrying sacks on their back. "Maybe they know something we don't know," Biggers said.

A few gunshots sounded from the south.

Harassing fire, Neff figured. *Doesn't sound like many weapons. They are feeling us out.*

Kilo had many Marines behind the walls. He expected they would push the gunmen off.

The incoming fire grew. Bullets snapped by, passing over the officers' heads.

Dozens of Marines opened fire. The rate of incoming fire seemed to build. Through their scopes, Marines saw Taliban gunmen to the south, moving into place.

"There's a shit ton of them!" shouted Private First Class Eric D. Currier.

A SAW gunner, Private First Class Joshua D. Horne, said he saw thirty or forty Taliban. He fired bursts until he had emptied a 200-round drum. "Reloading!" he shouted.

Captain Biggers watched his Marines firing back, distributing targets. This was bigger than the typical Afghan skirmish. Away from the gunfight, other Marines from Kilo were reporting to Biggers that they were watching men on motorcycles moving along their flanks, out of range. The Taliban was massing.

Biggers surveyed the two platoons around him. Marines were firing in multiple directions and the Taliban was spread out. But this still seemed manageable. Most of the Taliban were to the south. They would not be able to cross the open fields under fire and prevent Kilo from reaching its objectives to the north—the bazaar and the bridge.

Biggers consulted his GRG, the annotated satellite image, to determine the building numbers of compounds from where he thought Kilo was taking fire, and ordered Neff to move northward with Laney's squad, nearer the objective. He planned to arrange fire support and Second Platoon would fight off the Taliban to the south, then be ready to sweep through an area cleared by Neff's platoon and take the bridge.

Bullets were flying by and striking walls. Among them were machine-gun bursts, which flew by in a rush or tore up ground in front of Marines. Here and there the Marines heard the heavier crack of a well-aimed shot. Someone out there had a good rifle, and the skills to use it. Second Platoon spread out, sending Marines south and west to cover Kilo's flank. They met more precise gunfire as they moved.

The fight settled into a stalemate. After an hour it still raged.

Much of Kilo Company was arrayed in a C-shaped arc. Taliban fighters had pushed into the open center. Biggers had few good options. If it had been night, or if the fields had had walls and thicker crops, this would likely have played to the Marines' advantage. But the fields were bare, the walls were few, and the Taliban had chosen positions cannily. Many shot through firing ports, the murder holes the Marines had been warned about. Marines who crept forward were met by fire that fixed them in place. Along one wall, Lance Corporal Travis Vuocolo, a SAW gunner in Second Platoon, was nearly hit repeatedly. His squad leader, Sergeant Ryan Rogers, ordered him back. The man who owned the compound stood near his doorway, gesturing, imploring Marines not to trample his poppy plants.

The company had been told that the assault in Marja was necessary to stem the opium trade.

"Don't step on the poppy, don't step on the illegal shit!" shouted Corporal Jamie Wieczorek, a fire team leader, then muttered to Marines clustered with him against a wall. "This is what we're here to fight and they say don't step on it."

"He's giving us information," a Marine replied.

"So what?" Wieczorek said. To the west, Second Platoon had been attacked the previous day. "The last guy who gave us information put us into an ambush. Fuck him."

Marine training emphasized rushing attackers at the shorter ranges. But at longer ranges, by daylight, when an enemy was well positioned and behind its guns, rushing across the open spaces would be more than foolish. It would mean throwing away Marines' lives. Kilo Company settled into a fight.

Some of the Afghan soldiers were fighting, but others lay low, doing nothing. Sergeant Rogers urged an Afghan with a machine gun, Mohammad Sadir, to get up.

"Taliban! Taliban!" the Afghan soldier said to Rogers, nodding toward the far side of the field.

"You see Taliban," Rogers said. "You shoot him."

The two men bumped fists.

The machine gunner stayed low, and did not fire.

Another Afghan offered another English word. "Sniper," he said. But after each round flew overhead, he did not fight. Rogers returned to his squad.

A cry rose along the walls—"Corpsman up!"

Vuocolo had been hit.

He had fallen beside a line of Marines, who pounced and rolled him over to check his wound. A corpsman cut away part of Vuocolo's uniform, exposing a pair of holes on his left shoulder. The bullet had passed through his deltoid, missing bone. After the corpsman applied a pressure bandage, Vuocolo was back on the wall.

Another Afghan soldier shouted triumphantly, his voice tinged with glee. "Taliban!" he taunted. "Pussy!"

The company was stalled. Staff Sergeant Joseph Wright, Second Platoon's sergeant, was concerned. Kilo was using up ammunition. It needed to conserve what it had for a second fight, at the bridge. Wright paced as bullets passed over his head.

"Shoot only what you can see and what you can hit," he said.

Neff and his First Squad, led by Sergeant Laney, were on the northern edge of the fighting, waiting for it to subside, ready to shift focus to the bazaar and the bridge. But Kilo was halted. Its officers wanted more firepower to kill the gunmen across the fields, or at least convince them to leave.

Near Captain Biggers, Lieutenant Durbin, who led the company's fire-support team, huddled with a small group of officers, trying to organize mortar or artillery fire. He knew the pattern from his briefings: Once Americans concentrated firepower, the militants would disappear. If Kilo could get an aircraft overhead, or some artillery fire to splash down, this gunfight might end. The company could return its attention to the bridge. Captain Akil Bacchus, a pilot assigned as a forward air controller, was trying to arrange for an aircraft. Second Lieutenant Marvin Mathelier, an artillery forward observer, was working with him, relaying radio traffic through another forward observer, Corporal Christopher Herr, who was in Building 316 with Corporal Charfauros. Radio communications were spotty. The officers were frustrated. Kilo Company, in a large operation, was fighting alone.

One of the Marines, seeing the Afghan soldier with a machine gun was still sitting out the fight, put down his weapon and picked up the Afghan's weapon to use. He fired over the wall.

Durbin had regained radio communications and was discussing artillery support, when he was told to be ready to report on the damage for an impending HIMARS rocket strike. HIMARS rockets were large—more than twenty feet long, with warheads containing about 200 pounds of high explosives.

Durbin was startled. He had not called for a HIMARS strike.

"What HIMARS?" he asked into the radio.

"The HIMARS that you called for," the voice replied.

Durbin's surprise became alarm. Kilo Company was partially wrapped around the Taliban. If big ordnance was about to crash down, its Marines needed to know.

"Where are they coming?" Durbin demanded. "Where!"

Captain Bacchus grabbed Lieutenant Mathelier by the arm and spun him, pulling him face-to-face. Bacchus seemed shocked, too. "You just called for HIMARS without telling me?" he said.

If rockets were in the air, Bacchus needed to warn aircraft and pilots out of the way.

This was the first Mathelier had heard of a HIMARS mission. "I don't know what you're talking about," he said.

All three officers were flummoxed. The battalion had still not answered Durbin's question. He wondered what he had missed.

"Hey, confirm you got a rocket in the air," he said into his handset.

No answer came back. He asked again.

"Confirm you've got a rocket in the air."

Battalion did not reply.

Durbin changed handsets and broadcast a general warning on the company's tactical net. "All stations," he said. "We've got rockets coming in and I don't know where. Everybody get down!"

Shouts passed from Marine to Marine.

"Get the fuck down!"

"Rockets inbound!"

"Get the fuck down!"

The voices rang with elation and anticipation. This had been a rifle fight for too long. The fire support the Marines had hoped for was happening at last. *Those fucking Taliban are about to get smoked.*

On the roof of Building 187, Lance Corporal Adam Wallace was facing the center of the battle with his back to the bazaar. There had been a break in the shooting. He fished out a cigarette. He heard a loud whistle, which almost immediately became a rushing whoosh. Wallace looked up and saw a large rocket falling from the sky. He'd never seen anything quite like it. It resembled a section of utility pole with tailfins extended like small wings.

It landed on Building 284 and disappeared in a brilliant flash. A shock wave rushed past, followed by a noise like thunder. A second rocket landed behind the first, detonating in an identical blast. Marines like firepower, and being on the winning side. Several screamed with joy.

"Fuck yeah!"

"Get some!"

Wallace heard another shout.

"There was a family in there!"

The cheering stopped.

Across the fields to the west, where Vuocolo had been shot, Second Platoon had been facing the spot from which the sniper had been harassing them, expecting the spot to be hit. The rockets came down to the left, a few hundred yards away, at the next compound. They turned their heads and watched black smoke and hot dust climb. The platoon had not taken fire from that place but assumed someone must have. Marines cheered.

"You ain't got no fucking house!" one of them shouted.

There was a long pause. Something did not seem right.

Back in Building 187, Larry Lau, First Platoon's radio operator, was scrambling to figure out what had happened. He had heard a radio call just before the explosions—a warning to stand by for HIMARS on Building 284—and then felt the twin blasts shake the steppe. He knew immediately someone had made a mistake.

There was no enemy in that compound, he thought. *It was all women and children.*

Beside him, the executive officer, Colistra, was equally confused. *What the fuck was that?* he asked himself.

Colistra looked outside. He had not heard Durbin's warning, and was not sure what weapon had been used, or even who was behind it. His heart pounded fast. The family who lived in this building, whom he had asked to remain with the Marines, had gone there the morning before. *The women,* he thought, *all those little kids.*

Oh shit.

Oh no.

Around Captain Biggers, dozens of Marines faced the smoldering rubble, watching. Someone stepped out from the compound's door. A few Marines fired. The range was long. The bullets missed. The survivor froze, in clear view.

She was a child.

She stood motionless, coated in dust.

"Cease fire!" someone shouted. "It's a kid. Cease fire!"

Marines fell silent. For a moment the girl looked stunned. Then she ran, bolting straight toward her home, Building 187, which was about 400 yards away, and full of Marines.

She covered the distance quickly, determined, dashing across her own yard.

Marines met her at the compound door. Her face was smeared with blood. Her clothing was soaked in more. The corpsman put her on a table and looked for wounds. Her only visible mark was a small scratch on her face. The blood on her clothes had come from someone else.

Her father was brought to the room. He was First Platoon's detainee. He picked her up. She clung to him. The interpreter asked questions. "Who was in there? Are they hurt? Are they alive? Are there bad people in there?"

The girl looked terrified. She barely spoke. Colistra had seen enough. He knew who was in that compound. He had seen them go in the day before. He and Lau had work to do. He called Captain Biggers on the radio.

"Was that us?" he asked.

Biggers told him it was.

Shit, Colistra thought.

"We've got civcas," he said, using jargon for civilian casualties. "We need to get a squad in there fast."

Neff was with his First Squad, Kilo Company's northernmost unit, when the rockets hit. He had heard Durbin's warning that HIMARS were inbound and lifted his head over the wall and saw the rockets hit Building 284, right between his support-by-fire position, where he had left Second Squad, and Building 316, where Corporal Charfauros and Third Squad were fighting on the company's eastern flank. He was momentarily in disbelief.

"What was *that*?" he said. "We weren't taking rounds from that compound."

Neff remembered its occupants: an old man and a group of women and children. They had followed instructions and stayed inside. He heard confusion around him. Other Marines were as surprised as he was. He looked across the field at the drifting smoke and the shattered wall. Then he saw the girl. Through his rifle's four-power scope he saw her dirty hair. It was black and wild. He thought she might be three or four years old.

"We searched that building," said Lance Corporal Hummel, a fire team leader. "That's where they put their women and children."

"Who called that in?"

No one knew.*

The firefight had paused. Neither the Taliban nor the Marines seemed to know what to do next. Firing slowed.

Captain Biggers came to Neff on the radio. "I need you to get over there with your squad immediately and search that compound and give me a BDA," he said, using the acronym for battle damage assessment. "I need to know what's going on."

Neff scanned the field. It was an empty expanse, exposed to the same gunfire that had been holding Kilo Company in place all day. The ruined building was about seven hundred yards away. Any crossing on foot would be a charge across the open, potentially a death run. He gathered his squad and told them the mission: to get into that compound and render aid to anyone wounded inside. He stopped. He wasn't going to bullshit anyone about what would await them if they made it.

"Be prepared to see some shit," he said. "There's going to be some bodies."

---

* For most of those who were there, the origins of the errant HIMARS strikes remain uncertain to this day. The former company, battalion, and regimental commanders all agree that the rockets targeted the wrong building and killed unarmed civilians. They also agree the strikes were a result of human error, not a technical flaw. Public statements by a British major general in Kandahar that the compound was being used by the Taliban in the attacks were false. The Marine Corps investigated the mishap but did not publicly release the results. After repeated inquires by the author, spanning years, the Corps said it could not find a copy of its investigator's report.

The squad stepped from behind the wall into plain view, spread out, and hustled across the field, each man expecting to be shot. Neff figured the Taliban would wait until his Marines were far away from the walls, with no chance of returning to cover, then open fire. Their only ally was speed. They needed to cross fast. Heavy with equipment and wet with sweat, he jogged farther into the field, expecting bursts of machine-gun fire, accepting that at any second they could be cut down. Nothing happened. First Squad was unchallenged. Amped by the adrenaline that accompanies imminent death, they drew nearer to the broken building. Laney called out to his Marines. "You remember that messed-up training I made you do?" he said. "You're about to see some shit that's worse than that."

To his left Neff saw the support-by-fire position, where other Marines watched in astonishment.

The rockets had hit a corner room and blown out an exterior wall. Neff and Laney's Marines reached the gap the blasts had made.

First Squad's point man stopped, glanced inside, looked back at Neff. "Sir," he said. "We've got a whole bunch of bodies."

Neff inhaled a bitter, burning smell, a mixture of explosives, burned soil, and something else. He looked in. One corner of the compound had been blown asunder. The courtyard was a tableau of rubble, dead livestock, scraps of cloth, and human body parts. Shrapnel had gouged divots in walls. Twisted pieces of the rocket littered the ground.

His Marines swept into the place, weapons level.

Their training kicked in. They fanned out and dashed through the structure's mini-geography, covering one another and calling out as they opened doors, searched animal pens, assured themselves that the place was safe. They were looking for weapons or Taliban. The grounds were as still as a tomb. Haji Mohammad Karim, the old man whose family had been displaced the day before, arrived from Building 187 and stood dumbfounded, as if looking for something.

Several Marines rushed to a room where the HIMARS hit. A voice came out. "We've got bodies in here. Women and kids."

Neff entered a scene of abject destruction. The dead were spread about the room. Many were small, the same children he had seen alive at the gate earlier. Others were adults ripped partially apart. The roof and walls had collapsed upon them, covering broken frames or shattered skulls with earthen brick. All were coated in a tan dust that settled upon faces and pools of blood.

Someone said the compound was clear. First Squad had found no weapons and no one alive. It all confirmed what Neff already knew. The HIMARS had destroyed a civilian home.

His stomach tightened. He steadied himself.

His platoon had not done this. His Marines would have to clean it up.

The corpsman with First Squad knelt beside the body of a young woman. She had no legs and was missing an arm. A moan floated in the air. Neff found his voice.

"Doc," he asked. "Is she still alive?"

The corpsman nodded. "Yeah," he said.

Neff looked closely. The woman wore a blood-soaked maroon dress. Her chest rose and fell fitfully. Her remaining arm was held by a tissue of flesh.

From where she had fallen, she could not see the devastation in the courtyard or all of the bodies thrown around. She tried to sit up but could not. She turned her head, calling out names.

"She's looking for the children," the interpreter said.

The corpsman slipped tourniquets over her stumps and cinched them tight. Lance Corporal Dave Santana removed part of her dress, looking for more wounds. He saw the extent of the damage; she was mostly a head and torso. Santana had lost his sense of time but thought the rockets had hit about forty-five minutes ago. *How is she even alive?* he wondered. He felt a wave of empathy. A thought formed that he never expected to have: He wished that she would die. He wanted her suffering to end.

Outside, one of the Afghan soldiers had found a goat that remained alive. He drew a knife and slit its throat.

Haji Mohammad Karim stepped into the room. He was despondent and enraged, scolding the Marines. He yanked Santana back and pointed. Santana was standing on a piece of human skull. He had not seen it. He lifted his foot and apologized.

Colistra had crossed from Building 187. He pulled Neff aside. "We've got to do a BDA," he said. "We have to start counting bodies."

Neff agreed. He and Laney moved through the blast site, tallying the dead. Two were girls, maybe ten years old or a little older. One wore a royal-blue dress with gold sequins in swirls. She rested on her back on bits of straw, eyes closed, streaks of blood clotted beneath her nose, the right side of her dress soaked over a hidden wound. Her right hand was wet with dark blood, as if she had clutched her wounds as she died. The other wore a pink top and pink pants. Her brown eyes were opened, staring blankly at the cold sky. A boy about eight years old was missing flesh from his chin and part of the right side of his head. Two smaller girls were similarly wounded. One was a toddler. Neff kept counting. Shrapnel had cut the throat of a gray-haired woman in a blue dress. The old man who had greeted him at sunrise was dead, too, as was a younger man whose upper forehead had been split. There were more: three young women or teenage girls. He looked at the tangle of bloody clothing for a long while before deciding he could not approximate two of the victims' ages. It didn't matter. Not now.

At one spot a human foot lay alone. It had been sheared neatly from the shin. He had no idea to whom it had belonged.

Sergeant Laney shared his count.

"We're at ten," he said.

Neff thought Laney had missed one. He pointed to a limb in the dust. "I've got number eleven over here," he said.

"No, sir," Laney said. "That's this guy's arm."

Neff looked again. It was not an adult arm. It was a child's leg.

"No," he said. "Eleven."

The two men confirmed the count. Five dead children, two dead adult males, four dead women or teenage girls. Eleven, as best they could tell.

Neff passed the number to Colistra. Laney called Biggers and asked for a helicopter for the woman in the corner. Somehow she was still alive.

Mixed among the dead were chests holding the owners' possessions. It was all familiar by now, the same things the Marines had seen in each impoverished house: carpets, kitchen utensils, jugs of water, small glasses for tea, stacks of cushions and bedding. Afghan soldiers were arranging the bodies in a row and covering them in whatever cloth and blankets they could collect from the piles. After they lifted the body of one woman, they saw her abdomen had been torn open, revealing an unborn child. She had almost carried the baby to term.

Several Marines swore.

Neff felt a fresh wave of revulsion. He left the fetus out of his count.

He was functioning on one level, as an officer in command, staying on mission. On other levels he was switched off. So were the Marines around him. This was the second day of their Afghan war. He found himself grateful to the Afghan soldiers who were tending to the dead, sparing the Marines some of the worst. *They're stepping up their game,* he thought.

Santana was listening to Haji Mohammad Karim, who stood in the mess, demanding the interpreter tell them his words. It created an eerie delay. The old man would shout, and the interpreter would speak softly in English.

"You did this," he said. "My family. You killed them. You did this."

The Marines were almost as shocked as he was. They did not know what had gone wrong, other than this had been a mistake. At their level they had not been involved in the call-for-fire that had brought the rockets here, and had no authority or leverage to find out more. They had no answers, or at least none of any use.

Some of them tried to calm the man. "The Taliban did this," one said. The words infuriated the old man. His anger filled the roofless room. "You lie!" he shouted. "You lie!"

Neff felt his own anger rising. The rockets were not supposed to have hit here. *This was all civilians,* he thought. But he had to lead his platoon. He figured the company and the battalion would admit to the strikes. For now he had to hold his feelings inside. He needed to finish his mission and make sure his Marines were in position. *A platoon commander cannot check out,* he told himself. The battle was not over. Kilo Company had summoned a medevac helicopter. First Platoon would have to secure its landing zone.

A few hundred yards to the southeast, in Building 316, Niall Swider was taking another turn on post. The wall was head-high. He stood on a stack of two storage chests that allowed him to look over the top. The Taliban had gone quiet around the area where the rockets had landed. But at the blocking position where Charfauros's squad was holding its lone building, gunmen kept harassing the Marines. Taliban fighters were in buildings to the south, moving from spot to spot, firing as they pleased. Flat ground separated them. Neither side could expect to rush the other and succeed. The two sides traded shots.

Swider held an M4 rifle with a grenade launcher under its barrel. He was waiting for the Taliban to show again when he saw cigarette smoke rising from a shallow irrigation ditch that ran in front of a compound wall. He figured some of the Taliban gunmen were not religious. They smoked just like Marines. And this man had made a mistake. Swider could imagine it. The man must have been crawling through the ditch and now was lying there on his back, smoking, having a break. He had given his position away. Swider aimed his rifle. He figured he'd get this guy. The man popped up in a kneeling position with a Kalashnikov rifle. He wore a white top with a brown vest and ripped off a few bursts. Swider fired back. The bullets impacted in front of the man, just short. The man dropped out of sight.

Swider was irritated. He'd have to try another way. He looked at the tall wall directly behind where the man was hiding, and had an idea. Ducking from view, he loaded his grenade launcher with a 40-millimeter high-explosive round. He would lob the grenade against the wall, just beyond where the smoke had been rising. It would burst there and splatter the man with fragmentation, killing him in his hiding spot.

Swider slid the grenade launcher closed. He stood and swung its fat barrel toward the man.

A bullet struck the top of the wall beside him, dusting him with chips of dried mud. It came from his left, from Building 2. He ignored it, remaining fixated on the spot where he had seen the smoke.

His left arm went numb. His hand fell off the launcher's barrel. Something smacked his chest.

What the fuck, he thought. He had not gotten off his shot.

His left hand could no longer grip anything. His rifle pointed down. Swider did not feel pain. How had he lost function of his arm? He was perplexed. He turned around.

"Chief," he said, "I think I just got shot."

"Then get the fuck down," Charfauros said.

Swider stepped off the stacked chests and grasped what had happened: The Taliban gunman to his left had been watching him as closely as he had been watching the smoker. The man had made a shot before Swider could. A bullet had passed through Swider's left triceps, and been stopped by his vest's ceramic plate.

It was a wonder he was not dead.

Neff got a call from Charfauros saying Swider had been hit and Doc Harger had examined him. The wound, he said, was a through-and-through. The bullet had entered and exited without hitting bone.

Neff said he'd try to arrange a medevac. Colistra was on a radio asking for an aircraft. The company now had three wounded people who needed to be picked up: Vuocolo, the dying woman, and Swider. They were in three different spots.

The woman was growing quieter. Her breath had become faint, though she occasionally mumbled the children's names. The Afghan interpreter sat beside her, lost in prayer. Santana and the corpsman had moved her onto a litter and continued to work on her. The little girl had returned and was in the room, bawling. Another woman was there, too, asking the Marines not to take the child.

The wounded woman fell still.

The Marines lifted her off the litter. She was dead. Afghan soldiers took her body, to bundle it in cloth and rest it beside the others.

Helicopter rotors thumped to their south. Neff recognized the sound. *Black Hawks.* They were here to pick her up. Gunfire sounded. Someone was shooting at the aircraft as it approached.

We need to reroute the birds, Colistra thought.

He stepped outside and saw them. There was no longer anyone to treat. He assumed the Taliban had not pulled back. They had used the time since the HIMARS strike to change positions. He radioed to Biggers. "They need to push off," he said. "She's gone."

The two helicopters kept coming. One was descending, preparing to land beside the compound's southern wall—the side facing the Taliban. The other banked and circled, firing a machine gun.

Bullets snapped by. Colistra ran into the open, heading toward where the medevac aircraft was settling, waving his arms, warning the pilots off. Laney ran out, too.

Explosions shook the ground. *Shit,* Colistra thought. *We're getting mortared.*

Across the field, Biggers canceled the mission.

"Abort!" he shouted. "Abort!"

The gunfire grew. Colistra made eye contact with one of the pilots. He could see the man understood.

From the south, near Building 316, a rocket-propelled grenade sailed overhead toward Building 284. It exploded by the aircraft. The concussive blast jolted Marines outside the walls.

The helicopter lurched forward and pulled away, just above the ground. Gunfire followed it, then subsided. The aircraft banked and settled near Biggers to pick up Vuocolo.

The Taliban had missed. The Marines were listening to the Taliban on their radio frequency. A frustrated commander berated his fighters.

Neff called to Second Squad in Building 187 to give an update. "Everybody's dead," he said. He was spent but could not dwell on what had happened. The second day in Marja was ending and Kilo had not seized the bazaar and bridge. The company was low on water and ammunition. It would try again in the morning. The dead Afghans were arranged in a row in the compound's one intact room in a mix of white sheets, blue sheets, and gray and green blankets, many of them stained. Neff did not know what Kilo would do with them. Its mission was still the bridge. He gave instructions for the bodies to be guarded, and headed back to the support-by-fire position to plan for the next day.

Across the field, Biggers and his command group were moving west to the compound where Third Platoon waited with much of the company's equipment. The Marines would form strongpoints for the night.

Inside Building 187, by darkness, Neff remained in a methodical state of mind. The day had been a horror. Someone above the platoon had made a grave mistake. He had not joined the Corps to do such harm. He sat with Colistra to vent. *What the hell? That was crazy.* But Neff also knew his platoon was blameless. He needed to keep his Marines focused and sharp. He thought back to his training and how more experienced infantry officers had told him of his duty to stay on top of his platoon and to look after its well-being. Kilo's first big fight was already gaining a grim nickname: "The Valentine's Day Massacre." As shocked as he was, and no matter his preference for being understated, he knew he had to be a presence.

First Squad was tired, and a few of its Marines were dirty with blood. They were scattered inside the building. Neff trusted Laney and allowed the night's business to be done: issuing new ammunition, cleaning weapons, discussing the next day's missions, assigning Marines to watch. But he made the rounds, looking at each man. *Hey, what's going on? How you doing? Do you need anything? Talk to me. Do you have what you need?*

Activity continued as the hours moved toward dawn. Late that night a helicopter landed near Building 316. Swider walked on and was flown away to have his bullet wound treated. More helicopters arrived later still, leaving food, water, and ammunition in a field beside the compound where Captain Biggers and Second Platoon had fought. It would be too dangerous to retrieve the supplies by day, so weary Marines passed the last hours of darkness lugging all the crates, jugs, and boxes into a compound before the sun rose and the gunfire resumed.

The Marines guarding the bodies of the civilians had no food and little water. They had been sent to the shattered building so quickly that they left behind their backpacks with their supplies. It was a forlorn and eerie place, packed with dead animals and the family that had perished. The wind blew. The night was frigid. The Marines on guard huddled in the cold, night-vision goggles on, parched and famished until Afghan soldiers gathered the last eggs of the chickens killed by the rockets and cooked a meal to share.

In Building 316, Charfauros, like Neff, stayed awake. The Taliban had attacked his squad from three directions during the day. He was edgy, even though he saw no movement through his goggles, and the buildings across the canal seemed deserted. The opposing gunmen had disappeared. Charfauros had a feeling why: Around Kilo Company, beyond the range of a rifle shot, Afghans were mourning. Over the wind, in the blackness, he could hear women wailing.

Neff and his Marines were ready the next morning for a repeat push. Captain Biggers was returning with more Marines and Afghan soldiers to try again.

The Taliban waited along their route.

Biggers led a widely spaced column, walking from west to east. At the first long field, the canal ran parallel to its southern side. The field was coated in fine white dust, resembling confectioners' sugar, that silhouetted every man.

Gunmen opened fire from the opposite side of the canal.

From where he waited, Neff heard Kalashnikovs and PK machine guns, then American weapons replying. Marines in the kill zone were pouring fire into vegetation on the far side of the water. They suppressed the ambush as other Marines ran for Building 318, the compound to their east, and returned the favor.

Though rounds had cracked past helmets and thudded into dirt beside the Marines, no one was wounded. The company regrouped, faced the bridge, and kept walking, winding its way behind Afghan homes, which shielded the Marines from further gunfire. Soon Neff saw the first of the troops striding into the compound of poppy plants where Vuocolo had been wounded the day before. They did not hesitate. The Marines pressed farther north, up a low hill, within sight of the bridge.

Second Platoon, with a machine-gun squad and a contingent of Afghans, began its assault. Its Marines entered the last set of homes before the bazaar.

At last the Taliban put up its defense—the battle Kilo had been expecting for weeks. They had built several bunkers and fought back, spraying the Marines with fire. The Afghan company commander was looking over a wall at the maneuvering troops. A bullet slammed into his face. He went down.

The helicopters were ready. Neff saw a plume of the red-smoke grenade on the edge of the fight, marking where the casualty was waiting. A Black Hawk landed and flew away with the man. He was alive.

Cobra attack helicopters began strafing the main bunker. Second Platoon crossed the distance to the bridge, throwing smoke grenades to obscure its rushes, and reached the road with minesweepers and an explosive ordnance disposal team, then went across. The Taliban withdrew. The bridge was under Marine control. The shooting subsided, reduced to occasional harassing shots.

Some of the Marines had barely eaten or slept in two days, and most of the supplies that the transport helicopters had left had not been distributed. Inside Building 284, where Marines from First Platoon and a detachment of Afghan soldiers were guarding the bodies of the Afghan family, there was no water. Two Afghan soldiers ventured out with jugs to collect water from a canal. Neff was one building away, watching over the bazaar, when he heard a single shot, followed by shouts.

"Fucking ANA got hit!"

An Afghan soldier was down in the field. The other was dragging him. Neff, the corpsman, and a team of Marines ran out to help. Laney threw a smoke grenade. The wounded Afghan was a rifleman the Marines affectionately called King, for the gaudy gold necklace that he wore. He had been shot through the throat. They removed his helmet. It was full of hot blood. A team of Marines surrounded the man to protect him, looking for the shooter as others pulled him inside. There was little to do. King was unresponsive, struggling for breath on the floor, his necklace slicked with blood running from a large wound.

Neff figured the shot had come from about three hundred yards away. Whoever had done that probably was not using a Kalashnikov. *Hell of a good shot*, he thought.

King's labored breathing stopped. The corpsman worked a few minutes more before saying what everyone knew. King was dead.

That night King's body stayed in the open-air compound just outside where the Marines slept. His Afghan friends visited him to pray, weeping quietly. Neff tossed and turned a few dreary hours.

Two days later, on February 17, First Platoon made its first major move. Its original positions were no longer necessary. Kilo Company held the bridge and the bazaar, and the rest of the battalion was pressing closer to the croplands. The battalion's other rifle companies were approaching slowly, searching for hidden bombs as they moved, anticipating ambushes. But most of them—including an engineering unit to build a walled outpost beside the bazaar—would soon be inside Marja's green irrigated zone, allowing Kilo Company to relocate its forces.

The day before, Colonel Christmas had flown in and walked with Captain Biggers and an infantry squad to Building 284, where Christmas sat with Haji Mohammad Karim to offer condolences and disburse a payment for each of the dead. The battalion had owned up to the strike as a mistake. Christmas told the grieving elder that the mishap would be investigated and that the Marines would help bury the dead wherever the family wished.

Haji Mohammad Karim's anger was no longer visible. Twelve of his relatives were dead, lined up in a room across the courtyard, wrapped in blankets and sheets, and under the guard of foreigners whose errant firepower had killed them. He was powerless, subdued, and solemn. He sat on a carpet in the ruins with a quiet dignity. The girl who had survived the rocket attack was beside him. Through an interpreter he accepted the money and asked that his relatives' remains be transferred to Lashkar Gah, away from this place. Marines stood on watch outside. The dead animals on the ground were beginning to decay. The colonel said he would arrange for an aircraft to fly the bodies out.

The patrol left for a glum walk back to the company's temporary command post. Both sides were reorganizing; neither was looking for a fight. The Taliban and villagers were holding a funeral for one of the men whom Kilo had killed, and many young men—presumably the same fighters who had been firing on Kilo for days—were gathered at the gravesite. This left few militants to interfere with the colonel's business, and his patrol crossed the fields unmolested. On the return walk it faced a few harassing shots from a distant gunman. The large battles of Marja had ebbed.

Christmas was true to his word. Late that afternoon a Marine tilt-rotored Osprey landed. Neff's Marines loaded the bodies for a flight to the provincial capital for burial. The Taliban tried to destroy the Osprey as it sat on the ground, but again their shots were wide. A last RPG, fired after the Osprey lifted off, exploded beneath it, just far enough away that the aircraft and its crew were safe. The aircraft departed with its cargo, the bodies of the very civilians Marine commanders said the troops had come to protect.

First Platoon's job at Building 284 ended. Captain Biggers ordered its Marines and Afghan soldiers—less Corporal Charfauros and his squad on the flank—to move the next morning to the company's position to the west.

Neff and two squads left at dawn, bidding farewell to Haji Mohammad Karim. The walk was more difficult than those of the previous days. The Marines had to carry all of their equipment—the heavy loads they had brought with them by helicopter to Marja but had kept in their occupied compounds for days; the same immobilizing loads that Swider had wished to complain about to the commandant. They moved clumsily under the rising sun, weighted down like mules.

The platoon crossed the first fields without incident, and halted behind the cover of buildings, waiting for Sergeant Ryan Rogers from Second Platoon to bring two Marines who were going to walk with them. The sun climbed higher. Neff was feeling on edge. He did not like moving all of his Marines by daylight, slowed by full loads, giving the Taliban's spotters time to watch. And he was down to his last spare battery for his two-way radio and worried about losing communication.

First Platoon had about a kilometer and a half left to cover. Up to this point its movement had either been near compounds under Marine control or behind walls of buildings. Neff could route the patrol behind buildings for a few hundred more yards, but then they would come to the danger area. The final leg would be across a flat field, an expanse seven hundred or eight hundred yards wide. The company command cell waited beyond that. The southern side field was bordered by a canal. Other platoons had been fired on from there as they crossed this field.

Neff did not like the route. When they reached the last open area, the platoon halted. The field looked risky under any circumstances, but especially risky by day and with heavy backpacks. First Platoon had its orders. There were missions to perform.

The platoon began to walk.

Sergeant Laney's squad took point.

The Marines headed out tensely, with everyone watching the silent walls and vegetation to their south.

The point man, Private First Class Currier, was about three hundred yards out, almost in the middle of the field, when the ambush began.

First came a short burst from the south. The Marines dropped, ready to fire back. Laney thought it might be harassing fire. He ordered the Marines back up, to hustle for the buildings ahead. *Let's move forward and get out of this danger area*, he thought.

Multiple weapons opened fire in single shots and bursts. Neff heard the thumping of at least one machine gun. Marines fell. Neff was still at the compound wall, in a safe position. He dropped his pack and dashed out to the open, trying to reach the downed men.

Sergeant Laney had run toward one of them, to help drag him to safety as he ordered his teams back. The Marines were silhouetted on a barren field covered with white powder. Bullets skipped around them and rushed by in the air.

The Taliban had had days to prepare this position on Kilo's flank, and was firing from trenches and murder holes. Its fighters were unseen.

Marines spun out of their packs, dropped, and fired from behind them, using the packs as shields.

Private First Class Joshua Horne moved by Laney and said he was shot. Another Marine, Corporal Timothy Smith, had been struck, too. The two Marines had arm wounds. Neff reached Laney, who was beside the first downed Marine.

"Who's hit?" Neff asked. "Who is it?"

"Currier," the sergeant answered. He was holding Horne's squad automatic weapon and Currier's rifle, as well as his own.

Like Neff, Currier was a "Christmas present," one of the last Marines to join the platoon. He had been with Kilo only since December. He was from New England, also like Neff. He looked lifeless.

Horne was there, his face in pain. "Sir, I've been hit," he said. Laney told him to rush straight back to the compound. He could not fight or help move Currier. Neff picked up Currier's pack.

First Squad withdrew as Second Squad returned fire with 40-millimeter grenades and machine guns. Laney and Hummel dragged Currier across the white dust. Currier was not a big Marine, but with all of his equipment he was heavy, and they were carrying extra weapons. Laney's legs gave out two times.

When they reached the compound wall some of the backpacks had bullet holes. The corpsman rushed through a triage. Smith's and Horne's wounds did not appear life-threatening. He focused on Currier, pulling away his equipment to check his wounds. A bullet had struck him high in the chest, passing just above the top of his ceramic plate. He was dead.

A rocket-propelled grenade slammed into the wall, sending up a cloud of hot dust.

To their north, Staff Sergeant Wright, the platoon sergeant for Second Platoon, heard the gunfire. His instinct was to help, but he was short-handed and could not leave Kilo's supplies unguarded. Neff's voice came up on the radio.

"I have one KIA and two WIA," he said. Rogers radioed back and got no reply.

Neff sounded frazzled. Wright was not one to stand still near Marines under fire. He and Sergeant Rogers ordered four Marines to stay behind to guard the supplies, then sprinted toward the fight. They found First Platoon in the compound at the edge of the field, jumped over the low wall on its northern side, and joined them. Wright knew this place. Two days earlier Second Platoon had been ambushed in the same spot.

He projected composure.

"Hey, man," he said.

Neff was near the body of a Marine and two others who had been shot, trying to get his radio to function. He needed a helicopter. Wright's radio had a working battery. He told Neff they could divide the work.

"I'll do the casevac," he said. He urged Neff to focus on fighting the Taliban off and reaching the company command post.

From the west, Kilo Company began firing 60-millimeter mortars. Biggers dispatched a squad of Marines to flank the Taliban from the other side.

Wright called Colistra, who had lost contact with Neff when Neff's radio battery died. The two men began organizing a medevac. A short while later a helicopter landed near the compound's northern wall, shielded from the Taliban to the south. The platoon rushed out the wounded Marines and Currier's body. Attack helicopters followed and strafed the fields.

With gunships circling, the Taliban's firing abruptly stopped.

Wright urged First Platoon to move. "It's quiet now," he said. "Get across. We got you. Go."

First Platoon stood, shouldered packs, and prepared to try again. Covered in sweat and their friends' blood, they stepped out into the danger area. One of the Cobras passed low overhead. It was a menacing machine. Neff figured it would keep Taliban heads down.

Thank God, he thought.

He was carrying his pack and Currier's, a load of two hundred pounds. The Taliban did not fire again.

Several minutes later the Marines trudged into the compound where Kilo was set up. They filed past their peers angrily, gathered rations and water, and sat in knots. Neff left them to see Biggers. He returned with news.

"Say your prayers and do what you can for each other," he said. "But keep your head in the fight, because tomorrow we're going to push down to the south where you just got ambushed, and we're going to get some payback for Currier. We're going to be in a firefight again tomorrow."

Captain Biggers had issued Kilo their next order. Two platoons would cross the canal early the next morning and run down the Taliban harassing the company from the south. Most of the company would be involved. They would have mortars ready and air support. Neff laid out his plan. It was uncomplicated—a movement to contact. "Nothing fancy," he said. "We're getting on line and we're going." When they found the Taliban, they'd fight.

After issuing his order, Neff cleaned his rifle, replaced his radio battery, and sat alone, rehashing the ambush in his head. He needed rest but could not sleep. To anyone watching, he looked calm. Inside he was grilling himself, rethinking his decisions. *Would I have done anything differently?* He could have crossed the danger area farther north and stretched the distance between the Taliban machine gun and his platoon. But the northern side of the crossing was wider. The Marines would have been unprotected a longer time. There was no good answer.

Around him, First Platoon was in a foul mood, seething and grieving at once. Neff sat for three or four hours, his mind replaying the ambush again and again. At last he drifted to sleep. *Don't overthink it,* he told himself. *Go get some revenge.*

The Marines emerged into the cold air the next morning. They were about to change their pattern. The gunmen fighting them had developed an understanding of where Kilo did not go. These men had stacked up in compounds and canals and built fighting positions and holes through which they could harass the Americans on the northern side. Kilo intended to use the Taliban's confidence against it by rushing headlong into the enemy's zone before sunrise to catch them unready and rout them in place. The company had no plan to claim ground. This day was a hunt.

Biggers arranged two platoons side by side, with his command group in the center, and brought machine-gun squads, an explosive ordnance disposal team, snipers, and Afghans. Neff's platoon took the eastern edge. The 60-millimeter mortars stayed behind, on call to lob rounds into any resistance. The air officer, Captain Bacchus, had a lineup of aircraft and drones on call. Neff had all three squads arranged on line, like an exercise from infantry school.

On the eastern edge, Corporal Charfauros's squad exited Building 316 for the first time in days. They had been all but under siege, repeatedly attacked from three sides. A hamlet of villages was in front of them, across the canal, and Charfauros felt almost naked as his squad stepped into the gray dawn. The Taliban had kept up blistering fire against his squad. His Marines would have been mowed down from that hamlet if they had tried this in the days before. But it was early. Their foes did not seem to be awake. The word from Neff to get moving came over the radio. Third Squad crossed the field at a near jog. Within minutes they were south of the canal and entering their enemy's positions. They had not faced a shot.

It was as if they had captured an opposing army's trenches. Along the walls facing Building 316, Charfauros's Marines found murder holes littered with spent brass from the gunfights of the preceding days. Inside the buildings and compounds, they discovered that the Taliban fighters had hacked man-sized mouseholes through interior and rear walls, or had placed ladders and planks that allowed them to change positions quickly.

"Motherfuckers," one of the Marines said.

Unprompted, the Marines of Third Squad started ransacking rooms. They smashed furniture, shattered teacups, heaved bedding, broke doors.

Nothing was spared. An Afghan fighter picked up a Koran from the floor and complained in halting English. "No good," he said. "No good."

Charfauros realized that was a step too far. He apologized. His Marines could read neither Arabic nor any of Afghanistan's principal languages. They had not recognized the holy text. He had an idea. The Afghan soldiers seemed disgusted at the Taliban, too. He asked the interpreter to tell the Afghan soldiers they could help. "From now on, you guys grab the Korans," Charfauros said, "and then we'll trash the place."

The Afghan soldiers agreed.

The squad continued to tear through the deserted hamlet, kicking in doors. Charfauros's Marines were fit armed men rushing through someone else's maze, marking their path with a trail of broken goods. After days of being stuck under fire in a single building, they felt released. Half hunting, half raging, they were gripped by a hunger and a power that the architects of the Pentagon's counterinsurgency doctrine rarely acknowledged. One of their friends had been killed. Now they moved with a contempt that was timeless, exhilarating, satisfying, and channeled by youth—a living exhibit of why American soft-touch notions of counterinsurgency, pursued by conventional troops who had enlisted to fight, would almost never work. Circumstances for Third Squad had aligned. Officer catechisms had faded. They were not here to make friends. They were here to find the men who had been fighting them, and kill them.

If any of the Taliban's gunmen remained in the village, they withdrew in the face of Third Squad's advance.

As the squad reached the end of the hamlet, its excitement waning, the dynamic changed. The Taliban was filling in behind them, cutting off the route back.

Other fighters opened fire on the Americans from the fields, behind a new set of trenches or murder holes. They were off in the distance again. Third Squad stopped.

Marines took cover. Charfauros called Neff, who was more than a kilometer to the west.

Neff had information from the air officer. A Reaper pilot had seen gunmen leaving buildings on motorcycles not far from Charfauros. The

Taliban might be flanking his squad, trying to surround them, but they had made a mistake. They had been seen.

Neff described the route they were taking on the map. "You need to eliminate the targets," he said.

Charfauros knew the road they would be coming on, to his east. He arranged his squad and the machine guns and lay among them, looking through his four-power scope.

Motorcyclists appeared on five or six bikes, some doubled up with a second gunman on the back. They were far off but heading his way.

The Marines laid their sights on them, waiting for the sign from their squad leader. It was a moment they had waited for: the Taliban, out from behind walls, moving into range.

Charfauros fired. The rest of his squad opened up, along with an Afghan soldier behind a machine gun, who released a long burst.

Motorcycles veered and crashed as bullets struck. Some of the gunmen fell, stood, ran, and fell again. Others leaped into the nearby canal, alive.

Marines whooped and swore.

———

To the west, Sergeant Laney's squad had crossed the same canal and overrun the vacant firing positions used by the gunmen who killed Currier the day before. They found holes cut in walls. Looking back through the portholes to where the platoon had been attacked, they saw the kill zone from their ambushers' perspective. It was incredible, they thought, that more of them had not been hit. The scale of preparation was impressive, and so was the discipline. The Taliban had picked up their spent cartridge cases, and left the ambush positions clean.

The Taliban's fighters had not returned from wherever they slept.

First Squad searched the nearby houses. They were empty, too, except for the occasional snarling dog. Fire pits were cold. Vehicles were gone, leaving nothing but tread marks where they usually parked. The residents had moved out, surrendering their homes to war. The squad kept bounding forward. As the lead Marines approached a fresh set of compounds, gunmen from inside shot at them through more murder holes about two hundred yards away. The Marines took cover in a chest-high irrigation canal with ankle-deep water, in which they spread out and fired back with rifles and squad automatic weapons. More gunmen moved on the squad's right flank.

Lance Corporal Hummel pressed his chest to the dirt of the canal's southern side, assumed a braced firing position, and looked down the scope atop his M16. The compound to their south had high walls of dried mud and a small door. He settled his scope on the door and waited, ready in case the gunmen inside looked out. It was a good firing position. He felt steady.

To his right, a gunman jogged across from right to left, toward the door. Hummel shifted the 4-power scope slightly until its circle contained the trotting man. The scope's magnification brought him into view. He was bearded and wearing a dark blue-gray coat over gray clothes. In one hand he held a radio to his head, beneath his Afghan wool cap. In the other he gripped a Kalashnikov rifle.

He had almost reached the door.

The scope's reticle contained a small red chevron that indicated the expected point of a bullet's impact. Hummel tried laying the top of the chevron on the man's head. He eased back on the trigger.

The M16 fired.

The round struck the wall. Hummel saw dust splatter where it hit.

He fired again.

The second round missed. Hummel could not tell where.

He fired a third time.

The man dropped instantly and tumbled to a stop.

"I got one," Hummel said to Sergeant Laney, who was beside him.

"You get one?" Laney said.

"Fuck yeah," Hummel said.

Through the scope, he could see the man, in a heap, as motionless as a sack.

Neff was nearby on his own radio, talking with the company. This day was different. Neff did not have to defend compounds, watch a bridge, or guard bodies. First Platoon was maneuvering with all three squads and a sniper team, and the company command group was not far to the west, ready with fire support. Laney had relayed the compound's building

number to Neff, who passed the coordinates over the radio to the air officer, Captain Bacchus. The Reaper was still above them. Bacchus told Neff
it was armed with a Hellfire missile, could see the target, and would strike
the building in front of First Platoon.

"Roger, inbound," Neff answered.

He gave the squad a heads-up. A missile was about to hit the building,
he said. When it did, the Marines would rush forward in an assault.

Bacchus's voice came over the net again.

"Release," he said.

Neff and First Squad heard a screaming whoosh. The ordnance
slammed into the compound, near its north side, and exploded. It was
smaller than the HIMARS strikes they had seen, but still sent chunks
of wall and dirt spinning in the air. Its roar shook the field. Black smoke
rose.

The compound fell quiet.

Laney looked at the rising smoke and wondered if the missile had
struck outside the compound, at the base of the wall. The exterior walls
all seemed intact, except for a small section that collapsed. He was concerned it had been a near miss. He wanted a second strike before asking
his Marines to run across 200 yards of empty field. They had tried that the
day before. Three of them had been shot.

He ordered several of his Marines to form a base of fire, to suppress
the compound, and told two Marines—Hummel and Lance Corporal
Spencer Crowe—to be ready to run across the open with him and clear
the compound. Laney had a yellow smoke grenade, and told the Marines
who were staying back that when he threw it they should cease fire.

Minutes passed.

The Reaper pilot thought he had hit the place. Neff said there would
not be another airstrike. He told Laney to clear the compound. "Take
your squad and go, go, go," he said.

Laney, Hummel, and Crowe scrambled from the canal and began
running south. The field contained nothing more than the tan stubble
of the previous year's crop. It had not yet been tilled and did not offer
furrows they might dive behind for protection if the Taliban tried to cut
them down.

The rest of the squad fired as the men ran.

At about 100 meters out, Laney threw the smoke grenade. Its bright yellow plume rose and billowed on the still morning air.

First Squad ceased fire.

The three running Marines closed the last distance in seconds, hearing only their own breathing and thumping footfalls of their boots.

The man Hummel had shot was sprawled on the ground near the door. He had been hit just above the left eye. His radio was beside him.

Hummel rushed past.

They reached the wall, stopped briefly, then burst through the door firing.

Laney saw that Neff had been right. The missile had hit its target, exploding with a wave of heat and pressure and splattering the walls with shrapnel. Its blast had blown over an earthen interior wall and partly buried a Taliban fighter. The dead man's legs protruded from the rubble. An RPK machine gun was in the mess, unattended.

Hummel heard motorcycles outside, but not close, as if more fighters were fleeing.

The Marines tossed fragmentation hand grenades and cleared the remaining rooms. They found no one else within the building, and expanded the search.

Just outside another wall they found a third dead Taliban fighter. He sat upright in a shallow canal, head back, eyes closed, mouth open, in dark green pants and top. His left leg was twisted at a strange angle, as if broken multiple times. His right shoe was gone, exposing a sockless foot. His torso looked singed. Blood from his wounds seeped into the canal, tinting the water red.

Laney figured other Taliban fighters had been dragging their friend's body away and abandoned him as the Marines rushed.

The Marines returned inside and dug out the dead man. His head had been crushed. They made photographs of the two bodies killed by the Hellfire, for an intelligence report, and collected the RPK.

Hummel stood over the man he had shot.

He thought the Taliban fighters in these compounds were the same men who had killed Currier the day before. Currier had been a member of Hummel's team. Looking down at the corpse, Hummel felt as if he were settling a score. He had never killed a man before, at least not that he could confirm, and had wondered what it would feel like—if he would be sad, or scared, or angry. And now here he was, getting to find out. The sentiment registered: It was joy.

Hummel searched the dead man, taking his radio, rifle, and a chest rig holding several Kalashnikov magazines. He removed a wad of Pakistani currency from his pocket, and took a scarf. There was nothing left to do.

Laney radioed Neff and the rest of his squad to tell them they were coming back.

The three Marines ran across the field and rejoined the others.

First Squad was intact again, in the little canal, minus those who had been shot the previous day. Neff could sense his Marines' energy. They were sleep-deprived, parched, running on adrenaline, fueled by revenge. They were low on ammunition, and the barrels of their weapons were freshly cooled. They examined the weapons they had captured, and listened to the Taliban radio crackle with the sounds of their enemies' voices. It was a tongue they did not know. The meaning of the weapons seemed clear. The Taliban had fired that RPK, they thought, at First Platoon the day before.

"Hell yeah," someone said. "Fuck yeah. We probably got that piece of shit who shot Currier."

Marines surged with satisfaction and swore.

A Taliban fighter tried to cross the dirt trail on a motorcycle to their west.

One of the Marine snipers had been watching the spot through his scope. He shot the man. Another man stepped out to help the downed fighter. The sniper shot him, too.

Kilo company had moved far south, to the edge of the area where First Battalion, Sixth Marines were operating. Neff's mind worked like a checklist, processing the day, assessing his platoon's situation. He had a count of his Marines. *No one was hurt. No casualties.* To the east he saw armored trucks on the road. They were a familiar profile, the armored vehicles of one of the Marine companies that had entered Marja overland. They had caught up to Kilo. Their appearance meant that the rest of the battalion was arriving and First Platoon's flank was covered. Kilo would not be alone any longer, and the Taliban would know it.

Captain Biggers told the company to pull back.

Neff gave the word.

The snipers and the Marines of First Squad covered for Second Squad, to the west, as it began bounding north. Then it was their turn. They filed out of the canal and began walking briskly, weapons ready. This day had been for payback. Neff was proud of his Marines. They had been given a chance to fight on their terms, and they had fought well. *This is what I thought the Marine Corps was going to be like*, he thought. He felt good.

PART IV

Reckoning

Throughout 2011, the American military presence in Afghanistan remained large, at just under 100,000 troops. Officially the military said it was meeting its goals. Ground commanders and troops knew that the Afghan surge had not achieved what its organizers promised. Osama bin Laden was dead, killed by Navy SEALs in a raid in Pakistan in May 2011. And Mullah Omar remained in hiding, his relevance uncertain. But a new generation of Taliban commanders and local fighters, seasoned by a decade of war with the United States, held sway over much of the countryside, even as the surge crested and the Afghan government churned out new units. U.S. forces had spread out across the country, building bases and challenging the Taliban in remote areas, and now they were preparing to draw down and try passing responsibility to Afghan combat forces, which were unready. In Iraq, the Pentagon was completing a full withdrawal. The last American troops were due to leave the country by the end of the year.

ELEVEN

G-MONSTER

The Satisfaction of Restraint

"I prayed to be able to see action and be in combat. Now I pray I don't have to see combat and can avoid having to drop."

DECEMBER 31, 2011
Inside an F/A-18 Super Hornet over the Arghandab River,
Kandahar Province, Afghanistan

Commander Layne McDowell looked from the cockpit at the American military's battlefield presence below. He had returned to the Afghan war after an absence of a decade to find scenes and circumstances that bore almost no resemblance to the war he had left. When he departed the theater in late 2001, he hoped that his services as an attack pilot would not be needed over Afghanistan again. But in the intervening years there had been more war than he had foreseen, and a few hours before he had been catapulted off the USS *John C. Stennis*, a nuclear-powered aircraft carrier in the North Arabian Sea, to patrol an assigned sector of sky—a "kill box," in his community's jargon—to provide air cover to ground forces whose numbers had swelled and were roaming the Afghan ground. He expected a long day, at least seven hours in the seat, a flight requiring pacing between calls for help from ground troops and scheduled times to refuel.

For the moment it was quiet. McDowell scanned the ground through the infrared sensor of his targeting pod, listening to radio traffic.

He marveled at the changes, at how the urgent simplicity of the early Afghan campaign had been replaced by a ponderous, intricate, and entrenched military and air traffic control scheme. In 2001, McDowell had flown into Afghanistan stealthily. There had been almost no one to talk with on the ground. Usually he had an assigned target list, flew through nearly empty airspace, dropped ordnance, and rushed back to the ship, often without using his two-way radio. Now McDowell's F/A-18 worked in a sophisticated air-support system that rotated strike fighter and attack aircraft from multiple countries into Afghanistan's airspace; integrated them with drones, helicopters, and other attack aircraft operating from Afghan bases; assigned them to ground units and aerial fuel tankers; guided them to strikes or units in need; and then, after a mission, rotated them out. Afghanistan was a cluttered airspace. Pilots were at risk of violating air-control rules as surely as if they were flying over Atlanta.

Changes marked the ground below as well. Even when viewed from above 15,000 feet, Afghanistan looked different. It was as if a foreign force had colonized an arid planet. Rural provinces had been overlaid with American military bases and outposts. Even small positions were visible from the air, with linear blast walls and telltale gravel landing zones. Some bases were effectively small cities, with endless plywood shacks, motor pools, airstrips, and rows of palletized supplies. A few were watched over by blimps that swung far overhead, rooted by tethers and connected to video screens that gave soldiers live infrared feeds of their outposts' environs. The blimps angled up and away, pulled by dry Afghan winds. Convoys moved between them. The airwaves were busy with encrypted radio chatter.

McDowell was the executive officer of VFA-41, a strike fighter squadron from Lemoore, California. The Black Aces, the unit called itself. He was on his command tour, expected to deploy once with the squadron as its second-in-command and then return briefly to the States, become the commanding officer, and head back out to sea for a final tour in 2012 or early 2013. President Obama's Afghan surge was well into motion when he arrived. The American withdrawal from Iraq was under way. McDowell thought maybe the Afghan surge would be over before his next tour, though he sensed not. Even if the Pentagon was drawing down forces by then, airpower would be needed to cover whatever troops remained and to protect bases from being overpowered. Moreover, carrier-based aircraft offered the Pentagon an end run on its Afghan troop-strength cap. Naval aircraft were not stationed in Afghanistan. They did not count in the troop tally. For the Pentagon they amounted to an accounting trick—an expensive off-the-book asset that was present nonetheless. This almost ensured that as McDowell and the Black Aces would be back.

In the fall of 2011, before setting up off Pakistan's coast, the *Stennis* entered the Persian Gulf for what the Pentagon touted as the final air-support missions of the Iraq war. The campaign had shed its original name, Operation Iraqi Freedom, and replaced it in 2010 with an optimistic new label, Operation New Dawn. American combat brigades left the country that year, and during 2011, the remaining troops, many of them combat forces by training but assigned to "advise and assist" roles under the messaging of the day, were to leave Iraq, too. The war was not over. The country was ruled by a government class beset with corruption and sectarian tension. Al Qaeda in Iraq's descendant, the Islamic State of Iraq, lurked in Sunni neighborhoods and provinces, and the rest of the country remained crowded with militias of uncertain intentions. Its military and security forces were weak and often organized along sectarian lines. But the United States, determined to extricate itself from an unpopular war, was leaving.

Aboard the *Stennis*, F/A-18 crews were assigned to cover the departing ground troops on missions they called armed overwatch. The flights were long and the missions unliked. Communications with units on the ground were spotty. The Super Hornets left the carrier with little ordnance, and often, upon reaching the areas they patrolled above the desert, the crews would announce themselves over encrypted radios to ground forces that did not reply. Some of the younger aviators were miserable. They fit the same profile McDowell had fit as a younger pilot: aggressive, eager, hungry for action. They had trained to fly and to kill. Years of releasing precision-guided munitions had imbued their community with a peculiar form of confidence. The old bromides of general destruction through carpet bombing ("we'll bomb them back to the Stone Age") had been supplanted by the possibilities of their time ("we put warheads on foreheads"), but the mission over Iraq offered the Black Aces no chance to wield such power. The flights were boring. McDowell, as a senior pilot, was one of the most experienced aviators on the ship. He remained soft-spoken, thoughtful, self-contained. His job involved mentoring new aviators. One lieutenant junior grade, Sasha Young, flew the first combat flight of her career as his backseater. Between flights, she had heard him telling younger aviators that they were fortunate to see a war nearing its end, to look down from the cockpit at convoys of American troops headed home. "The campaign is over," he said. "We're here just in case." Young had been as bored as her peers. But she respected his view. For all of the strikes behind him, he was no braggart. She came to see him as a modern fighter, cerebral and mature, a leader who was not looking for action for action's sake. *Our job in Iraq,* she thought, *is to close the door on a war.*

Afghanistan would be different. In December, as the *Stennis* prepared to depart the Persian Gulf to take up its station in the North Arabian Sea, the aviators studied their squadron's next role. McDowell reviewed the change. In 2001 the Taliban held territory openly and had familiar infrastructure to strike, right down to airfields and bases. In 2011 military infrastructure in Afghanistan was held by NATO or Afghan government forces. The Taliban and other militants were almost invisible from the air. News reports and the briefings on ship described them all around the outposts, keeping government forces in a state of low-grade siege. But they rarely massed. They moved in small numbers and were almost impossible to distinguish from civilians. Outposts were kept alive by convoys on primitive roads and by helicopter support. The details cohered into a bleak picture. NATO officials rarely stated it, but Western airpower kept a far-flung American enterprise alive. Without aircraft to deliver precise and powerful munitions in less than an hour, the Taliban would be more assertive and bold. Outposts would be overrun. The officially sturdy but actually flimsy position that Afghan soldiers and small groups of Americans could hold remote territory would then unravel, along with the public relations messages and morale, which was already low.

Across the country the joint Afghan-Western hold was tenuous and sparse, challenged by patient enemies who had studied the Americans and their tactics for a decade. Obama's surge had pushed fresh forces out into much of the country only to meet populations that often did not want them there. Airpower helped reduce Western casualties. It bought time. But it could not win the war, much less foster real peace, and the statistics about its use could be reassuringly deceptive. The data showed that air strikes were relatively rare. This was not because violence was down. It was because the rules for releasing weapons were more restrictive than they had been, and the Taliban, so familiar with American response times, often attacked and withdrew before aircraft showed up.

In the cockpit of one of the most lethal tactical weapons the world had ever seen, McDowell faced the limits of American conventional military power. He framed his squadron's place in the Afghan war of 2011 in frustrated terms. A mission from ship to shore, he thought, was like flying in airspace around LAX, one of America's busiest airports, and then trying to find and attack a gang member with high-explosive weaponry and cause no civilian casualties—in greater Los Angeles. This was not how to defeat a gang.

His sentiments about being an attack pilot had evolved. In his first two tours, as a younger man, when he was dropping bombs he felt like he belonged. But after his first son was born the nightmare started—of entering a building he had struck and finding his own child in the rubble. The nightmare was occasional. It never intruded upon his sleep when he was in a busy flying schedule; McDowell assumed that this was because his mental and emotional bandwidth was fully occupied with the schedule's demands. It also never went entirely away. Its effects on him worked into his thinking. During his tour to Iwakuni he was grateful to be deployed away from the wars; the assignment meant he would not be asked to drop weapons where civilians and combatants were mixed.

Later, McDowell took a Navy posting in Alaska, working for ALCOM, the Pentagon's Alaskan Command. It was a non-flying staff job. He enjoyed it. He and Jolene bought land and built a house in Wasilla, along Cottonwood Creek, and they now had a second son, Grayson. When McDowell was not working, he hunted big game and fished with the boys for the Pacific salmon that ascended the watersheds and sometimes passed almost through his family's yard. Outwardly he was the archetype of U.S. Navy success. He cleared NASA's initial screening for the astronaut program, and was rated highly enough to be in the pipeline to command an aircraft carrier. The Navy signaled that it had big plans for him and that his horizon was boundless. He was selected for F/A-18 squadron command, and had only to decide which course to choose after his next flying tour. And yet sometimes, in spite of this success, McDowell thought of a major life turn. He contemplated a final squadron tour, followed by retirement to Alaska with his family. He'd been away enough to know the costs his Navy life had exacted on those he loved. He knew how it hurt. He kept his hand up for career-enhancing assignments. But a simpler life appealed to him. His mind moved down parallel tracks—the impeccable aviator's career beside a simpler, comforting dream.

He was assigned to VFA-41 in 2010 and sailed in 2011 aboard the *Stennis*, the third carrier he had deployed on in his career. When the ship steamed off Pakistan's coast, he was not eager to use his weapons. American air-to-ground tactics had changed in ways he generally approved of: Aviators covering ground units under fire often did not attack. Instead they flew down from high elevation and showed themselves, trying to drive the Taliban off by signaling their presence. These tactics were an explicit recognition that in the haste of fast-moving gunfights both pilots and the ground controllers orienting them had erred too often for too many years, killing Afghan civilians as well as Western and Afghan troops. Action, reaction, counteractions. The war's puzzles were ever harder to solve. Tighter rules reduced risks to civilians but also gave the Taliban more confidence that it would not be targeted, and introduced layers of supervision that could delay aid to ground forces in need. McDowell was not a pacifist. If a unit called for his bombs and he could be sure of his target, he would release them. He remained a product of the warheads-on-foreheads culture in which he had been raised. But he was older now, a veteran of many campaigns. Violence was more complicated than it had been.

On December 31, McDowell was directed west of Kandahar to patrol over a network of outposts along the northern bank of the Arghandab River. This was the literal birthplace of the Taliban, and since 2010 the Army had expanded its presence in the cropland to confront the Taliban in another of its rural strongholds, much like the Marines were doing to the west. Local fighters, familiar with the trails and walls and irrigation canals, had fought the American offensive ferociously. The valley had become one of the most dangerous locales of the Afghan war.

McDowell checked in by radio with a ground controller near Forward

Operating Base Wilson who used the call sign Heartless. The F/A-18 squadron's call sign was Vengeance. Heartless and Vengeance exchanged greetings and plans.

After the first portion of the flight, McDowell and his wingman departed to rendezvous with an aerial tanker. They returned to a unit in contact. Grunts had come under gunfire from across a farmer's field and wanted air support. Through his targeting pod, McDowell could see American vehicles moving slowly down a dirt road as troops checked for bombs. The Taliban was hidden from the pilots' view. The F/A-18s circled the fight. Heartless radioed more information. The grunts said they knew a building where attacking gunmen had hidden. They directed McDowell toward one structure, then changed the coordinates. At last they pointed him toward a different place. McDowell did not know which building to watch most closely. The grunts told him it was a hut used for drying grapes.* They fired a yellow smoke grenade at it, hoping he would see.

From the air, set against the tan earth and light-colored walls, yellow smoke did not offer enough contrast. McDowell could not see it. He kept his targeting pod on what he thought was the correct building, knowing that Heartless could see the feed live. The fight wound down. The radio traffic stopped.

McDowell circled, watching, seeing little, waiting for follow-up. There was nothing more from Heartless. With fuel running low, Vengeance had to leave. The Taliban had fought directly underneath them and ghosted away.

Back on ship, McDowell wrote of his hesitation and of the satisfaction of restraint.

> *Both us and the troops were thinking the same thing I think. Inside that grape hut are two insurgents who deserve to die. But we didn't know if they were alone. I thought about that house back in Kosovo I accidentally struck 12 years ago . . . this felt a lot like that, except this*

---

* In areas with large grape harvests, Afghan insurgents often used grape-drying huts—thick buildings of dried mud with ventilation slits—as firing positions. This made sense. The drying huts were ideal bunkers. Their walls stopped bullets and light shrapnel, and the slits doubled as parapets.

time I wasn't going to drop . . . who might be inside . . . kids? . . . maybe
more insurgents, but who knows, and the hut was surrounded by other
mud buildings. Who knows, maybe a school, maybe an orphanage.

Funny how things have changed in how I view things. As a JO* I
prayed to be able to see action and be in combat. Now I pray I don't
have to see combat and can avoid having to drop. Though I don't think
about it much, or try not to, there's still a lot of blood on my hands
from my first two deployments . . . all from people we intended to kill
(as far as I know), but it's the not knowing for sure that always makes
me pause. Glad I didn't drop today. Hope I can make it through this
deployment without dropping.

Happy New Year, Afghanistan.

A few days later McDowell was back over Afghanistan, this time far
west in Farah Province, near Iran, supporting an Italian unit searching a
mountainside for arms caches and rockets. The planes descended and
buzzed the mountain, hoping to flush out any Taliban fighters. Nothing
happened. The Taliban did not show. But the flight left an impression on
its pilot. A former farmer himself, McDowell was moved by the scenes he
saw at low altitude—a village on a riverbed amid brown, sun-scorched
terrain. The poverty seemed extraordinary. He wondered how Afghans
managed to raise anything there. He wondered how people ate. He wondered about his role. Some of the world's most expensive attack aircraft
were being applied to small and seemingly unsolvable tactical problems
in remote corners of the earth.

The next week he performed a similar role, flying low down the
length of a canyon northwest of Kandahar to help an American unit that
had been airlifted into the canyon earlier in the day and come under fire.

The *Stennis* was soon to be replaced. On January 11 the squadron
flew its final supporting flights of its Afghan tour. McDowell had not
dropped a bomb. Depending on the carrier's next tour, when he would be
a commanding officer, his service in war might have ended for good. In
his stateroom, taking notes to himself, he admitted to feeling relief.

---

* Acronym for "Junior Officer."

I can't bear the thought of injuring anyone who doesn't deserve it, es-
pecially if a child were injured during an attack. I think back to the
house I accidentally bombed in Kosovo and wonder who was in it. . . .
I hope no one. But I don't want that kind of haunting anymore. I'm
glad it's over. I hope my days of flying in combat are over.

On January 13, clear of its requirements to have planes over Afghanistan, the ship had a no-fly day, and sailors passed their hours with maintenance. The *Stennis* sailed away from its box in the North Arabian Sea. The
next day McDowell was scheduled for a flight in which his Super Hornet
would serve as a tanker to pass fuel to aircraft awaiting turns to land on
the ship's flight deck.

It was a routine mission, and potentially boring compared to the
more complicated flights over Afghanistan. But as the evening light grew
soft, something special happened. Out in the pattern around the ship, far
above the surface of the sea, McDowell encountered a flat and level deck
of clouds.

He felt a rush of joy. Clouds, in his experience, were usually dynamic.
They tended to have vertical development. They did not often settle into
stable pancake shapes. The clouds before him were something he rarely
saw, much less when he had time to spare. He descended and closed on
them. He was happy—even elated.

Although F/A-18s can fly at supersonic speeds, in many flights there
are no visual cues that give an aviator a frame of reference. Aside from
the g's experienced, a pilot often has little sense of how fast an aircraft is
moving. High-speed, low-level flights change all that. Cues appear outside the cockpit's windscreen. The ground in its myriad details, or waves
on the ocean's surface, whip by in an extraordinary and constantly changing view. A pilot literally *sees* speed. It registers in the brain like danger,
a threat. The body reacts involuntarily, feeding the pilot adrenaline with
such intensity that it creates a sensation with its own nickname. Ground
rush, aviators call it—an unmatched high. Supervisors frown upon pilots
who get hooked on ground rush. Chasing its fix is a fine way to lose an
aircraft and get killed.

As a younger man McDowell sometimes chased it anyhow. It was an
exhilarating thrill, the experience of flying in a hyper-stimulating fashion.

As a commander by rank and an executive officer by position, he was expected to behave differently. His seniority and flight hours attuned him to his place in the machine. He emanated self-control. His days flying fast and low over sand were behind him.

But clouds? This was something else. The cloud deck gave him a substitute for the ground, and a means to realize that old high. This, too, had its nickname: cloud surfing. By dropping his Super Hornet just above the top of the clouds, he could skim along the surface of this horizontal barrier, soak in visual feedback resembling what he'd get flying close to the dirt, and stimulate adrenaline flow. He could fly even lower to the cloud than he would dare to the earth, so close that it seemed as if the skin of the Super Hornet would scrape the clouds and be peeled away. And there was no danger of striking anything, nothing to fear.

McDowell made his first pass.

No matter what his mind knew, his body could not be convinced.

Adrenaline poured into his bloodstream. He was electrified, supercharged, ecstatic. He reached the end of the cloud, climbed, turned around, dove, and surfed back. Racing above vapor just below his feet, Commander McDowell was happier than during any of his recent flights above Afghanistan. He was alive.

On the first flight of his life, as a child taking off out of San Diego on a passenger jet, McDowell had looked out the window as the plane entered thick gray clouds from below. He was still staring out when it broke through into light. The sight of the tops of the clouds, a brilliant vista he had never seen before, cemented his desire to fly. It helped set his life on its course. Cloud surfing above the North Arabian Sea, filled with rapture and wonder, seduced by a spontaneous pleasure, McDowell was carried back to that moment.

For thirty minutes, in an attack aircraft with no bombs, he raced back and forth, the wars behind him, soaring as if through a celestial place. It was as close to heaven, he thought, as a living man could get.

President Obama won reelection 2012, and as he began his second term the war in Afghanistan, upon which he had focused the Pentagon four years before, remained a brutal contest against a Taliban that had survived his surge. But the Afghan forces were more numerous, and since 2011 the American military had been leaving its Afghan bases and returning home. By late 2013 its force in Afghanistan had fallen below 50,000 troops, with plans to fall below 20,000 by the end of 2014, and perhaps a nearly complete withdrawal for 2016. Both Iraq and Afghanistan were sliding back toward violence. The Islamic State of Iraq, the Sunni terrorist organization that had not existed prior to the American invasion, had expanded into Syria and was gathering strength under yet another name, the Islamic State of Iraq and Syria, or ISIS. It held American hostages, was luring recruits from abroad, and was soon to break out and encourage terrorist attacks across much of the world.

TWELVE

THE FIGHTER

Gail Kirby's Demand

"I am not the same Mom who sent her son to Iraq."

NOVEMBER 4, 2013

Inside the George W. Bush Presidential Center in University Park, Texas

Former president George W. Bush opened the door to his office and looked upon his guests. The entire family of former Navy corpsman Dustin E. Kirby—Doc himself, along with his parents and his brother and sister—stood before him. They were eager and anxious, unsure what to expect from the man who had sent Doc to war.

Bush extended his hand. He was the picture of a gracious host. "Thank you for coming," he said. "Welcome, welcome."

The invitation to visit the presidential center, extended at the Texas Motor Speedway the afternoon before, left no time for the family to gather dress clothes. Doc had come to Texas to be honored at a NASCAR race. He was dressed for speedway stands. He stood in front of the former president in jeans, a plaid shirt, and a black baseball cap. A 7.62-millimeter rifle round dangled from a necklace made of parachute cord.

Bush wore a suit jacket. He chided Kirby for the hat. "You're wearing a cover indoors?" he said.

Kirby had voted for Bush in 2004 while Iraq spiraled deeper into violence. In only a few seconds of seeing the former president in person, he noticed things he could like. The man opened his own doors. He greeted guests without staff. His eyes looked sincere. Nothing about him was officious. He had less attitude than some of the officers and first sergeants Kirby had known. But life had carried Kirby past protocol. He was not going to apologize for his look. He kept the hat on his head.

"I'm not on active duty no more," he said. "I'm retired, sir."

Bush did not take the bait. He led the family into the room.

It had been almost four years since Bush left office and nearly seven since Kirby had been shot. Time had been kinder to the former commander in chief than to the corpsman. Kirby had endured more than two dozen surgeries. His jaw had been rebuilt with a bone graft, screws, and plates. The work had not set him right. His bottom teeth did not align with those on top, and a section of his mouth was a food trap that he often had to clear with his index finger when he ate. He was in constant pain and self-conscious about his appearance. He had gained fifty pounds. He was medically retired, unemployed, divorced, and disfigured. He was also on probation in the state of Georgia for a reckless-driving conviction. Years of drinking had left their mark.

A battlefield corpsman with two Purple Hearts, Kirby matched a stereotype revered in the American imagination and celebrated in official discourse. And yet he was not entirely free. He needed permission from his probation officer to cross the Georgia state line.

He sat in a chair across from his old commander in chief. He'd taken a long road here, and experienced Bush's war from a perspective a president would be unlikely to understand. So much had happened. It was late now. What could either man say?

Beside him, his mother, Gail, looked on. Her son might not know what to say. She did not have that problem. She had prepared for this moment. She waited anxiously, biding her time.

Dustin Kirby woke in Landstuhl, Germany, on December 27, 2006, two days after the bullet slammed into his face. He had been unconscious since the anesthesia washed through him on the first operating table in Iraq. He slept through a pair of flights and returned to consciousness slowly, with no idea where he was. He did not feel like himself. He felt heavy, as if something were pressing him to the bed.

As a trained health care provider, he forced himself to assess. An understanding of his circumstance formed. He was alive. He recognized that he was in a hospital. He was not sure where but it did not feel like Iraq. He was breathing, but not through his nose—a tube entered his trachea. He remembered: the rooftop bunker, the blow to the face, his teeth and a piece of his jaw in a bloody pile by his knees, a helicopter ride, trying to stay awake as the blood rolled from his chin to his chest to his thighs. A nurse walked into the room.

"Oh, you're awake," she said. "Let me go get the doctor."

She hurried away.

Doc thought she sounded nervous. His mind was foggy but working. *She's trying to stay calm.*

A doctor appeared. He was accompanied by a staff sergeant Kirby did not know and a younger Marine from Doc's battalion who had been wounded before him. Both men were looking at their feet.

Kirby did not have to be told what it meant. *They don't know what to say.*

The doctor did. He caught his patient up: He'd been shot in the face two days ago and was stabilized in Iraq before being flown here to Germany, where the staff was assessing him and planned to put him on a flight to the United States soon. The doctor described what the bullet had done. Kirby's mind seized on stray words and phrases: "missing bone," "fractured jaw," "lost teeth."

What the hell is this guy saying? he thought.

The doctor asked him if he understood.

He didn't. But he was busily taking in more details than the doctor had shared. His eyes followed the breathing tube to the ventilator. He was a serious case. He nodded, to make the doctor go away.

The two Marines remained.

A rolling table with a mirror stood by the bed. Kirby wanted to see his face for himself. He leaned forward, dragging hoses and tubes as he moved. Vertigo spun him. The room rolled upside down.

He dropped back onto the bed. The two Marines watched him, unsure what to do. The younger Marine decided. He pushed the mirror toward him.

"I don't think that's a good idea," the staff sergeant said.

Rank meant nothing here and now. The younger Marine adjusted it so Doc would have a full view.

Doc looked. A face stared back at him, swollen to enormous size. He did not know it.

That's not me.

Both of its eyes were darkened; one a deep blue, the other a light green. A hump of skin and flesh protruded from the face's right cheek, as if the cheekbone had been broken and its ends were angled up and out from a mound of meat. Beside this strange lump he saw a large hole. He categorized it immediately. *This must be where the bullet had exited*, he thought. He noticed thick sutures, gauze, and dried blood, and the ventilator tube. He kept scanning—part patient, part provider—looking for anything familiar, a sign of himself, of the face he used to know.

He thought he recognized the top of his forehead.

He was not even sure of that.

He looked back at the hole where his right cheek had been. He heard an echo of the doctor's words: "missing bone."

Bones that are missing are gone.

This is bad, Kirby thought. *What will I grow to replace that?*

He pushed the mirror away.

He settled the back of his head into his pillow. He had already classified his case: He was not going to be one of those wounded vets the magazines write about, the maimed soldier who rebounds to run marathons and scuba dive. His face was broken. Part of it was gone, just as if someone had scooped it away with a jagged spoon. He could not speak. One part of his mind wanted to scream. Another was a corpsman still, trained in medical care.

This is going to be an extensive process, far beyond dentures and wiring the mouth shut, he thought. *This is going to be years.*

He calmed himself. His face hurt. He could see that he was hooked up to the IV drip. *Painkillers*, he thought. He'd soon be dosed again, and back asleep. These were the first minutes of his new life.

Anger flashed through him, momentarily overriding fear. A lot was headed his way that he did not yet understand. In his last conscious hour he had been in an outpost in Iraq, ringed by militants waiting with rifles and bombs. He was not ready to be a patient. He was still wired to fight.

What the fuck ever, man. I don't care.

Kirby slept.

———————

Doc's mother, Gail, woke Christmas morning feeling crushingly sad. For months she had dwelled on her son's second tour in Iraq. The news from the war was unrelentingly grim, and unlike his first tour, which he spent mostly on ship, he now was serving the entire time in one of Iraq's most violent provinces. Fear was her companion. It followed her everywhere.

Gail had started a new job at the Kmart in Hiram in the summer and she had been trying to learn the position. But she felt distracted, worn down by mental and emotional fatigue. The Christmas season drained her further, with its streams of shoppers and long hours. She closed the store Christmas Eve and was late getting home, where she discovered she had missed Doc's holiday call from Iraq. He had spent Christmas Eve on Camp Fallujah, a safer place than out on Route Chicago. She did not know he had gone back, or that he had been assigned to a rooftop post. She felt heartache. She wrote him an email, reminding him of the Christmases they had shared and promising good things to come. At last she went to bed.

In the morning the holiday took an unexpectedly upbeat shape. One of her cousins, who had three young children, was spending Christmas at Gail's home, filling the house with energy. Doc's new wife, Lauren, visited with a gift. Lauren and Doc had been married just before Doc left for war. By afternoon Gail had an uplifting realization: She was having a good day.

In the evening she stepped down into the basement to have a cigarette out of sight of the children. She was due back at Kmart in a few hours to open the store for the overnight stockers. Its shelves had been picked bare and needed to be filled for a December 26 sale.

One cigarette, she thought. *A moment away.*

Destiny, Doc's sister, rushed down the stairs. She was holding the telephone.

"It's Camp Lejeune, and they won't tell me anything," she said.

Gail took the phone. A Marine staff sergeant identified himself in a flat tone.

"I am calling to inform you that your son, Dustin Edward Kirby, has been hit by enemy small-arms fire in Iraq," he said.

Gail's mind stumbled over the language. *Enemy small-arms fire? What does that mean?* She thought she knew.

Her mind would not let it stick. *Enemy small-arms fire.*

Then it registered.

"What?" she asked. "He's been shot?"

The staff sergeant repeated the sentence like he was reading from a note card.

She raised her voice. "He's been shot?"

She didn't hear an answer. *I am his mother. He is my kid. They have to tell me.*

She shouted the question: "HE'S BEEN SHOT?"

The basement was becoming a blur of disassociated motions and sensations. Her husband, Jacko, stood at her side. She had not seen where he came from. She was screaming uncontrollably. "You promised!" she shouted. "You promised!"

Someone was trying to hug her. She struck whoever it was.

"Mama, please stop," she heard.

She recognized this voice. It belonged to Daniel, her younger son.

Regret mixed with her grief. She had to take care of Daniel, too, and of Jacko and Destiny. She was more than Dustin's mom.

Why have I been so focused on just Dusty?

Dusty.

Jacko took the phone and walked into another room.

She had not heard the details. *Dusty. Is he dead? He's dead?*

IS HE DEAD?

Jacko returned. He was somehow under control and able to talk in the clipped language of a man clinging to facts he had just heard. He spoke as if everything would depend on him sharing a verbatim account. Dustin had been shot through the face, he said. He was alive and in critical condition. Doctors had stabilized him in a military hospital in Iraq. The Marines planned to move him to Germany, then home.

The words meant one thing to Gail.

He's alive.

She still had little idea of what it meant. *Shot through the face?*

The phone rang again. Her family was crossing into a new world, passing into the territory of the grievously wounded, a place of its own. She had no sense of time. Doc's battalion commander called from Iraq. Between calls she and Jacko notified their larger family. They had a duty of notification. People needed to know. The family already had one wounded corpsman. Now it had two. There was so much to share, and yet so little. *Dusty got shot in the face. Dusty's hurt, but Dusty's alive.*

Calls went out. More calls came in.

Already everyone was talking about how to relocate to Washington to visit Dusty in the military hospital, to help him, to learn the contours and customs of the new universe pulling them in.

For a while, Gail and her mother, who was nearing eighty, sat away from the others. Curled into a fetal position on a swinging bench on her back porch, Gail laid her head across her mother's lap. They rocked slowly back and forth in the cool Georgia night. She was speechless, feeling her mother's hand running softly through her hair, and then it was time to go.

Gail did not have her Kmart manager's home number. She had to drive to the store, find it on the call list, and ask for time off. She drove wordlessly through the empty Christmas night, let in the workers for the overnight shift, made the call to her manager, and headed home. It was late when she stepped back into the house. Most of her family was asleep. The lights on the Christmas tree were bright. She was waiting to find out what had become of her son, and of her family's life.

My Dusty, she thought. *What does it mean to be shot through the face?*

———

Most people struck in the head by military rifle fire die instantly or soon after, and never reach the operating table. They leave nothing for surgeons to do. Doc Kirby's wounds were among the rarest seen. The bullet blew through his mouth from left to right, ripping through bone and tissue but missing major arteries and veins. One minute Kirby was intact. The next he was dying. Then he was saved by a trauma team. He was wheeled into Bethesda Naval Hospital a few days later as the newest member of a tiny cohort—those who survived rifle shots to the face. He was more than a man now. He was a living exhibit of chance and the blind indifference of ballistics. A sniper making a thousand shots might not manage to replicate the result. Had Kirby's head been turned slightly, if the angle of the shot had been different by a fraction of a degree, had it entered his face an inch higher or farther back, he would have been killed. Instead the bullet cut a left-side entrance hole, hit teeth and tongue, and blew through the right side of his jaw and out his right cheek, ripping open a hole. The impact cracked his lower skull near the roof of his mouth and damaged his sinuses.

Gail and Jacko arrived at Bethesda Naval Hospital as their son, fresh from evacuation from Europe, was being wheeled down the hall. Gail had a glimpse. She thought he looked agitated but was not sure. She stood in a waiting room until the staff had moved him to a room and allowed the couple in.

She rushed the bed, scanning his face, crying. At first she focused on his eyes. They were expressive. His eyes told her he was there. Then she looked him over more closely. For four days she had wondered what he would look like. She had not anticipated this. His face was so swollen that it looked like he was hiding a bowling ball in his mouth. His bandages were stained with seeping blood.

He could not speak but wrote notes on a pad of paper. His mother was a fresh source of information. They talked past each other. She wanted to know how he was. He wanted to know about his battalion and whether everyone else was okay.

"Have you heard from my boys yet?" he asked, then asked again.

Doctors explained the procedures ahead. His surgeries would require more than reconstruction. They would require replacement of rows of teeth and a chunk of jaw. Soon after his return, they began. They removed his right fibula and grafted part of it to the right side of his jaw. With screws and plates, the transplanted bone created a hybrid mandible where the original had been. His face was being remade.

Lauren, his wife, took turns at his bedside with his parents. His pain was excruciating, lessened by drugs administered through an IV machine that he reset when the staff was not looking. In this way he could decrease the time between doses and exceed the prescribed amount. Nurses fed him nutritional shakes. He vomited many of them, sending them back up through his wired jaw in frame-shaking heaves.

A week passed. Then two. His face healed. The rest of him grew weaker. He lost weight. When he stood, he felt dizzy—a mix of drugs, exhaustion, a disrupted sleep schedule, and the lingering effect of the jolt to the brain. The physical-therapy staff urged him to leave the room for walks around the hospital floor, in family areas and outside. He resisted. When he made eye contact with strangers, he felt them squirm.

He was taken off the ventilator and breathing through a hole in his trachea. He still could not talk. His family and nurses hand-bathed him. Privacy was stripped away. Depression gripped him, along with a narrowing sense of hope. *Getting shot in the face in some ways is the worst wound possible,* he thought.

Some of his handwritten notes reflected irritation, discomfort, and pain. "I itch," he wrote. "I am nauseous." Hospital life required endless small adjustments. "I just want a better pillow," he wrote, between requests for more medication or changes to the bandages over a sore on his backside.

Other notes were electric with insecurity and fear. "If I stop breathing, will you help me?" His mind could feel fevered with anxiety. "It scares me so bad. Could you give me some low grade anesthesia to keep me from freaking out."

At times he summoned humor.

"I am gonna vomit," he wrote one day. "Would you prefer I used the term 'oral discharge'?"

Guilt stalked him. Kirby had been flown home early. He believed he had let Weapons Company down. On this theme he would write and write, scribbling on loose sheets of printer paper or a yellow legal pad. "I could never stay out of the fight. I am a warrior and I just feel like a failure. I should be there. I should be fighting still. I just wish that everyone else would get to come home."

Dignitaries made their rounds through the hospital to visit wounded troops. Kirby observed the rituals, replying like the faithful prop his circumstances forced him to be. "Honored to serve," he'd write, or something similarly accommodating. Inwardly he was angry. The visits felt like mere formalities, senior officers checking a box. Some of them presented him with challenge coins, medallions with military unit insignia or sometimes a general's name. Self-referential junk.

"Put this coin with the rest of my coins," he wrote, after one officer left.

He vented later to Gail that it was as if these visitors did not understand military service, or that he was part of a company of Marines: "Something gets on my nerves about all these congressmen and generals and bigwigs, like all these people, they don't ask anything about my unit or how they are doing or feeling or anything like that."

One officer was different: Major Justin Constantine.

A Marine reservist and lawyer who had volunteered for a tour in Iraq, Constantine had been shot through the mouth by a sniper about two months before Kirby. The bullet hit the back of his jaw beside his left ear and exploded out his mouth. He was further along in the reconstructive process than Kirby and an outpatient who returned to the hospital for surgeries, therapy, and follow-up care. He was learning to talk again.

One day after Doc's reconstructive surgery, Constantine arrived at his bedside and introduced himself, in slightly slurred and labored speech. He explained his own wound, although the description was almost unnecessary. His face was a calling card.

Kirby had never met another patient who had been shot in the face. He could talk differently to this officer than he could to the others. He took up a pencil and apologized.

"Not much to look at, sir," the note said.

Constantine had been warned to expect something negative.

He opted to be stern, telling Kirby that while the bullet had gone through Doc's face from left to right, the one that struck Constantine had gone through his head at a worse angle, from back to front, and caused more damage. But in spite of the severity of the wound, he had done whatever his doctors told him to do, and was making progress.

He summoned Kirby's sense of duty, reminding him that he was a corpsman. He asked him what he would tell his Marines if they had been wounded the same way.

Kirby said that he would tell them to do their therapy and rehab.

Constantine said they both knew guys who didn't come home from Anbar. They owed it to them, he said, to make the most of every day.

"You are going to get better," he said. "I am an old man and I am doing it. You're a young man and you can do it, too."

Kirby watched the major closely. Constantine's speech was imperfect, but he was articulating words. Kirby could understand him. And Kirby could see the major was living a life. He was not hospitalized. He was eating real food. He walked the corridors alone. He projected no self-pity. He radiated determination. It all suggested possibility and hope. The major told him to concentrate on small steps and immediate problems, and not to be overwhelmed about what he had lost or how long his recovery might take.

"Don't think about before, or too far ahead," he said. "Think about the here and now."

Kirby wrote back, "Thank you, sir. Thank you for everything."

After the major left, Kirby took his first shower. He examined himself in the mirror a second time.

His face remained huge but his body had shrunk, wasted from weeks of inactivity and limited food. But this time, after the first rounds of reconstruction, he could almost make himself out. A row of sutures ran along his jaw, holding together a wide purple scar. *Big ol' zipper face,* Doc thought. His face looked as if it was under pressure from within, like it might burst. He knew the surgeons were just beginning, and that his remade jaw needed time to set and heal. His windpipe was still an open vent through which he was breathing. Soon it would be capped. Then, Kirby thought, he would breathe through his mouth and nasal passages and try to speak again. The mirror was loaded with information. He was coming out of early trauma.

Okay, this is me, he thought. *I'm stitched up; I am plated and screwed together. This is the beginning of this journey. Shit is happening now.*

Now when I am getting out of here?

Second Battalion, Eighth Marines, was scheduled to return to the States in February. Doc made it his goal to be there to greet them. By late January, doctors closed his tracheotomy and he began breathing through his mouth and nose. His voice was clumsy and thickly slurred. But to talk at all was relief. Suddenly he was not scribbling notes. After a swallowing study to ensure he could ingest soft foods and liquids, he was discharged from the hospital and returned to Georgia on medical leave. He had weighed about 180 pounds on Christmas Day in Iraq. He left the hospital at 137.

He bought a Chevy pickup truck and was issued Georgia license plates bearing an image of a Purple Heart. He was a wounded warrior now—a member of a class. He and Lauren drove to North Carolina to meet the Marines of Second Battalion, Eighth Marines, as they returned to Camp Lejeune.

The Marines had flown back to the States and were bused to the battalion area to return their rifles and equipment. Wives, children, girlfriends, and parents swarmed the grounds, looking for their Marine. Seabags were in piles. Doc found Weapons Company and strode to its small mountain of green bags and started moving them, just like the working parties he had been part of throughout his enlistment. He was wearing jeans and a black fleece over a gray T-shirt. His short hair was gelled. He had shaved and was regulation. He had been eating solid food again and had pushed his weight back up near 150, but his frame was still skinny, his face outsized and creased by a large purple scar.

No one recognized him.

No unit likes it when a stranger touches its kit. Corporal Upton strode up to him to ask what he was doing in the blunt-speak of grunts.

"Who the fuck are you?" he said. The two men had been in a truck together when it was hit by an IED. But Upton could not place him.

"Who the fuck am I?" Doc answered. "Who the fuck are you?"

Then it happened.

"Doc?" Upton said. "Doc Kirby?"

Marines from Weapons Company rushed them. Pressed tight among his Marines, Kirby was encased in the biggest hug of his life.

The joy of the reunion, for all of its authenticity, did not last. Dustin Kirby's wound and the bitter undercurrents of Weapons Company's Karma tour were the ingredients for a crash.

Doc was no longer a member of an infantry battalion. The damage to his head ensured he would never join a line unit again. The fragility of his rebuilt face, his speech difficulties, the absence of a fibula—these disqualified him from combat duties. Being a corpsman had been his identity. He clung to it. But his circumstances required him to trade infantry duties for life as a recovering sailor.

At first the routine held promise. He and Lauren rented an apartment, he joined the battalion that tracks the rehabilitation of wounded Marines and corpsmen, and soon he was splitting time between treatment centers on or near Camp Lejeune and the naval hospital in Bethesda. But physically he was diminished. He was unable to run and could not work out. He had few responsibilities beyond healing. For a man of his intensity, the official aimlessness of his new status was maddening. The wars in Iraq and Afghanistan continued. He wanted a meaningful role.

In pain, beset with anxiety, prone to rage, and at risk of seizures, he began unraveling. Doctors prescribed pills: Ativan, Seroquel, and Depakote, along with Percocet and morphine sulfate. The cocktail disagreed with him. He had not joined the Navy to be a junkie, and he wanted to stop using anxiety and seizure medications. *This will turn you into a zombie and make you fat,* he told himself. But doctors kept prescribing more pills, and his pain did not relent. He put on weight, slowly climbing over 200 to 215. Painkillers became an accepted staple of his life, the engine of a grim logic: Fear of letting the pain get ahead of his meds kept him glued to the dose schedule. He was reliant on his pills, physically and psychologically. His leaner, agile self was gone.

Old friends from his infantry battalion visited him, but the reunions often were not uplifting. He remained dedicated to most of Weapons Company's Marines. Many of them were trying to grasp the meaning of their combat tours. Had it been worth it? Had they helped? Why had they been ordered to fight the way they fought? Doc tried pushing aside any larger assessment of the war. He was of two minds. He accepted that he did not understand all the reasons behind the American occupation, or the Marine Corps' tactics, or their prospects for success. He had not seen much in Karma that he thought worth fighting for and no longer bought the idea that what the Corps was doing in Karma was tied to American security at home.

He could not dwell on this. He opted to remember his own reasons for serving: to care for Marines in combat. His entire being was invested in that. But sometimes calls and visits from his friends came with ugly whispers, the agonizing rumors of a combat tour, including that Doc had been shot by one of Weapons Company's M4s. The stories varied. In one, an Iraqi sniper had obtained the rifle the sergeant had lost in Karma and used it to shoot him on the roof. In another, a Marine had tried to kill him, either because of a rivalry or a grudge. The rumors formed a dispiriting mash of postwar barracks gossip. They were unverifiable, corrosive, and profoundly cruel. Doc was unmoored, unsure whom or what to believe.

It was bad enough to have been wounded while standing extra duty as punishment. It was worse to be haunted by other questions. Was he a victim of negligence? Attempted murder? Cover-up? Or had one of Karma's snipers simply set up with his own weapon near OP Omar on Christmas Day and waited for a clear shot? The last scenario was more than plausible. Snipers around Karma were hitting Marines before their company lost an M4. With no firm or conclusive answers, he passed days believing he had been ruined by error or crime, then cast aside by the unit he had faithfully served.

He and Lauren were young, new to marriage, and under extraordinary strain. Their bond weakened. They fell into quarrels. Recriminations piled up.

Officially, Doc Kirby was a hero. Personally, he was in a spiral, racked by anger and doubt, like a man who wondered whether he had been betrayed by his own church. The Navy assigned him to a small medical clinic for boot Marines attending their first infantry school. It was an out-of-the-way post, a satellite shop.

Doc understood that he had been sent there because his bosses did not want him around. He managed to enjoy some of the duties. He often ran morning sick call, treating and documenting minor injuries and common illnesses. Sometimes he instructed new Navy corpsmen on what to expect when they went to war, assuming the mantle of battle-scarred veteran holding forth. He was an imposing presence, teetering toward a fall. By 2008 he was drinking heavily and ignoring warnings that his painkillers and alcohol should not be mixed. He filed for divorce and slid further into a funk. Trash, laundry, and dirty dishes accumulated in his apartment. He

kept cold beer in his pickup truck in the parking lot and in a small refrigerator at the clinic. Some days, after seeing patients in the morning, he
would sit in his shop and drink. He knew this was wrong but it alleviated
pains he could not quell.

He wanted to recover, and tried. At least twice a month he attended
PTSD therapy or biometric feedback, to train himself to recognize his
triggers and learn to calm down. He stopped taking the anxiety medications. He could not dispense with painkillers or alcohol. Lauren returned.
They tried to reconcile. They parted again.

One night after she had moved out for the last time, Doc was alone
in his apartment when he accidentally called his mother on his cellular
phone. It was a pocket call. Gail was shocked by what she heard. "We're
going to see him," she told Jacko. They drove to North Carolina and found
their son, the decorated combat veteran of Anbar Province, alone in a
state of squalor and with a refrigerator low on food. His parents remained
for the weekend, doing laundry, taking out trash, cleaning rooms. Gail was
scared and mad. She blamed the beer and the booze. She rejected the idea
that it was anything more, and would not hear any suggestion that Doc
suffered from PTSD.

They're not going to put that tag on my kid, she thought.

She left, determined to pray harder for her son.

A weekend of mothering was not enough. Doc Kirby did not change.
The gunshot had stolen his identity and purpose, and saddled him with
unceasing pain. His years after Iraq extended into a blur of surgeries and
duties that did not challenge him, all while he jealously watched fresh
crops of Marines training for wars that would not end. Years passed bleakly
by: 2008, 2009, 2010. He had trouble telling them apart. Battalions returned from Iraq, refitted, restocked with new officers and boot Marines,
and flew off for Afghanistan. He worked in an infantry-producing machine. Younger faces filed by, as yet unbroken. He stayed put, shattered.

He had not joined for this.

Gail and Jacko were unsure how to help. *He's drinking his wages,* Gail
thought. They invited him home to Georgia for weekends and holidays,
to remove him from an environment where he was embittered and stag-
nating. She asked God to help her son find his way.

In June 2010, on a trip back, he met Brandi Smith, a single mother with two daughters, one four years old and the other a newborn. She was separated from the girls' father. They began dating. Brandi moved to North Carolina to be with him, not long before the military decided it could neither do more for his wounds nor expect him to be able to serve abroad. The Navy retired him medically in early 2012, severing him from the active-duty forces for good.

The return home was jarring. Five years of bouncing between Bethesda Naval Hospital and Camp Lejeune had left Doc semi-functional and struggling with substance abuse. But active-duty service had organized his life, coming with a regular paycheck, an apartment, and daily proximity to people who understood. It gave him a partial sense of belonging, enough to prevent complete collapse. In Georgia, however, it was as if he were starting adulthood over, with no routine at all. He had been somebody in North Carolina, surrounded by sailors and Marines. In Georgia, surrounded by civilians, he was no one. He felt unknown. The downward slide was swift.

Doc moved into a bedroom in his parents' house and began drinking prodigious amounts of booze. Soon his room was lined with empty green Jägermeister bottles. Brandi had a job at a convenience store. He spent days sitting on the front lawn, often alone, tending bonfires. To keep the fires burning, he removed the trees and bushes beyond the house and fed them to the flames. He abandoned the military's grooming standards and let his hair and beard grow. Sometimes he wore a long knife sheathed at his side.

Joe Dan Worley, Kirby's cousin, had gone back to Georgia years before him. He had survived the IED blast on the bridge in 2004 but lost his left leg above the knee. His right leg was damaged, too. But he seemed to thrive. He had a job and was active at a Baptist church, where he was a youth pastor and deacon. He was committed to fitness, and often in the gym. Years after the blast, he was muscular and lean, with a torso and shoulders like the Superman that Dustin had always thought him to be.

One night, the two men met at a family gathering, a pair of cousins, both medically retired corpsmen from the Marine Corps' Anbar campaign. They talked about their respective wounds, and about how each man had been injured in ways that undermined his particular sense of self. Worley, the athlete, lost a leg and his mobility, and the ability to participate in his favorite sports. Kirby, handsome and confident, had suffered a disfiguring trauma to his face. He was prone to drooling and felt unsightly. He told Worley that he felt disgusting. "We both just got hit in our vanity," Worley said. He looked at Kirby with worry and concern. Five years had passed since he had been shot, and he was not adjusting.

Gail was a devout Christian. She knew her son was in there, but she did not know how to reach him, and disapproved of his drinking, which she considered the source of his troubles. She saw positive signs when he was with Brandi and her children. His enthusiasm returned, along with a playful and upbeat demeanor. He could exude pleasure. But it was never enough. Brandi had to return to work. And Doc returned to his fires and his bottles. Some days he was drinking before lunch and continued until he passed out, late at night.

His neighbors did not know what to think. In April 2012, a few weeks after returning to Powder Springs, Doc stood in front of his house in a sleeveless T-shirt and torn blue jeans, wearing black work boots with his knife. He weighed about 220 pounds. His arms were covered with tattoos, and his beard was patchy and long, partially hiding the scar that traced his indented right jaw. The fire burned a few feet away.

Three girls, about ten years old each, rode down his quiet street on bicycles. When they neared the Kirby house they spotted him on the lawn. Like a school of fish, they abruptly turned and crossed to the opposite side of the street, giving him wide berth. Doc watched, knowing that they saw him as grotesque, a human eyesore on their residential street. He was used to it. He remembered people's reactions the first time he stepped into the halls of Bethesda Naval Hospital. They had turned their eyes.

"All the kids who ride past the house each day, they look up here at me on the lawn and they think, 'What a weird guy,'" he said. The fire burned at his feet, crackling and snapping, sending smoke into the warm Georgia air. "Adults drive by here and think that, too."

He had been sipping rum and soda over ice since morning and eaten nothing but a slice of pizza. His doldrums seemed complete. His pay stopped when he left the Navy. He was due for a medical pension, but there was a delay before it kicked in. He was behind in his bills. At the pace he was burning the foliage in the yard, before long the Kirby property would be bald. He still wondered who had shot him and whether he'd been hit by an American weapon. He loathed what he had become. *I went from being an independent, capable person to being nothing, living on my parents' couch.*

In early May, Doc was in Marietta, spending an evening with Brandi at her brother's house. He had a few drinks at dinner, played with her daughters, gave them their baths, and helped them to bed. He was brooding. After the kids fell asleep, he and Brandi quarreled about how she was using her phone. It was a harsh argument, more than he could bear. He shouted at her, so loudly that a neighbor called police. Shortly after midnight, before the police arrived, he stormed out of the house in pajama pants and unlaced sneakers, started his pickup truck, and drove away. He wore no shirt. He was not sure where he was going. He eased his pickup onto U.S. Route 41 North and sped through town. He was crying and blaring emo music. Tears rolled down his face, over scars. He shouted, then screamed. He drove through the commercial corridor at more than 80 miles an hour.

At the intersection with the Ernest W. Barrett Parkway he turned left and headed west. Barrett Parkway is a six-lane country road, and often clogged with traffic by day. It was deserted in the darkness before 1:00 A.M., a veritable speedway now. Doc's mind opened in an exhilarating rush. He pushed the accelerator to the floor. His GMC pickup had a 350-cubic-inch eight-cylinder engine. Its speed climbed quickly to 90 miles per hour, then slowly kept rising beyond that. He came upon a red light, could not stop, and blew through it, still accelerating.

Oh, great, now I am going to get a ticket I can't fucking pay, he thought.

He kept the pedal pressed to the floor.

The speedometer moved past 100 to 110.

It finally stopped at 120 miles per hour, pegged.

The asphalt hissed by underneath. The road was a wide and gently turning ribbon and he managed to make its turns. Time felt distorted. He was amazed. No one had stopped him, he had not crashed, he was in control of the truck at an almost impossible speed.

"Fuck it," he said.

He'd die right here, right now.

There was a spot ahead where the road turned slightly to the right and the shoulder fell away to a downhill incline that led to a stand of trees. Behind them was a row of houses. Doc usually slowed before the turn.

He kept the accelerator floored.

The distance closed.

Eyes fixed ahead, he saw there was no guardrail at the turn.

There.

That would be the spot.

He did not turn or release his foot from the gas. He removed his right hand from the steering wheel and reached down and released his seat belt.

The truck's front tires hit the curb with a jolt and burst.

Its front end seemed to lift into the air as the ground sloped away beneath it. He was airborne, gliding in a truck cab at more than 100 miles an hour. The truck hit. It snapped the trunks of small trees. Glass shattered. Metal twisted. The truck banged to the ground, crumpled around him, and stopped.

His troubles were no more.

The night was still. He heard no sound.

Except for the small driver's compartment, which had wrapped around him like a bubble, his pickup truck was destroyed. Kirby sat in the wreckage, waiting for blood and pain, expecting to discover his bones were shattered and it was impossible to move as he bled out. Death would carry him off. He had seen the Reaper before, and knew the color of his eyes.

But he had barely been scratched. He was alive.

"Fucking shit!" he screamed.

His phone rang. He rummaged around in the darkness until he located it. It was Brandi.

"What the fuck!" he said.

"Where are you?" she asked.

"I don't even know. I just got in a car accident."

A police officer was with her, she said, and she was going to pass him the phone. The officer asked him which road he was on.

"I am on Barrett Parkway somewhere," he said.

The officer told him to stay put. The call ended.

Doc stepped from the wreckage, walked uphill to the parkway, and called his parents. Jacko answered.

"It didn't work!" Doc said. "It didn't work."

A police car, emergency lights on, eased beside him. The lights made him squint.

"Are you Dustin Kirby?" the officer asked.

"Yes, sir, I am," he said.

The officer asked what had happened.

"I tried to kill myself, man," Doc said. "And it didn't work. This fucking blows just like everything else."

This was the bottom, and even here he thought he had failed. In the glow of the police lights, the wreckage of his truck behind him and down the hill, Doc started telling the officer a little bit about everything—about Iraq, about his wounds, about his discharge, about his absence of a mission and sense of self-worth. The officer was a former Marine. He said he understood. Doc's phone rang again. His parents were calling back. The officer asked for the phone, told them where Doc was, and urged them to come for their son.

Two more police officers arrived, and a wrecker.

The first officer told Doc it was time to leave.

"Look, I am going to place you under arrest," he said. "Are you going to fight me?"

"No," Doc said.

The officer was courteous. "Well, you're pretty a big guy and you had a rough night and we don't know," he said. He turned Doc around and cuffed him.

His parents arrived as Doc was being taken into custody. Gail pleaded with one of the officers. "That's my son, let me go to my son," she said.

She was not allowed near. She watched from afar, looking at her beautiful first boy. He was ungainly. He moved as if in slow motion. When he had enlisted in the Navy, he was nothing like this. He had been gorgeous before. He was cuffed, tattooed, bearded, stuffed into a police cruiser, gone.

The police took him to a hospital, where he was found to be unhurt, and then to the Cobb County jail.

Kirby was arraigned on a reckless-driving charge in the morning. His suicidal wish had faded with the crash. He felt as if a burden had been lifted and he could discuss his pain. He returned to his parents' home. His mother and he began to talk. She said that for the first time she was aware he suffered from PTSD. She admitted that she had not wanted to acknowledge this before. He heard an understanding he had not found in the past. That day he did not drink. He stayed sober into the night, and the next day, too. He did not drink in the weeks after either. The court soon sentenced him to probation and therapy. His face hurt, eating was hard, and he remained self-conscious. He was weighed down with agonizing emotions and bouts of crushing doubt. But as he attended therapy he was moving toward acceptance. He was seeking peace of mind.

Gail was changing, too, growing into the roles her life as the mother of a wounded corpsman demanded. She was reading up on PTSD and becoming involved with veterans' support organizations and conversant in their work and their causes. Her perspective changed about her son's return from the war. She realized that even if he had not been shot in the face, he would still have PTSD and difficulty reintegrating into civilian life. She began speaking at veterans' events, sharing details of her family's suffering. And she looked for chances for Dusty to be honored, so he might hear gratitude and encouragement from people outside his immediate circle.

In the fall of 2013, through the Armed Forces Foundation, she nominated him to be a guest of Kurt Busch, a NASCAR driver, at a race in Texas. He was selected and received permission from his probation officer to leave Georgia for the trip. The entire Kirby family was at the speedway when one of the organizers, who had worked for President Bush, said he was trying to arrange a personal meeting with the former president, whose office was not far from the NASCAR event. The follow-up was fast: Bush would see them, Gail was told, the next morning. She slept fitfully. This was an audience every veteran's mother should have. She did not intend to squander it.

———

President Bush looked fit for a man nearing seventy. He offered coffee to his guests and thanked them again for visiting. He was interested in veterans and their families, he said, and pleased to meet Doc and his family and hear about his service and their lives since the war.

He seemed to have a format, and went around the room. He turned to Daniel and Destiny and asked them about their work and school.

"Attaboys" all around, Doc thought. He knew his turn was coming and was not sure what he would say when asked. The whole meeting felt over-the-top.

What do you say to the president of the United States?

Doc knew the truth: He had not been doing much since the Navy sent him home. He had little to report and did not want to complain. Nor did he want to disclose all that had gone wrong, including the fact that to visit Texas he had needed permission from a parole officer in Cobb County.

The president turned to him. Doc was a sight, with his black cap above his beard and scars. He had been a fighter once, well groomed and lean.

"How about you?" Bush asked. "Are you going to school?"

"No," Doc said.

He had thought about his answer, about finding a balance between honesty and a happy progress report.

"I'm not doing much of anything really," he said. "I'm living my retired life, trying to keep myself together.

"I kind of fell out of the military and sat where I landed," he added.

He left it at that. It wasn't Bush's job to fix his life.

Bush pressed. Doc said he'd been in an accident but was better now.

Bush nodded thoughtfully. He thanked Kirby for his Navy service and his work with Marines, and talked about the value of his commitment and sacrifice. Doc was surprised. The man seemed like he really was trying to get through.

This is the guy who was making all the big calls, and he's talking with me?

He knew Bush met many veterans of the wars. It seemed as if he had learned something, Doc thought, and understood Weapons Company's time in Karma—even though he couldn't possibly know the details. He told Kirby that after what he had done, he needed to get up and live his life and not waste it on meaningless days.

Doc nodded back, the way one does to a boss. "Thank you, sir," he said.

Bush smiled at Gail. It was her turn.

"Hi, I am Gail," she said. "The mom."

All the barriers were gone. She was having a one-on-one with the man who had sent her son to war.

"What are you doing?" the president asked. "Do you work?"

"Yes," Gail said.

She wanted to push past small talk. She had practiced what she would say, and she was annoyed by what she had just heard from her son. Dusty had downplayed his troubles and his mistakes. He'd allowed himself to be charmed, and had not given the president the real information. She looked at Dusty dismissively.

"Did you hear him?" she said to Bush. "He told you about that truck accident like it was nothing."

She wanted Bush to know the truth. Too many people must sugarcoat things for him. Why should the Kirby family hide what it had endured?

"He tried killing himself by driving his truck into a tree at speeds in excess of 120 miles an hour," she said. "I am not the same mom who sent her son to Iraq. I'm different now."

Doc squirmed in his chair. *Buzzkill,* he thought.

She was ruining the ritual and undercutting him in front of his former commander in chief. *Damn,* he thought. *He was proud of me.*

Gail did not stop. This was her turn. "It would have destroyed us if he'd been killed," she said.

"I know," Bush said.

She took her eyes off Bush to look at her oldest boy.

"Dustin," she said.

"Mom," he answered.

"It would have destroyed us."

Bush looked at Doc, too. The former president had turned serious and set his face.

"Were you drunk?" he asked. "Or just being stupid?"

Dustin remembered the drive that night, the desperation, the last miles before the deliberate crash, the sound of the tires hissing on the road, the release as he chose the moment to die. He could feel that depression. People did not know what coming home from war is like, much less coming home maimed and in ceaseless pain. He was displeased with his mother—*Here she is, blaring all my shit at the president,* he thought—but nothing that could be said in this meeting would be as bad as that wearied despair.

"I wasn't really thinking about anything other than giving up on my situation," he said. "I didn't feel like I had anything going. I felt like I wasn't what I was, and I didn't have anything left."

And that's it, he thought. *Honesty.*

He waited for Bush's reply. None came. The meeting had turned. Gail was driving now.

She kept going, talking fast, seeking assurances that Doc's wounds had not been for nothing. She needed to know that this man had really been in charge. "You did know what you were doing, right?" she asked Bush. "Because let me tell you what it is like for a mom when her son goes to war."

Gail had prepared a monologue and practiced its lines overnight. The president would listen to her script.

"I realize that you may not understand what we are going through as parents while our child is serving in a foreign country during a war. You may not have a son that is serving. But you do have that grandchild that you are completely in love with."

She stared at the president, and held his gaze. He looked back. She plunged on.

"Now picture that baby being out in a car seat and put in the middle of the highway, a very busy highway, with hundreds of cars that are zooming past him all day long.

"You know in your heart that that baby will be safe as long as no cars swerve even just a little bit. You pray every minute of every day that those cars stay away from that yellow line and your baby in that car seat.

"That is exhausting enough.

"But to make it harder, we will put you in an office with a TV that is playing the footage of those cars driving past your baby every minute of every day, for weeks on end. To make it even more realistic, there must be hundreds of babies, dressed exactly like your baby, in the same state-of-the-art car seat, lying on that yellow line as far as your eyes can see.

"You know in your heart that every baby has a mom praying as hard as you that their baby stays safe.

"But you pray even harder now."

She kept talking, barely allowing time for breath, allowing no pause for the president to interrupt. She was looking into Bush's eyes.

"You get absolutely exhausted, watching that TV every minute that you can, only leaving when it is necessary.

"And then it happens: One of the cars swerves just enough to clip a baby.

"Is it yours?

"Is that baby dead?

"Oh, God, tell us something!

"If it is, the phone will ring or there will be a knock on your door.

"You wait and pray even harder, dying a little every second that passes.

"The special report comes on and it is not your baby.

"Thank you, Jesus.

"Thank you, Jesus.

"Then the road is cleared and the cars are speeding past those babies again.

"So you go back to watching all of the cars again.

"You are so thankful that it is not your baby that you celebrate for a minute.

"And then it hits you: It was someone else's baby.

"Then the guilt pours over you like a heavy blanket, adding to the exhaustion that you already feel.

"But all that you can do is watch that TV, because you know that it very well could be your baby the next time.

"Then one day a car swerves, and it's your baby.

"It's your baby that was hit."

Gail stopped.

She turned to her son. He sat bolt straight in his chair. He couldn't believe what he had heard. His mother was going after the man, the commander in chief, like she was in charge, not him. *Damn*, Doc was thinking. *Wow.*

She turned back to Bush. He had sat through her monologue silently, maintaining eye contact and shifting slightly in his chair. Now he looked around the room, at all the tense faces. Each member of the Kirby family was waiting for him to react. Jacko was braced for anger, expecting a thunderclap.

That's a president of the United States right there, he thought. *Nobody talks to him like that.*

Gail did not care. Her son had been shot. She had not come here for ceremony, or to be denied her agency or right to speak.

Bush's demeanor was gentle. He leaned forward.

"That's quite an analogy," he said.

"I am sorry," he said. "I am responsible, I know. I sent him there."

Gail had grown used to people changing the subject. The aftermath of the wars was beyond what many people had the time or heart to hear. The Kirby story was too big, and it was just a small part of it all.

But she had unloaded on Bush and he was still there listening. Her family's experience was being validated. She was exalted, carried away by the experience of being heard. *He's not like so many people,* she thought. *He respects us.*

These veterans deserve respect, she thought.

Gail Kirby felt herself relax. Her concentration drifted. The rest of the meeting was a blur of small talk and coffee before Bush asked his guests if they would like to have their picture taken with him. This was their signal to go. Gail led Jacko and Doc's siblings to an anteroom for the shoot. For a moment Bush and Doc were one-on-one. The president had shown his disappointment in Doc's postwar slide. He seemed alarmed at Gail's description of a man who had saved others' lives and later chose to drive his truck off the road to end his own. Not many people stepped into presidential offices like this. With his scars and tattoos, his beard and baseball cap, Kirby could be mistaken for anger personified. He was not. He had survived his leaders' bad ideas and Karma's efforts to kill him to come through a chain of disasters alive. His mouth was a mess. His eyes retained the brightness of youth. Bush suggested that no one should waste such a gift. Countless mistakes had brought them here, along with crimes to shame the world. The former president smiled, held up his right hand, and gave the former corpsman a fist bump. "Make better decisions," Bush said.

Epilogue

The chaplain arrived at Tanja Slebodnik's door early in the afternoon of September 11, 2008, not long after she had put her three-year-old son to bed for his afternoon nap. He was accompanied by an Army officer Tanja did not know. He said something about Mike having been shot in the leg. *Oh, thank God,* she thought. *We can handle that.* They kept talking until she understood. Her husband was dead.

They stayed with her for about two hours as she notified Mike's world. First she called his parents in Western Pennsylvania. Then she called her mother. She called Mike's ex-wife, and a few others, and it was done. They explained some of what would follow: the return of her husband's remains, the inventory and return of his personal effects, death benefits that would be paid, arrangements for his funeral. Ben, Mike's youngest son from his previous marriage, returned home on the school bus at 2:45. She took him upstairs to share the news.

The weeks that followed proceeded in a gray procession, punctuated by anguish and frustration and fear. The Army did not bring Mike's body home for more than a week; there was some sort of complication, the casualty assistance officer told her, about finding all of his damaged leg. Two more senior officers visited. They spread out maps to show her the flight routes on the day Mike died and described something of his last mission, and something else about the long route to the hospital in Bagram and the efforts to resuscitate him. If they had gotten him there faster, he might have survived, they said, because they did have an adequate blood supply on hand. After they left, she was perplexed. *Why did they tell me this? What was the purpose?*

She withdrew. She discovered she could not bear the sound of the doorbell. Each time she heard it, she thought of the chaplain on her step. She disconnected it so it would not ring again.

Before the burial at Arlington National Cemetery, Spencer, another of Mike's sons, put a Bible Mike had given him on his father's chest.

The return of Mike's personal effects was a special form of torture. His possessions arrived in black plastic footlockers with inventory sheets. She opened the first box. A foul odor rose to meet her. Everything had been sanitized. It was hideous to Tanya, but she followed her duty to her husband methodically. The casualty assistance officer instructed her to mark each item off the lists as she unpacked, and she did this, down to the Army's maddening level of detail, right down to the last half-used disposable pen. When she lifted his laptop, she felt hopeful. Here would be the things she would cherish and want—his journals and photographs—and that would allow her to glean some sense of his last tour.

The laptop would not switch on.

The Army told her it had wiped his hard drive clean. It did this, she learned, for everyone who died.

When the last crate was empty, she realized the Army had not returned his wedding ring. She called the casualty assistance officer, who said there was no record of it.

She could not understand. The Army had accounted for every scrap in Mike's pocket, had logged in and registered even his toothbrush. *How could they lose his wedding band?* Tanya pursued it for months, calling and sending emails up and down the Army chain of command. As time passed she sensed she was driving people crazy. She did not relent.

In early 2009, at home, she was looking for something else when she opened a small, heart-shaped porcelain box she had kept for years. The wedding ring was inside with a note written by her husband's hand.

"I love you," it said. "Mike."

Viper Company suffered no more fatalities after Private First Class Richard Dewater was killed on April 15, 2009, and in the weeks that followed, Second Platoon's ambushes—one outside and one inside the kill zone—came to seem like seminal events.

The platoon shifted some of its tactics, working more often at night or in larger, company-sized operations. The violence in the valley declined. Intelligence units tracking the Taliban and listening in on their communications began to hear some of the valley's commanders participating in attacks outside Korengal. Fighting continued around the KOP, but the clashes were less frequent and intense. It may have been that the Taliban changed its focus, or that the Korengalis were playing things smart and were less inclined to fight Viper Company at the end of its tour, when its experience level was highest and its fire-support reaction times were dialed in. Or it may have been that the ambush on the ridge had proved costly to the Korengalis, or that the uptick in American night patrols and the larger operations left them off balance.

One linchpin of the American strategy had been to fight the Taliban away from population centers, in part through outposts the military called blocking positions. The troops understood that the assumptions in this strategy were weak. The Taliban was not really blocked. Its fighters had no trouble leaving the valley, and the soldiers in the outposts, bound by strict rules of engagement, had almost no chance of stopping them.

Aware of these limits, Captain Howell and Lieutenant Rodriguez were quietly recommending to their superiors that the Americans depart their outpost. They did not propose a retreat. They favored a negotiation in which the Taliban would make concessions. They sent a letter, via the elders who came to Captain Howell's *shura*s, to Nasrullah, the Taliban's leader in the valley. They proposed a measured American withdrawal in exchange for a Taliban commitment to reconcile with the Afghan government and a pledge not to allow the Korengal to be used as a staging ground for attacks.

Viper waited for a reply. At last a letter came back, saying perhaps the Taliban and the Americans could work out a deal, but only if the Americans would convert to Islam. Until that time, Nasrullah said, New York and London would have to burn.

Rodriguez did not think this was necessarily a bad start. At least Nasrullah had replied.

Soto knew nothing of this. He was busy with the patrols and his duties as the platoon radio operator. He noticed the difference in Viper's tactical posture. His platoon moved more by darkness and less by light, and no matter the prohibitions from Kabul about entering Afghan homes, its soldiers sometimes searched homes in the deep of night, trying to capture the able-bodied men who formed the bulk of the local insurgency.

These missions reaped few results. The houses almost always held only women, children, and elderly men. But many soldiers appreciated doing them. Night raids made them feel like they were fighting rather than role-playing a failed doctrine. They beat walking on presence patrols by daylight to talk with elders who gave scripted responses.

In the spring a new crop of soldiers showed up at the outpost. They were from the Fourth Infantry Division, assigned to replace Viper Company. Soto watched their numbers grow. They were neatly shaved and noticeably fit, wore clean uniforms, and carried new rucksacks and CamelBak water bladders. They looked fresh, charged with an energy Viper Company faintly remembered about itself. Soto felt a mix of sadness and goodwill. *I want them to succeed,* he thought. *We all want them to succeed.* But there was so much to tell them and not enough time, and some of them, self-conscious about filling in behind a seasoned unit, bristled at instruction. Viper took them on patrols, and in June the two groups pored over inventory sheets together and Viper handed over much of its equipment. *These are your radios now,* Soto thought. *These are your vehicles.*

He felt especially keyed up in the last weeks. A photograph of him running out of the kill zone seconds after Dewater had been killed had appeared on the front page of the *New York Times*. Word of his combat service rushed through his circles in the city. Friends wrote him on Facebook and email. For almost a year Soto had shrunk his world to a grunt's regimen. Sometimes he assumed a fatalistic view and was all but certain he was going to be killed in the valley. This made his job easier. He had accepted that he would not be going home. Now he felt pressure not to die. He passed the last days with a heavy understanding: The new unit was not going to win over the locals, much less quell their resistance. Some missions, including one when the platoon was instructed to search for bombs along the road, still seemed like a suicide lottery.

In mid-June, Soto walked his final Afghan patrol beside his replacement, giving advice. He was packed. All that was left was a helicopter ride to Bagram. It would be by darkness, to reduce the chance of having another aircraft shot down. That night he and a small group of Viper troops sat on the dirt of the landing zone, under a bright moon, the seats of their pants on gravel and dust, their backs pressed against stuffed rucksacks. They were near the mechanics bay, where the remains of their peers who had been killed had waited in body bags for their own flights home. Soto was outwardly still. His mind churned. The very nature of his existence, the routine by which he stayed alive, was changing. It was minutes from being over. *My life is not going to be the same, when everything is calm and I am supposed to act normal, whatever that means,* he thought. Something did not feel right. He was jolted when he realized what it was. *I know I am going to miss this place, for some fucking crazy reason.*

A soldier gave them a heads-up that the aircraft was inbound. Soto heard the low thud growing to an engine noise, which became louder and was joined by the aircraft's high-pitched whine. Just before it landed, the company first sergeant appeared. He was handing out unit coins. It was dark. Dust swirled as the aircraft descended, and no one could see anyone else's face.

The first sergeant grabbed Soto and shouted at his helmet.

"Who's this?"

"Soto!" he shouted back.

"Soto?"

The first sergeant pressed the coin into his hand. "Man, you really deserve this."

Soto cherished the words. He had been respected. This was worth more than any medal. It was authentic, unlike so many medals he had seen.

He belted himself into his seat in the aircraft and switched on his iPod. The bird lifted away. It banked and accelerated down the valley.

Soto felt momentarily jittery—*This is where they shoot*—but the helicopter cleared the danger area quickly and settled into a fast, even flight.

Back at Fort Hood, he adjusted poorly to garrison routines. The base seemed a hot and dusty wasteland. His peers gradually departed, either leaving the Army or heading off with new orders. He asked for an assignment to jump school and a transfer to the 82nd Airborne Division, so he could get back into the action. The Army granted his requests and in early 2010 he checked into his new unit at Fort Bragg. Soon after arriving, he overheard that one of its brigades had been assigned to earthquake relief duty in Haiti. He volunteered the same day and was sent to Port au Prince.

Soto was in Haiti when the Army announced that it was closing the Korengal Outpost and withdrawing from the valley. On one level, he understood. American plans for the Korengal had failed and American lives were being lost in a pointless stalemate. But he was crushed. Multiple units had passed through the valley, losing lives. And now the Army had decided, *Never mind*? Why had it taken years to acknowledge mistakes?

When he returned to Fort Bragg in the summer, Soto did not fit in. The 82nd could seem like a ceremonial unit on post, invested in toy soldiering. In 2011 his unit was sent to Iraq for Operation New Dawn, to help with the withdrawal of American equipment and combat forces. He was a sergeant now and leading a fire team. His Iraq was nothing like his Afghanistan. His team was part of a base security force with a narrow mandate, and spent much of the time guarding the perimeters of airfields as planes carried away troops and whatever else the Pentagon wanted to keep. He never patrolled in nearby villages and had almost no exposure to Iraqis. The country had entered a period of relative calm. The insurgents appeared to have decided to let the Americans go. Soto saw no direct action but had learned to doubt official military narratives. When he flew to Kuwait in late 2011, among the last of the American soldiers to leave Iraq, he did not feel as if peace had been assured.

Soto separated from the Army with an honorable discharge in 2012.

In 2013 he moved in with his grandmother in the Bronx and enrolled at Monroe College. In 2014 he transferred to Columbia University and graduated in 2017 with a degree in Political Science underwritten by the GI Bill. He was back to chasing the dream he had held before enlisting: a career as a performer. He was twenty-seven years old, gaining distance from the war and traction in his life. War had come to his city when he was a child. Now he was a soldier returned home. He was ready to try peace.

After Kilo Company, Third Battalion, Sixth Marines, pushed south and avenged the killing of Private First Class Currier, most of its Marines returned to the village where Captain Biggers had made his command post. Their stay lasted only days.

Lieutenant Neff was given a few last missions near the landing zones and bridge. His platoon cleared a hilltop with a radio tower, unwittingly crossing through a belt of IEDs that had been badly made and failed to explode. The hilltop was a former Russian military position where a cracked and empty inground swimming pool was ringed by trenches. Another Marine, Matthias Hanson, from Second Platoon, was killed in a gunfight the same day. More Marines were pouring into Marja overland, including combat engineers with heavy earthmoving equipment and lumber, who began constructing crude outposts. The first position, Forward Operating Base Hanson, was made just below the hill and radio tower, near the intersection and bridge that Kilo Company had been ordered to clear. It looked directly upon Haji Mohammad Karim's home, where the HIMARS rockets had struck.

The company was ordered east, along the road that connected Marja to Helmand's provincial capital, Lashkar Gah, to another newly constructed outpost at Five Points, a road intersection in open farmland. The Marines spread out, with platoons on each side of the dirt track and a convoy of trucks proceeding down the center, but they were delayed when a vehicle broke down and by the slow process of clearing the road of hidden bombs. It was two days before they filed into the outpost. Another Marine company was there and had the place under guard. For the first time since being helicoptered into the landing zone almost ten days before, Kilo could relax. Its Marines fell asleep on bare ground.

Five Points, and a string of small observation posts along the road between it and Forward Operating Base Hanson, became Neff and his Marines' world for much of 2010. Spring came. Temperatures climbed, then became stifling. The poppy crops rose around them, and bloomed in fields of red flowers. Neff and his platoon rotated through duty in the observation posts and walking small patrols. Often they were drawn into quick gunfights. There was a lull in May, when Afghans harvested poppy for the opium trade, but by late that month the violence resumed.

Kilo Company's presence kept the road open and its frequent patrols created a reasonably safe corridor in a stripe of farmland on either side. Outside this belt and similar areas around other Marine outposts, the countryside remained thick with Taliban fighters. The road to Lashkar Gah, Neff thought, was "the Wild West." A British and Afghan army outpost out that way had limited influence, and felt isolated, too. To the south, the other Marine battalion was engaged in regular fighting also. Marja had not been quieted. It was a perilous combat zone, not a liberated community grateful for a foreign military presence.

The American government chose not to interfere with the poppy harvest; senior Marine officers said they would nudge local farmers into growing alternative crops the following year. Their decision was a concession. If the Americans took on the poppy farmers, they'd face open warfare from the people the generals said they had come to Helmand to protect. Neff let others worry about plans. He and his Marines focused on patrols. He was suffering from large painful cysts, including one on his tailbone that could make it hard to walk. He refused to take time for treatment. He would not miss a day while his Marines were outside the wire. In July an Afghan soldier at the British outpost attacked the British command post, killing three members of the Royal Gurkha Rifles. The attack sent a chill through Kilo Company, which suffered strained relations with the Afghans living at Five Points. This was the real Marja. By the time First Platoon's tour was over, the conditions the Corps had said it would create—a Taliban on the run, an economy uncoupled from the drug trade, Afghan security forces capable of independent operations—sounded in retrospect as naïve or dishonest as the propaganda of Soviet Union's Afghan try.

Not long after Kilo rotated home, Neff turned over his platoon to a new lieutenant, checked into a hospital, and had the cysts removed. He was on medical leave until November, when his time in the Corps was almost over. He hung around Kilo Company's office for a few weeks, a lieutenant without a job. No one knew what to do with him, but among many of the Marines who had fought in Marja he was accepted—the officer without officer ambitions, who sought no perks, trusted enlisted Marines, and shared every risk. He kept to his original plan: to go home and pick up his life where he'd left it, and to become a cop.

Neff checked out of the Corps in early 2011 and spent much of the year in the gym and on the beach in North Carolina, living on his savings while pursuing police jobs in Massachusetts and growing closer to his girlfriend, Brittany Everett, whose family lived outside the base gate in Sneads Ferry, where they had worked for generations in commercial fishing. Neff filled out applications, took tests, and underwent background checks for police jobs near Boston. This time, with his veteran's status, his application was viewed differently. He was hired by the Massachusetts Bay Transit Authority before the end of the year and started the police academy in 2013. He graduated on a Friday in July, proposed to Brittany at a Red Sox–Yankees game in Fenway Park that Sunday, and started on the police force the next day. (The Red Sox won, in extra innings.)

In 2017, Neff and Brittany moved back to North Carolina, and he began a job as a civilian police officer on Camp Lejeune, where he remained in the Marine Corps reserves.

By then Marja had flipped to Taliban control. The place was as dangerous as it had ever been, and maybe more so.* The American government was again debating what to do about Afghanistan. Many of the Marines from Kilo Company were civilians. Some wondered why they had been asked to do what they had done. Questions lingered, too, including about the HIMARS strike on Valentine's Day, which the Corps never bothered to explain to the young men left to clean up. Niall Swider, who was shot in the first days of the fighting, remembered the pre-assault pep

---

* The Marines' presence served to harden the Taliban and perhaps improve its skills, including in fielding more sophisticated IEDs. Among them were directional fragmentation charges that could be detonated by remote control with receivers that were offset and away from the device. These could be used against patrols equipped with portable jammers.

talks from the generals, the sell. It was as if the brass had decided before the operation that Marja was to take its place beside Tarawa, the Chosin Reservoir, and Hue—a battle to be recorded as institutional legend. *Forever you will be known as Marja Marines,* they had said. Many units passed through the same fields. The Taliban outlasted them all and reasserted its primacy when the Corps drew down. Except for abandoned outposts that stood over the fields where Marines like Currier and Hanson had died, and for the loss of Afghan civilians killed by errant fire, the place was little changed. What changed was the Marine Corps' enthusiasm for the place. Swider said that when so-called Marja Marines mentioned their campaign, senior Marines "told you to shut the fuck up."

Neff took an accommodating view. He accepted that the Marja push had not been a strategic success. He kept his thoughts on his platoon, a group of tough grunts he had come to know only because another officer was arrested for driving drunk. They fought hard and looked out for one another. As he saw it, that was all a grunt could do. Higher-ups had failed. They had not. He was proud.

———

Layne McDowell's break from the Afghan war did not last long. The USS *John C. Stennis* and the aviation squadrons aboard returned to the United States in early 2012, and McDowell became the commanding officer of VFA-41 soon after. By summer the Navy notified its units that the *Stennis* strike group would sail back to the Middle East ahead of schedule. Mc-Dowell and VFA-41 turned around fast and were back on another deployment late that August, this time for eight months.

Soon he was above Afghanistan again, flying his third tour over the country. The American war effort had crested. A troop drawdown was at hand. The Taliban had not been defeated. It remained part of the Afghan social, political, and military fabric. Aircraft could punish its forces when they dared mass, and the aircraft's presence also helped prevent remote outposts from being overrun. But these were supporting roles. The war had hardened into patterns that F/A-18s could not break. Sophisticated targeting sensors, guided munitions, and tactics refined through a dozen years of air-to-ground war could not change facts on the ground. There was no clear end to any of it, and few people had expectations otherwise.

On one flight north of Kandahar, McDowell and the other aircrew accompanying him were not assigned to a ground unit. He was flying in his
kill box, scanning the ground through his FLIR, when he saw an American convoy making its way down a road. One of the vehicles was hit by an
IED. McDowell saw the flash.

The vehicle stopped.

Troops rushed out.

High above them, McDowell wanted to help. But they were not part
of his mission and he did not know their call sign or the radio frequency
they were communicating on.

There was a building near where the troops scrambled. McDowell
suspected someone inside had detonated the bomb.

He wondered if the Americans were wounded.

For a half hour he tried calling nearby ground controllers and the
air traffic authorities, to volunteer his services. He never managed to
make contact with the soldiers on the ground. He was not even sure the
troops realized he was watching. They were looking at the same things
at the same time, but apart. He ran low on fuel and left them to fight
their own war.

It was the closest he came to dropping ordnance on that tour. Some
of the younger F/A-18 pilots in the squadron had not released a single
missile or bomb in combat during two deployments overseas.

McDowell never dropped a bomb again. The *Stennis* returned to the
States in mid-2013 and the aviators departed once more for their airfields.
McDowell led his squadron home in a thirteen-aircraft flyover formation
in the shape of a spade. That summer he turned over command of VFA-
41 in a two-plane flyby that marked his last flight as a strike fighter pilot.

The rules that codified restraint were malleable, and did not last. As
McDowell finished his career in the cockpit, the Islamic State was rising in Syria and Iraq, asserting its presence and gathering strength. Upon
its breakout in mid-2014, when it drove American-trained Iraqi forces
from much of the Sunni territory in Iraq and seized the city of Mosul,
the group occupied a large swath of territory in two countries. From this
self-declared caliphate, it held American and European hostages, produced snuff films and other extreme forms of online propaganda, and
trained jihadists for international terrorism and war—all while fighting

a ground war on multiple fronts. Soon it was claiming responsibility for terror attacks across the world, including in the United States. The group, forged in Sunni insurgency during the American occupation, had not existed before the United States invaded Iraq in 2003. Eleven years later, and roughly three years after McDowell and his fellow pilots had been told they had closed the door on the Iraq war, it drew the United States back into Iraq amid a broader conflict in the Middle East. The new campaign was pursued with less restrictive rules. Calls for warheads-on-foreheads were back.

The war against the Islamic State was not McDowell's to fight. He had been a contender for aircraft carrier command, and was a member of the tiny ring of his service's rising leadership class, on the cusp of Navy royalty. But he retained the sensibilities of the Texas cotton farm where he had been raised. Before the Islamic State became a household name, he had already opted out, and asked not to be considered for high-profile command. He wanted to see more of Jolene and their two sons, Landon and Grayson, who had spent much of their lives with their father away. He sought stateside jobs in the Navy and by 2017 was a captain in the Department of Defense's Alaskan Command, the director of its plans and policy shop, seeking to finish his career in the state he had chosen for a home.

In the summer, the water that flowed along the McDowell property sometimes filled with spawning Pacific salmon. He tried to take time off during the runs.

Leo Kryszewski recovered from most of the wounds he had received in the rocket attack at Balad. The first months were difficult. Soon after arriving home, he attended a memorial service for Major Syverson, who had been killed at his side, at a chapel at Fort Campbell. Kryszewski had been in Iraq nineteen days. Many of his Special Forces peers had not been aware he had been overseas. Others heard rumors that he had died, and were startled to find him in the chapel alive. He was bandaged, in pain, and sedated. He struggled through the ceremony. One moment he was trying to remain awake. The next he was in tears.

The road back was long. Kryszewski needed three surgeries to remove large pieces of shrapnel and six other outpatient procedures for smaller metal bits that remained in his flesh. He was racked with survivor's guilt. By the fall of 2004 he had worked himself back into shape for full duty and was assigned for two years to a special mission unit in Virginia and prohibited from discussing his new work. His duties occasionally took him back to Balad Air Base, and on the one-year anniversary of the rocket attack he returned to the PX where the rocket had hit him, Major Syverson, and Master Sergeant Crowder. It was a rare experience. Few soldiers have the chance to revisit the ground where they were wounded, much less within a year. He walked the area outside, stopped at the small staircase by the entrance, and wandered the aisles inside the store. The blast damage on the exterior wall remained. The front door had been replaced.

Try as he might, Kryszewski could not force the ground to match his memories. It felt as if he had never been there before.

The following year, after being promoted to master sergeant, he transferred back to the Fifth Special Forces Group at Fort Campbell and was assigned as team sergeant of ODA 591. (The team was later redesignated ODA 5331, as part of Fifth Group's expansion.) In 2007 the team was sent via Balad to Nasiriyah, where it partnered with a six-hundred-member Iraqi SWAT unit. The contest for control of Iraq had divided into wars within wars. Much of the American conventional military effort was in or near Baghdad or the Sunni population centers north and west of the capital. Kryszewski's team and several others were ordered to help Iraqi security forces against Iranian-backed Shiite groups in the south, most notably against Jaysh al-Mahdi and the small Soldiers of Heaven cult, which was trying to gain control in Nasiriyah. After a series of pitched battles in 2008, the team returned to the States, and Kryszewski was assigned to the group's support company as its first sergeant.

In late 2009 Kryszewski retired, ending a twenty-four-year career. In 2010 he joined the police department in Clarksville, Tennessee, and passed an unhappy run of months as a traffic cop, ending with his divorce and a dismissal from the police job. He considered both events blessings. As a police officer responding to a traffic accident, he had met Cindy Russell, the daughter of a career Navy sailor who was volunteering with the Special Forces Association, and had just helped arrange an association reunion. Russell had been part of the military community her entire life. They dated, fell in love, and were married. She helped him to rethink his post-Army career. Soon after leaving the force, where he earned about $30,000 a year, he joined a private contracting firm, Wexford Group International, which paid him as much as $1,200 a day. He returned to Afghanistan as an armed embedded civilian adviser and worked alongside Special Forces teams.

Kryszewski stayed with the firm through 2015, spending most of his time deployed, often in outposts that were rocketed. He remained a combatant even as his hair grayed, and was involved in several more raids or other actions. He finally had enough. One night, after a pair of rockets landed near where he was sleeping, he decided to return home for good. He was offered a job with another firm, Quiet Professionals, that allowed him to work in the States. He and his family relocated to Tampa.

Pain still plagued him. The wars were not far away. Sometimes in bed he would find sores on his skin. When he rubbed them they would bleed. These were small pieces of shrapnel or debris working their way out years after being blasted in. He was attuned to life in a deployed team, to the rhythms of readiness and the habits of wariness that keep soldiers alive. He struggled to fit into a quieter life, and became angry. Cindy loved him and knew he needed her. She watched her husband closely, and studied PTSD on her own time. She urged him to understand that dark moods and short temper, along with constant vigilance, did not have to be his normal. With her at his side, he enrolled in care at the VA in Tampa. He started therapy to unpack his memories and reset his behaviors, to accept the past and adjust to the present. He knew the wars had not succeeded. He wondered if it would have been better if the United States had not invaded Iraq. But after all the violence and close calls, he had learned to separate his personal service from the larger march of American foreign policy. He had not picked his missions, much less the reasons Washington chose to go to war. *As a soldier it's not up to me to decide,* he thought. He had done his duty and given his best, and if his service had helped anyone, even a single person, he felt his role was worth it.

Leo moved forward. He considered his treatment superb and by 2017 he thought he was feeling better. But he was not done. In August of 2017 he and Cindy were driving home from a movie in Tampa, when they were caught in a thunderstorm. It was a summer Florida classic. Rain came down in sheets. Wind roared. Lighting flashed, then flashed again.

Thunder shook the car. Leo was activated. The rocket that had hit him in 2004, and all the near misses by other rockets in the years after, had left him rewired.

Behind the wheel of his Dodge Ram 3500, he began shaking.

He was too rattled to drive. He pulled over. He and Cindy switched seats so she could drive the rest of the way home.

It was pouring still when she pulled into the driveway of their home. Leo stepped out of the truck's passenger-side door. He intended to dash through the downpour to the open garage. Lightning flashed again. It seemed almost to hit him. His defenses crumbled. He panicked. He dove to the ground and stayed there, pressed flat to the soggy lawn as an explosive roar encased him. He cupped his hands behind his head.

Facedown, trembling, crying, he was waiting to die. *Hurry up and come kill me*, he thought.

Cindy was on the other side of the big truck and did not see him drop. But as she gathered her purse and made her way to the garage, she noticed Leo was not inside. She spun and saw him in a fetal position on the lawn, shaking violently in the rain. Her reaction was as instantaneous and involuntary as Leo's. But it was different. She was not fighting fear. She was compelled to save him.

She bounded across the driveway, dove onto her husband, and covered him with her body.

For a moment they lay there, in the wind and driving rain. She felt him beneath her. He was tensed, terrified, and curled up in a protective posture, his muscles flexed tight. His breathing was deep and fast. She pressed her mouth close to his ear, telling him she was there, and that he was safe.

"It's okay, baby," she said. "It's all right. It's okay."

Leo did not answer.

She stayed sprawled atop him, shielding him from the lashing gusts. She repeated the words, soothing him. Rain soaked her clothes and hair.

"I'm not going to let anything happen to you," Cindy said.

After a few minutes Leo's muscles started to unclench. He was still breathing with an animal fear. But he was returning to himself. She kept comforting him.

Leo stood up.

Cindy stood with him. She took his hand, led him to the open door, kicking her purse toward the garage until they were inside. She walked him through the house to the bathroom, where she removed his soggy clothes and put a dry robe around him. She guided him to their bedroom, and gently had him lie down.

The room was quiet. Neither of them spoke.

She took her place on the bed and placed her mouth close to his ear again, so he could hear the rhythm of her breathing. She waited. She knew he needed time. She just breathed, purposefully, steadily, signaling security and calm.

Gradually his breathing matched hers.

After a while Leo knew it was over. His wife was holding him. In her embrace he recognized an unusual sensation: He felt safe.

He was back.

I have my protector, he thought. *She's not going to let anything hurt me anymore.*

He remembered this kind of feeling. It was the same sense of security he had once drawn from his Special Forces teams, even when in danger, all across the world. He admitted it: He needed more help. The next day Leo went back to the VA to start the rest of the work. Cindy was beside him.

All that war, all that time, all the ways he had changed. Her love, Leo thought, was bringing him home.

————————

After meeting President Bush, Doc Kirby returned to Georgia and served the remainder of his probation quietly.

His despair dissipated. He and his family grew closer. His anger at Lauren eased, and he reached an understanding about the failure of his marriage. *I don't even hold no ill will. I truly don't look at it for anything but what it was: We were really young, and if we had managed to meet our expectations it might have been different. But we both lost a lot. We thought things were going to be different and it didn't work out that way.* He thought the sergeants whose actions Marines in his platoon said had wronged him—whether for losing a rifle, or for putting him on the rooftop post as punishment for urinating in a bottle—deserved peace, too. Blame games would change nothing for the better. They would only cause more pain.

As he moved toward accepting the ugliest episodes of his past, he and Brandi grew closer, and he took on a larger role in her young daughters' lives. He began introducing himself as their father. By 2014, Brandi had delivered two more daughters. Kirby was the father of four. In a few short years he went from crushing loneliness to being a partner with Brandi in a busy family. He was recovering emotionally, adjusting to his life outside the Navy and away from the Marines at last.

Physically he was in decline. Insomnia drained him, leaving him fatigued, which was amplified by the hypervigilance associated with his PTSD. He was worn down by migraines, and his mouth's chronic pain was almost unbearable. He had learned to compensate in his speech and could communicate well enough, even over the phone. But his surgeries, which once held promise, did not carry him as far as he or his doctors had hoped. He could eat only soft foods, and had trouble with each bite. He drooled. His remaining teeth ached; the bare gums were tender. His lower jaw did not quite align with his upper palate. Nurses had always asked him where his pain was, on a scale of 1 to 10. On a good day, he figured he was a steady 7. Often he was worse, including when his mouth shed tissue or debris. One day it was a small shard of bone, another a tiny screw. In early 2015, faced with throbbing pain, Doc extracted two teeth while standing before a mirror. He pulled them out with the pliers on his Leatherman tool.

His mother, Gail, was despondent. She could see that even as his family life improved, he was at risk of unraveling. She was tired of the simple narratives of recovery that formed part of the military's presentation of its wounded veterans. Her son was suffering. He was backsliding. The Veterans Administration was not doing enough. The president had seemed an ally. The rest of the government did not.

In 2007, while his wounds were fresh, Doc had been hosted by Jack Doyle, an investment portfolio manager, at a gala benefit dinner given by the Marine Corps–Law Enforcement Foundation, a private organization that provides scholarships to children of Marines and law enforcement officers killed in the line of duty. It was a grand night at the Waldorf Astoria, and during the ceremonies Doc met a pair of brothers, a dentist and a doctor, who told him that if he ever needed medical attention, they would help.

He thought little of it at the time but had mentioned it to his mother. Eight years later, Gail found Doyle's email address and asked him for help. Doyle's brother-in-law had been killed in the World Trade Center attacks. He felt personally connected to the veterans of the wars in Afghanistan and Iraq. In less than two weeks he found a dentist willing to shepherd Doc through a fresh round of reconstructive surgery in New York.

In the spring of 2016, three surgeons led by Dr. David L. Hirsch, the reconstruction director of maxillofacial surgery at the New York Head and Neck Institute, removed the hardware that held Doc's rebuilt lower jaw together for almost a decade and replaced it with a titanium plate fashioned through computer-assisted design. Doc felt the change immediately. His bite was properly aligned. The throbbing ended. For the first time since a bullet passed through his head, the moving parts of his face seemed to fit. In follow-up procedures he received dental implants to replace his damaged teeth. No longer self-conscious about his scar tissue and mismatched jaw, he started smiling again. Sometimes his smile was outsized. In the autumn of 2016 he did something he once thought he would never do again: He bit an apple, clean through.

Gail Kirby kept an autographed copy of President Bush's book in her home. She remembered something he had told her in his office. "You speak with passion," he said. That much was true. But passion had limits. Gail wanted to support the wars, to believe they were right not only in ambition but in practice. Al Qaeda, after all, had attacked the United States, setting in motion the huge and lethal machine that descended upon Afghanistan and Iraq. Hunting down al Qaeda was just. But much of what had happened since perplexed her, and the war machine seemed to have no Off button. She knew things had gone wrong, but most of all she knew that the people who had answered Washington's call had come home to a government that did not give them adequate support. Her passion could not overcome that.

Questions burned in her. Why had her son's face been rebuilt with pro bono private care? Was this the country we wanted to be?

Gail's aversion to politics spared the government her wrath; there was only so much one person could take on. She looked for good where she could and then goodness appeared. The private doctors who stepped in where the government had failed gave her a phenomenon to marvel at: the return of her oldest son. She was in awe of Dusty, at how he had turned it around. She saw it in his eyes. *I was always proud of him, but now I am proud of every part of him,* she would think. *He's got a grip. He's got a grip.* She could call it many things. Blessing in catastrophe, grace amid horror, salvage from waste. Compassion where coarseness and indifference had reigned. God's hand. Luck. Whatever it was, her son had been restored. She wished it could be extended to the rest, to those for whom it was not too late. How many lives had these wars wrecked?

Author's Note
Regarding the Cover

The photograph on the cover of this book captures the beginning of the ambush of an American foot patrol on the afternoon of April 15, 2009, beside the Korengal River in Afghanistan. It shows three soldiers from Second Platoon, Bravo Company, First Battalion of the Twenty-Sixth Infantry. Specialist Robert Soto, the platoon radio operator, is in the foreground. Specialist Robert Oxman and Specialist Dustin Parkison, a M240B machine gun team from Third Squad, are crouched together in the upper right. The image was made seconds after an improvised explosive device had exploded under a trail, killing a fourth soldier from the platoon, Private First Class Richard A. Dewater, and as the Taliban began firing rifles, machine guns, and rocket-propelled grenades against Americans in the ravine. Specialist Soto, who had been walking with Dewater and was blown over by the blast, had regained his feet and was running for cover. Specialist Oxman and Specialist Parkison were scanning the hills and stone houses above, looking for the gunmen firing on them, and about to move to a better position from which to fire back. The image was made by Tyler Hicks of the *New York Times*.

Author's Note on Sources

The reporting of this book was initially organized around firsthand observations in the United States, Afghanistan, and Iraq, and aboard the USS *John C. Stennis* and several military aircraft. It began with being present during the attack on the World Trade Center and continued with repeated cycles of work in Afghanistan and Iraq, including in Afghanistan in late 2001 and early 2002 (overlapping with Leo Kryszewski*) and in Iraq in late 2002 and 2003, followed by reporting in the field alongside other characters—Dustin Kirby, Robert Soto, Jarrod Neff—during certain events described in these pages. These include the rocket attacks that killed much of the family of Haji Mohammad Karim, the sniper shot that struck Lance Corporal Colin Smith during the daytime raid on the outskirts of Karma, and the explosion that killed Private First Class Richard Dewater beside the Korengal River. In 2012 I was in the backseat of an

---

* Kryszewski and I did not meet in Afghanistan, although at one point we may have been about twenty feet apart on the streets of Jalalabad when his team was returning to a safe house in the city and passed by me as I worked.

F/A-18 combat sortie behind Layne McDowell as he was catapulted from the *Stennis*, flew up the boulevard in Pakistan, and patrolled over southern Afghanistan. During the sortie, McDowell flew a low pass to suppress Taliban fighters harassing a ground unit below. I was also present at Doc Kirby's home in Georgia immediately after he was medically retired from the Navy in 2012. In 2016 I observed Dr. David Hirsch and two other surgeons perform the surgical reconstruction of Kirby's face in an operating room in Manhattan.

None of this was enough. To supplement what could be seen and heard firsthand, I interviewed any willing participant of events portrayed in these pages, including Navy aviators and Army pilots who flew with Layne Mc-Dowell and Mike Slebodnik, and a long list of ground combatants. I then interviewed multiple family members. Some of these sources wished to remain anonymous. Others are listed in the acknowledgments pages.

I also traveled to many of the locales where action in this book occurs. In Afghanistan this included trips into the Helmand River basin and the Kunar, Pech, Korengal, and Watapur Valleys, as well as the cities and almost all of the bases or outposts described (many of which are now destroyed), and in Iraq to the al-Kaed bridge, the highways where Wade Zirkle and Joe Dan Worley were wounded, Outpost Omar (also now destroyed), the police station in Karma, and the Balad Air Base, also known as Logistics Support Area Anaconda, where Kryszewski was wounded in 2004 and Slebodnik was assigned in 2005 and 2006. Travels in the United States included the Bethesda Naval Hospital, Walter Reed Army Medical Center, Fort Campbell, Camp Lejeune, MacDill Air Force Base, Arlington National Cemetery, and Fort Benning.

Field notes and observations were further developed with official documents, and with the letters, journals, emails, videos, maps, prayers, and personal collections of characters involved, or those of their peers and families. These include but were not limited to "The Good Friday Ambush" by Colonel Dennis Mroczkowski, a U.S. Special Operations command historian who made a record of the ambush on al-Kaed Bridge in 2003; the 101st Airborne Division's "Take Away" note after the militant raid on Muqdadiyah on March 21, 2006; an email from Colonel Jeffrey N. Colt to Major General Thomas R. Turner about the battle damage to the Kiowa helicopters that responded to the same raid; a PowerPoint presentation titled "Optimized IED 20 SEP 2008," prepared by Viper Company after a fatal attack on its soldiers on Route Victory; and the Marine Corps' photographs of civilians killed in the HIMARS mishap on February 14, 2010, the so-called Valentine's Day Massacre. Among other official references consulted were TM 1-1520-248-10, the Operators manual for the Army OH-58D Kiowa Warrior helicopter, and the Navy EODB/Army Technical Manual F-44-2-1-2, Explosive Ordnance Disposal Procedures, Brazilian Rocket, 127-mm HE, Surface-to-Surface, SS-30 (ASTROS). In places I referred to WikiLeaks' Iraq and Afghan War Logs, for example, Reference Number IRQ20040604n394 (about rocket attacks on Balad) and Reference Number IRQ20040201n125 (about a discussion of insurgent tactics in Iraq, and the difficulties and confusion inherent in some of the American military's response). And there were many more.

The second quote on the epigraph page, about America being at the mall and not at war, is from a photograph taken in Ramadi, Iraq, in January 2007 by John Moore of Getty Images. In places where sources recall different translations of the same psalm, this is because different translations of the Bible circulated through the wars.

All of the primary characters in the book, save one, cooperated with repeated interviews and the sharing of personal materials. The only primary character I was not able to talk with was Slebodnik. In fall 2008, soon after Slebodnik was killed, the photographer Tyler Hicks and I were passing through Jalalabad after a reporting trip up the northeastern valleys and stopped to meet members of his cavalry troop and discuss Slebodnik's life and career. While a staff sergeant was checking to determine the availability of his peers, we learned that a fellow reporter from *The New York Times* had been kidnapped in another province. We were recalled to Kabul. Over the next three years I spoke with many soldiers about him, until, upon flying aboard Dustoff medevac helicopters in Helmand Province and along the Arghandab River during the troop buildup ordered during President Obama's first term, I met several pilots who knew him, including Matthew Cole, Jason Davis, and Joe Callaway. With these pilots' help and more from Jeremy Woehlert, I started reconstructing the events of his service, and ultimately was assisted by the grunts and a medic and the chaplain who cared for him in his last hour, and by Slebodnik's family.

In a few places I also referenced the work of other journalists or news organizations, including, as mentioned or quoted in the book, a PBS interview with Raad al-Hamdani, a former Republican Guard commander, and "Into the Valley of Death," by Sebastian Junger, which appeared in *Vanity Fair*, January 2008. Junger's work was relevant, because many conventional enlisted soldiers, provided limited pre-deployment intelligence by their services, consume news media accounts of wars they will soon find themselves fighting. Junger's story was passed among soldiers headed to the valley and who were eager to know what to expect.

Aside from Slebodnik, each of the primary characters assisted in the fact-checking of the chapters in which they appear, as have a majority of the other named sources, along with a set of technical reviewers and proofreaders listed in the acknowledgments section.

Verification was furthered by Rob Liguori, a professional fact-checker granted unfettered access to reporting materials, sources, and primary characters.

No matter the above, responsibility for any error in this book lies solely with me.

Acknowledgments

This book would not exist were it not for the patience of Jonathan Karp, Alice Mayhew, and Stuart Roberts of Simon & Schuster, who allowed years for it to come together. The wait, episodically maddening, in hindsight was necessary. Many of the people who shared their memories needed time—time to process and feel comfortable discussing wartime experiences that were still fresh, time for the arc of their lives in combat to end, time to leave uniformed service and be able to speak freely. Some needed time for all three. Throughout it all, Jonathan, Alice, and Stuart endured long pauses and tolerated my travels—to Afghanistan, Libya, Syria, Iraq, and Ukraine—with more than graciousness. They remained eager and were ready at each juncture with encouragement and counsel, as was Stuart Krichevsky, my agent, who stayed enthusiastic and involved, relieving me of burdens as he urged me on. All this allowed many of the characters to evolve, to reach conclusions about what happened around them and what they did, and for the book to assume a form. At the end, David Chesanow's copy editing, Jackie Seow's art direction, Lewelin Polanco's interior design, David Lindroth's cartography, Al Madocs's production contributions, and Rob Liguori's fact-checking made a collective effort cohere. I don't have enough thanks for the privilege of working with you.

To the extent that the many events in these pages managed to be realistic or accurate, credit and gratitude must go to a list of veterans and their family members who gave their attention and their time to inform the research. A few asked for anonymity. Others can be named. In no particular order, and with ranks removed for those who served (in part because many of them held multiple ranks across the years they helped), they include Jason Sharp, T. J. Rios, Lori Hill, Jeff Runion, Chris Hume, Cindy Russell, Jacob Lewis, Michael Meaney, Matthew Dalrymple, Patrick Greene, Justin Constantine, Thomas Schumacher, Darrin Crowder, Ray Charfauros, Sokol Cela, Hayden Archibald, Wesley Laney, William "Jacko" Kirby, Gail Kirby, Daniel Kirby, Destiny Kirby, Wade Zirkle, Joe Dan Worley, Angel Worley, John Trylch, Jimmy Hathaway, David Lemoine, Tanja Slebodnik, Amber Smith, Jeremy Woehlert, Mariko (Kraft) Callahan, Daniel Strauser, Sean Riordan, Donterry Woods, Joseph Menas, Joshua Rosales, Andrew DiMarca, Jesse Leach, Michael Leslie, Anthony Santos, Juan Valdez, Kenneth DeTreux, Shawn Dempsey, John Lynch, Robert Minton, Jonathan Miller, Brian Meyer, Joseph Callaway, Ryan Craig, Emmitt Furner II, Matt Cole, Pamela Paquet, Steven Halase, John Rodriguez, Sean Conroy, Jimmy Howell, Robert Oxman, Cory Colistra, Lawrence Lau, Josh Biggers, Adam Wallace, Zach Whisenhunt, Dave Santana, Niall Swider, Justin Smith, Edwin Harger, Mark Hummel, Joseph Wright, Brian Christmas, Randy Newman, Mike Grice, Marvin Mathelier, Daniel Durbin, Junior Joseph, Maureen Krebs, Jason Davis, Jonathan Cooney, Drew Upton, Peter Sprague, Drew Fanning, Troy Rathke, Christopher Herr, Craig Tanner, Callie Ferrari, John Gay, Ryan Craig, Jody Slebodnik Barnes, Kevin White, Brandi Smith, T. G. Taylor, Craig Faller, Jeremiah Foxwell, and Sasha Young. The book was also assisted by the U.S. Navy's Chief of Information, which in 2011 gave Layne McDowell permission to cooperate with research.

The effort was also helped over the years by Iraqis and Afghans, who volunteered information and good judgment, and shared rides, meals, and conversations. Like most Americans who journeyed through these wars outside of a government's employ, I would not have been able to work without the friendship and help of Iraqis and Afghans. In some cases, absent their advice and alertness, I might not have survived. Abu Malik, Abdul Wahid Wafa, Nasir Ahmad, Sangar Rahimi, Duraid Adnan, Mazin Jawad, Karzan Mahmoud, and Taimoor Shah—knowing you has been a blessing.

The work was further aided by a long list of *Times* bureau chiefs who put up with my comings and goings, including John F. Burns, Carlotta Gall, Alissa Rubin, Tim Arango, and Steven Lee Myers. Mujib Mashal, of the Kabul bureau, provided helpful guidance and a necessary translation from Pashto. Karam Shoumali, of the Berlin bureau, helped with translations from Arabic and a bottomless reservoir of inside jokes. Tyler Hicks and Joao Silva, both staff photographers, were companions in the field and were present at many of the events. Someday, somehow, their own stories should be told.

When things went wrong, as they inevitably did, having support and wisdom from Roger Cohen, Susan Chira, Michele McNally, Beth Flynn, Alison Smale, Rick Gladstone, Ian Fisher, Bill Schmidt, Janet Elder, Michael Slackman, and David McCraw was repeatedly invaluable. There is little feeling as fortifying as knowing that the Sulzberger family and Bill Keller (the executive editor during most of the years covered in these pages) have your back. They never wavered, not once. After Bill retired, Jill Abramson and Dean Baquet upheld this standard.

Once draft chapters were complete, critical readers stepped in to offer technical review, operational context, or fact-checking—all in the service of accuracy. Among them are Major Joshua Rosales, the executive officer of Weapons Company, Second Battalion, Eighth Marines in Karma in 2006 and 2007; retired Lieutenant Colonel Sean Riordan, the executive officer of the same Marine battalion during the same time; Lieutenant Colonel Jimmy Howell and Major John Rodriguez, respectively the commanding and executive officers of Viper Company in the Korengal Valley in 2008 and 2009; former Major Cory Colistra, the executive officer of Kilo Company, Third Battalion, Sixth Marines during Operation Moshtarak in 2010; retired Chief Warrant Officer Jeremy Woehlert, a former Kiowa pilot and friend of Mike Slebodnik; Jody Slebodnik Barnes, Mike's sister; retired Colonel John Lynch, a former Kiowa pilot who commanded Task Force Out Front in eastern Afghanistan in 2008; retired Chief Warrant Officer Matthew Cole, an Army Black Hawk pilot who flew as a chase helicopter pilot on Dustoff medevac missions in Iraq and Afghanistan, including on the flight to evacuate Slebodnik after he was shot; former Specialist Steven Halase, the platoon radio operator for much of Viper Two's Afghan tour; Andrew DiMarca, a turret gunner who served with Dustin Kirby; and Cindy Russell, the wife of Leo Kryszewski.

Several other early readers examined the entire draft manuscript and provided comments and corrections. These included retired Colonel Dave Edmond Lounsbury, a former Army doctor and coauthor of an American military compendium of battlefield trauma and its treatment; retired Colonel David Fivecoat, a former Army infantry officer and paratrooper who served as a battalion operations officer in Iraq and a battalion commander in Afghanistan before commanding the U.S. Army's Ranger School; Colonel Kenneth DeTreux, who served as the commanding officer of Second Battalion, Eighth Marines from 2005 through 2007 and as the operations officer for the Second Marine Division from 2010 through 2012, including during its command rotation in Helmand Province; Mark Warren, the editor I formerly filed to at *Esquire* magazine; and three of my editors at *The New York Times Magazine*—Jessica Lustig, Shreeya Sinha, and Charlie Homans. Nancy Sherman, a professor of philosophy at Georgetown University, affiliate at the Kennedy Institute of Ethics, and author of *Afterwar: Healing the Moral Wounds of Our Soldiers*, also reviewed a draft manuscript, as did Ian Fisher, an editor worthy of blind trust.

Three veteran friends working in journalism offered suggestions as well. Two of them work for the *Times*: John Ismay, a former U.S. Navy explosive ordnance disposal officer who served a tour in Iraq, and T. M. Gibbons-Neff, a former Marine grunt who served two tours in Afghanistan, the second as a scout sniper team leader during Operation Moshtarak, and beyond. The third, Brian Castner, a former Air Force explosive ordnance disposal officer, served two tours in Iraq and is now a magazine writer and author, including of books on the same wars covered here: *The Long Walk* and *All the Ways We Kill and Die*. Their recommendations improved the book.

Long before reaching that point, I was blessed with love and tolerance from my family: Jack, Mick, Elizabeth, Willie, and Joe, along with Honey and Jack, and Jim, who held us together through it all.

Last, and first, were the grace, encouragement, and understanding of you, Suzanne. Your love carried and finally saved me, while you held a place for me in your heart and in our home across an absenteeism of years. And then, as I wrote, your incisive intellect and sound judgment, and your suspicion of power, helped focus my sometimes scattered thinking about the wars that claimed so much, and that I had at times navigated without understanding. All that coffee, all those talks, all your selflessness. How can I have had this luck? I cannot say, even as I know that such debts cannot be repaid with words.

Index